EUGENE DE MAZENOD

Founder of the Oblates of
Mary Immaculate

JEAN LEFLON

This fourth and final volume of the
English-language edition of Monseigneur Leflon's biography of Eugene
de Mazenod brings the prelate's life
and work to a close. His final years
saw further strengthening of the diocese of Marseilles. Bishop de Mazenod's emphasis on higher levels of
education for his diocesan clergy and
greater attention to parish life effected
for a time considerable parochial and
social advances which proved beneficial
to the entire city — and, in fact, to much
of Provence. His own beloved congregation of Oblates flourished, at times
almost beyond expectations. What had
been started as an organization intended to evangelize Provence became
an almost world-wide missionary corps.
During his lifetime, Eugene de Mazenod's spiritual sons preached the Gospel
in Canada, the United States, and
Mexico, in England and Ireland, in
Ceylon, in South Africa, and through-

(continued on back flap)

at the Institut Catholique in Paris, and
his works on Emery and Bernier have
been crowned by the Academie Française. The translator, Rev. Francis D.
Flanagan, O.M.I., is a former member
of the faculty of Our Lady of Hope
Seminary at Newburgh, New York.

Eugene de Mazenod

(1782-1861)

TRANSLATED FROM

Eugène de Mazenod: Évêque de Marseille, Fondateur des Missionnaires Oblats de Marie Immaculée, 1782–1861.

Tome III: L'Oeuvre Pastorale et Missionaire, Adaptation et Extension, 1838–1861 (Paris, Librairie Plon, 1965); chapters ten through fifteen.

ALREADY PUBLISHED:
Eugene de Mazenod: Bishop of Marseilles, Founder of the Oblates of Mary Immaculate, 1782–1861.
Volume I: *The Steps of a Vocation, 1782–1814* (Fordham University Press, 1961).

Volume II: *Missions of Provence, Restoration of the Diocese of Marseilles, 1814–1837* (Fordham University Press, 1966).

Volume III: *Pastoral and Missionary Work, Adaptation and Extension, 1838–1861,* part one (Fordham University Press, 1968).

1805

1821

ca. 1851

EUGENE DE MAZENOD

JEAN LEFLON

TRANSLATED BY

Francis D. Flanagan, O. M. I.

EUGENE de MAZENOD

Bishop of Marseilles

Founder of the Oblates of Mary Immaculate

1782-1861

IV

Pastoral and Missionary Work
Adaptation and Extension

1838-1861

PART TWO

FORDHAM UNIVERSITY PRESS · NEW YORK

Nihil Obstat: AMATUS PETRUS FRUTAZ
Subsecretarius S. R. C. pro Causis
Sanctorum
Romae, 26 Mart, 1968

Printed in the United States of America

To
ALL THE MISSIONARY OBLATES OF MARY IMMACULATE
laboring
in home or foreign mission fields
to evangelize
God's
poor.

ABBREVIATIONS

MANUSCRIPT SOURCES

A.A.M.	*Archives Archevêché,* Marseilles
A.D.M.	*Archives Départementales,* Marseilles
A.G.R.	*Archives Générales O.M.I.,* Rome
A.N.P.	*Archives Nationales,* Paris
A.S.V.	*Archivio Segreto Vaticano,* Rome
P.R.	*Archives Postulation O.M.I.,* Rome
Arch. Propaganda, S.C.	Archives of the Sacred Congregation of the Propaganda, *Scritti riferiti nei Congressi,* Rome
Yenveux, *Saintes Règles*	A. Yenveux, o.m.i., "Commentaire des Constitutions et Règles des Missionnaires Oblats d'après la correspondance et le Journal de Mgr. de Mazenod." Manuscript in P.R.
Aix, Hôtel Boisgelin	Aix-en-Provence, Hôtel de Boisgelin, private archives of the Boisgelin Family
Saint-Martin	Chateau of Saint-Martin de Pallières (Var), private archives of the Boisgelin Family

PRINTED SOURCES

Missions	*Missions de la Congrégation des Missionnaires Oblats de Marie Immaculée* (quarterly booklets published since 1862 for the use of the members of the Society)
Rambert	Toussaint Rambert, o.m.i., *Vie de Mgr. Charles-Joseph-Eugène de Mazenod, évêque de Marseille, fondateur de la Congrégation des Missionnaires Oblats de Marie Immaculée.* Tours, 1883. Two vols.
Rey	Achille Rey, o.m.i., *Histoire de Mgr. Charles-Joseph-Eugène de Mazenod, évêque de Marseille, fondateur de la Congrégation des Missionnaires Oblats de Marie Immaculée.* Rome-Marseilles, 1928. Two volumes published posthumously.

NOTE: A complete listing of the sources used for the material in the present volume will be found in Volume III, Bibliography, pp. 501–516.

TABLE OF CONTENTS

Volume IV

Pastoral and Missionary Work
Adaptation and Extension

(*1838-1861*)

PART TWO

Chapter One

Parishes, Seminaries and Clergy

PAROCHIAL EQUIPMENT

The pastoral problem posed by Marseilles' growing population became more and more acute after 1836. In 1836, the city's inhabitants numbered 146,239; the number rose to 154,035 in 1841; 183,186 in 1846; 195,257 in 1851; 233,817 in 1856, and 260,910 in 1861.[1] From 1831 to 1841, the growth in population slackened because of cholera; beginning with 1841, however, it quickened its pace with an increase of 29,151; slowed down somewhat from 1846 to 1851 with an increase of 12,071; picked up between 1851 to 1856 with 38,560; lessened from 1856 to 1861 with 27,093; then jumped to 39,221 from 1861 to 1866. Marseilles then ranked second among the cities of France in population. Now, because of its area, which was still that of the ancient commune and comprized almost nine square miles—that is, three times the size of Paris[2]—Marseilles' expansion varied greatly from canton to canton. *Intra muros,* from 1836 to 1866, the rate of increase for the cantons was as follows: 0.4% for the middle canton, 45% for the north and 68% for the south; *extra muros,* the rate of increase was 286% for the north and 525% for the south, but only 44% for the middle canton which was still rural. The commune of Allauch remained practically stable. The northern and southern cantons *extra muros,* which comprised only 13% and 8% respectively of Marseilles' population in 1836, now totaled 23% and 25% of it. They benefitted from the push of the city towards the north and south, Porte d'Aix and Quartier Longchamp, and Place Castellane. The conglomerate population which stretched out, in star fashion, along the road to Aix, toward the Vale of Jarret, into

3

the Huveaune Valley found better air and more space in those sections. Elsewhere, the inhabitants were crowded together in ancient quarters where there was no more land available for building and where the layout and narrowness of the streets were entirely unsuited to the demands of traffic which had become uncommonly more active, especially during the time of the Empire.

Numerous two- and three-storey houses were rebuilt: they had three front windows and were typical of houses put up since the turn of the eighteenth century; a few oblique avenues were opened to relieve the congestion of the center of the city which was still the business district. However, radical steps which alone would have made an orderly layout of the city possible encountered a two-fold obstacle: high elevations and local conservatism. "The steep slopes, greatly prized for their defensive value when cities were founded," [3] forbade any geometrical street-plan. This was especially the case with the three hills in the parishes of Saint Lawrence, Les Moulins, and Les Carmes, which isolated the new port from the old one and from the Cours Belsunce. Mirès, the noted financier, had wisely proposed leveling them in order to provide a site for creating a vast section with wide avenues.[4] Bishop de Mazenod favored this plan highly since it would have been advantageous for his new cathedral then being constructed near the old one. However, fear of the mistral from which the old port would no longer be protected, and the agitation of thousands of inhabitants who would be forced to move and to find lodgings elsewhere, brought opposition from the municipal council; a half-measure was then adopted by opening a street, la rue Impériale, connecting la Joliette with les Augustins.

This demographic evolution affected the diocesan program all the more seriously since it ensued not from an increase of the natives of Marseilles, but from the arrival of immigrants. In fact, the excess of births over deaths in the city was practically negligible; in the better years, 1859–1861, the number of births never exceeded 2,000; at the time of the depression noted in France under the July monarchy, and especially during the general crisis of 1846–1851, the death rate actually surpassed the birth rate: 6,836 deaths as compared with 4,975 births in 1837, the year of the cholera epidemic; in 1841, 5,198 deaths to 5,099 births, and in 1842, 5,222 deaths and 5,209 births. "Thus, it could only have been through immigration that Marseilles' population increased." [5] Now, from a religious standpoint, this influx of outside elements little by little changed the situation and the mentality of the city. Some people having come from urban or semi-urban districts, migrated to the shops, the artisan studios, and the stores, rather than the mills, while others of rural origin, lacking any technical skill, remained day-laborers, carters, loaders, and unskilled laborers[6]; in each case, however, they found themselves out of their element and uprooted. Although the pastoral supervision in their former communes had kept them faithful to their devotional practices, in Marseilles they felt isolated and reduced almost to anonymity in that immense city where the pastors did not know them, were not known by them, and supervised thousands of souls. Gaston Rambert may assure us that Marseilles quickly assimilated the immigrants, that there was no problem for Provençals, who were almost rural Marseillais, and that there was hardly any problem for the large majority of foreigners,[7] particularly if they were Mediterraneans; but, judging from a Christian standpoint, one can wonder who was changed more by this mixture of classes: the urban community or these new diocesans of Bishop de Mazenod.

The influx of these immigrants did more than merely help to change the complexion of the parishes in the older section of the city. Although these parishes grew numerically as a result of the newcomers, they lost a portion of their traditional flock; abandoning the neighborhoods that were becoming heavily populated by the lower classes, the middle class, especially the upper bourgeoisie, settled in the residential sections on the perimeter of the city. In spite of the financial problems posed by this exodus of the wealthier families, the ranks of the curates had to be increased, and the pastors had to be persuaded to accept added responsibilities. Above all, both pastors and curates had to be convinced that their pastoral program needed adaptation to a milieu that was changing completely.

Compared with that of Marseilles, the population increase in the rest of the *arondissement,* comprising three cantons, was relatively unnoticeable; the canton of Aubagne rose from 10,818 inhabitants in 1836 to 11,354 in 1861; Roquevaire's population, during that same time, went from 10,658 to 11,602 and la Ciotat increased from 8,543 to 11,746. But the increase in the last-named canton, much greater than that of the other two, began only after 1851 and was due almost exclusively to the growth of the chief town where construction of steel ships was increasing.

The steps Bishop de Mazenod had already undertaken during the first part of his episcopate to reinforce the pastoral equipment of his diocese by founding thirteen new parishes had been halted by the 1848 revolution and the subsequent political crisis. In 1850, once the situation became stabilized and finances were reorganized, the regime of Prince-President Louis Napoleon, who was favorable to the Church, allocated budget funds for one hundred additional succursal parishes. The prelate took immediate advantage of it, and following the principle that to be sure of obtaining the essential one should ask for much more, he submitted several requests. Only one was honored: that which concerned Saint Michel's parish. This was a section in the rapidly developing eastern part of the city, and it was too distant from Saint Vincent de Paul Church to which it belonged. Two other parishes were subsequently created in the city proper: Saint Jean Baptiste near the Place Castellane in 1853, and Saints Adrian and Hermes on the Prado when le Rouet parish was suppressed in 1859. Five others were also created in the districts surrounding the city: in the northern suburbs l'Estaque in 1853, and Saint Mauront in 1860; in the southern suburbs Saint Eusebia in Montredon and Saint Cassian in 1854, and Saint Anne in 1861.[8] In the rest of the diocese, where the population increased very little, only Cadolive was given preferential treatment, but for reasons entirely foreign to demography: "the state of antipathy and irritation"[9] which existed between Cadolive's inhabitants and those of Saint Savournin necessitated the independence of that hamlet from the rival village.

Another problem—that of churches—presented itself, not only in the new succursal parishes which needed new places of worship, but also in a certain number of old parishes where the churches had become decrepit or inadequate. Between 1848 and 1861, eleven churches were rebuilt: two in the canton of Roquevaire (Auriol and Saint Savournin); one in the canton of Aubagne (la Penne); two in the northern suburbs of Marseilles (Saint Barthélemy and Saint André de Séon); three in the southern suburbs (Saint Marguerite, Mazargues, and Saint Peter); lastly two in the city proper (Saint Vincent de Paul and the cathedral). The old Church of the Reformés of the Strict Observance, which had been allotted to Saint Vincent de Paul parish in 1802, was considered not only inappropriate on the tree-lined Meilhan Promenade but also unsuited to the population of a quarter which was as active as it was favorable to commerce. As for the old cathedral, although it was very venerable historically and archeologically, it was criticized even more than the Church of the Reformés, as unsuitable opposite the magnificent new port. The second city of France, spread out so majestically along the Mediterranean and so bursting with vitality, deserved much better than the skimpy, decayed, austere, and lusterless old cathedral. For the prestige of Marseilles and the honor of his see, Bishop de Mazenod felt more strongly than anyone else that it should be replaced by another vast, modern, and majestic cathedral. Consequently, he was tireless in taking steps and making requests to the mayor, the prefect, the minister of cults, and the government. He finally won his case with Napoleon III, although he failed to gain his choice of a more central and favorable building site. And yet, his was the wiser choice. Sufficient proof of this can be found in the letter he sent to Berryer, commissioning him to handle his case:

I could give many other reasons for opposing the choice of the Saint Martin locale [for the cathedral], but my letter is already too long and I want to say a word about the Cours du Chapitre as the best location. This is reached by way of a magnificent ready-made avenue, les Allées. It is easily accessible from all points of the city. It is a favorite promenade; on holidays, everyone goes there. With far less demolition and at a much smaller cost than elsewhere, the façade of the cathedral could be exposed to view and could be seen from the Place Noailles. The edifice would extend along another beautiful promenade, the Cours du Chapitre; it would be set apart completely from everything else, and no demolition would be necessary. Surrounded by a parish of 18,000 souls, whose number will soon reach 25,000, it would not be at the extremity of the city, as has been claimed; beyond it stretches all the land occupied by the houses that were built parallel to Longchamps Avenue. One need not be a prophet to foresee that the city will grow rapidly in that direction and eventually will reach as far as les Chartreux. More and more construction is going on in that direction, and a combination of new circumstances is going to increase this building activity east of Marseilles. Lastly, to the right of the future cathedral, there is a very suitable location for the seminary, and to the left is the site of the present Church of the Reformés, which would be ideally suited as a site for the episcopal palace. The Church of the Reformés is in such pitiable condition that the city will have to build another for that large parish. With the cathedral near by, such a need would disappear and the municipal treasury would be saved more than 600,000 francs; the majority of the municipal council must appreciate this fact and rightly so! [10]

All these arguments, which were inspired both by a consciousness of pastoral obligations and by an expert understanding of town planning, were brushed aside by other arguments which experience proved to be far less valid. The prelate had been altogether correct in wanting the new cathedral built on the Cours du Chapitre; today, it is the crossroads of the city proper.

The demographic growth of Marseilles demanded more than merely the establishment of succursal parishes and the building of churches. It also demanded additional ecclesiastical manpower for the increased population. It was therefore of vital importance for the diocese to recruit clergy and to give them a solid and suitable training so that they might exercise the ministry under rather difficult local conditions. Both quantity and quality were needed.

What the official statistics reveal regarding quantity is more alarming than reassuring. These statistics show first of all a deficit between 1837 and 1846; in fact, the number of deaths (63) exceeded the number of ordinations (61): the year 1846, with twelve ordinations, marked the start of a noticeable improvement, but although it continued, it also dwindled very quickly, since from 1846 to 1860 ordinations exceeded deaths by only 24. In 23 years, therefore, the major seminary's contribution provided a surplus of only 22 subjects.[11] It should be pointed out, of course, that these fluctuations tallied with the general movement verified by Nigon de Berti, the Secretary General of the Ministry of Cults, in the statistics he drew up in 1861 for the whole of France—the same periods of slump from 1841 to 1846 and from 1855 to 1860, and the same period of recovery from 1847 to 1854.[12] Nonetheless, Bishop de Mazenod was more adversely affected by it in comparison with the other bishops; in France as a whole, where since 1822 the number of ordinations had always exceeded that of deaths, the increase in ecclesiastical ranks was "proportionately greater than that of the population": 2/5 to 1/5.[13] But in rapidly developing Marseilles, there was a noticeable and growing disproportion between the poorly reinforced local clergy and the steadily increasing total of inhabitants.

Because of the paucity of local recruits, Bishop de Mazenod, like his uncle before him, had to call upon a large number of foreign priests. This explains why, in 1860, he had 378 priests at his disposal, even though his own seminary had furnished him with a surplus of only 22 during his episcopate. More keenly than anyone else, he was aware of the disadvantages of a system which urgent necessity had obliged him to adopt. It was not only the unity of his priestly corps which suffered from this admixture; although some of these immigrants showed exemplary regularity and were capable of adapting themselves to a milieu far different from their native country, a certain number of them were prompted by motives other than pure love. Some had left their countries for political reasons (as for example the Italians and the Spaniards who had been expelled either by the liberal revolution or by the counter-revolution); some liberals had slipped in among them and were considered dangerous by both the prefect and the bishop; others had to leave their countries after moral lapses; still others, guided solely by self-interest, were seeking advantageous situations for themselves and their families. But the prelate, although he had resigned himself to this foreign contribution, would not assign these priests as pastors, rectors, or curates.[14] With few exceptions, these appointments were given only to the local clergy. Besides, the local clergy expected these concordat posts to be reserved to them. Priests who had come from outside dioceses remained on the sidelines as chaplains, professors and proctors of colleges, assistants in parishes, or confessors. In this way, the manpower needed for the erection of succursal parishes and for the reinforcement of certain curacies became available.[15]

This importation of clergy may have eased some of Bishop de Mazenod's manpower problems, but the Marseillais clergy which he concentrated on the parishes was hardly being rejuvenated, since the number of ordinations remained so small. Of the 167 priests whose ages we know and who filled the 173

posts which existed in 1861, 93 (that is, more than half) were from
40 to 59 years of age; 12 were from 60 to 71 years of age, and
only 62 were from 24 to 39.[16]

The proportion between the total number of priests and the
total number of people at first declined and then improved
slightly. In 1823, there were 171 priests (that is, 1 for every 832
inhabitants); the diocese, therefore, was slightly below the mean
established in 1821 for the whole of France, namely, 1 for every
814 inhabitants[17]; this proportion fell in 1836 to 1 priest for every
938 inhabitants, and improved again in 1861 with 1 for every 791
inhabitants—a figure slightly below the general mean which at
that time was 1 priest for every 700 inhabitants.[18]

Meanwhile, to avoid the necessity of resorting to foreign elements and to step up the recruitment for his too limited clergy,
Bishop de Mazenod did his utmost to develop his seminaries,
hoping that they would provide him with the reinforcement he
so badly needed.

THE SEMINARIES

His minor seminary gave him many disappointments. We
have no data regarding its effectives other than the official statements of the episcopal administration which are found in the annual reports drawn up for the Ministry of Cults. Now, before the
Falloux Law, the avowed quota was prudently maintained, with
a certain uniformity, at about the maximum of 150—a quota set
by the ordinances of the Restoration period; in 1851, however,
it was stated that the number suddenly rose to 260 and in 1852 to
334. Such an abrupt and considerable increase suggests that beginning with these dates the exact figure was recorded. Beginning
with 1853, the total subsided, for it comprised aspirants for the
priesthood exclusively: 68 in 1853; 56 in 1854; 47 in 1855; 42
in 1856; 60 in 1858; 50 in 1859, and 69 in 1861.[19] From this time
the number of nonseminarians was not included in the reports, as
had been the case when, even in spite of the regulations set down
by the Ordinances, the Minor Seminary of the Sacred Heart admitted boarders and day students who were not destined for the
priesthood. This explains why, from 1837 to 1850, the seminary
furnished the diocese with so few priests. Even in 1836, at the

time of the first Villemain Bill, Bishop Fortuné bemoaned the fact
that "scarcely one out of every ten young students eventually entered Holy Orders." [20] In 1843, his nephew likewise figured that
only 7 or 8 of every 20 pupils enrolled each year embraced an
ecclesiastical career.[21] Officially listed as a seminary-college after
the Falloux Law was passed, the Minor Seminary of the Sacred
Heart furnished even fewer recruits than before, and, in 1853, the
prelate rebuked the seminary superior "for the almost total loss
of vocations" in his establishment.[22] In 1859, only four of its
rhetoricians entered the major seminary.[23]

Evidently wishing to compensate for such feeble returns, the
bishop decided to seek other sources of supply. Not only did he
encourage and support the rectory schools—concerning which
there is no desirable information before 1853[24]—but he also
made use of the cathedral choir school and the other parochial
choir schools, particularly that of Allauch. Finally, in 1851, he
opened Holy Family School at Rouet with the help of Father
Bruchon; in fact, this school became the official minor seminary
and was formally recognized as such in 1862 by Bishop de Mazenod's successor, Bishop Cruice. Such great effort had encouraging
results toward the end of Bishop de Mazenod's episcopate, and
even more so after his death. In 1854, 10 entrances into the major
seminary were recorded, 12 in 1855, 15 in 1857, 16 in 1858, and
17 in 1860.[25] Of the 18 who were admitted in 1859, Holy Family
School alone supplied 8 recruits.[26]

Information regarding the spiritual and intellectual training
of the minor seminarians is either lacking or is limited to vague
and conventional generalities. The only data regarding their intellectual training concern the last two years of Bishop de Mazenod's episcopate. Now, if we were to judge the level of studies by
what we know of the new philosophy students at that time and
if we disregard the fact that they were by no means excellent
students, we would be forced to conclude that the level was rather
low. A letter sent to Father Fabre, the superior of the major seminary, by Father Rey, one of the major seminary professors, ac-
knowledges the poor impression he received during the commence-
ment exercises he attended at the Holy Family School and at the
Sacred Heart Seminary. At the first named of these two establishments, he was amazed by the "inferiority that was revealed" by

the selections that were read. At the second, where awards nonetheless abounded, "those who are to enter or who have entered
the major seminary, gained little or nothing from their studies." [27]
Far from finding his correspondent's pessimism inordinate, Father
Fabre was even more pessimistic:

What you say of the two ecclesiastics who entered the clerical ranks at
Easter is not too encouraging, especially when it is viewed alongside
what you told me of the rhetoric students of the Holy Family School.
Ah me! what kind of students are we getting! [28]

The following year a similar lament was voiced regarding the
entrance examination given to the new recruits:

We spent yesterday and the day before with our new arrivals. . . .
Oh Lord! what sorry days, and what sorrier results! The passage you
had chosen from Tacitus, the burning of Rome, was unintelligible to
all of them. They had to be given another from Sallust, and several of
them scarcely understood that one. . . . I'm very much afraid that
three or four of them will be casualties.[29]

To soften these judgments, should it be supposed that Fabre and
Rey were prone to belittle the very difficult work accomplished
in the minor seminaries, as is often the case with directors of major
seminaries? And yet, even if their appraisals were truly objective,
they should not astonish us. Although we do not yet have a docu-
mented and critical general study regarding the ecclesiastical establishments in the nineteenth century which taught grammar
and the humanities to young men studying for the priesthood, certain perspectives nonetheless are beginning to emerge. The first
period of that century, 1802–1850, retained the system of improvizing invented after the Revolution. Because trained and schol-
arly teachers were lacking, it mattered little who did the teaching or what was taught. Not until after Bishop Affre founded
the Carmelite school, and after the Falloux Law, did competent
professors with degrees become available in certain dioceses, and
even they were limited to a few cases. It was only in the last quarter of the century, because of the creation of Catholic universities,
that conditions generally improved. In 1850, the sole exceptions
to that unfortunate situation were the seminaries of Saint Nicho-

las and Saint Mesmin, the result of the brilliant initiatives of Bishop Dupanloup. At the time this prelate assumed the see of Orléans, a certain number of his pastors did not know even the elementary rules of spelling,[30] as was only too evident from the pastoral survey he launched. Bishop de Mazenod, therefore, like all his colleagues, was faced with the difficult task of finding competent masters for his minor seminaries. Too frequent changes, rather than remedying this difficulty, succeeded only in aggravating it. With more stability, those who had the capabilities would have been able through trial and error to acquire a certain measure of the pedagogical knowledge they lacked.

Although the files on the major seminary have more information than those of the minor seminaries of the Sacred Heart and the Holy Family, they nonetheless have their gaps. The lack of data concerning effectives makes it especially difficult to formulate precise statistics. In the seminary archives and those of the diocese, there is no record of admissions and withdrawals and no attendance records. The personnel lists of the clergy which were sent to the ministry do supply us with the official figures for each year, but for certain periods these figures do not give the real picture, since they include a number of Oblate scholastics who were pursuing a course of studies at the seminary. Now, although the registers of the Oblates give us the number of these scholastics, the periods during which they appear are not all clearly determined. Lastly, some withdrawals occurred during the school months, and the correspondence alludes to them by simply mentioning a vague plural. However, in spite of a margin of uncertainty the general trend is evident. After the abrupt shortage of seminarians following the Revolution of 1830, the total remained approximately thirty until 1840; from 1842 to 1854, it varied between thirty and forty, with a brief decline after 1848, and then slightly and regularly increased until 1860.[31] The curve for Marseilles corresponded to that established by the Ministry of Cults for the dioceses of France as a whole.

The data on the geographical origin of the seminarians show that two-thirds of the seminarians who came from the diocese were from the City of Marseilles and that one-sixth of the total number of seminarians came from the outside dioceses.[32] Vocations were exceptional in the aristocracy, in the wealthy bour-

geoisie of the business world, in manufacturing circles, and in the
liberal professions which had been largely dechristianized; similarly, only a few vocations came from the lower classes since poor
families in country towns as well as in cities sent their boys to
work as soon as they were able—at which time they ceased going
to school, and, in fact, ceased attending catechism classes. For
the most part, therefore, it was the middle class which gave its
sons to the Church; in the country it was the well-to-do farmers
and in the city the "store-keepers." [33] Father Allemand's society,
which consisted of young men of this middle class, gave more
than a hundred priests in sixty years (1799–1857), while Timon-
David's working-boys' society, restricted to the working class, gave
only four in ten years.[34] Other major seminaries, like that of Marseilles, were entrusted to the Oblate fathers at that time, but, until 1854, the Marseilles major seminary was the only one open to
the scholastics of that congregation, since, in order to economize
on professors, Bishop de Mazenod had his young professed
scholastics take their course of studies there; in fact, during certain periods, he even had them board there. It was only reasonable, therefore, that fears would arise regarding either a lack of
conformity or too wholesale an assimilation. The Marseillais
seminarians had the impression that they were not in their own
seminary and they so complained; the Oblate scholastics, on the
other hand, complained of not being able to live in their own
community. In 1853, Vital Grandin, who later became the heroic
and saintly bishop of Saint Albert, wrote of this togetherness: "It
is not the most agreeable thing," [35] and in 1851, the *Correspondance de Rome* had voiced the complaints of certain priests
of the diocese.[36] In 1854, even the provincial of the Oblates regretfully admitted that the piety and studies of the scholastics had
suffered from this system,[37] and twenty years later Rambert agreed
that "the seminary was more a novitiate than a simple diocesan
seminary." [38]

This criticism from both sides was justified to a certain extent, since there was a need to maintain the proper equilibrium.
Now, every equilibrium is inevitably unstable, but under the
circumstances a certain number of similar elements made it easier
to maintain this balance. The regulation adopted in the seminary
harmonized with that of the congregation founded by Bishop de

Mazenod, and both were modeled after the regulation followed at Saint Sulpice in Paris, even in its hourly schedule. The spirituality of the Parisian seminary was no different from that which animated the interior life of all French major seminaries. All were marked by the style of an era in which, in the Church in France, asceticism and mysticism were not being modernized any more than was Christian thought. Nourishment was derived from the heritage of the past, without holding to any specific school. Contrary to Saint Francis de Sales' theory, however, the bee did not draw its honey from every flower; Tronson's system had prevailed over that of Olier and those of the great Masters of the seventeenth century; special recourse was made to the famous rules set down by the author of the *Examens particuliers,* since, in striving to shelter the future priests more surely from the essentially depraved society which issued from the Revolution, directors and superiors deemed it indispensable to surround them with a web of prescriptions and observances more numerous than those imposed during the golden era. Instead of allowing their students to develop their personalities through a liberal education, superiors were firmly determined to channel all liberty. Conformity did its part in suppressing spontaneity and in causing attempts at independence to be discouraged, and, superiors were strict in imposing their authority.

In spite of these elements which made it easier to maintain an equilibrium, the fact still remains that Father Tempier and his successor Father Fabre could not exercise the same authority over the future priests of the diocese as they could over the members of their congregation, bound as the latter were by their vow of obedience and obliged by their rule to confess their faults openly. Then too, in the training of the secular clergy, the Sulpician spirituality which, under Father Émery's direction, had left its mark upon Bishop de Mazenod, put stress upon the grandeur and sanctity of the priestly state, while in the training of the Oblate students the perfection of the religious state as well had to be emphasized. Lastly, pupils destined for such dissimilar ways of life and such dissimilar ministries could not be given identical preparation.

In spite of its disadvantages, the unique character of this combined seminary-scholasticate had its advantages. To be sure, the regularity and fervor of the young Oblate scholastics edified their Marseillais fellow-students, and must have fostered the latters' own regularity and fervor, as all testimony indicates. Though Bishop de Mazenod's major seminary did not differ from the other major seminaries in France in its methods of formation which held to the style of the era, from a spiritual standpoint it ranked among the best.

Considering it from an intellectual viewpoint, however, one can find nothing about the major seminary of Marseilles to justify changing the harsh opinions formed about the insufficiency of ecclesiastical studies in France during the nineteenth century. As elsewhere, the same causes were producing the same results. Like the bishop himself, the teachers naturally insisted on the obligation of competence in the sacred sciences. But although profane sciences were constantly making new advances and their methods were being perfected, the sacred sciences remained at a standstill. Did the apprehensive defense-mechanism against modern society, which explains the barriers accumulated in the moral and spiritual training of the clerics, likewise intervene to preserve them from being contaminated by the ideas of the day? There are some who think so. It does seem, however—and if it were so, the error would have been all the more egregious—that, in conforming with a tradition inherited from the eighteenth century, so much attention was paid to issues of the past that there was little, or at best a poor, appreciation of the issues of the day which affected the Church much more vitally. Thus, by coping with the problems of bygone eras, the seminarians were spared any intellectual upheavals; but, at the same time, upheavals of a far more serious nature were being prepared for the future. The clergy thus lost contact with the changing realities of its times.

Such a regrettable defaulting, however, should not be imputed solely to the teachers whose task was beyond their capabilities. They themselves were the casualties of a historical situation which dated from the days following the Revolution, when, in the reopened seminaries, bishops relied on the survivors of the *ancien régime* who utilized the textbooks of their distant youth. Those who succeeded them, after a hasty course of studies, walked in their footsteps by maintaining obsolete teaching methods, since competent personnel were lacking and the improvizing of teachers

was becoming an established system. This was the case at Marseilles, where Bishop de Mazenod would eventually blame himself
for having changed his seminary professors too frequently and
before they had time to become proficient.[39] Undoubtedly, after
long nights of intensive study they were able to increase their
store of knowledge, but, though they labored mightily, these self-
taught men could not labor efficiently, since they had never enjoyed the benefit of qualified teachers who would have shown
them how to work systematically. Father Rey certainly excelled
in learning, as is evident from his biography of Bishop de Mazenod, but he had no idea of synthesis or of vivid presentation, the
marks of a true professor.

In Bishop de Mazenod's major seminary, because of the
rather low intellectual level of certain students and their less than
excessive thirst for knowledge, as elsewhere and as always, it was
essential to remain simple without weakening the foundation,
and, on the other hand, to arouse interest so as not to discourage
the listeners. If we consider the textbooks in use at that time, we
can see how necessary it would have been to master the course and
to possess to a very high degree the art of animating a cold and
dry text. In the philosophy course, they used the Oratorian
Valla's *Institutiones philosophicae,* which date from 1782 and
combined "scholastic theses useful to theology with a simplified
Cartesian philosophy." [40] This work was later replaced by the
Institutiones philosophicae et theoreticae of the German Jesuit
Rothenflue; Tempier considered this work "too deep," [41] and
when Father Baret was asked to give his opinion of it, he stated
that it contained "more thorns than roses." [42]

For dogmatic theology, they resorted to Bailly, Bouvier and
Liebermann successively. It was not until 1851 that the principal
tracts were studied from an abridged edition of the *Summa* of
Saint Thomas.[43] In moral theology, the doctrines of Saint Alphonsus were to be taught by order of Bishop de Mazenod. Controversial questions touching on modern issues were limited to
Gallicanism, rigorism and papal infallibility. In the old textbooks,
marked by the rationalism of the eighteenth century, there was
such a concern to render the faith reasonable that mystery faded
away and the essentially vital nature of Christian dogma was
forgotten. In the tract *De Ecclesia,* the institutional forms of the

Church were fondly emphasized to the detriment of its profound realities. The social problem posed by the Industrial Revolution was not even mentioned in the treatise on justice which had been devised for the old economy. New teachings in moral theology, therefore, were limited to the introduction of Liguorian principles, and in dogma to what certain professors, during their studies at the Billens scholasticate in Switzerland, had learned from the new German theology then in full vigor. However, since they had no grasp of the German tongue, the only works of this new theology which they could utilize were those which had been published in Latin. For the same reason, the numerous and challenging works of Biblical criticism which were published in German were also eliminated. Consequently, although the seminary statutes declared that knowledge of scripture was "absolutely necessary and indispensable for ecclesiastics," the courses that were devoted to it remained too irrelevant to the problems of method and interpretation then being posed. They simply gave an introduction to the scriptures, with a synoptic table for each book, and briefly explained certain passages in their literal and mystical meaning.[44] Bishop de Mazenod was aware of these deficiencies, as he indicated in a letter to Bishop Dupanloup,[45] but he evidently failed to effect any improvement in the teaching of this subject in his major seminary. As was the case elsewhere, the professors were little concerned with technical questions; their primary concern was to teach the students how to utilize the sacred text for their self-edification and their preaching.

Thus, although his own intellectual training had been rather summary, the Bishop of Marseilles was vitally interested in raising the level of ecclesiastical studies, and it must be acknowledged that, with his very intuitive mind, he had some rather modern ideas in this regard. In the above-mentioned letter to Bishop Dupanloup who had consulted him, he stated that the programs of studies in seminaries, which were too limited to theology, had to be broadened; he maintained in particular that a special course should be devoted to Church history, since the seminarians learned this subject only from monotonous readings during meals in the refectory, where, as Cardinal Baudrillard observed, "the jaws and the stomach are more active than the brain." In fact, he took the initiative in inaugurating this course in his major seminary, and he determined precisely how it was to be conducted: the professor's role was not to teach the pupil dates and events; on the contrary, he was to bring out their importance

in relation to dogma and especially to the discipline which comprises the Church's mode of existence and government in each epoch, her activity at home and abroad, her relations with temporal governments, her means of defence against heresy, and her guiding spirit under varied cirumstances.[46]

This was his way of giving honor to a branch of learning which, until then, had been largely ignored, and it gives evidence of a comprehension all too rare in ecclesiastical circles at that time. Moreover, he made a wise choice in appointing his friend and collaborator, Jeancard, as history professor. Receptive to new ideas, cultured, and effervescent, Jeancard did not excel in learning and in the art of criticism, but he knew how to gain the interest of his pupils and how to imbue them with an ambition to become historians. The diocese would one day count among such as these Canon Albanès, author of *Gallia christiana novissima.*[47]

The prelate, however, had little relish for canon law, since, like the civil law of the *ancien régime* before the Napoleonic Code, its complexity gave rise to disputes that were interminable and prejudicial to discipline, and the Code itself had not kept pace with the evolution in progress since 1789. In his letter to Bishop Dupanloup, he wrote:

To me, a course in Church history seems of more value than one in canon law; in most cases, canon law cannot be applied to present situations and tends to teach ecclesiastics how to rebel against authority, or, by placing too many conditions upon obedience, restricts the perfection of the ecclesiastical spirit to what existed within the clergy in times of laxity when the Church could obtain no more than what the canons prescribed. In my opinion, canon law today tends to make the letter of the law prevail over its spirit and to make us regress to an era when reforms were assuredly not so perfect as those which divine Providence had effected through the revolutions.[48]

Conforming to the decisions of the Council of Aix, however, Bishop de Mazenod inaugurated a course of canon law in his major seminary, and, moreover, imbued it with an ultramontane spirit. Completing the program of studies there were sacred oratory, plain chant, and pastoral theology; the profane sciences were strictly outlawed.

How highly did the seminarians of Marseilles esteem the teaching of their professors and how greatly did they benefit from it? It should not be astonishing that some of them, during their courses of philosophy and theology, experienced the same dull boredom which La Menais claims was experienced by many of their contemporaries. Every professor has had students in his classes who resignedly wait for the bell to liberate them. Vital Grandin toiled over Bouvier and Saint Thomas and worriedly prepared for his examinations with the prospect of undergoing "a half-hour of humiliation, . . . not only before all the professors but before the whole community." [49] However, the future bishop of Saint Albert, who was so rich in other endowments, was no intellectual genius and was somewhat exhausted from having to work harder at the Marseilles seminary than at the seminary of Mans where he had begun his ecclesiastical studies. On the other hand, there were others such as Carbonel who took delight in the Angelic Doctor.[50] These individual cases, which can be duplicated everywhere, cannot warrant any general conclusions. The only general appraisals, gathered from official reports, concern Oblate students; these reports state that, in 1843, the latter achieved "more than ordinary success"; in 1850, that they "applied themselves to study and to the success which goes with it"; in 1856, that they made "satisfactory progress." [51] Nonetheless, if one takes into account the lively emulation between the Oblate scholastics and the diocesan seminarians to which Rey attests,[52] it can be presumed that the diocesans did not lag behind. Moreover, the works published by a certain number of Marseilles' secular clergy, the high posts they filled in universities, the important positions they held in academies and local learned societies, all suffice to prove both their personal ability and the profit they derived from the education they received during their ecclesiastical training.[53] Thus, the efforts of the bishop and teachers, who were intent upon forming intellectually and spiritually zealous priests, had not been in vain. The deficiencies cited above were the result of an historical situation and of an era, and they were found in the other major seminaries of France. Whatever was accomplished and improved in the Marseilles seminary can be credited to the bishop of Marseilles and his Oblate colleagues.

Bishop de Mazenod was aware that the shortage of priestly recruits was partially the result of priests' material plight; on September 23, 1846, he wrote to Bishop Parisis:

To my way of thinking it would be of advantage to religion if reputable families had no repugnance toward allowing their sons to embrace this holy career; to effect this without appealing to cupidity, religion would have to offer a suitable living, at least to those who have reached the highest ranks of the minor clergy, and not the meager salary which is given today to lesser administrative employees. . . . Otherwise a kind of discredit is put upon the priesthood itself by the seemingly little value attached to ecclesiastical services.

What had been happening in France since the Concordat was, in his opinion, "opposed to right order." In the first place, the system in force was unfair to "those in the highest positions" since they were placed "on a level with the lowest subordinates." In fact, vicars general and canons were reduced to a much lower state than were pastors as far as income was concerned. They received an annual salary of only 1,500 francs plus a small supplement from the *département*. They were given no living quarters nor did they receive an allowance for any.

In Marseilles, the large amount of currency in the hands of the masses very often enables the common laborer, the working man, to enjoy better living quarters and more comfortable living conditions than the canon, who, in both respects, is placed in a truly miserable and therefore extremely indecent condition.[54]
[Thus,] to appoint a pastor to a higher position is to ruin and practically to punish him. For this reason, some have refused the honor of being admitted to the chapter, and because of this, the bishop is at present encountering the most trying difficulties in filling certain vacancies.[55]

The prelate sent warning after warning to the minister of cults, the prefect, and even the municipal council regarding this matter, pointing out in 1852 that soon, as compared with the canons of Lyons, Bordeaux, and Toulouse, only the canons of Marseilles would be "poorly salaried." [56] Since his observations achieved no results, he established a fund for the chapter which would assure a fee of 2,000 francs a year for attendance at choir. Now, there were no sources for this fund, and, since the collections prescribed for this purpose yielded little, the bishop gave the chapter the exclusive right to preside at the burials of foreigners who had died in the city; needless to say, this did not please the city's parochial clergy. The vicars general were given the stole fees from the vacant parishes in their archdeaconry, but this was a meager compensation and merely accentuated the disorder without remedying it.

Nonetheless, although the pastors were certainly better salaried than the vicars general and the canons, "the system of equal salary for ecclesiastics fulfilling the same functions" resulted only in a "great inequity." It would be necessary, therefore, instead of standardizing pastoral salaries, to compute them "according to the importance of the place of abode," as had been done for magistrates and prefects. The same principle, moreover, would have to be applied to the salary of bishops, so that the "urgent requirements" of very different situations might be met. This provision had been rightly inserted in the budget for the archbishop's palace in Paris which was now enjoying a substantial supplement. Why not extend it to the archbishops and bishops of cities which totaled hundreds of thousands of inhabitants? [57]

Although the government progressively increased the annuities of simple succursal pastors who were the most poorly salaried, it refused to initiate the equalization which Bishop de Mazenod specified for the purpose of making the living conditions of first- and second-class pastors more equitable. Failing to obtain satisfaction on this point, the prelate therefore set down rules for the distribution of stole fees for the City of Marseilles—that is, the stole fees over which he had jurisdiction. We have already seen what measures had been taken in 1831 under his aegis to create a common fund into which each parish of the city had to pour this casual income every month. During his episcopate, he continued to improve and to supervise personally the functioning of that system which established a parity between rich and poor parishes and which was of special advantage to the curates. Previously they had been receiving a mere 500 francs a year, but with the new system they received the same amount of stole fees as pastors and rectors, save for about 100 francs. The shares of both pastors and curates varied according to the years; they increased continually from 1833 to 1847; in that latter year they decreased, making it necessary to raise the stipends. To make the parity more complete, Bishop de Mazenod, in 1858, described in detail what each type of marriage in every parish would demand in the way of "essentials" and "extras" so that there might be uniformity in ceremonies as well as in stipends.[58]

It seems that the prelate was less plagued by this financial problem in parishes outside the city. Pastors of succursal parishes had been granted increases in salary; in the "important localities," the casual income more than met the need; in the country places, the living conditions of the priests "are, more often than not, affluent in comparison with the financial means of their parishioners."[59]

Lastly, financial help had to be assured to priests who were sick or aged and to those active priests who were completely destitute. The bishop of Marseilles established a relief fund for this purpose, the money coming from donations, collections, and subsidies granted by the government, the *département,* and the villages. He himself donated part of the funds he had at his disposal and, when the need arose, dug into his own pocket. There is no statement, however, to provide information regarding the functioning and resources of this relief fund.

Bishop de Mazenod's solicitude was not limited to guaranteeing a decent livelihood for his clergy as required by canon law. Intent upon raising the intellectual level of his seminaries, he was determined that curates, administrators, and pastors pursue ecclesiastical studies. The yearly examinations prescribed for the newly ordained answered this purpose. To stress the importance he attached to them, the prelate presided over them, taking care, however, not to be more severe than the other members of the examining board. He also wanted to organize ecclesiastical conferences where papers would be read and views exchanged. Before deciding on this, however, he wanted to find a way of making

them effective, since the results he had carefully observed in the
surrounding dioceses had convinced him

more and more of their uselessness. The priests at these conferences
are not making any progress in the sacred sciences, and, for that reason,
they are not seriously disposed toward study, and their priestly spirit
gains nothing. For the most part, the only ideas they exchange are
those of little or no edification; conversations at these affairs are often
idle and, in fact, sometimes even unpleasant. In one diocese, for example, a proposal was made to stage a demonstration against the
episcopal administration. They eat well, however, and sometimes there
is an abundance of food—which is more or less out of place. Perhaps
the exceptional circumstances of my diocese will allow me to organize
the conferences along different lines.[60]

Whether he succeeded in establishing them along the lines he
wanted, we do not know.

We have abundant information, however, on the steps the
prelate took to assure the apostolic effectiveness and the sanctification of his clergy, and about the obstacles he met in pursuing this
twofold objective. Bishop de Mazenod never ceased to profess the
great love he had for his priests; his letters and his *Journal* contain
multiple and explicit declarations on this point. Looking beyond
their human nature, he saw Christ perpetuating the infinite value
of the divine priesthood in them in spite of their natural deficiencies. He felt the plenitude of his own priesthood overflowing
upon the Lord's ministers to whom he had personally transmitted
this dignity and character, and this spiritual paternity endeared
them still more to him. Consequently, he allowed no one else the
privilege of ordaining all candidates from his diocese. In the case
of Gaduel, who had been permitted to enter the Society of Saint
Sulpice, his *Journal* states his "resolution" on this point, and sets
forth his reasons at great length:

How can a bishop forego the privilege of begetting for the Church all
those whom the good God has given him to be his cooperators in his
great mission? Were one to reflect upon the sublime effects of the
imposition of hands, upon the marvelous process of communicating the
Holy Spirit, upon the intimate, incomprehensible, but deeply felt
and very real relationship established between the soul of the bishop

and that of the priest by virtue of ordination, upon the supernatural union which results from this fruitful emanation, and upon all the spiritual and correlative treasures which flow from it, I think that the happiness of being the instrument of such great prodigies would not be yielded to anyone. Personally, each time that I ordain, I feel that I can say with Our Lord that virtue goes out from me. Sinful and unworthy as I am, I feel inwardly something I shall never be able to express. And if God were to permit a priest ordained by my hands to experience, if not the same impression, at least a kindred feeling proportionate to what this operation of grace makes me feel, I think that he would remain inseparably united to me, that he could not help but feel an affection for me greater than that which a son feels for his father, that he would want in some way to share in my life as I want to share in the life of Christ Jesus who is the original source of this spiritual generation which produces the priest through the bishop. I cannot express it as I want to, and so perhaps it will be difficult to understand me. My singularity will be excused, however, when one considers that my way of acting in this matter is the result of a deep-seated conviction which penetrates and dominates my soul; it is a way of acting to which I adhere with all my soul as being the sweetest and most consoling duty of my difficult and fearful ministry.[61]

Was the reciprocal affection and intimate union he hoped to receive always found, even in the young generation which had received the priesthood from him? Would that it were so! The facts, however, are quite the opposite. Although Timon-David readily acknowledged that his bishop "was a saint and at the same time a man of the world," that he "had a tender love for his priests," and that he left behind "a few friendships . . . which remained loyal, even excessively so," the founder of the Working-Boys' Society, who with his customary independence paid Bishop de Mazenod the most moving and most objective homage, went so far as to write: "Bishop de Mazenod, in spite of his great qualities, was detested by the majority of his priests." Even allowing, under the circumstances, for the rather general abuse of superlatives on the part of southern Frenchmen, and taking into account especially the purpose which the founder of the Working-Boys' Society had in compiling his confidential memoirs for the use of his religious family,[62] it must be admitted that the clergy was very unevenly divided about the prelate. All, of course, acknowledged his superior virtue, his piety, his austerity, and his zeal. No one denied his justly deserved esteem, but many feared him too much to love him. His manner of administering the diocese and of handling pastors and priests gave rise to very sharp criticisms, and provoked an opposition which, although it was often more passive than overt, was no less substantial.

Why were such distressing misunderstandings created, in view of the fundamental kindness of a prelate who was guided solely by supernatural viewpoints, and in view of the undeniable improvement of a priestly corps which he had purged and sanctified? Obviously, part of the answer lies in the prelate's very marked partiality towards members of his religious family and in the very important role he reserved for them in Marseilles. Local pride was offended, and very deeply so, by the fact that Oblates comprised the majority of the diocesan council, where the few representatives of the secular clergy were eclipsed or reduced to mere figureheads. Was the second city of France so poor in talent that it was impossible to find men there who were capable of forming the episcopal administration? The local pastors refused to admit this, being all the more mortified that the bright lights of a religious congregation founded to evangelize the peasants of the countryside had been borrowed from the rival city of Aix. Besides complaining that the Oblates were striving for control, they accused them of supporting their congregation with funds from the diocesan treasury,[63] of allowing only Oblates the right to preach parochial missions, of recruiting vocations from the future priests at the major seminary, and even of monopolizing *la Bonne Mère* at Notre Dame de la Garde. All this produced a slogan which became prevalent in the rectories and synthesized protests and resentments: "Marseilles for the Marseillais!"

Then too, only with difficulty could the clergy gain access to the bishop. The poor seculars ran into certain obstacles: the prelate's manservant was by no means a model of courtesy and felt that his master was too easy-going—a dupe in fact; the private secretary—chosen, of course from the Aix congregation—turned visitors away with the claim that His Excellency was too busy (one such was Father Aubert, and more than any of the others he had the reputation of being overly protective, thereby "making a nuisance of himself" [64]). No doubt, at Marseilles as elsewhere—even more than elsewhere—it was necessary to screen callers in order to get rid of undesirables. Still, the diocesan priests felt they were entitled to be received by the bishop. Moreover, it was the bishop's wish to be at their disposal, and when pastors and curates, barred from seeing him by his vigilant bodyguard, were lucky enough to meet him as he came out of his office, they were immediately invited in by the prelate. Timon-David verified this from his own experience after cooling his heels for a long time in exasperation.

Once these obstacles were surmounted, one had to contend with the prelate's initial brusqueness, if it happened to be one of his bad days; for, when Bishop de Mazenod "got up on the wrong side of the bed," wrote Timon-David, "and this often happened, he was detestable." Whether it was a case of being upset or preoccupied, "he displayed a beastly mood"; such was the case when he returned in his carriage from a visit to *l'Oeuvre de l'Étoile,* still fuming from everything he had seen there; "he even vented his anger on our society, which was too stunned to make any reply," relates the same witness.[65] Should the sorry impression which his priests retained regarding his brusque manner be attributed solely to the prelate's outbursts of temper, as Timon-David seems to indicate in this passage from his memoirs, after relating all that had preceded the incident? It does not seem so, for his manner of dealing with matters and of making clear-cut decisions by bearing down on essentials was no less disconcerting than the brusqueness of his greeting. Naturally, a conventional attitude—in fact hackneyed pious expressions—would have been more agreeable, even if they were meaningless. But, because he was straightforward, honest, direct, and sincere, especially when dealing with religious matters, the prelate was determined to remain truthful, even should it mean taking the bull by the horns, and not dodging questions by beating about the bush. Although on the surface his manner did not seem very ecclesiastical, it really was, and in the best sense of the word: more so, in fact, than many of his priests thought it to be when they regretfully compared it with that of his uncle, Bishop Fortuné. Brassevin, the historiographer of the Sacred Heart Fathers, wondered whether the prelate's character which Gregory XVI described as "ardent as the noonday sun," and his qualities which "were those of a good and holy missionary," would not have made him better suited for the conquest of souls than for "taking over their government." [66] Was the sorry impression his clergy retained the result of the fact that, being on his own, he had not practiced obedience before exercising authority; that, since he had been a young priest he had practiced the ministry separate from the other clergy, and that as a founder of an order he began by being superior general without having progressed through a novitiate and scholasticate and without having started out as a simple religious? Was his manner affected by the haughty and yet familiar nonchalance with which aristocrats rather often treated inferiors? Was it modeled too closely on the rather general behavior of the French bishops of his time, since liberals like Affre and anti-liberals like Gousset were equally autocratic and were none too gentle in dealing with pastors, administrators, curates, and professors? Valid as all these explanations may be, it seems that they should be reinforced by another which, even then, was too seldom invoked. Far more blameworthy, at that juncture, than his flashes of temper and his austere virtues, was his weak understanding of the mentality of the secular clergy.

Bishop de Mazenod belonged to a social milieu quite different from the one in which the young clerics of Marseilles had been raised since the Revolution; he had not been trained in a diocesan seminary, but at Saint Sulpice; he had not practiced the parochial ministry within the ranks. At Aix, he had surpassed his fellow priests in every way, not without suffering much opposition from them. Moreover, his religious status helped to set him even further apart from them. Finally, when he was appointed to direct the diocese of Marseilles without having shared the life, labors, and difficulties of his subordinates, he lacked the experience which is acquired from such a sharing; his method of handling the members of his clergy was inevitably affected by this. The impression he made on them when they called on him in no way corresponded with the one he wanted to make; in fact, more often than not it was the direct opposite. Rather than providing access to his heart, he closed it to them. Many left his office embittered and unforgiving.[67] Misunderstandings were intensified by other causes of a higher order which should have counted in the bishop's favor by offsetting the sudden flashes of his character and the errors of his ecclesiastical psychology. His administration often appeared to be a series of impulses and to be supported by an autocracy which relished giving orders. This was failure to realize that the so-called impulses bespoke a very high and well-pondered ideal, and that, as Aillaud expressed it, Bishop de Mazenod's concept of authority was "more supernatural than natural." [68]

Certainly no one should be astonished that the prelate failed to "satisfy everyone." No more than any of his colleagues in the episcopate could he pretend that his appointments of pastors, canons, and curates met with general approval. Far from entertaining any delusions in this respect, the "saintly bishop," Timon-David tells us, "went so far as to say: 'Whenever I make an appointment, I make 99 malcontents and one ingrate.' " [69] Consequently, he relied solely upon his conscience and considered only what was in the best interests of his diocese. In fact, in governing his diocese, just as in regulating his personal conduct, views of faith preceded everything else; if the common good demanded something, it mattered little to him that the measures he deemed indispensable for it would be unpopular; Bishop de Mazenod fearlessly adopted them and refused to retreat in the face of criticism and opposition; as has been evident before, such criticism, rather than stopping him, made him all the more energetic and fearless in pursuing his objective, even if it meant losing the good will of some of his priests: "The good called it vigor and the others rigor." In all truth, although the bishop of Marseilles was exacting and severe, these traits should be "attributed solely to his firm determination to see his clergy steadily improve and his diocese become better organized." [70]

During the long vacancy of the see of Marseilles some unfortunate practices had been introduced there, and they had to be eradicated; in fact, abuses had crept in, and they were in even more urgent need of being corrected. Now, Bishop de Mazenod was not a man to tolerate what he deemed to be vacillation or disorder. Anxious to muster forces for a broad and concerted action, he had to contend with the individualism of a clergy entirely opposed to a new regime which would not allow everyone to act as he saw fit. However, a Marseillais dislikes being "bossed"; according to Timon-David, he is "a monarchist at heart and a republican by conviction; he is completely in favor of a power which permits him to govern himself as he pleases." [71] The priests of the diocese were no exception to this contrast which, in the days of legitimism, characterized the people of that part of France. The episcopal administration, on the other hand, could not be content with merely retaining the *status quo* in a changing city; in completing structures and adapting methods, it had to make innovations. And the prelate, whose aim was to be a missionary bishop, refused to admit that one should be content with merely assuring the perseverance of the faithful and increasing their fervor; he burned with a desire to bring the lost sheep of his immense flock back to the fold. His exactingness which some deemed excessive quite simply suited a program whose apostolic aims were inspired by the prelate's spirit of faith.

We have already noted what obstacles his resoluteness pushed aside when he changed the system of appointments to rectorships in spite of petty quarrels and private interests which favored the adage *melior est conditio possidentis*; and the obstacles he had to contend with in building or restoring churches and in assuring the financial and material resources necessary for religious worship and its ministers. This expansion of the diocese and this perpetual motion which was troubling their tranquility disconcerted and even exasperated those who were comfortably settled and those mediocre individuals who were satisfied with things as they were. Because, "like the mistral, Bishop de Mazenod compelled one to do his best," [72] and like the mistral forced open doors that were firmly closed, certain old-timers sighed for the peace and quiet of the good old days; their dissatisfaction infected some of the younger priests who found it difficult to match the pace set by their tireless bishop. In Marseilles, which gave no proof of originality in this respect, opposition emanated from the upper ranks, just as it did in many other dioceses. The pastors of the episcopal city banded together; some of them impeded progress and, in fact, more or less openly fomented dissension. Naturally, the chapter, into which Bishop de Mazenod brought his sympathizers including the Oblates, was perfectly docile; contrary to the tradition of the *ancien régime* which was so faithfully observed by so many others, it showed no fighting spirit, and remained so much in the background that it exerted little or no influence. It took the death of the prelate to bring it out of its passivity; only then did the venerable canons regain their courage, and, during the following episcopate, they even defended Bishop de Mazenod's reputation with a loyalty and a sense of justice that were all the more praiseworthy since they were rather exceptional at that time. The new priestly generations, as a whole, however, more closely approximated Bishop de Mazenod's expectations. To name only those who were outstanding, the following should be given special mention: for apostolic endeavors, Fathers Fissiaux, Vitagliano, Timon-David, and Louis Guiol; for deep spirituality, "Father Chauvier, chaplain of the Holy Name Convent where he died in the odor of sanctity in 1882," "Father Plumier, the saintly chaplain of *les Grandes Orphelines*," Father Tassy, "a man of great interior recollection," Father Demore, "the good angel" of the Poor Clares, and Father Baussier, "a venerable priest" and the spiritual director of the foundress of the Victims of the Sacred Heart.[73]

In all justice, Bishop de Mazenod should deserve nothing but praise for having wanted "an exceptional clergy." [74] Canon Brassevin did this in the long passage he devoted to Bishop de Mazenod in his excellent history of the Sacred Heart fathers, and he did it with an objectivity that is especially meritorious since the good canon belonged to the Society of the Sacred Heart fathers which was suppressed under painful circumstances.

Completely captivated by the excellence of the priesthood, he felt the sharpest pain and the liveliest indignation whenever he learned of any misfortune which befell it, and in his ardor, he mercilessly banished from the sanctuary those who were compromising its honor.

He was criticized, of course, "for neglecting on rare occasions to gather all the facts and for believing calumnious denunciations too easily." [75] However, when he became better informed, the prelate did his best to make reparation for his honest mistakes. Undoubtedly, some have regretted that he was sometimes guilty of "excessive severity," but they added that such cases probably involved subjects who were "more difficult to manage." [76] Thus, for the number and harshness of his severe measures, a distinction must be made between the young vicar general at the outset of his administration and the old bishop in the closing years of his career. The age difference is not the only explanation for the smaller number of his interdicts or his softer manner of chastisement. The situation had changed completely and improved notably because, to his credit, the prelate instituted in 1823 a necessary purge, and continually worked for the sanctification of his priests. In 1823, when the ecclesiastical ranks had been increased by foreign elements, fugitives of the Revolution, refugees from poverty-stricken areas, or victims of political disturbances, moral standards necessarily suffered, with no possible assurance that after such a troubled period everything would be perfect with the native clergy of the diocese. However, from the Restoration period on, the efforts expended on behalf of the seminaries (of which the prelate was especially solicitous) had undeniably borne fruit. In speaking of the major seminary directed by the Oblates, who were nonetheless strongly criticized, Canon Brassevin paid the prelate just homage:

By his unswerving determination to give his helpers a good training, by monitoring their progress, by nourishing them with sound doctrines, by imposing hands on them only after he became personally acquainted with them and was assured that they shared his feelings, particularly on the question of papal infallibility and the doctrine of probabilism as taught by Saint Alphonsus Liguori which he introduced to France, [Bishop de Mazenod] refined the priestly ranks and prepared pastors mighty in word and deed for the parishes whose number he increased.[77]

Not only had the old bishop softened his manner when his conscience forced him to act severely, but there were fewer and fewer occasions when he resorted to canonical punishments with the Marseillais clergy; about the only ones punished in this way were transient priests or priests who had taken refuge in the diocese.

Besides, even in his early manner, he carefully differentiated between disciplinary cases and those involving morals. The odd behavior of the famous Jonjon would suffice to prove this. As uncompromising as the Bishop of Icosia proved to be toward the two loose-living priests whom this morally blameless man had chosen as his collaborators, he proved conciliatory to an equal degree in his efforts to find a happy solution to the case of their director who was a difficult man to handle and an inexhaustible lampoonist, but basically a very upright priest. It was the Bishop of Icosia who settled Jonjon's problem, and in the process proved to be much more flexible and lenient than his uncle, Bishop Fortuné, who was nonetheless considered the very personification of mildness and pliableness.

At least Jonjon had the courage to sign his pamphlets. Other members of the clergy who like him wanted to arouse the public were less courageous and resorted to anonymity. When one of these pamphlets was erroneously attributed to a priest who was dissatisfied with his new appointment, the accused cleared himself with the bishop; however, since his unruly conduct lent credibility to such a grave accusation, he felt that he should also explain that conduct. The Bishop of Marseilles answered him with these words:

I would be greatly to be pitied were I to doubt the truth of your statements. I am therefore very gratified that you deny responsibility for the shameful letter that was written to me at the time of the appointments of the pastors of X and Y. . . . I will not say anything about the other matter because it is more difficult to overlook; that doesn't mean, however, that it cannot be pardoned. Oh! if only a father's heart could be understood! You yourself know whether or not the words *Quis tam pater* can be applied to me. I am going to prove it anew by allowing you, in spite of the extreme need of the diocese, to spend a year at X, not for the purpose of seeking relaxation from the labors of the ministry, but for continuing your studies there.

The bishop made it a point to say that he would have preferred it, had the ecclesiastic come to talk it over with him instead of stating his case in a letter.

You should have discussed it with me at length since you must have known that I would be very distressed by it. You know only too well that I hate to see my children doing wrong. Learn to go straight to the point with me. You see that nothing is lost by doing so.[78]

On the contrary, if the trouble were one that could result in scandal, Bishop de Mazenod never showed leniency. Nonetheless, it should not be fancied that he acted thus out of sheer wantonness or out of heartlessness. In fact, his one wish was to make his punishments salutary. Far from cutting the half-broken reed in two or extinguishing the still-flickering candle, he did everything possible to rehabilitate anyone who, through discouragement, indifference, or weakness, had fallen by the wayside. He softened his vehement reproaches with such paternal and touching pleas for reform that he actually wept in giving them. Once the desired result was obtained, everything ended with a fatherly embrace. Unfortunately, the prelate was not always able to effect the necessary amendment; in such cases, he sorrowfully resigned himself to the extreme measures which he would have preferred to avoid, and then ceased giving the least consideration. To an incorrigible offender who had exhausted his patience, he wrote bluntly and harshly:

Begone! leave my diocese immediately; I hereby suspend you from all ecclesiastical functions. . . . Don't even bother to visit me; I have no wish to see you. Depart from here and mend your ways! It is with that last remark that I bid you farewell.[79]

Far from being satisfied with an "irreproachable clergy," the Bishop of Marseilles wanted to draw his priests closer to his own spiritual and apostolic ideal, and, in his opinion, nothing was more effective in achieving this than the introduction of common life in the rectories. The pressure he personally exerted during retreats and visits to rectories, and the influence of a special group of his own. choosing, were not, in his estimation, sufficient to bolster the efforts of favorably disposed priests. Individuals had to be brought into line and organized. Even as vicar general, during his uncle's episcopate, Father de Mazenod had extolled a return to this "salutary discipline" [80] in the *Monita* which were prompted, if not actually composed, by him; however, he was quickly informed of the opposition facing this reform, which was such a departure from local mentality and local traditions: the chorus of protests and criticisms which arose when the antiphon was intoned was enough to convince him that it would be wiser not to continue such a revolutionary theme. He still clung firmly to the idea, however, feeling that it would eventually find favor. As bishop, he set about realizing his plan, and proceeded gradually. Earlier, we saw that when vacancies occurred, the appointments

of pastors outside the City of Marseilles were made on the condition that the appointees live in common with their curates.
To one such pastor who objected to the idea, the prelate justified
his determination and defined the system he intended to follow
in attaining his goal:

You know the motives behind my firm determination to carry out
this measure; the only difficulties connected with it are those which
spring from considerations of a far different order from those which
concern me. It boils down to a conflict between nature and grace.
Judge for yourself whether my convictions can yield before such an
obstacle. It must be clearly understood that it is only a matter of time.
I do not want to force anything because that goes against my grain;
however, as long as my conscience always proposes the same principles
for me to follow, I feel duty bound never to deviate from them. I hope
that eventually people will realize that rather than force the bishop
to use this authority to fulfill his obligations it is more suitable and
more just to support him zealously and devotedly, and more in
harmony with the spirit of religion which must animate the co-workers
of a bishop whose only wish is the welfare of souls, the honor of the
priesthood, and the uniformity of discipline.[81]

With the same patience and perseverance, therefore, the prelate
continued to push his plan, but only in individual cases, without
making it compulsory for everyone. In effect, he hoped that
gradually, through private arrangements, the trend would begin
and that, with a change in mentality, persuasion would bring
about convictions, and thereby dispense him from imposing his
authority. In 1848, the idea actually seemed to be catching on;
the pastors who had been forced to agree to take their curates into
their rectories were on the whole passively resigned, and certain
priests even exceeded his desires. Brunello, Guiol, and Timon-
David took a vow in his chapel and in his presence "to live together
so that they might the better devote themselves to the sanctification of young people." [82] All three, because of their priestly
qualities, enjoyed a high reputation and as high an influence.
Undoubtedly, they were only a *pusillus grex,* but their initiative
was an example to others and an effective support to the bishop.
And yet, the prelate still held back and, for the time being, concentrated on clearing a new obstacle, this one concerning parishes

where there were no vacant pastorates and where, therefore, he could not introduce his system with a new titular. He prescribed, therefore, that a room be reserved in these parish houses for the curate on call; he would sleep there during his nights on duty so that there would always be a priest available in cases of emergency. Cases had actually occurred in which the sick had died without the last rites because no one could be found to administer them.[83] It was not until 1856 that the prelate deemed the time ripe enough for enforcing the "salutary discipline" which was so dear to his heart. Moreover, his old age made it urgent that he bring the work to completion; at seventy-five years of age, he knew that time was running out and he honestly felt that he had tried long enough to rally minds to his pastoral concepts. Lastly, it seems that the effusive affection which certain priests bestowed upon him, and the perfect confidence which these apostles, enamoured of perfection, professed to have in him, had nurtured fond illusions. Aging superiors often feel the need of being surrounded by faithful subjects. The consolation and encouragement which they find in a restricted circle of friends put them in danger of accepting as true what these individuals tell them. Furthermore, devotion and attachment, even when prompted by identical supernatural motives, are often somewhat unconsciously tinged by personal motives. Now, the clergy of Marseilles included others besides the Timon-Davids. The latter, who was highly esteemed by his bishop, never curried favor, and, in judgment as well as word, maintained an independence made possible by a complete lack of self-seeking. This total disinterestedness explains why he, at least, remained loyal to the deceased prelate and why he defended his name so courageously during the violent reaction which followed the death of the "saintly bishop," as he called him.

The same credit, it appears, cannot be given to Father Louis Guiol, who greatly influenced the 1856 decision to make common life mandatory in the rectories. Bishop de Mazenod, whom Guiol had chosen as spiritual director, rated him among the "excellent priests" because of his fervor and zeal and had made him "his favorite son." [84] Through a letter which this "favorite son" sent the prelate on July 27, 1854, we know that Guiol, who was then curate at la Trinité, voluntarily offered "to establish a community" and to devote himself with his confrères "to the parochial ministry and to everything connected with it." The sad experience of his failures had convinced him that "parochial reform" was "urgently needed" and that this reform demanded "the common life of the parochial clergy."

I formed a men's society; it has not amounted to much. The ladies' society failed even more quickly. I organized a sewing school for the poor; it is accomplishing nothing. . . . For three years, I gave conferences to the men; you, better than anyone else, know that they were not well attended. . . . I submit all these reflections to you with no other desire but to know the will of the Lord through the mouth of one whom he loves as a father with all the respect and spirit of faith he bears his bishop, and who likewise loves him so tenderly.[85]

One deduces from this letter that the bishop and the priest had been attuned beforehand to react to these proposals and declarations with confidence and affection. In fact, two years later, the pastorates of Saint Charles and Saint Theodore parishes in Marseilles were vacated simultaneously, and hence they provided Bishop de Mazenod with the opportunity to proceed still further with the execution of his plan. Because of a general reshuffling of curates demanded by the choices to be made, the prelate established new communities in these two parishes and added a third one at Saint Martin's. Since Guiol was highly in favor of the "indispensable" parochial reform for which he had offered his personal services, the "favorite son," who had already been awarded a canonry, was therefore appointed pastor of Saint Charles' parish.[86] Such was Guiol's influence and favor with the prelate at that time that the latter commissioned him to "prepare the decrees" which were to be proposed to the synod when it convened "in accordance with the canons" passed by the provincial council of Aix.[87]

This synod opened Sunday evening, September 28, and closed October 1. Although the representatives of the clergy were not allowed to "deliberate or vote" on the statutes that were presented to them—since "the bishop alone decides," as Bishop de Mazenod reminded them—they were nonetheless invited to comment "modestly and moderately," as their conscience "dictated," [88] on the four sections of the ordinances to be promulgated: ecclesiastical life and morals; spiritual administration of parishes; temporal

administration of parishes; sacraments. But the section dealing
with the spiritual administration of parishes devoted such a
lengthy passage to common life that the adoption of that kind of
life seemed very clearly to be one of the essential objectives of a
gathering meant to uphold "ecclesiastical discipline, procure its
strict application in every detail, and above all else make its spirit
prevail." [89] The whole passage began by compiling the arguments
which showed the advisability of common life—in fact, its necessity: authority and prescriptions of the popes, all of whom were
listed; likewise the authority and prescriptions of Saint Augustine,
Saint Charles Borromeo, the general councils of the Church, the
recent provincial councils, particularly that of Aix; the example
set by men like Bérulle, Ollier, Condren, Bourdoise, and Vincent
de Paul; the union of pastor and curates in charity and in works of
zeal, and the avoidance of all vain association with the world,
both of which are indispensable conditions for the conquest of
souls and the spiritual renewal of parishes. A simple paragraph,
on the other hand, was all that was devoted to rejecting the "vain
excuses" which "worldly prudence or purely human wisdom
always offers in rejecting a disciplinary practice which opposes
their inclinations." Everything ended with the following conclusion:

We gladly profit from the solemn occasion of our diocesan synod
to reaffirm our express intention of successively establishing common
life: that is to say, having pastors and curates live together and take
their meals in common in every parish except those where the lack
of room or similar material difficulties oblige us to postpone its institution. In several parishes of our episcopal city and the rest of the diocese,
priests have been living in common for some time. The number of
these parochial communities will increase with each nomination of a
new titular, and only when all the parishes of our diocese have adopted
this practice will our conscience as bishop be at rest.

However, the measure already adopted in parishes where vacant
pastorates had to be filled, and which was now to be made general
for any future replacements, was not

retroactive. Nonetheless, we hope that through their good will and
piety, present pastors and rectors will strive to see things as we do by

drawing as close as they can to the common life. We should be only too glad to have them take the initiative, and we shall always be ready to do everything we can to further the realization of their noble desires.[90]

The bishop of Marseilles, who was depending upon the adhesion of his priests henceforth to support a measure that had been highly criticized until then, felt that he had unanimous approval. In fact, the jottings in his private diary agree with what the official report of the synod relates and with what he himself asserts in his pastoral letter promulgating the new statutes. His diary states:

I think there will be a report of the proceedings of this memorable synod which will leave a permanent impression upon all who had the good fortune to take part in it. For that reason I shall not write down an account of it here. I simply say that, after being called, if not to deliberate, at least to assist through free and open discussion in the preparation of the synodal statutes, this very large gathering of priests could not possibly have acquitted itself of its task with more conformity, wisdom, and moderation. Not one reprehensible word was heard, and not the least idea contrary to the respect due authority was expressed. It was really a family reunion. Joy reigned supreme during recreation, free time, and meal time; piety was evident at all the spiritual exercises, at the chanting of the Divine Office, at adoration, and especially at the Mass which I celebrated and at which the clergy received Communion.[91]

Deeply moved, he had closed the synod with an improvised address, which, in its simplicity, its straightforward tone, and its warmth, may be rated as one of his finest discourses:

My very dear sons, I am your father. My age, my episcopal character, and my heart make me so, and I have an added claim to that title with some of you, inasmuch as I have imposed hands upon you at ordination. I confess, however, that I am at a loss for words to tell you what is taking place in my heart today. I swear that I can find no expression that can adequately reveal what I feel. I have known you for a long time, of course, but during these past days filled with blessings and graces I have come to know you better; I have been with you almost constantly and I have seen that fraternal harmony, that mutual respect, and that trust in your bishop which are so characteristic of you. I have become acquainted with everything that was on your mind. I have gladly listened to every observation you made and I shall keep them in mind because they are worthy of great consideration. In short, observing all of you more closely, I felt my love for all of you grow stronger. Oh! my sons! my dear fellow-laborers! may God, who has so visibly presided over our gatherings, give you a hundredfold the same ineffable consolations you have given me and the days of happiness with which you graciously enrich my last years! Presently you will leave this cenacle to resume the multiple duties of your sacred ministry with renewed fervor. You will be even better equipped, I think, to discharge them worthily. Before we leave, however, come! let me fold you in my arms. You have made me the happiest of fathers.[92]

The official report states in the style of the times:

At these words, the venerable old man, descending his throne, knelt before the holy tabernacle, asking God to grant his wishes; he then sat in front of the altar, and all the participants of the synod, their eyes bathed in tears, came to receive the sweetest reward for their labors, their bishop's kiss of peace.[93]

Now, according to what took place immediately after the death of Bishop de Mazenod, unanimity at that juncture was very likely simple passivity rather than sincere adhesion. No one would have dared to propose substitutes for the synodal articles which Guiol had composed and submitted to its members. They were all restricted to making observations about minor details and form; as far as the essentials were concerned, each of them knew that the prelate was determined, and that wanting to change them would only get him into trouble. Unanimity would be realized five years later, but in an inverse sense, for no sooner had Bishop de Mazenod rendered his soul to God than pastors and curates retrieved their freedom; there were not enough furniture movers in all Marseilles to take care of transporting ecclesiastical belongings. Wrote Father Rey:

Besides witnessing the stirring scene which brought the synod of 1856 to a close, we also witnessed the obsequies of Bishop de Mazenod and the attitude of the Marseilles clergy in 1861 under the administration of the capitular vicars. Rectory communities were seen breaking up immediately. What had become of the feelings expressed by the orator as well as by the recording secretary of the synod? [94]

Even Canon Guiol, the compiler of the synod's statutes and its secretary, was in no less a hurry to turn against his beloved father. This earned him the bitter diatribes of Jonjon, the incorrigible pamphleteer, who did himself credit at that time by defending the prelate's good name against his detractors.[95] However, Guiol's turn-about earned him the confidence of Bishop Cruice and the title of vicar general under an episcopate which contradicted everything its predecessor had done. In spite of the precautions which Bishop de Mazenod felt he should take, his efforts to make common life in the rectories a reality—which were laudable in themselves —ended in absolute failure, and this innovation had made him extremely unpopular in ecclesiastical circles. He thus lost the benefit he would have gained when, with time and prolonged effort, "he had smoothed the sharp edges of his temper which was so formidable in his young days." [96] At the very time when, better understood by his clergy, the Bishop of Marseilles might have hoped to finish his career in a climate of mutual trust, relations became more strained than ever. The ordinance obliging pastor and curates to live and take their meals together explains far better than do the misunderstandings cited earlier why Bishop de Mazenod was, in the words of Timon-David, "detested by the large majority of his priests." Did he weigh sufficiently the personal risk he was taking by going counter to inveterate habits of individualism and independence? We know that when the general interest was at stake, it was of little import to him what might be said or thought of him. His completely supernatural lack of self-interest left him unaffected by the all-too-human furor which can be provoked by initiatives supernaturally demanded by the salvation and sanctification of souls. None of those initiatives which the prelate had undertaken up to that time had brought him more opposition, more enmity, or more bitterness. In his opinion, however, the establishment of the common life was the keystone of his entire work; since he considered this keystone indispensable, Bishop de Mazenod was determined to set it in place, at whatever the cost.

Chapter Two

Pastoral and Social Organizations

ECONOMIC EVOLUTION OF MARSEILLES

The reform which Bishop de Mazenod wanted to effect by having priests live in common in rectories aimed at more than securing the sanctification of the clergy; it likewise sought to coordinate the clergy's efforts so that the religious problems created by Marseilles' economic and social evolution might be more successfully resolved. It was a question not only of meeting the needs of a growing population, but of complementing the traditional ministry and adapting it to changing situations. The hitherto sturdy parochial framework, which Dufourcq termed the fortress of the French Church during the Revolution, was no longer adequate to sustain the practice of religion and prevent de-Christianization. Too many elements were eluding it as a result of the influx of foreigners, or were breaking away from it due to the influence of an entirely new mentality. Although the change, which was about to transform large modern cities, was less rapid in the city and diocese of Marseilles where many traditional structures remained firm, it was nonetheless becoming noticeable enough to require finding new means to revitalize the pastoral program and, at the same time, extend it.

Certain areas were scarcely affected. This was particularly true of the rather extensive agricultural area in the three outlying cantons of the *arrondissement,* and in the canton of Marseilles, since, of the 70,790 acres of land in the city, 35,627 were under cultivation in 1853;[1] even as long ago as 1848, it had been foreseen that irrigation, made possible by the Durance Canal, would permit increasing this acreage of cultivated land by fertilizing

43

the sandy soil of Montredon and the barren table-land of Chateau-Gombert. According to the 1851 census, which provides precise data regarding the socio-professional classes, agricultural workers, both men and women, constituted 35% of the Marseilles population at that date and workers in industry and commerce, 32%.[2] This percentage would later decrease with the growth of the city population, although it seems that the percentage of the rural population remained unchanged. The city proper counted a certain number of "vacheries" (cow-barns), where cattle and people shared the discomfort of foul-smelling stables; in many cases these were located in cellars; but in view of the long-standing practice of the inhabitants of seeing their needed supply of milk drawn from the cow at their very threshold in order to guarantee against fraud, the Board of Health hesitated to order the said vacheries transferred to the country.[3] Hygiene certainly gained nothing, but at least the quaintness of the local scene was not marred.

In agriculture, the social problem of the *ancien régime* persisted. Much of the land was occupied by the numerous country estates of wealthy merchants. Peasant landowners were few in number; those who tilled the soil, farmers or tenants, owned only small parcels of land, and very often hired themselves out as day-laborers during the wintertime in order to augment their resources. Their methods of farming were old-fashioned, and the soil barren and stony. Because of their lack of funds, a more or less camouflaged usury was widespread. Since the farmers lacked any organization for selling their produce, the major part of their profit went to middlemen. Thus, poverty reigned among the farmers, and *a fortiori* among the "brassiers," or farm-hands. The statistics show that in Marseilles, in that "entirely commercial environment," "a low value was put upon agriculture"; it paid so poorly that, "in the public eye, farmers occupied almost the lowest rank, and were resigned to that position." [4]

This resignation of the peasants, moreover, was a source of comfort to law-abiding men. Accustomed to their traditional destitution, the peasants were hostile to any innovations, and their illiteracy protected them from subversive ideas. In 1849, scarcely one-sixth of them knew how to read, for, although city-workers' children could not be hired until they were twelve years of age, peasant children in the country worked from the time they were eight or nine years old, and, consequently, ceased attending school. While noting that the economic and social situation was far from ideal, the committee formed in Marseilles in 1848 to study the problem accepted the *status quo* which, in its eyes, was not entirely without some advantages: "to protect agriculture in Marseilles," it stated, "there is nothing else to do, therefore, but to favor commerce and industry . . . , to spread sound information in the country districts . . . , to distribute free of charge . . . some literature of a very simple nature"; the country pastors, who were in a good position to influence the minds of the peasants, "were expected to preach and exercise their influence accordingly." [5] Insofar as one can draw definite conclusions from the official surveys which used different classifications from 1856 to 1861, it would seem that the number of farmers remained the same, as did that of the overseers; but, the total number of tenant farmers and farm hands, particularly the latter, lessened dramatically, decreasing from 13,083 to 1,537.

For Marseilles' commerce and industry in the 19th century, we have no comprehensive survey which would meet the demands of modern sociology, and, the statistics which were recorded from 1848 to 1861 are not particularly useful in establishing the professional units of the population. The 1851 census is the only one which lists the "chief categories into which the wage-earning population was divided"; the other enumerations simply give the sum totals of those who gained a livelihood from each profession: namely, the head of the family, his wife and children, the relatives living in his home, his employees and domestic servants and their families. But even in these successive surveys, the terms employed are unreliable and do not fit present definitions;[6] in Marseilles, for example, hairdressers and barbers are included among the small industrialists, as were café owners. It is likewise surprising to find office holders, landlords, and people living on their income classified among the liberal professions. Even the term "industry" covered very important manufacturing as well as simple hand-work.

An evolution was occurring nonetheless. In Marseilles, which had traditionally been a commercial city, commerce continued to dominate, and very much so. However, industry was being modernized and was expanding, especially after 1855. Undoubt-

edly, industries still depended upon the port—particularly metallurgy which was essential to steamship navigation—but they were
no longer limited solely to converting imported goods; mechanization was progressing and striving to supplant the small workshops.
It took several years to recover from the financial crisis provoked
by the revolution of 1848. The figures for ship traffic, as well as
for customs receipts, are good proof of that. The economic depression came to an end in 1853 and an era of prosperity began.
Ships crowded into the new dock; large companies came into
being: the National Sea Transport Company and the Imperial
Transportation Companies in 1852, and in 1853 the Marseilles
Steamship Navigation Company and the Combined Shipping
Company. The Crimean War and the Italian War brought a
further increase in transit. In 1853, the prefect stressed that "commercial transactions are numerous and are easily handled; the
port is crowded with ships, salaries are very high, and all classes
are enjoying great affluence." [7] Furthermore, the statistics regarding this affluence were given in round, and consequently inaccurate, numbers: increase in the number of people making a
livelihood from the building trade went from 16,529 in 1856 to
26,569 in 1861 (activity in the building trade is always a sign of
prosperity); increase in the number of people who made a living
from professions connected with agriculture, commerce, and industry: namely, credit bureaus, insurance, banking, stockbroker-
age, commercial brokerage—this increase went from 6,117 in
1856 to 12,968 in 1861. The number of people who made a living
from transportation was doubled from 1856 to 1861: 21,484 in
1856 and 41,906 in 1861. Money which was hoarded in 1848
became plentiful and was now being put into circulation and
invested.

Under the category listed as Industry, those connected with
literature, science, and art show a decrease; the total number of
people making a livelihood from these diminished from 3,085 in
1856 to 2,454 in 1861. Industries producing articles of luxury and
amusement made scarcely any progress: 3,059 in 1856 to 3,463 in
1861. The city's traditional industries prospered unevenly; although clothing and dressmaking benefited as a whole from the
increase of population (28,154 in 1856 and 35,596 in 1861), and

tailors and seamstresses became more numerous (7,716 in 1856, 11,700 in 1861), the hat-makers held to the *status quo*. The leather industry increased from 1,571 in 1856 to 3,091 in 1861, although boot and shoe manufacturing declined, dropping from 8,643 to 7,508. For the lighting industry, the volume of wax and tallow candles persisted because of technical improvements, but gas companies were forced to amalgamate.[8] The food and chemical industries, which had difficulty surviving the 1848 crisis because of competition from beet sugars, inferior-grade soaps, and taxes levied upon salt, recovered after 1855: people making a living from foodstuffs numbered 21,089 in 1856 and 25,792 in 1861; those whose livelihood depended upon the chemical industry numbered 6,485 in 1856 and 7,071 in 1861.[9] The man most responsible for the recovery of the sugar industry was Joseph Grandval. He set up a block of mills (a refinery, a smelter, a molasses distillery) which covered an area of about $3\frac{1}{2}$ acres; these mills employed 1,500 workers, and, in 1852, the daily output of sugar amounted to 120,000 barrels.[10] For their part, the soap factories benefited from the progress made by the oil works which, at the urging of Falguière, made use of cereal fats instead of olive oil and perfected their mechanization. Although the number of soap factories did not increase noticeably (40 in 1849 and 47 in 1855), the same was not true of their output which rose by $33\frac{1}{3}\%$. The number of oil refineries rose from 13 in 1849 to 21 in 1861.

But the greatest sign of the evolution then taking place was the rapid rise of new big industry. Metallurgy provided a livelihood for 4,408 people in 1856 and for 11,133 in 1861. Although the manufacture of goods was still spread out among a number of small shops, at least it was the one industry to which this term can be truly applied in its modern sense, when one considers the importance of a few large factories established on the perimeter of the city. Even in 1849, lead-sheet workers at the Figueroa plant numbered 210; in 1855, the Long foundry employed 100, and Taylor's machine works employed 389 in 1851 and from 900 to 1,000 in 1861; the factory of Benet, Peyruc and Co. employed 250 in 1850.[11] The movement had begun and was to increase its pace steadily; thanks to Marseilles, "the Bouches-du-Rhone *département* ranked fifth among all the industrialized *départements*

of France." [12] With the exception of Marseilles, La Ciotat was the
only city in France which experienced a similar evolution because
of its shipyards.

How much this evolution changed the mentality of the people
and how great a social problem it posed is difficult to determine
precisely. In attributing the leftist leanings of the popular classes
to the subversive activities of republicans, socialists, and secret
societies, the official reports dealing with public opinion are
limited to political views. The strikes which broke out in 1861
at the bakeries, the Mediterranean Ironworks ánd Shipyards, and
at the Gréasque and Saint-Savournin coal mines, were all attributed to the same cause, and, as such, were prosecuted as a
breach of public order.[13] In spite of their limited nature, however, these reports are exact in stating that

although demagoguery, deprived of its ringleaders and lacking any
newspapers to spread its propaganda, had lost much of its effect in
country towns, . . . there were still many troublemakers among the
artisans and workers, particularly at Marseilles; the skilled-labor
groups most affected by demagoguery were the bakers, the hatters, the
mechanics, and the workers in the metallurgical factories and the
shipyards.[14]

The same reports, discussing the religious situation from the
same political viewpoint, establish, in regard to the extreme right,
a similar identity between legitimism and Catholicism.

The legitimists are far more numerous. They may be divided into two
groups: the political legitimists and the religious legitimists. The
former are striving for the return of the legitimate monarchy and use
religion as a means; the latter, on the contrary, are striving for the
ascendancy of the clergy and use the legitimate monarchy as a means.
The political legitimists are in the minority; for the most part they
belong to the upper classes of society; that is where the influential
members of the party are found. . . . The religious legitimists are led
by the clergy in the country towns and, in Marseilles, by the Jesuit-
controlled *Cercle religieux*. These legitimists include a few men of
high social level, but most of their recruits come from the peasantry,
and, in Marseilles, from the dock workers and artisans.

As for the Orléanists, who are bourgeois, liberal, and de-Christianized, they "wield no great political influence and have no power over the masses." [15] Even in this distinction, another regarding the evolution has to be made between the native Marseilles population and the immigrants whose crowding into the city was responsible for its demographic expansion. Of these immigrants, the Italians were a special cause of concern to the prefect (in 1851, of the 18,778 foreigners in the city, 16,109 were Italian[16]): "The Italian political refugees are very numerous in Marseilles," wrote the prefect Crèvecoeur.

The events of the Orient and the possibility of war between the great powers have nurtured their hopes which are given expression in heated agitation. Many of these foreigners are rabid demagogues and they pose as enemies of all governments; they conspire not only against their own country's government but even against that of France, which has given them refuge. They have frequent dealings with the so-called French patriots; it is absolutely imperative that the number of these refugees in Marseilles be reduced.

The Polish and Spanish refugees, on the contrary, "are generally very peaceful and do not appear to be engaged in political intrigue." Of those from the Basses-Alpes *département* and the Provençals, whose numbers were considerable, Crèvecoeur made no mention of them.[17]

Unfortunately, only one report of an ecclesiastical source has been found regarding the religious evolution that took place within Marseilles' population. But since it concerns a Menpenti parish in which the great Taylor factory was built and expanded, and discusses only the foreign workers, its value is limited: "Saint Jean Baptiste's parish deserves very special concern because of the great number of workers in it," wrote the diocesan commission.

These workers, who have come from all parts of France, are entirely different from those of Marseilles. They have a certain amount of education, they are well-read and they continue to be. Unfortunately, their reading matter is bad books and bad newspapers.[18]

Thus, this industrialized section was being led astray sufficiently to cause concern. Although those who conducted the survey were rather short-sighted in imputing this area's de-Christianization to

evil notions, the difference they set down from a religious viewpoint, between workers native to Marseilles and those from outside Marseilles, must nonetheless be admitted. It agrees not only
with the prefect's assertions but with the entirely different living
conditions of the two groups. The "pure-blooded" Marseillais
workers were not in foreign surroundings; their traditional jobs
were still open to them. In their native city, they formed a "labor
aristocracy": the jobs of "fisherman, stevedores, caulkers, carpen-
ters, packers, soap-makers" were their "exclusive privilege." Jobs
in the factories "were left to the Alpine mountaineers and the
Genoese," since "these two emigré races" were "willing to work
for the lowest wages." [19] Furthermore, in the event of a crisis or
a period of unemployment, the workers native to Marseilles were
shown preference; layoffs affected the immigrants first and the
Marseillais last.

One could foresee, however, that eventually small trades and
old corporations, which had been more or less officially restored,
would gradually disappear in favor of centralization, and that
this would bring about a mixture of the two elements which were
still distinct from each other; in fact, opposed to each other. The
situation was already beginning to change, particularly for the
stevedores who still remained conservative in their political,
social, religious, and economic viewpoints. Because of the opening
of the new Joliette dock, where the major bulk of transit goods
would henceforth be handled, the monopoly of unloading boats,
which the dockers had enjoyed in the old port, was losing its
advantages and importance. In 1859, the stevedores were greatly
upset over the forthcoming functioning of the Joliette docks,
which would put an end to their privileged status and, consequently, would put them in danger of losing all their benefits.
"A wise arrangement seems to have put an end to these quarrels,"
reported the procurator general. "It was agreed that the new
dock would hire the stevedores." [20] Although the latter, therefore, were not excluded from working at the new dock, they still
lost their autonomy. Thus began the decline of the most powerful
and most formidable of all the corporations, which by its attachment to the past and by its solidarity had so effectively contributed
to the continuance of Marseillais traditions.

Both Bishop de Mazenod and his priests were aware of a

very noticeable falling away in certain parishes of the city, and they realized that a work of re-animating the faith was imperative. The problem, however, lay in deciding what means were to be used to stem the tide of de-Christianization. It was not a problem that was peculiar to Bishop de Mazenod's diocese. In the diocese of Orléans, where de-Christianization had already occurred in certain areas, pastors were searching for an answer to the problem, and were straining their ingenuity in devising "zealous activities," without being able to put them into operation.[21] At the time of the survey made at St. Jean Baptiste parish in Marseilles, the one who formulated the report was not concerned with finding the methods best suited to the transformation of that entirely new milieu:

In order to bring back to their religious beliefs and practices [the foreign workers who have been led astray by evil doctrines], there must be edifying and learned priests who, by the sanctity of their lives and the soundness of their sermons, will succeed in doing away with their prejudices and giving them an exact knowledge of the truths of religion.[22]

Persuaded that the pastor and his curates were fulfilling this indispensable condition, which he deemed sufficient, he concluded with this encomium: "The clergy of this parish understands its mission perfectly and is fulfilling it worthily."

"Perfectly understanding" the mission of the priest in this sense was not uncommon at that time. The Marseillais clergy, more than those in other cities, was in danger of not keeping pace with the economic and social evolution; the latter evolution was less rapid and less easy to discern, for many of the old structures were stubbornly holding their ground and it was not just the façades which remained. There can be nothing but praise for the clergy that had faithfully retained the eternally sound principles received during its seminary training, principles which are the supernatural bedrock of priestly life and priestly work. But that same training in Marseilles, as elsewhere during the 19th century, had imbued the clergy with a very strong aversion toward the changes which had occurred since the crumbling of the *ancien régime*, and had filled it with fear by warning against all the changes that might ensue. The clergy of that time looked upon the evolution of modern society as an evil and a calamity. In their eyes, the Church, which had suffered so greatly from it, could only suffer still more since the evil doctrines spread by her enemies had brought on these deadly changes. Good Tempier, who swore by Bossuet, had very little to say about Saint Paul's *praeterit figura hujus mundi,* and one surmises that the history course at the major seminary was intended to preserve the illusions of the future priests regarding the *belles époques* rather than to enlighten them regarding the instability of human empires and institutions. An established Church militating against all changes was their ideal, not a missionary Church which constantly uses new methods in evangelizing different and successive generations. Within the clergy of Marseilles, this love of the *status quo* in the religious domain was intensified by a sentimental and earnest legitimism, and, although since 1837 its bishop's approval of Louis Philippe's regime and later of the Second Republic of the Empire had officially kept it in a state of political neutrality, its hearts remained loyal to the old monarchy, as did those of the "pure-blooded" Marseillais, and, in fact, even that of Bishop de Mazenod. Therein lies the reason why the pastoral program had made scarcely any innovations, either in the parishes or in the societies, which were intended to complement the formers' work.

TRADITIONAL PASTORAL PROGRAM: MUTUAL AID, CHARITABLE, TEACH-
ING SOCIETIES

Parish missions always remained dear to the heart of the aging prelate, for they brought back memories of his robust youth. Although reports on those preached in Marseilles and the country places between 1838 and 1848 have been preserved, unfortunately the same is not true for the period between 1848 and 1861. No list of the parishes where missions were given can be found, either in the episcopal archives or in those of the Oblates. Rey, making use of Bishop de Mazenod's *Journal,* refers to only four: Gréasque in 1849, les Aygalardes in 1858, Saint Cannat in 1859, and Auriol in 1860.[23] Is this sudden drying-up of such a spiritual wellspring to be explained by the decline of the aggressive type of ministry which had been so much in vogue until then? There might be cause to think so if one did not know how indispensable and efficacious Bishop de Mazenod considered these missions. This type of mission had been his own creation, and he was not likely to allow it to fall into decay. The diocesan statutes of 1856 are proof of this. After reminding the pastors of the decrees of the Council of Aix and citing his "own personal experience" regarding the "immense good that can be accomplished by the Missions," the bishop of Marseilles ordered them "never to allow a period of ten years to elapse without having a mission preached to the faithful of their parishes." [24]

Likewise linked with methods of the past was the Association for the Defense of the Catholic Religion which he supported and encouraged. The brochure printed in 1852 for the use of its members declared: "This is not a new creation"—and rightly so, since the association was merely resuming the work of a society founded in 1824 under this same name to spread religious instruction; it had died out in 1830 after contributing greatly to the religious movement gradually winning minds back to Catholicism. With a different horizon, however, the revived association intended to broaden its activity and to perfect its organization. Its aim was threefold: to secure the keeping of the Sabbath, to prevent blaspheming, and to spread religious teachings; in this way, the members would

counteract the ever-increasing ravages of impiety and scandal with a sort of pious league which would be composed of fervent members of the faith and to which a consciousness of Christian honor would eventually lead the indifferent and lukewarm.

This association was divided into groups of tens and hundreds; each group of ten had a leader called a "zelateur"; although the zelateurs already belonged to other societies—St. Vincent de Paul Society, Archconfraternity of Notre Dame des Victoires (devoted to making reparations for blasphemies), *Cercle Catholique,* and pious societies formed in Marseilles—, they still had "eagerly and joyfully agreed to the plan suggested to them by their venerable bishop," since they were convinced of the "immense value" of "a collective protest inspired by respect for God's law," and of concerted action on the part of thousands of participants.[25]

It was on this association that the prelate relied in the campaign he waged in behalf of the Sabbath day of rest. To be sure, this campaign coincided with the others which the majority of his episcopal colleagues undertook at that time to halt de-Christianization and secure return to the practice of religion. At Marseilles, however, where even the spiritual was tied in with the port commerce, the campaign came up against special difficulties and thereby took on a unique character. It must be stressed, in fact, that the sole determinant of the prelate's offensive was the unloading of ships on Sundays and holy days of obligation. Even though certain factories, in defiance of the divine law, continued to operate on these days, they were not the direct targets of Bishop de Mazenod's attack. On the wharves, the stevedores' corporation, which stood for tradition, was the party involved, and the bishop refused to allow that particular tradition to be discredited.

Now, in 1853, a poor harvest brought about the arrival of many ships loaded with wheat. To guarantee that the nation would be supplied, the cargo of three merchant ships was brought ashore and shipped by rail on the last Sunday of October. On All Saints' Day, an additional forty-three freighters were unloaded. The bishop immediately protested to the mayor for allowing the weighers, who were under his jurisdiction, to discharge their duties; he also protested to the head of the customs house who had not suspended operations—for if each of them had respected the customary ruling for Sundays and holy days of obligation, the unloading would have been impossible. The workers would not have been forced to work, nor would the prelate have been subjected to granting a dispensation for the sake of easing their consciences.[26]

Failing to obtain satisfaction from the mayor's office or the customs house, both of which took refuge behind the orders of the prefect and of the government, Bishop de Mazenod then sent a circular letter to his clergy on November 8th, reaffirming divine law and specifying each one's obligation. He even dared to raise an official protest because of the success of a petition which had been circulated by the Association for the Defense of Religion; the petition had been signed by more than 4,000 members of all the industrial and the labor societies, demanding that the 1814 law regarding the observance of Sunday be enforced.[27] The bishop said nothing about the government's measure to allow the unloading of ships on Sunday, except to point out that by re-moving a material obstacle on an administrative level it licensed each worker to judge according to his private interests or his own conscience; however, his office as bishop urgently required him to make clear the "exceptional" arrangements he had to make for circumstances which, by their very nature, were extraordinary and temporary. The commandment which forbids servile work on Sunday and which "the Church has never intended to be taken in an inflexible and Judaic sense," may lawfully admit of excep-tion only in cases of "special and grave" emergency. Therefore,

the unloading, the weighing, and the transporting of grain on our wharves [must be regarded] as a violation of this precept unless it would be impossible to delay this work either because of critically urgent needs of the people or because of an imminent danger that a great part of the ship's cargo would be spoiled.

With this rule laid down, "a distinction had to be made, in the present situation, between the workers and seamen who were com-pelled to work on our wharves, and the merchants or anyone else who ordered this work to be done." The former, who are "not expected to judge for themselves the degree of urgency in such cases" and who cannot refuse to do the work without rather grave inconvenience to themselves and their families, are "entitled to the maternal condescension of the Church."

Consequently, taking into account a situation in which I am vitally concerned, I declare that these workers, subjected at least indirectly to a pressure which I deplore, may comply with the order to work at their trade on holy days of obligation and on Sundays for the duration of the present crisis; this, however, does not constitute a permanent and fixed rule.

And they are still obliged to hear Mass on these days.
The case is entirely different for "heads of commercial houses and other individuals who are responsible for the unload-ing of wheat." Church law does not authorize

granting them the same latitude; they are not under any outside pressure; they are free to defer operations. Merely saving money, if

such should be the case, is not sufficient reason for dispensing them
from the precept, since this reason could always be invoked and since
the postponement of work until the day after a Sunday or a holy
day has always been taken into account by commerce and it has not
hampered commerce from attaining its objective and being successful.
[However,] if the merchant sincerely feels that an emergency exists
and that he is entitled to an exception, the way is always open to him
to refer his particular case to the proper spiritual authorities. He has
no right to decide his own case, but must ask for a decision from the
bishop who is the rightful interpreter of the sacred precepts binding
upon the faithful of his diocese.

In showing himself stricter toward the employers than toward the
employees, the prelate made allowance for their respective states,
and, by that same token, averted the danger of seeing the viola-
tions of the law regarding Sunday rest being made general.

Why, in ordinary times, the worker, by common consent, is obliged to
sacrifice a seventh part of his earnings to the observance of this law,
whenever that seventh part is not absolutely necessary for his and his
family's subsistence; why then should not the Christian merchant be
obliged to make a similar sacrifice, one which has always been accepted
in the past and which, in proportion to his circumstances, is not any
way near that of the common laborer to whom he pays a salary! Why,
if I permitted that, I would be establishing an odious inequality in
the very scale established by the Church, and would be incurring the
just condemnation which sacred Scripture pronounces against him
who uses one set of weights and measures for one person and a different
set for another. In fact, I would be abolishing the precept binding
upon everyone, and very soon, instead of seeing quiet on the Lord's
day, one would see all the hubbub of the great amount of work
carried on in our great city; this would cause outsiders to doubt the
city's Christian faith, astonished as they would be by a spectacle too
similar to a general apostasy. Please God I will never agree to such a
scandal! . . . Since the matter of keeping Sunday holy is, in this in-
stance, linked to the commerce of our city, ask yourselves, what commerce will turn into if it has no regard for religion; ask yourselves
whether it will then afford any great security and whether it will be
trustworthy. Vast as the sea which washes our shores, our commerce
is the means through which the most powerful elements of an unlimited prosperity flow into our city from all parts of the world. But,

will these elements develop fully, as we hope they will, if the Lord does not bless them? No one wishes more than I that Marseilles, which is so prosperous in every respect, will become even more so. And that is why, with exception of sin, nothing disturbs me more than the thought that people might blind themselves to such an extent that they will not fear bringing chastisement upon our city; a chastisement I want to avert so that she might be assured the blessings which I constantly call down upon my flock with all the power within me.[28]

This circular caused a few flurries in government circles. The prefect, Crèvecoeur, who had refused to "discuss the matter with the promoters of the petitions" and to yield to their "demands," denounced the circular in a report to the minister of cults as a political maneuver. He claimed that by exonerating "local authorities of all responsibilities" so that he might place all the blame "upon the government," the bishop of Marseilles was striving to get back into the good graces of the legitimist party, which since December 2nd "had not forgiven him his conduct." He was also intending "to create a lamentable antagonism between the workers and the merchants" in order to assure the royalist party the support of the popular classes. This "act of war," furthermore, was prompted by some personal setbacks he had received; to lure him from legitimism, stated Crèvecoeur, Suleau, the former prefect, had allowed him to hope for a cardinal's hat; now "this hope has not been realized and does not seem as if it will be." Then too, he had been promised a new cathedral, and no work on it had begun. He asked for an allowance larger than that usually granted to a bishop, claiming that his status as bishop of a great metropolis incurred higher expenditures; this request was refused: "whence a displeasure which was waiting only for an occasion to express itself. . . ." Summing up, the prefect concluded:

I think that the bishop of Marseilles, who has been a questionable friend of the government until now, will be its declared enemy in the future. That, of course, is regrettable, but at least it will be clear how things stand, and the government will not be subject to making concessions which basically profit only its enemies.[29]

The minister of cults did not even deign to answer him. The memorandum which had been drawn up was not sent, for reasons which were given in a marginal note in Fortoul's own handwriting: "The prefect's letter does not contain anything serious or well-grounded." As a matter of fact, a statement composed by the minister's office concluded: "The pastoral, or, more accurately, the circular letter, . . . is very moderate and merely states the teaching of the Church." [30] Crèvecoeur had gone to all his trouble for nothing.

Besides, the emotion that had been stirred up by the association's campaign of 1853 had subsided rather quickly, and the Association for the Defense of Religion became inactive. "It is merely a relic of the past," wrote Father Guiol to Bishop de Mazenod on March 21, 1855, in proposing a complete plan to reestablish it on new bases. However, this plan, submitted to the prelate by his "affectionate son," seems to have remained just that,[31] since there is no record of any committee which Guiol proposed setting up. Whether it was felt that the cause had been won or whether Marseillais opinion, which is easily aroused, had become indifferent, the association existed only in a few parishes and even there it scarcely functioned.

On the other hand, the charitable societies, far from merely functioning, expanded and prospered. In a report to the bureau of statistics, Timon-David wrote that every year new charitable societies were

being added to the old ones. It is an endless progression. . . . They all exist without hurting one another's interests; rather, they improve one another through emulation. Justice, even more than my priestly status, compels me to add that the main credit for these new societies belongs to the present bishop of the diocese. Before the see was reestablished in 1824, there were no more than three or four charitable organizations in existence. Today, by comparison, they are innumerable. They were all established through the advice, approval, and leadership of Bishop de Mazenod. He never discouraged any of them, and he can justly boast that this diocese, which was once so deficient in charitable societies, is now provided, more than any other, with organizations of every kind.[32]

The prelate's zeal in behalf of these charitable societies was not prompted solely by an evangelical concern to ease distress; in supporting them, he hoped to ensure their Christian character so that their charitable activities might foster the apostolic endeavors of his clergy.

This increase in mutual-aid societies, which assured financial help to workers in times of sickness, was not the result of any initiative on the part of the prelate. The prosperity which these societies enjoyed in his diocese was consonant with a general movement which, at that time, effected their extension throughout France. In his *Les Débuts du catholicisme social en France*, J. B. Duroselle points out that Napoleon III, "who at one time had written *L'Extinction du Pauperisme*, took an interest in the labor problem." [33] A law of 1850 enabled these societies to be recognized as the proper concern of the state: "through the efforts of mayors and pastors," the decree of March 28, 1852, envisaged the creation of these societies in the communes "where their public function would be recognized." Each of these mutual-aid societies included active members, i.e., dues-paying members who benefited from the society, and honorary members, i.e., benefactors who generously underwrote whatever other funds were necessary.[34] Marseilles had not waited for this new legislation to make use of this method of assistance: as early as the beginning of the century, it had been using this method to camouflage the reactivation of the trade guilds of the *ancien régime*. However, the following statistics prove how much faster these societies progressed, beginning with 1850:

Number of Mutual-aid Societies: 1820——34
1840——47
1850——102
1852——138
1860——183

Number of Members: 1820——2,600
1847——3,500
1850——7,400
1852——10,500
1860——15,000

Reserve Capital: 1840——88,000 francs.
1850——350,000 fr.
1860——1,188,000 fr.[35]

A very large majority of these societies were controlled by the Supreme Council of Mutual-Aid Societies in which legitimists dominated, and this supreme council exerted "a certain religious influence over them"[36]; Maurel, its executive secretary, was a member of the Saint Francis Xavier Society (although practically all bore the names of saints, they were not, by that token, all Catholic). Using A. Maurel's work as his authority, J. B. Duroselle lists as specifically Catholic only seven of the 200 controlled by the supreme council. Moreover, several "parish confraternities or associations" had "their own relief funds" over which the supreme council had no authority; these associations were simply "private societies, similar to the Toulouse confraternities." [37]

While these mutual-aid societies were multiplying, the complement of Catholic hospital and teaching societies in the diocese of Marseilles was also increasing. In the City of Marseilles, the number of nuns devoted to the care of the sick reached a total of 471 in 1861.[38] In 1852, the Little Sisters of the Poor joined the numerous congregations devoted to the relief of physical, moral, and spiritual destitution, and soon became very popular among the fishwives; as did the Sisters of Saint Joseph of the Apparition. Their motherhouse was established at Marseilles after some painful settlements in other places, and for them it was a harbor of refuge. Their foundress had suffered many setbacks in Gaillac, Alger, and Toulouse, where the bishops had attempted to change the rules of her institute regarding points she considered sacrosanct; from Bishop de Mazenod, however, she received understanding and support. He encouraged her to carry on her work, invited her to settle in his diocese, approved her constitutions on December 6, 1853, without changing one iota of them, and, finally, proposed that her sisters assist "the Oblate fathers in their mission fields," particularly in Ceylon. "Through his intelligent understanding of things pertaining to God and through his exquisite charity," the prelate "so eased the last years" of the foundress, who died at Marseilles in 1856, that her daughters insist on ranking him high among the distinguished protectors of Madame de Vialar.[39]

On the contrary, the prelate's views and those of Canon Vitagliano differed concerning the group of women who were to direct the boys' orphanage founded by Vitagliano in 1849. Bishop de Mazenod took the initiative in persuading the four helpers of his spiritual son, who were serving as mothers for poor homeless boys, to join the religious life. "We shall make them Oblate Sisters of Mary Immaculate," he enthused. Vitagliano and his helpers gladly accepted; this hearty agreement, however, was based upon a misunderstanding. What Bishop de Mazenod actually intended was that the new recruits join the Oblate Sisters of Mary Immaculate founded by Father Guigues at Notre Dame de l'Osier in the Isère *département*. Since he had inadvertently neglected to say so, and, since Elizabeth Reinaud, her companions, and their director, Vitagliano, were ignorant of the Oblate sisters' existence, all five felt that they were being established as an autonomous congregation devoted exclusively to work with the orphans. On discovering that it was a case of something entirely different, they lost their enthusiasm. Allowing themselves to be adopted by an institute of entirely different geographic origins, which would impose its spirit upon them, by no means appealed to them; coming under an authority other than that of Father Vitagliano made the four postulants even more reluctant; still, obedience triumphed. Since the bishop had mapped out the path, they agreed to follow it, and, on February 26, 1852, the prelate presided at their investiture. The preacher for the occasion was Father Vincens, an Oblate, and Vitagliano relegated himself to the background. Thus it became clear under whose jurisdiction the orphans and their "mothers" would find themselves. The arrival of the Oblate sisters, who had come from their motherhouse of Notre Dame de l'Osier to take charge of the Marseilles community, was intended to complete the amalgamation. Instead of effecting the hoped-for amalgamation, however, the mixture of these much too different elements provoked such grave discord that their incompatibility became all too apparent. "The virtues of each of them were not enough to smooth the way," wrote L. Giraud; "material of different colors cannot be fitted together willy nilly, even though they may all be of rich velvet." [40] With heroic detachment, Vitagliano maintained a reserved attitude and left everything to divine Providence, since it had never failed a work that had begun and was continuing despite human wisdom. Like a good Marseillais, he repeated the maxim of the women of Saint John: *"Co que lou bon Dieù bagno, lou bon Dieù lou seco"*

(The face God moistens with tears, He also dries). However, after waiting patiently for a few months, and convinced that prolonging such an unhappy experiment would result only in compromising and embittering everyone, Elizabeth Reinaud, who had become Mother Marie Elizabeth, talked to the bishop in complete candor. After giving him proof that the experiment had been a failure, this able and good-hearted woman even laid down an ultimatum:

Moreover, Your Excellency, if I fail to get a favorable decision in this matter, which is so essential to the welfare of the orphanage, then my daughters and I must beg you to allow us to leave and work for the glory of God elsewhere, since we cannot divorce our interests from that of our founder.[41]

The prelate, who had a reputation for insisting on his authority and obstinately holding to his own views, admitted that he had made a mistake; although at times this improviser went ahead too quickly, he also knew how to extricate himself and turn back. He therefore renounced affiliating the Oblate Sisters of the Orphanage with the Oblate Sisters of Notre Dame de l'Osier who were under the control of his own dear congregation; he authorized the orphanage sisters to use their original name and to remain devoted exclusively to caring for homeless children, specifically the orphans of Marseilles. The prelate returned their spiritual father to them, and Vitagliano once again took charge of his house which steadily expanded; in 1854, it was doubled in size, and a second house established at Jarret, where workshops were added for teaching the oldest orphans a manual trade.

The prelate was less fortunate in initiating the creation of a religious society which took the name of Brothers of Notre Dame de Bon Secours; its purpose was to care for sick men, both rich and poor, in their homes. Bishop de Mazenod wrote in a circular letter to the bishops of France:

However laudable the services rendered by the different religious orders of women are, I have been convinced for a long time that it would be more advantageous in many cases to assign men religious rather than women religious to care for men stricken with illness, since women religious cannot always supply the care that is needed.[42]

This society seemed so indispensable to him that he hoped to extend it to other dioceses; moreover, while waiting for returns from the collections he had requested of his colleagues to cover the initial expenses, he sold the two country places he owned "in the Banon section" of Aix.[43] On December 16, 1856, five brothers received the habit from his hands. Although they were "well meaning" and wholeheartedly approved the prelate's aims,[44] their congregation, in which he had placed so much hope and for which he had made such great sacrifices, soon deteriorated and eventually disappeared under distressing circumstances; in 1858, the bishop of Marseilles found himself forced to complain to the imperial procurator regarding "collections taken up by former Brothers of Notre Dame de Bon Secours." [45]

By way of contrast, the restoration of the Brothers of Saint John of God was a success with the opening of their first establishment in the southern part of France, since the order benefited from a long-standing tradition and age-old experience. Personal reasons also came into play to facilitate its restoration. Father de Magallon, who undertook the task of restoring this order suppressed by the Revolution, had, in days gone by, been a close friend of the de Mazenod family; moreover, his Aix origins inclined him to prefer Marseilles where from 1819 to 1823 he had enjoyed the "great consolation" of caring for "the sick and wounded soldiers of the Hôtel Dieu"; Marseilles had also been the cradle of the institute's renascence in France. Bishop de Mazenod, for his part, earnestly desired to see this congregation implanted in his diocese. On February 2, 1852, after a succession of abortive attempts, his desires were finally realized, when the first brothers dedicated their hospital on a large tract of land they had acquired in the Saint-Barthélemy quarter.[46]

The Holy See's approval sought in 1854 for the Notre Dame de la Compassion Sisters did not signal the birth of a new religious family, since this congregation had been in existence for ten years. As previously seen, Bishop de Mazenod himself had taken the initiative for its creation in order to provide an urgently needed shelter for poor servant girls who had no lodgings, either because they had not yet found employment "after arriving from their mountain homes," or because they had been dismissed from their place of employment. Up to then, there had been no religious community devoted to this special apostolate, and, for lack of a house which would have sheltered them, those poor homeless girls, with no means of support, had been falling prey to "abominable women who led them astray and plunged them into a life of vice." [47] The idea of instituting the Sisters of Notre Dame de la Compassion, therefore, came from the bishop of Marseilles who presided over their inception on April 12, 1844; however, credit for bringing the group to reality belongs to Father Barthès, the Jesuit, whose collaboration the bishop had sought. The prelate acknowledged this in his *Journal* in 1845: "Evidently, the good God is helping this good Father Barthès to succeed in undertakings where more clever men would fail." Nonetheless, Bishop de Mazenod pointed out, at that time, that one of the ends of this congregation—a very minor end, in his opinion—that of conducting schools for the poor, was prevailing too much over its primary end, that of caring for servant girls. "It was essentially for this work that I adopted this new order, or, to put it better, that I allowed it to be formed under my auspices and authority." [48] He therefore made the necessary criticisms regarding this point. Undoubtedly, they were heeded, since for several years "the house was always filled with servant girls who greatly benefited from the advantages procured for them." [49] Moreover, the community of Notre Dame de la Compassion steadily increased. Still, there could have been trouble when the "good Jesuit father," without saying a word to the prelate, decided to give the community "a rule, or rather constitutions, in conformity with those of the Jesuit society." "In these new statutes, the bishop was out of the picture completely," wrote Bishop de Mazenod to Cardinal della Genga in 1855, "but I let it pass; as long as good work was being done, I was satisfied."

In 1854, however, he had not been so tolerant when the prefect of the Congregation of Religious sent him the said rules, for which Father Barthès was seeking Roman approbation. Although he was completely surprised that Father Barthès was credited, in the request sent to Rome, with being the founder of the institute, Bishop de Mazenod merely shrugged it off without taking any exception to it. He remarked: "It doesn't matter who the founder is, since good is being done in the house of God." What disturbed the prelate, however, was the fact that there was not "a single word regarding the essential purpose" he had proposed for the institute—that is, caring for servant girls. "I would never have even considered forming a new community of sisters, either for educational work, or for running schools, or even for hospital work; there were enough of those already." However, there was no community devoted to helping poor servant girls.

I have no desire to establish a religious community of women whose purpose, according to what I read in the document, is to engage in every kind of work that can be found in the world: *Our special vocation is to go into divers localities and to live in any part of the world wherever there is hope of serving God better and of working more effectively for the salvation of souls.* This purpose is fine, although it seems a bit peculiar for a community of women.

Notwithstanding that peculiarity, however, the prelate was willing to "approve" the rules drawn up by Father Barthès if the Holy See requested it, but only on one condition, as he wrote to Cardinal della Genga:

I cannot do it unless the rules state that the sole purpose of the institute, or at least the most important one, is to care for servant girls, whom they will have to take into their houses and to whom they will give religious instruction and skill in the work of their profession.[50]

An agreement must have been reached, since the bishop of Marseilles continued to preside over the religious professions of the Sisters of Notre Dame de la Compassion, as he did over those of all the other sisters in his diocese. As for settling the question whether the title of founder should be reserved to Father Barthès or whether it properly belongs to the prelate, it is still being argued today, as though the prelate had taken that "paternity suit" seriously. As far as he was concerned, the only thing that mattered was that real good was being done; certainly, on that point, Father Barthès agreed with him.

There was no such problem with the Sisters of Mary Immaculate, who were founded to care for blind children, since the initiative of this foundation came from an Oblate, Father Dassy. While Bishop de Mazenod fully approved this specialized and needed ministry, he counseled Dassy, who was superior of the Calvaire, against creating a new congregation. Instead of a scattering of forces, which was then taking place among the numerous new foundations, he wanted concerted effort. For that reason, he preferred to have Father Dassy's collaborators affiliate with a congregation already in existence, instead of setting itself up as an autonomous institute. Attempts were made on this score with the Holy Family of Bordeaux, the Sisters of Saint Vincent de Paul, and the Sisters of Notre Dame de l'Osier, but they all failed. The prelate then allowed Father Dassy's helpers to form a lay community and later, in 1859, a religious community. Their constitutions were modeled on those of the Oblates. The prelate's final illness prevented him from approving their rules, but at least he gave this last foundation a blessing *in extremis* on his death-bed; later, the congregation extended its ministry to the deaf and dumb.[51]

While all these charitable societies were expanding, there was an equal expansion of teaching societies, at least for the communities of women. In 1861 women religious of the thirteen congregations devoted to teaching numbered 610; of these, 562 were stationed in Marseilles and 48 were outside the commune, while the members of charitable societies numbered 504 in all. As for congregations of men, the fathers or brothers of the six congregations in charge of public or private schools numbered 236; 223 of them lived in Marseilles and 13 lived in the other divisions of the *arrondissement*.[52] Secondary schools numbered only two, Holy Family School and the minor seminary college which also admitted pupils not studying for the priesthood. In 1848, Father d'Alzon had considered transferring his school at Nîmes to Marseilles because of the difficult situation being created there by the university inspectors; but the bishop, fearing this would antagonize his clergy and result in a loss of boarding students of well-to-do families which supported the Sacred Heart Seminary-College, was unfavorable to the idea. The plan was then abandoned.[53]

Nor were the Jesuit fathers any more successful in establishing a school at Marseilles. The gentlemen belonging to their *cercle*, had, since 1830, been sending their sons to study at Fribourg, Switzerland, under the tutelage of the Society of Jesus; however, profiting from the Falloux law, they were determined to provide their sons with the same cultural, moral, and spiritual advantages at Marseilles and under the same teachers, thereby avoiding the inconvenience of lengthy, difficult, and expensive traveling. To this end, they had formed a committee to collect the needed funds and, during the absence of the prelate, who was in England at the time, had collected 120,000 francs. On returning from his travels, the bishop expressed "his complete dissatisfaction" that such an initiative had been taken while he was so far away, without consulting him beforehand. Since the committee refused to be deterred, and, on the contrary, declared that it would "go ahead with its plans," Father Tissier, a Jesuit superior, visited the annoyed bishop in an effort to mollify him. Father Tissier reported:

He told me: "They are placing me in a difficult position. It seems that they wish to force me to allow a Jesuit college here. Father, you know how deeply I love your society and how pleased I would be to see a college formed here under the direction of your fathers. Tell these gentlemen to hold off on this matter for a while. Soon, I shall be the first to ask your fathers to establish a college here." This reply was entirely unsatisfactory to the members of the committee; they felt duty-bound to continue their campaign, and forthwith decided on the means to be taken to force the bishop to give in. They were sure they would succeed.

However, Father Roothaan, the Jesuit General whom the bishop of Marseilles had treated so kindly during the former's stay in Marseilles after the Roman revolution, took an entirely different viewpoint, and advised waiting "patiently for the propitious moment." The Jesuit General "had hopes that it would come, and that, when it did, Marseilles would be more than compensated because of the experienced professors who would be carefully chosen for its college." [54] Only after the death of Bishop de Mazenod were these hopes realized.

SOCIAL ACTION

All these mutual-aid, charitable, and educational groups which were expanded, albeit in varying degrees, produced no innovations and remained linked with the past. The same was true for the various associations which strove to safeguard the faith of their members and complement their religious formation within parish or confraternity limits: penitent groups of every shade; sodalities of men, women, boys, and girls. Nonetheless, it was becoming evident that, although these spiritual associations continued to be efficacious among classes that were still Christian, they were not reaching the de-Christianized classes. Moreover, as the parish surveys of 1862 show, the associations of men and boys were scarcely functioning; in fact, in a certain number of parishes, they no longer existed. Thus, it was thought that other methods, better suited to a changing situation, would have to be devised. It is true that these methods were not discovered immediately and that priests and laity did not perfect this type of association in Marseilles, even though they were amenable to societies of a social nature; but, at least an orientation had begun. A system of patronage, which has gone out of vogue today, was still being used, but at least a socially oriented apostolate began to devote its efforts to a class of people which had broken away from the Church.

Prominent among the societies which evidenced this more or less social character were the *saintes crèches,* or day nurseries, which were established in Marseilles in 1844 and were modeled after the Parisian society founded in that same year by François Marbeau; the purpose of these day nurseries was two-fold: to take care of children of poor families during the day by placing them under the supervision of ladies, and to leave mothers free to engage in profitable work. By 1860, there were three such nurseries in Marseilles and 500 babies were being cared for annually.[55]

Although the diocese had no agricultural school for training children to work on the soil "so that the overflow from the cities might be transferred to the country," [56] mention should be made of a very original group which had been established in the *arrondissement* of Aix by Father Fissiaux as a branch of the penitentiary. Fissiaux's settlement, which was both agricultural and industrial, provided professional training for future farm and industrial workers[57]; although it could not be called a trade school in the modern sense of the term, at least it gave the juvenile delinquents practical preparation for a trade that would help to set them on the right path and provide them with a future livelihood.

The Saint Vincent de Paul conferences also engaged in social action in Marseilles. The bulk of its membership, of course, belonged to high society, as Bergasse stresses in his *Histoire d'un siècle*, when referring to the conference of Saint Joseph's parish:

The membership always came from a high social level: industrialists, merchants, landlords, professional men, army officers, magistrates, public administrators; this conference was one in which the original tradition of the Saint Vincent de Paul men was best preserved.[58]

The excellent Christian gentlemen who composed the Marseilles parish conferences may not have always broken away from the concepts of their environment and their times, but homage must still be paid to their inexhaustible charity. The investigations, which the conference of Saint Joseph's parish conducted regarding the standard of living of men and women workers in a neighborhood which was never considered "one of the more destitute," regarding the influx of immigrants, and regarding the moral and religious condition of the working people, all testify to the solicitude of these men, and, from a sociological viewpoint, furnish extremely valuable information.[59] Moreover, their activities were not limited solely to visiting the poor and bringing them food; they devoted their time as well to finding jobs for the unemployed, and furnishing tools for those who wanted to set up a small workshop. In one case, they bought baskets for a mother employed as a domestic in a house of ill repute, thereby enabling her to ply her former trade of selling second-hand goods; they also made it possible for poorly-housed people to move out of the slums. The Saint Vincent de Paul men also cooperated with other societies: the *Cercle religieux,* the Association for the Defense of Religion, the Catechetical Society for Adults; finally, they promoted two special organizations, one called the *Militaires,* which assured Sunday Mass, retreats, and evening instructions for the soldiers, and the other called *Apprentis,* founded by one of the members, Major Lion; in 1860 it had a membership of 251 teenagers.[60] Now, when one considers that these men were gentlemen of high society, much of whose time was taken up with business, work, family and social obligations, one can see what devotion and spirit of sacrifice must have been needed to assume such added burdens.

And that was why, after first taking a somewhat reserved attitude toward the Saint Vincent de Paul conferences, which he suspected of laicism, Bishop de Mazenod put his complete confidence in them. Moreover, he was very flattered that Marseilles was chosen, in 1853, as the seat of the regional council of the society in the dioceses of Marseilles, Aix, Fréjus, Digne and Ajaccio. On July 17th of that year, he celebrated the Mass for the inauguration of this council and then presided at the open-air banquet tendered to the out-of-town conferees by the members of the Marseilles society at the country estate of one of its members. "Towards the end of the meal, His Excellency arose and . . . walked around the table," which was set for 215. "As he passed in front of each man at the table, His Excellency spoke a few paternal words to him. We were all deeply moved by such great kindness." [61]

Two months later, Ozanam arrived in Marseilles at the point of death. The confrères of the city had the consolation of "accompanying the holy Viaticum and of being present at the administration of the last sacraments which the dying man, in complete possession of his faculties, received with an admirable display of faith and love." He answered "all the prayers with a loud voice." [62] It was indeed fitting that Marseilles had the privilege of witnessing this perfect example of a holy death, one which had been lucid, quietly courageous, and marked by fervent charity, just as his saintly life had been. Next to Paris, Marseilles ranked first among all the other cities of France in the number of Saint Vincent de Paul conferences at that time. By 1860, the total number of conferences reached 23, with 407 active members, 139 honorary members, and 52 applicants; in that same year, they had taken care of 1,001 families, regularized 23 marriages, legitimatized 14 children, sponsored 251 apprentices, and instructed 269 poor children, 25 workmen, and 500 soldiers.[63]

The societies which were grouped around the Jesuits' *Cercle religieux* and which were termed "social"—Saint Joseph Conference for the Workers, Circle of Clerks and Store Workers, Saint Vincent de Paul Conference for Craftsmen—showed originality in being willing to adopt new methods, allowances being made for their different social milieux. However, they were all controlled by the said *Cercle religieux,* composed of the benefactors who provided these groups with the means of meeting their obligations, and by a "board of trustees" which supervised their budgets.[64]

The *Cercle religieux*, whose foundation and purpose have already been discussed, had not been affected by the 1848 revolution, since its members came from the upper bourgeoisie. Its director, Father Tissier, observing that it had grown steadily since that date, wrote, on September 19, 1852: "Its numbers, and their social value, are always growing." [65] At that time, it numbered 500 associates. On the contrary, the Saint Joseph Conference for the Workers, which had been established in 1846 and which had a membership of 700 in 1847, was on the brink of "dying out in 1853 when Father Tissier took it over with the aid of twelve men chosen from among the most influential members of the *Cercle*." "Under this beneficial patronage, the Conference realized such an expansion that it soon had a membership of 2,000 workers." [66] These workers were organized into tight groups of tens and hundreds; the advantages provided by their mutual-aid society were increased, in proportion, as the members were promoted to the higher ranks which Father Tissier devised in order to encourage greater observance of the rules of the organization. The rank of "elder," which was bestowed after five years of faithful observance, entitled the individual to "twice the amount of help" allotted to the sick each week by the conference, that is, six francs; the rank of "veteran," conferred after four more years of the same faithful observance, trebled the same weekly allowance, i.e., nine francs; the rank of "faithful dignitary," bestowed upon those who faithfully carried out the duties of "decurion," "centurion," and "divisional chief," assured them a further supplement of one, two, or three francs respectively.[67]

The conference sought to assure the material as well as the spiritual welfare of the members; hence the care that was lavished in times of sickness: special medicines, financial assistance, visits by fellow members and by benefactors . . . —in short, everything helpful to the admirable system which was devised to raise the moral standard of the working class and to consolidate its social equilibrium.[68]

Thus, after a rather long crisis, the society, which had been originally founded by Father Barelle and the coachman Joseph, when he became the legitimate husband of the famous Babeau, began to prosper. All the evidence agrees that it accomplished much good, both materially and spiritually.

Still to be provided for was an intermediate social class, that of clerks and other store workers. In 1854, Father Tissier had favored opening the *Cercle religieux* to this group, but the president of the *Cercle* opposed the idea. "If we adopt this policy," he replied, "the merchants and their sons will leave us; they will not tolerate being put upon an equal level with their employees." It was then decided to create a separate association for the clerks and store workers; like the Saint Joseph Conference for Workers, it would be sponsored by a group of men within the *Cercle* and would have its own group of benefactors. It shared a building of its own with the Saint Joseph Conference. At its disposal were "two large rooms with newspapers, card and billiard tables, good drinks at moderate prices, a library and reading room." In times of sickness or unemployment, they too profited from a mutual-aid society, doctor's care, a dispensary, an unemployment agency, and a night school. In 1858, this association had 250 members and 118 benefactors.[69]

In addition to all this, the Jesuit fathers had "contrived to have a Saint Vincent de Paul conference formed" under the direction of the Jesuit Fathers living in Marseilles;[70] it was composed solely of artisans and numbered 160 members who visited and brought help to a large number of sick and unemployed workers. Lastly, the Jesuits continued to direct the Saint Anne Sodality, founded by Father Barelle and his convert, Babeau. These ladies, evidently, were not too easy to manage; poor Father Barelle, whom they had brought to his wits' end, was obliged to ask for a transfer in order to escape their misguided zeal. Father Tissier, the superior of the Marseilles residence, wrote:

Their sodality is very large; it does much good, but it is also very noisy, especially during religious ceremonies, what with its band music, its bombs in front of the church, and all its other noisy contrivances. However, there is less cursing at the fish market and many of these women have become pious. In short, this sodality makes itself both respected and feared in the city; it does much to prevent the sick from delaying the reception of the sacraments. It is the Marseillais heart pure and simple.[71]

A problem, far different from that of the Saint Anne Sodality, was posed for the Jesuits by the *Cercle religieux,* the Saint Joseph

Conference, the Association of Clerks and Bookkeepers, and the Artisans' Saint Vincent de Paul Society, and it was far more difficult to solve. With Babeau and her associates, the lively elements which had to be controlled were at least homogeneous. The men's societies, on the contrary, were composed of such different social elements that harmonizing and coordinating the ensemble was no easy matter. In Marseilles, as elsewhere, certain workers and artisans resented the system of patronage which kept them under the control of the gentlemen of the *Cercle* and in an inferior position. Father Grangette, who appreciated their resentment, had valiantly striven to gain acceptance of their viewpoint, but he was quickly and politely dismissed. Father Tissier wrote to the provincial:

He wanted everyone to be on an equal level. He preferred having the *Cercle* and its board of directors no different from his Workers' Circle, the men's sodality. This gave rise to petty disputes which brought a halt to the financial assistance our society men had begun to give him; it also gave rise to some slight mistrust which, I hope, will disappear under the influence of the new father who is to be appointed, and which will be completely dispelled from the hearts of a few members of the Workers' Circle who are more restive than the others. For some time now, through the efforts of Father Pitron, there hasn't been any sign of this mistrust; but since the two directors of the circles cannot combine the administration and the means of stimulating competition between the two societies, not enough good is being accomplished.[72]

It was equally difficult to coordinate the three groups of workers, artisans, and the Saint Vincent de Paul Society. Father Tissier wrote to his provincial:

It would be much better if these three groups were not rival societies or were not indifferent to one another, [and] if they did not have different directors but only one who would see that everything went along harmoniously, since, in many cases, the same workers belong to all three groups. Because of a lack of unity and cooperation, each association is less effective. . . . I believe that the only thing needed for complete success with these three groups is a firm determination on the part of the father in charge of these three groups to establish this unity; up to now, these workers have had fine spirit. . . . I have always felt, and I have always told our fathers so, that the priest who devoted his efforts to this end would achieve far greater results than those achieved by the *Cercle religieux,* not only in the number of members but also in their fervor, because his influence with the working class would be greater and more productive than a father's influence with high society. More good is always accomplished with the poor than with the rich; not that working with the rich is not a special and very beneficial work.[73]

Despite these difficulties, which are common to all organizations, and which were particularly unavoidable at that time of groping, when efforts were being made to hit upon the right orientation, the men's societies, which the Jesuit fathers were directing, wielded a powerful influence upon the different classes they sought to reach. In fact, Father Tissier acknowledged that the *Cercle religieux* enabled the Jesuit fathers in Marseilles "to wield as great an influence over all the city's classes as would be wielded by a college with a large number of fathers." [74] That influence continued until 1870 when Father Poncet, the superior at that time, admitted that the *Cercle* was on the wane; he felt only a moderate regret, however, over its decline, since he deemed that the *Cercle* was "too concerned with externals and was actually a bit pretentious; although it had rendered real service in the past, its day was over." [75]

THE WORKING-BOYS' SOCIETY

Bishop de Mazenod gladly encouraged all the associations directed by the Jesuit fathers, and he presided at their ceremonies and celebrations; however, he did not take as direct or as active a part in their creation and their activities as he did in the creation and activity of the Archconfraternity of Working Boys which had been instituted and animated by his esteemed friend, Timon-David. In fact, the latter felt that "next to God," the prelate "was the real founder" of his society. He wrote that, instead of "being guided by the dictates of worldly wisdom," and mistrusting innovations, this holy prelate

considered things from a supernatural viewpoint. His whole life was devoted to good works; he had a perfect appreciation of them. . . .

Consequently, his policy was not to oppose them. "If God wills them," he used to say, "nothing will be able to prevent them; I, certainly, would not want to be responsible for their destruction. And if God does not will them, they will fail of themselves without any interference from me." Acting on these principles, he did not want to oppose the work to which I was attracted when I was ordained a priest, even though there was an extreme shortage of priests in the diocese at that time; in the space of two months, four priests had died sudden deaths.[76]

Timon-David encountered more than one disappointment in the work which his bishop had allowed him to undertake. We have already seen the reasons for his breaking away from Father Julien and the project at La Loubière. Father Allemand's Infant Jesus Society, charitable as it was, did not suit the purpose he had in mind, since it affected only the lower middle class, and the evolution of the lower class urgently demanded that effort be expended upon the children and teenagers of that especially neglected milieu. After directing a group of working boys, which had been added to Allemand's society in 1847, he eventually abandoned it in 1849 in order to organize his own independent society of boys from the working class. The 1848 revolution had "suddenly" revealed "the power of the workers" with "all its terrors," and the introduction of universal suffrage put a new class, "whose numbers assured it an undeniable numerical superiority, on the same level with the higher classes"; these two events convinced the young priest that perspectives had to be widened to "an entirely new horizon" and that "special needs" had to be met.

It was no longer enough to preach love for the humble life and for the most beautiful Christian virtues to young fellows who scarcely believed in God, and not at all in the Church, and who were fighting on the barricades with a wantonness, zest, and lack of scruples that were truly inconceivable.

Timon-David clearly perceived the necessity of a specialized apostolate for boys of the lowest class, but, unlike Ozanam, he did not perceive the true character of the crisis that began in 1848, or the social remedies it required. His efforts were limited to the religious domain, since, for him as well as for Catholics of his time, everything was blamed on the evil doctrines corrupting the working man and giving him an "insatiable desire for pleasure," with the result that the worker was demanding "more than society could give him."

Knowing, therefore, that my poor youngsters were being fed perverse teachings at home and in their workshops, and that the only counteragent was my working-boys' society, I strove mightily to give them that soundness of doctrine, that love for the Church, that respect for all authority, and those fine principles which, thank God, have become the distinguishing marks of our society, its individuality and its greatest claim to glory.

Faith and Catholicity were "the special characteristics of our house and its members. Thus it was that, in its small sphere, our society achieved a truly social purpose." [77]

Moreover, without allowing his society to be patronized and controlled by a committee of benefactors, Timon-David, through necessity as well as through principle, still intended to interest the

middle class of Marseilles in the society since that class was being threatened with respect to what it prized most, i.e., its wealth. [78]

Wealthy people came to our help through their donations which I requested as little as possible. In return, solely through the influence of our priesthood and the means provided by our holy Catholic religion, we molded a generation of laborers and clerks who were upright, honest, and thoroughly imbued with sound principles.[79]

In this way, he stayed free of the patronage system which was then prevalent, since he wanted to be master of his own house; this does not mean, however, that this admirable apostle, who stands out as one of the glories of Marseilles, was free of environmental concepts. Certain others in Paris took a broader and more farseeing viewpoint and, in a more social spirit (taken in the modern sense of the term), conceived a confederation of working-boys' societies; they also favored following the example of the German Kolping Society, and even envisaged the creation of a special religious order for the lowest class;[80] Timon-David, however, like a good Marseillais, mistrusted Parisian bureaucracy. It required an express order from Bishop de Mazenod to force him to attend the

Second Congress of Youth Organizations at Saint Nicholas du Chardonet in 1859, since he had little taste for these meetings at which "pettifogging directors" abounded and during which the speeches were "interminable and mostly theoretical." [81]

The nature of his society remained essentially local; it had its own by-laws, composed and edited by the founder himself, and had, as its essential purpose, the religious training of the sons of working people. Timon-David explained its objective as follows: "A group of boys and young men belonging to the laboring class of society, who, in their leisure time, meet to enjoy wholesome recreation and to sanctify their souls through practices of Christian piety." [82] A building was put at their disposal and was open all day Sunday; during the rest of the week, schoolboys used it after classes, and working-boys after work. However, the term "laboring class" must be taken in the sense that was given to it at that time in Marseilles. Using the society's membership book as his authority, J. B. Duroselle states that, of the 352 youngsters enrolled, scarcely ten had parents who worked in the factories, and that none of the teenagers was employed in those factories at that time; the majority were clerks. He thus concludes that "the class which was affected was by no means a real proletariate." Nor could it have been, since the proletariate "had barely come into being in Marseilles in those days." [83] Timon-David's group, therefore, bore the stamp of its environment as well as of its times. It bore the even more pronounced stamp of the personality of its director, whose priestly excellence matched his knack for organization. The training was thorough; it excluded those petty devotions that were over-prized in the 19th century, so that everything might be focused on the essential mysteries and on the liturgy, the virtue of faith cultivated, and the members learn responsibility by playing games, by fulfilling the tasks confided to them, and by promoting comradeship. Quality was more important than quantity. It was not enough merely to assure the perseverance of the group as a whole; special effort was made to prepare an elite corps within the laboring class.

If our working-boys' clubs achieve this goal, they will effect a real social good, not by reforming the entire working class—that will probably never happen—but by molding, within all the cities of

France, a nucleus of true Christians who will carry the banner of their faith proudly and fearlessly.[84]

That explains why Bishop de Mazenod was so devoted to this youth organization and to its director. Besides, there were enough things in common on the natural and supernatural plane between the two men to foster a mutual understanding, even though at times their views differed—since, by their very contrast, their personalities attracted them to each other. Both belonged to the land of the mistral, and they knew that, in addition to doing other things, the mistral swept clouds away; both were determined to devote themselves principally to helping the poor and to assuring secure foundations for their societies; lastly, both employed the authoritative system and were determined to maintain hierarchical order. The prelate, therefore, might well have applied to himself what Timon-David wrote of his style of management: "I had to have helpers and not equals." [85] By his direct manner, Timon-David also excelled in disarming the prelate in order to achieve his goals. He relates, with typical Marseillais flavor, how he went about securing Bishop de Mazenod's consent to consecrate the working-boys' chapel, which had been built for them at great expense:

Mustering up my courage, I went to the bishop's palace. As usual, I had to cool my heels for a long time in the waiting-room. Canon Carbonnel, the bishop's personal secretary, happened to pass by.
"Did you want something?"
"I would like to see His Excellency."
"He is very busy." (The usual answer.) "Perhaps I can help you."
"I wanted to ask him to consecrate our new church."
"You mean bless it."
"No, consecrate it."
"Oh? But that's impossible. His Excellency is too old for that; it would be too rough on him; don't ask him to do it." There I was, completely blocked. Fortunately, the door opened at that moment and there stood the bishop. I knew of his petty foible about old age and I took advantage of it. Bishop de Mazenod, who was seventy-five years of age at that time, was in the best of health; he was tall, strong, well-built, a fine-looking man in every respect, and at that time he gloried in this more than he had in the days of his youth.

"Your Excellency," I said to him, "I was just arguing with Father Carbonnel."

"About what?"

"I was talking to him about an invitation I wanted to extend to you. He told me that you are too old and that it would be too tiring for you. I protested, however, that you were not afraid of any kind of fatigue."

"He's the one who's afraid of getting tired," answered the bishop; "since he has to accompany me, he is using this pretext to avoid it. I am healthier than any priest in my diocese. What is it you want?"

"Your Excellency, I have come in my own behalf, and in behalf of my whole society, to implore you to consecrate our church."

This was his answer, exactly as I found it in the *Journal de l'Œuvre,* written undoubtedly at that very time:

"It is neither the richness nor the elegance of your chapel which makes me consent to consecrate it; my sole reason for doing it is to prove my affection for the Society of the Sacred Heart." [86]

The Working-boys' Society had not only become an arch-confraternity affiliated with the original Confraternity of the Sacred Heart on July 17, 1852,[87] but it had also given birth to a religious community under the same name, that of the Sacred Heart; Bishop de Mazenod had canonically erected it on November 20 of that same year, and placed it under his "direct superiorship" in order to ensure its direction and continuance.[88] Besides, it was the prelate who initiated the founding of this religious community. Timon-David bears witness to this in a delightful account which deserves to be quoted in its entirety, since it gives a striking picture of the two men who understood each other so well:

One evening in November, I was in Bishop de Mazenod's modest office. Providentially, he was less busy than usual and he kept me there for a long time, listening to me with the closest attention. It was a Friday evening. I was still there when it came time for his supper; what a supper! It did not even interrupt our conversation; his servant brought him a glass of water and a piece of bread on a tray; that was his regular collation for every Friday of the year. When I expressed my astonishment, particularly because of his age—he was then seventy—he said: "God has given me good health; I must do penance for my sheep." It was easy to speak of supernatural things with a prelate who was so harsh on himself. I brought out everything I have

just mentioned above: the difficulties I was meeting at that time, the
fears I had for the future; I had begun the Working-boys' Society
only on the express assurance that I would receive help from Father
Allemand's institute; everything had failed me and some decision now
had to be reached; the remarkable results of the society urgently demanded it; the society could not be exposed to the vicissitudes of sub-
sisting by itself. Up to then, the excitement and sudden changes of
the battle had prevented me from becoming discouraged, but such a
thing could happen; I could fall sick or I could die. Such a fine
society needed a better future; I requested his permission, therefore,
to give the society over to some religious community.

As I said, His Excellency listened to me with the closest attention,
without interrupting me. He reflected for some time in silence, and
this is the answer he gave me, almost word for word, since I wrote it
down the very next day:

"You wish to confide your society to a religious community; I give you
permission—that is to say, I will not oppose it. I can see why you cannot
carry on such a great work all by yourself. However, I do not approve
the plan you just mentioned. You will apply to a religious congregation, and it will be very willing to take over your house in order to gain
a foothold on the Mediterranean opposite Rome and certain missionary countries, but it will understand nothing about the running
of your society, will give it a subordinate place, and you will have the
sorrow of seeing your society die out during your lifetime, whereas
you want it perpetuated after your death."

"But, Your Excellency, I will still remain with the society; I will continue to direct it."

"That's what you think! I am the founder and superior general of a
congregation; I know religious better than you do; you won't be able
to reach an understanding with them; either you will dismiss them or
they will dismiss you."

"But, Your Excellency, that means, therefore, that there is no hope
for me."

"No, there is another and a much wiser solution: pick out a few of
your most pious and most zealous young men; certainly you can find
some among such a large number. Gradually, you can train them yourself; that will be much better than seeking the help of outsiders; these
young men know our customs and our language."

Since I began to raise countless objections, Bishop de Mazenod added:
"At any rate, I don't forbid you to try. Seek help elsewhere, but you
will not succeed, because this plan does not have your bishop's
blessing."

On leaving, when I asked for his blessing, he replied:
"You, I bless with all my heart, but not your plan." [89]

However, even though Bishop de Mazenod's views seemed so
wise and correct, it took Timon-David some time before he came
over to them, since he lacked confidence in his own capabilities
and could see nothing but difficulty on all sides. Forestalled by
Bishop de Mazenod's ordinance of November 20, 1852, he felt
that he "would gain so little advantage from it that" (on the
notice he posted in the church of the confraternity) he "substituted
dots for everything pertaining to the society, mentioning only its
canonical institution." [90] Eventually, however, after this first experiment Timon-David decided in 1856 to make a second, this
time more seriously; he "drew up a broad outline of his future
community,[91] without deciding whether it would be religious or
secular. With his first three recruits, he bound himself by vow
'to go through' with the plan he had outlined, which left enough
leeway for any future changes," since the "society we were founding was not then a religious community, but a sort of pious association of men who intended to devote their whole lives, within
this society, to helping working boys." In 1859, "a third experiment which grew out of the second" resulted in the permanent
establishment of the Society of the Sacred Heart.[92]

Beginning with 1855, the Working-boys' Society, which was
first established in Saint Vincent de Paul parish, extended successively to four others within the city and its suburbs, viz., Saint
Victor's, Saint Joseph's, Saint Barnabas', and the parish in Belle-
de-Mai, but it was unable to endure in any of these four. Of all
the many societies, which were striving at that time to improve
the religious life of the diocese, none, it seems, was so auspiciously
oriented toward the future as that of Timon-David, even though
it was limited to working boys of the old Marseillais population.
Nor did any of them cooperate so wholeheartedly with Bishop de
Mazenod and so loyally preserve his memory. Timon-David himself acknowledged what his society owed to the prelate's initiative
and affectionate protection. Although the remembrances which
this admirable priest has recorded reveal "the episcopal administration" as one of the sorrows which enriched his apostolate with
crosses, the pages he devoted to the "saintly bishop," by way of

contrast, pay him singular honor. Few of Bishop de Mazenod's contemporaries have left such sincere, touching, and vivid testimony; it does honor not only to the one who merited it, but also to the one who gave it with complete objectivity, with a familiarity that was entirely filial, and in a style that was typically Marseillais.

RELIGIOUS STATE OF THE DIOCESE AT
THE DEATH OF BISHOP DE MAZENOD

The preceding pages have attempted to give as clear a picture as possible of the demographic, economic, and social evolution of Marseilles, and of the resources of the diocese both in individuals and in societies; they have also tried to bring out the rather relative success in adapting the pastoral program to a changing situation. It now remains to summarize the results achieved in order to assess the religious life of the diocese—a delicate task, demanding strict recourse to statistics and to their interpretation. But the statistics regarding the practice of religion in the diocese during Bishop de Mazenod's episcopate are as fragmentary as those we have for the early days of the diocese. In fact, they are limited almost exclusively to notes the prelate jotted down during his pastoral visitations to what were called country parishes.

When he succeeded his uncle Fortuné, Bishop de Mazenod launched no inquiry such as Bishop Dupanloup, desirous of knowing the exact condition of his diocese, had made immediately on his arrival at Orléans, after being told his diocese was in a "frightful" state. Nor, from 1837 to 1861, did he ever resort to this system which anticipated our present-day methods. However, the information he did gather about the cantons of Aubagne, La Ciotat, Roquevaire and the suburbs of Marseilles, proves that he was anxious to have precise data on each of these country parishes. Since he was less directly and less constantly in contact with this part of his flock, he perhaps felt that he was not as well acquainted with these parishes as he was with those of the city proper. As for the latter, he may have relied on his personal investigations, on the information he gathered from visits he made or received; he may have felt he was sufficiently posted on the city parishes not to have to record on paper what he had in his head; he may have judged that if questionnaires were sent to his clergy, they would be given only vague and inexact answers, or, in fact, that certain rectors would put up a passive resistance to what might seem to them a sort of episcopal inquisition. We know that Bishop Dupanloup failed to gain any information from the pastors of the Orléans diocese. As Bishop Cruice later discovered, the pastors of Marseilles formed a solid bloc.

Bishop de Mazenod's notes about thirteen country parishes, and the few extant letters written by the rectors, furnish information that is too fragmentary and too vague to reveal anything but simple clues. In the suburb north of Marseilles, the pastor of St. Henri de Séon parish smugly stated in 1840 that his parish had the greatest number of Easter communicants, that is, more than 800 out of a total of 2,040 souls.[93] In 1844, although the pastor of Saint André de Séon parish rejoiced over an increase of twenty Easter communions, he pointed out, nonetheless, that "not one foreigner came to the communion rail," and, in 1855, he deplored the increase of immigrants, which, in the space of six years, had "changed the complexion" of his excellent neighborhood. On June 17, 1855, he wrote:

[This] shift from good to bad dates back to the mass of workers from every country who were brought in to build the railroads and the canal. . . . I hardly know the people in my church any more. People here are calling this progress, but, to my way of looking at it, it is a progress that is disastrous to the salvation of souls. . . . Immorality is increasing, young people are being lost. . . , even the children are being spoiled. All they talk about here is their sweethearts. There is no longer any reverence in church. When I carry out Saint Paul's advice, *argue et increpa,* people quake with fear, but it doesn't change things. For the last six years the disease has been making frightful progress.[94]

On the contrary, the situation in the middle suburb, where the population had decreased, remained stable, if one is to judge according to the total number of Easter communions; in 1833, it amounted to almost half the inhabitants, and in 1840 to a little more than half, i.e., 218 out of 416. Since the pastor furnished the exact numbers of married men and women, widows and widowers, and young men and young women who made their Easter duty, the proportion can therefore be established, and it is actually very high: 47% of the men and 87% of the women.[95] At Mazargues in the southern district, out of a total of 3,500 souls, 200 men and 500 women fulfilled their Easter duty in 1856 [96]; in the same district, in Saint Marcel's parish, Bishop de Mazenod noted that in 1856, although practically all the women continued to fulfill their Easter duty—that is, 400—the total of men dropped to 120 as compared with 300 in 1834.[97]

Allauch, which alone comprised a distinct commune bordering on Marseilles, had edified the bishop in 1838 by the "marks of piety and faith" shown by all its inhabitants. "It must be acknowledged," he wrote, "that such a well-disposed population could not be found in any other parish of the diocese." In 1851, however, out of a population of 2,500 souls, only three to four hundred men fulfilled their Easter duty, although, save for a few rare exceptions, all the women and girls were faithful to their obligation. In 1852, "there were more communions at Easter," but in 1856 the prelate noted that, although there were few women who did not frequent the sacraments, the majority of men neglected them. The picture contains some other dark spots: in 1838 Bishop de Mazenod noted: "The people would be perfect if the priests occasionally reminded them of the respect due their bishop. Only a few people were seen kneeling to receive his blessing." In 1851, he was far more concerned over the harm being done by a bad mayor; the said mayor was "hostile to the clergy, was doing nothing to curb licentiousness," and was in collusion with the gambling establishments "where up to 4,000 francs were lost in one night." He had dealt severely, and without justification, with the *Cercle du Droit Commun,* even though it was composed of "upright men incapable of conspiring against the government, . . . because they had voted against him." In spite of complaints, the municipal authorities took no action against the gambling houses: "the police colonel will have to be notified so that the gamblers can be caught redhanded at 'le Chalet' or in the other cafés." [98] There were other disorders, such as tobacco smuggling and blatant reading of cheap literature. At Plan de Cuques, which belonged to the commune of Allauch, only 80 men out of a total population of 750 made their Easter duty, although almost all the women received.[99]

Of all the chief towns in the districts outside Marseilles,

Aubagne was the most fervent. In 1854, the number of men who fulfilled their Easter duty was still as high as it had been in 1833, that is, 500. The number of women was beyond count.[100] In the parish of Cuges, which belonged to the same deanery, the situation was far from dazzling: only 20 men and 30 women of its 1,700 inhabitants received at Easter. "This is the result of impiety rather than of indifference. . . . The people work on Sundays and eat meat on Fridays." [101] In that same year, Bishop de Mazenod noted that there had been "a falling off of men's communions at Roquevaire since the start of the Republic: only 100 men at the most made their Easter duty"; as for the women, "the number of those who did not receive was so great that it could not be counted." [102] At Auriol, the number of parishioners had decreased because La Bourine was made a separate parish; in 1833 it had numbered 5,400 and in 1851, after the La Bourine separation, it totaled 4,200; even so, the number of men communicants still remained the same while that of the women rose to 700; however, "there had been dancing all summer long," and morals were being corrupted.[103] At La Ciotat, in 1851, of its 5,600 parishioners, 260 men communicants and about 1,500 women were counted.[104] Cassis, which belonged to the deanery of La Ciotat, had seen an increase in Easter communions: 1,000 in 1850 as against 490 in 1841; but, in 1851, the total dropped to 840.[105] Cyreste, which also belonged to the Ciotat deanery, was in a truly sad state. In 1856, the rector, Father Rouden, wrote: "I need God's holy grace to keep from becoming disheartened. Only two men made their Easter duty, and only seven go to Mass on Sundays." [106]

It is obvious, therefore, that, in his notes, Bishop de Mazenod attached the greatest importance to Easter communicants, since in his eyes this practice was the essential gauge of the religious state of a parish. With the exception of Cuges, where the number of men who went to Mass on Sundays amounted to barely fifty, there is no indication that he stressed the number of those fulfilling that obligation. As for confession and communion outside the paschal season, there is only one indication, and that refers to Mazargues: "There are more than 100 communions every Sunday, and 200 for the big feast days." The prelate paid particular attention to sodalities of men, women, and young girls (his notes make no mention of the sodalities for young men); their meetings were more or less well attended, depending upon how well staffed the parishes were. As for the Penitents, in 1838 they were not very active at Allauch, and in state of complete distintegration at Cassis. A certain number of them at Aubagne did not even fulfill their Easter duty. At Mazargues, only seven out of forty-seven received communion at Easter. In 1856, the bishop listed Auriol as a happy exception, noting that all the Penitents there remained faithful to their Easter duty.

Interesting, and at times revealing, as this data Bishop de Mazenod gathered may be, they still furnish us with only incomplete information as to his personal knowledge of the religious state of his diocese. Surveys were undertaken in 1861 and from 1862 to 1863 by his successor Bishop Cruice, who had everything to learn and had been left no official figures in the required form; these surveys fortunately allow us to fill in the gaps with a whole set of data which precisely fixes the *terminus ad quem* of Bishop de Mazenod's twenty-five years as chief shepherd of his diocese.

The first survey, which was prescribed in September 1861, was limited to a brief questionnaire with three general headings: Parishes, Diocesan Clergy, and Religious Communities. The first heading, which concerned purely pastoral matters, merely requested the number of parishioners, the capacity of the church, the approximate number of those who attended Mass on Sundays and of those who fulfilled their Easter duty, the arrangements made for teaching catechism, the number of first communions, the list of charitable societies, and the makeup of the parish council. Each pastor was required to "answer with the greatest possible precision." [107] This first survey, however, was unsatisfactory. When it was completed, it was considered much too general, and it was noted that far from being "as precise as possible" the reports were carefully designed not to reveal too much. One might also justly suspect that the bishop's initiative had encountered passive resistance since only one parish in Marseilles made a report, that of Saint Cannat; the 18 others are lacking. In 1862, therefore, Bishop Cruice decided to complement his initial survey —in fact to organize a standard system of enquiry which would keep him informed of conditions year after year.[108] He created two committees, one for the city and the other for the rest of the diocese; these committees would go into each parish and would use a very detailed set of 332 questions. Although more than half of these questions (174) deal with material matters (churches, sacred vessels, sacristies, archives, cemeteries, rectories, parish councils) the others furnish information regarding not only the practice of religion, but the parochial organization and its effectiveness as well: 85 of these questions concerned the state of the parish (reception of the sacraments, preaching, catechism, pastoral activity); 39 pertained to spiritual societies (choir schools, seminary and youth societies, sodalities of adult men and young men, and of women and girls, Penitent Societies, Holy Childhood and Propagation of the Faith societies); 13 concerned charitable organizations, and 19 concerned schools.[109]

Of the reports from the 80 parishes comprising the diocese, we possess 73; seven of those for Marseilles are missing: five for the city proper, one for the northern district *extra muros,* and one for the southern district *extra muros*; there is no way of determining whether the reports were lost or whether it was impossible to obtain the necessary data. The system, therefore, was an improvement. Most of the time, no doubt, the committees simply transcribed the answers given by the pastors, without enlarging upon the information. There were even occasions—as the erasures and insertions prove—when, to save time, the committee allowed pastors to fill in the questionnaire themselves, and even to add to or correct what the committee found too vague or too inaccurate. In spite of these defects and gaps, this survey, even with all its too summary information and its inexact global figures, permits us nonetheless to make a few general conclusions, albeit with "due reservations." [110]

In spite of these reservations, which one could have regarding the method then being followed and regarding the approximate figures furnished by the pastors, the percentages of those who attended Mass on Sunday and those who fulfilled their Easter duty give, on the whole, a fairly accurate idea of Christian vitality. Making allowance for the infant population and taking into account the civil statistics and the difference between the percentages established by Father Sarazin according to the totals submitted by the pastors and those established by Father Charpin, we can state that both these men agree on the general picture of the religious situation in the City of Marseilles.

The city's thirteen Latin Rite parishes, whose questionnaires we possess, may be rated as follows, according to the percentage of those attending Mass on Sunday, which is always higher than the percentage of those making their Easter duty, since the latter obligation demands greater effort and implies purpose of amendment:

> 51%—Saint Michel
> 40%—Saint Charles; Notre Dame du Mont
> 31%—Saint Joseph
> 30%—Saint Jean Baptiste; Saint Adrien
> 29%—les Carmes
> 25%—Saint Theodore; Holy Trinity
> 20%—Saint Cannat
> 19%—Saint Lazare
> 17%—Saint Laurence; Saint Victor.[111]

For the three other Latin Rite parishes of the city we possess only the numbers of those who fulfilled their Easter duty: the Cathedral, 600 men and 2,500 women out of a total of 16,000; Saint Vincent de Paul, 550 men and 2,500 women out of a total of 18,000; Les Chartreux, between 200 and 300 men, and 1,500 women out of a total of 6,000.[112] There are no data on the parishes of Saint Martin and Saint Ferréol. As for Saint Nicholas de Myre, a parish of the Greek Rite, which numbered 300 souls scattered throughout the city, the rector declared that all his parishioners fulfilled their Easter duty, and almost all of them attended Mass on Sunday.

In attendance at Mass on Sundays, therefore, a change had taken place on each side of the Vieux Port; north of it, the section between Saint Cannat's and Saint Lazare's parishes, on the one hand, and the section between les Carmes' and Saint Theodore's parishes, on the other; south of the port, the section between Saint Victor and Saint Charles *intra muros*. As for Saint Laurence's parish, it seems very likely that it could not be included in that area of slackened religious observance which tends to form a sort of belt along the western part of the city, since the number of those attending Mass on Sunday and those fulfilling their Easter duty, as recorded by the pastor, did not present a true picture; the pastor pointed out that many of his parishioners made their Easter duty at the Calvaire or at the Jesuit house; moreover, Saint Laurence's parish was considered one of the better parishes of the city: the rector boasted of its excellent spirit;[113] in fact, Father Charpin, in his survey on delayed baptisms, noted that

the fishermen residing in Saint Laurence's parish (and they comprised the majority of the parishioners) maintained a percentage of early baptisms superior to that of fishermen living elsewhere. . . . This fine preservation of tradition among the fishermen residing as a compact group in the same district in Saint Laurence's parish is a sure indication of the effective influence which surroundings have upon the religious attitudes of individuals.[114]

It should also be pointed out that there was a large number of communions in this parish on great feast days, viz., 800, and an especially large number of frequent communions, viz., 600; considered from this angle, it ranks second.

In the nonconglomerate population which resided in the commune of Marseilles and comprised its suburbs, the situation was as varied as it was in the city proper. In the still-rural central suburb, those attending Mass amounted to 66%; of the total of those fulfilling their Easter duty, the men numbered only 30%. In the southern suburb, the percentage of those attending Sunday Mass decreased to 31% while out of the total of those fulfilling their Easter duty, the men amounted to merely 24%. In the northern suburb, 27% attended Mass on Sunday, and 23% of the total number of those fulfilling their Easter duty were men. It should be noted, however, that in the northern and southern suburbs, the greatest falling off was in attendance at Sunday Mass; the proportion of men making their Easter duty persisted. Allauch, which formed a distinct commune, although it was attached to the canton of Marseilles, held true to its reputation. All its parishioners attended Sunday Mass; of the total of those fulfilling their Easter duty, the percentage of men was 36%. In the three deaneries outside Marseilles, of the total of those fulfilling their Easter duty, the percentage of men was about the same for each deanery, i.e., 22 or 23%; in the same three deaneries, however, the percentage of people attending Sunday Mass varied for each deanery: 55% for the canton of Aubagne, 39% for the canton of Roquevaire and 38% for the canton of La Ciotat.[115]

Father Charpin's study pertaining to delay in baptisms in the commune of Marseilles very fortunately complements the data supplied by the episcopal survey of 1862, and corroborates them entirely. In fact, there is a striking correlation between the percentage of those who had their children baptized immediately and the percentage of those who attended Mass regularly. The lists drawn up by Father Charpin show this very clearly.[116]

The two zones, B and A, which Father Charpin entitled "suburbs" even though they included some city parishes, actually constituted an area of slackened religious practice. Zone B took in the parishes of Saint Mauront, Saint Lazare, Saint Adrien, and La Capelette; Zone A took in those of Saint Victor, Endoume, Saint Jean Baptiste, Saint Michel, and les Crottes. Of the total number of parishioners in each of these two zones, only 21.4% attended Mass in Zone B and 28.6% in Zone A, and the percentages of those who delayed baptism were in keeping with these figures. The difference between the city and the surrounding territory was therefore very sharp, with an intermediate zone where the situation appears to have deteriorated considerably.

Father Charpin's study, furthermore, furnishes us with information regarding the socio-professional panorama which the episcopal survey did not consider. This information justifies stating that the farmers remained faithful to the tradition of having children baptized within three days after birth; the same was true for fishermen and seamen. Within the liberal professions, however, and within the classes of industrialists, merchants, police, army, clerks, and city and state employees, there were many delayed baptisms; as for the stevedores, the curve of those who attended to this duty quickly took a downward direction after 1851, when their corporation experienced the crisis previously mentioned and, as a result of which, part of its members went to work on the wharves of the La Joliette dock; artisans and merchants remained about average; on the whole, factory and construction workers also maintained it; their percentage of promptness, however, was lower than that of the numerous other trades.[117]

One cannot but rejoice that the physical and professional panorama of the city of Marseilles could thus be pictured, albeit roughly, for the year 1862. However, it would be much more desirable to know the extent to which this panorama had changed from the time of Bishop de Mazenod's accession to the See of Marseilles, since classes and parishes in every era and in every diocese differ in the style and quality of their Christian living. The main thing would be to determine whether throughout the whole diocese or in any particular section of it the situation remained stable, improved, or deteriorated, such as was determined for the diocese of Orléans from 1850 to 1877. In spite of its deficiencies, Bishop Cruice's survey enables us with some certainty to determine roughly the *terminus ad quem* for Bishop de Mazenod's episcopate; however, there is no such survey which would allow us to determine the *terminus a quo*. The only source for making a comparison between the two extremities is the data found in Father Charpin's study regarding delays in baptism; to do so, we must start with his fairly valid assertion that there is a certain correlation between the percentages of prompt baptisms and those of regular attendance at Sunday Mass. Now, after reaching a high of 80% around the end of the Restoration period, the number of baptisms three days after birth averaged around 70% in the commune of Marseilles until 1846; beginning with that date, however, there was a noticeable decrease in that percentage which dipped as low as 44 in 1861; this raised the percentage of those which were delayed for a week from 22% to 43.6%, and of those delayed for two weeks from 2 to 12. A trend toward delayed baptisms had thus begun, and after 1870 became more and more pronounced, particularly in delays of two weeks; "until 1869 the delay of baptism rarely exceeded a month"; "in 1861, there was a rather large disproportion between the number of those who delayed baptism for a week and those who remained faithful to baptism within three days, with most families adhering to the latter practice." [118] Thus, using delayed baptisms as a criterion, one must conclude that the general situation had been deteriorating for twenty years.

Nonetheless, it seems that the old Marseillais population was not seriously involved in this falling away, particularly in those parts where the old social structures remained intact. Father

Charpin noted this in speaking of the fishermen of Saint Laurence's parish who were more fortunate than the stevedores, and
the same assertion might be made for the rural areas in the eastern
suburb and in the country. The pastors did, of course, denounce
dances, theaters, cabarets, and city amusements, and the pastor of
Saint Laurence's parish even denounced the three thousand prostitutes, the hardened sinners of his flock. The children received
adequate religious instruction in catechism classes and in school;
unfortunately this instruction was not very well supplemented by
adult catechism classes or Sunday sermons. Almost everywhere,
sodalities of girls and women, which, on the whole, were flourishing, and sodalities of men, assured their perseverance, in fact, the
fervor of an elite class. The only parish societies lacking almost
everywhere were boys' societies, but those of Vitagliano, Allemand, and Timon-David more than compensated. Exposition and
perpetual adoration of the Blessed Sacrament, which Bishop de
Mazenod prized so highly, were attended with great devotion; the
number of feast-day communions and frequent communions recorded by certain parishes was very high for those days. The columns of the 1862 survey, concerning the refusal of the sacraments at the hour of death, are practically empty.[119] Traditional
faith was maintained, and in spite of all the flamboyant and noisy
displays of their processions, one should not underestimate the
solidity and depth of the people's faith.

   The fact remains, however, that the Catholics of Marseilles
had not kept pace with the economic and demographic evolution
of their city. The pastors unceasingly pointed out the harm being
done by the factories, the ships, the railroads, and the increased
influx of foreigners; like the pastor of Saint André de Séon's parish, they denounced the so-called progress. The clergy and faithful, who clung to the past and to the traditional pastoral system,
were entirely unprepared for the shock of the upsetting changes.
Actually, the harm came not so much from these changes as from
the problem created by the lack of religious leadership for the
new population which soon outnumbered the native Marseillais
population; in effect, they shied away from the traditional-style
parish, where they felt alienated, and adapted themselves outside
the parish to laboring groups whose faith was growing weaker.
In view of the difference in mentality and the lack of priests, the

problem was indeed difficult to solve. Even Timon-David, who was more sympathetic to the laboring-class apostolate, could not solve it by means of his working-boys' society; admirable as it was, it was still too limited to local personnel. At the same time, it must be recognized and understood that all these sociological components had in those days escaped those who, like Timon-David and Bishop de Mazenod, were bent on devoting themselves principally to the ministry of the poor. In certain contingencies, situations are beyond the control of even the most intelligent men who are sincerely eager to do good. Our own contemporaries, who today are grappling with even more complex difficulties, and who so often grope about in the dark, might do well to weigh their own success against their efforts before judging the men of that day.

Although Bishop de Mazenod's episcopate did not effect an unbroken rise in the spiritual life of his diocese, and although the curve for that diocese corresponds only too closely with that recorded for the other dioceses of France at that time, he must still be credited with having accomplished magnificent work. If the rather anarchical state in which he found the diocese in 1823 is compared with the cohesion he gave to it, if the number of parishes he created and the societies he inspired or zealously supported is totalled, and if it is kept in mind that his diocese throve for more than fifty years on the organization and structures with which he endowed it, then, what Timon-David wrote of the prelate does not seem to be Marseillais exaggeration: "Everything had to be done over again; he did it. . . . And in his thirty-seven years of administering the diocese, he rebuilt what had formerly taken fifteen centuries." [120]

Chapter Three

Oblate Missions in Canada and
the United States (1848–1861)*

PROGRESS IN WESTERN CANADA; ABANDONMENT OF OREGON

The pastoral activity Bishop de Mazenod sponsored in his diocese in no way dampened his enthusiasm for the missionary expansion of the Oblates. In effect, the year 1848 marks the beginning of a period when this expansion achieved the most progress. Not only were the first foundations which proved viable permanently strengthened and developed, but others were added to them in the United States, Ceylon, and Natal. Foreign missionary work, undertaken at the behest and under the direction of the prelate, had already extended into America and was beginning in Asia and Africa. From then on, his congregation would be permanently established on three continents outside Europe.

This development, however, was not always in one direction. Obstacles arose and, for a time, were deemed insurmountable, causing the superior general to re-station his available subjects on more favorable terrain so that he might put his still-too-meagre effectives to better use. Moreover, his sons on their own initiative practiced this system of transferral in the Canadian Northwest which had been entrusted to their zealous efforts; this they did by temporarily abandoning the evangelization of the obdurate prairie Indians in order to devote their efforts to more receptive tribes. Whenever the need arose, the founder employed the system on a large scale.

He had almost found it advisable to do so in the Red River mission, on the basis of pessimistic reports inducing him to withdraw his religious from that mission. Bishop Taché wondered who was responsble for those "fabrications" which he termed "deplorable." Afterwards, he had no wish to know who it was, but he nonetheless discovered the sorry influence they had exercised on the decisions of the general council of the Oblates. In his charity he excused their author who, he felt, was perhaps more clumsy than malicious. "One is so little and so poorly understood when one is far away," he wrote; "especially when one is as far away as we are, that it is almost impossible for us to know what interpretation will be given to what we write." [1] For that reason he himself hesitated to write, even though he excelled in minimizing his trials, because of his pleasant and spiritual manner of brightening the picture. There were others, however, who felt they should darken it, as though the facts could not speak for themselves.

This explains why Bishop de Mazenod was ready to abandon the missions in the West of Canada; he made his motives known later to Guigues on October 8, 1852:

The difficulty of maintaining correspondence with this mission; the system (directly contrary to our Rule) of sending missionaries alone into these savage regions, and cut off from everyone—so much so that one of them was left for more than a year without being able to find a priest to hear his confession; the insignificant results these missionaries reaped from their labors and their daily sacrifices: all these were more than sufficient motives for recalling our fathers so that they might be employed in a more fruitful and less dangerous work of the ministry.[2]

To these "more than sufficient motives" were added others, to give an unfavorable picture of the Canadian missions: the Quebec archbishop's delay in bringing the Oblates into his episcopal city where they settled only in 1853; the suspicious and critical attitude of the clergy; the disappointments in vocations following an encouraging beginning in New France (the novitiate then had only one postulant). Lastly, the 1848 revolution, in view of the economic, financial and social crises which had caused and aggravated it, was diminishing the funds of the Lyons Propagation of the Faith which, until then, had been subsidizing the Oblate establishments, at a disturbing rate. All these considerations disposed the prelate to believe the pessimistic reports reaching him from Red River.

Fortunately, before the resolution to abandon the Red River mission was made known to the Canadian bishops, they, who had no suspicion of any such measure, had taken an initiative which forced Bishop de Mazenod to reconsider the situation. They too were concerned with the problems which extension toward the North was posing, and they intended to solve them, but in a way entirely opposed to a general withdrawal. Their plan consisted in strengthening and organizing the whole territory through a new arrangement of dioceses. This plan had been submitted to the Holy See, and the bishops had offered several proposals for redistricting without consulting or even informing their Marseilles colleague. Instead of increasing the number of sees in the Northwest and creating a metropolitan, the Curia on June 4, 1847, simply established Bishop Provencher's vicariate apostolic as a diocese. This was entirely consonant with the views of the latter who felt it was a bit ridiculous to be "an archbishop in the middle of this desert." [3] He would have been satisfied with becoming "a bishop like the others and enjoying no special consideration" [4] if he had not felt his strength failing. Aware that he was no longer "young enough to travel great distances," the prelate therefore requested a "coadjutor" so that he might fulfill all his obligations.[5] The problem was whom to propose. Bishop Provencher deemed it essential that the candidate be "a native" and that he speak the "Indian tongue: were it not for that, the least of his clergy, acquainted with that language, would have been better received than he." [6] Obviously, among the religious and secular clergy of his diocese, there were few choices. His first choice was Father Laflèche, who was worthy of this honor in every respect and well qualified to carry out such a burdensome task. When the papal bulls arrived, however, the electee had been stricken with severe rheumatism, and asserted that he was in no position to accept: "You want a vigorous coadjutor and I am crippled; you need a coadjutor who will be able to take your place in visiting these vast regions, and I am less capable of traveling than you." [7] Thus, he had to be eliminated.

The bishop then reviewed the list of his scanty forces and,

through the process of elimination, found only one man qualified for such arduous duties—Father Taché. The only possible objection to the choice would be his age, 27, but the bishop of Saint Boniface overruled that objection, declaring that youth is the one fault that is sure to be corrected, and all too quickly at that.[8] Moreover, the prelate felt it would be extremely advantageous to have the diocese

pass into the hands of the Oblates, for, otherwise, it would be impossible to supply it with priests. . . . What can be done when there is no clergy and no means for building one? A religious bishop would be able to obtain priests from his order and everything would proceed with a oneness of views.[9]

In union with his colleagues of eastern Canada, he therefore urged the Congregation of the Propaganda to substitute the name of Father Taché for that of Father Laflèche in the bulls that had arrived in Canada, and Rome offered no objection. On June 24, 1850, Pius IX named Father Taché Bishop of Arath *in partibus infidelium* and coadjutor to Bishop Provencher with the right of succession. "I felt I was making a good move by asking for him," wrote the latter to the archbishop of Quebec. "I hope that God is as pleased as I am." [10] As a matter of fact, it was not only a good move, but a good one on two counts: not only did he guarantee his diocese a shepherd of the highest type, but without knowing it he prevented the withdrawal of the Oblates who, Bishop de Mazenod felt, had ventured uselessly into western Canada. Without intending it, Provencher had forced the latter's hand.

At the time the superior general had decided to withdraw his religious, he had no idea that Bishop Provencher was thinking of requesting a coadjutor; even less would he have thought that the prelate's choice would fall to Father Taché in view of the latter's youth. The bishop of Saint Boniface had taken pains, however, to inform Bishop de Mazenod of his intention, so that he might obtain not only his approval but his support as well at the court in Rome in order to hasten the procedure.[11] Unfortunately, through a regrettable misunderstanding, his letter, containing well-founded reasons, was detained at Quebec and did not reach the bishop of Marseilles in time. The prelate therefore learned of Taché's promotion through the newspapers. At first, he was inclined to take offense, feeling that Bishop Provencher had surmised his resolve to deprive him of the Oblates and had contrived to face him with a *fait accompli* in order to prevent the departure of his co-workers. However, this spontaneous and all-too-natural reaction was quickly followed by thoughts stemming from faith. Seeing the will of God in this "move" which had astounded him, the founder readily reversed his decision, admitted that he had come close to making a grave mistake, and wrote immediately to Bishop Provencher, informing him that he agreed with him; he then wrote to Bishop Taché, telling him to accept; not, however, without adding pointedly that his personal approval was unnecessary since certain people had felt it could be ignored.

Although Rome and the bishop of Saint Boniface had agreed upon the new prelate's promotion without Bishop de Mazenod's knowledge, the latter was determined that at least his right to consecrate the new bishop be respected. Writing to Bishop Taché, he pointed out that "sacred ties and a sacred union which nothing will ever be able to weaken" will thus be established "between a son of my family and the father of that family. This occasion will give you the opportunity to identify yourself with the brothers you do not know." He also pointed out that the interests of the foundation in question demanded that the coadjutor of the Northwest visit the superior general to enlighten him regarding that foundation.

I do not know enough about the Red River mission; I must admit that it was pictured to me in such an unfavorable light that I felt our subjects should be taken away from there. . . . Come, then! That is not too much to ask of a beloved son at the very moment when the dearest interests of the congregation are to be entrusted to him; by that I mean the guidance of its sons in one of the most difficult of missions.[12]

Bishop Taché meekly accepted the promotion; he admitted later, however, to the qualms of conscience he experienced when he received news of his promotion to the See of Arath; it was "like a bolt out of the blue." [13] He wrote: "The newly elect, sad to say, had enough vanity in him to be flattered by the choice." Notwithstanding this vanity, "even notwithstanding a kind of noble self-complacency" because of the "undeniable" mark of esteem his superiors had shown him,

the newly elect still had enough sense to feel that the burden of the episcopate, which is so heavy by its very nature, was indeed a crushing burden for the head and shoulders of a twenty-seven-year-old. He had labored conscientiously enough to know how burdensome duties are and that it would be simply bringing torture upon himself to accept greater responsibility.

However, "the bishop of the diocese, with the bulls of the sovereign pontiff in his possession, commanded his coadjutor to yield; his religious superior wrote in the same vein." He could do nothing but comply. As soon as he arrived in Marseilles, hesitation again took hold of him, and for the second time, Bishop de Mazenod had to intervene to extract a definitive acceptance from him. In his *Souvenirs,* Bishop Taché gives a stirring account of the circumstances, and recounts under what conditions and in what way it was done. Writing to the superior general of the Oblates in 1866, he relates:

You, my Most Reverend Father, who had the happiness of living near our deeply lamented Founder, do not need to be told what deep affection that great heart felt even for the least of his sons, or what spiritual joy was afforded those who were privileged to observe at close range the excellent gifts which the Lord had bestowed upon him. I will not speak, therefore, of the emotions that welled up in me when I found myself in the presence of my Superior General. But, instead, let me tell the Congregation of one of the conversations with which he honored me; using the affectionate *tu* form, the Founder said:
        "You will be a bishop."
        "But, *Monseigneur,* my age, my failings. . . !"
        "The Soverign Pontiff has appointed you, and, when the Pope speaks, it is God speaking."
        "*Monseigneur,* I want to remain an Oblate."
        "Of course! That is exactly what I expect."
        "But the episcopal dignity seems to be incompatible with religious life."
        "What! Do you mean to say that the plenitude of the priesthood would exclude the perfection to which a religious must aspire?"

Then drawing himself up with that stately pride and spiritual grandeur which characterized him, he added:

"No one is more a bishop than I, and, most assuredly, no one is more an Oblate. Do I not have the same spirit I wanted to inspire in my Congregation? You will be a bishop! I insist on it. Do not oblige me to write to the Pope. And for this very reason, you will be all the more an Oblate, since, as of this moment, I appoint you to be the religious superior of all our members in the Red River missions." Tears streamed down my face and my heart felt as though it were going to burst.

"Take heart, my son," said that good father to me again, as he put his arms around me; "Your election, it is true, was made without my knowledge, but I look upon it as being wholly providential, and it saves the missions in which you have toiled so arduously. Some letters I received had pictured these missions in such an unfavorable light that I had decided to abandon them and recall all of you. When I learned of your appointment to the episcopate, the decision had already been made in the council. I want you to obey the Pope, and I, too, want to obey him. Since the Vicar of Christ has chosen one of our members to be the future head of this newborn diocese, we will not abandon it. I will give myself the joy of consecrating you, and Bishop Guibert, another Oblate, will share my happiness." [14]

On November 23, 1851, Father Taché was consecrated bishop by his illustrious and beloved founder and spiritual father, in the cathedral of Viviers.

Bishop de Mazenod's joy in becoming better acquainted with Bishop Taché was even greater than that which he derived from transmitting the plenitude of the priesthood to him. The day after the consecration, the founder wrote to Father Farand, a missionary at Red River:

My heart is so full of joy, so dilated with happiness, that it must reach even as far as you. . . . What a worthy subject you sent us to represent your mission! Everyone is charmed by him, and I, the old patriarch of our numerous family, I love him as though I had always lived with him. That is because he has shown from the very start that he is a true son of the family and in spite of the high dignity to which he has just been raised, in spite of his inclinations, has made no change in his attitude toward the Congregation and all its members, especially yourselves, who have been the companions of his labors. On his return, you will find that he is the same as you have always known him.[15]

The new coadjutor, who was not lacking in ingenuity, capitalized upon the impression he had made upon the founder, to obtain some critically needed reinforcements: "So persuasive has he been," wrote Bishop de Mazenod to Bishop Provencher, "that I am granting him four new missionaries to help you in your arduous mission." Thus, instead of discontinuing it,

I am fortifying it with four new subjects. They will be a crown of glory for you, *Monseigneur*, you who are truly the founder of this mission. You will bless these dear sons whom I place beneath your crozier, or, better still, in your heart. You will be like a father to them while they are so far away from him who had adopted them on the day of their religious profession.[16]

The Red River mission, therefore, was not merely saved; with a constantly increasing staff of personnel, it steadily grew and spread its roots in the vast expanses of the Canadian Northwest, under the direction of young Bishop Taché who, two years after his consecration, succeeded Bishop Provencher on the latter's death, June 7, 1853. Mission stations sprang up along the lakes and rivers: Fond du Lac in 1853; a permanent mission at Lac Labiche in 1854; Grand Lac des Esclaves and Fort Resolution in 1856. Added to these were four subsidiary missions, i.e., Grande Ile, Fort Simpson and Fort Raë in 1859 and Fort des Liards in 1860. The intrepid Father Grollier reached the Arctic Circle in 1859 with the founding of the Mission of Good Hope, to which were added two subsidiary missions, Fort Norman and Fort McPherson in 1860. At the time of Bishop Taché's consecration, however, only the Indians living in the forests had been converted to Christianity. It took long years after the foundation of Saint Albert in 1861 to evangelize the forbidding and bellicose tribes of the *Grande Prairie*. This evangelization was the admirable accomplishment of Bishop Grandin, who became coadjutor to Bishop Taché in 1857, and of Father Lacombe who was as skilled a diplomat as he was an ardent missionary. Grandin's radiant sanctity and Lacombe's influence over the redskins, together with his skill in understanding and handling them, made it possible for him to persuade the Indians to permit the "iron horse" which frightened away their game to pass through their reserves; even long before the noisy locomotives had greatly simplified travel into *la Grande Prairie,* that same influence and skill made it possible to infuse the life and grace of the redeeming and sanctifying Christ into souls hungry for prayer. The "old patriarch" of the congregation did not live to praise God for the achievement of an apostolate that had begun with so few resources. But to him will always belong the merit of having laboriously inspired its foundations with that supernatural discernment, that awareness of opportunities and possibilities, and that tenacious and courageous perseverence which are the marks of great missionary founders and true men of God.

Although Bishop de Mazenod after reversing his decision had ultimately left his religious at Red River, the same was not true of Oregon: it was permanently abandoned in 1858. In spite of an unpromising and stormy beginning, the mission nonetheless gave the founder great hopes. They soon withered. Contrary to what might be thought, the major difficulties came not from the Indians who welcomed the Oblates in truly primitive fashion, but from the prelates who had so urgently sought the help of the fathers. The bishop of Marseilles had put full confidence in his colleagues of the American Northwest, convinced that, following Bishop Bourget's example, they would treat his sons as they would himself. The facts proved just the opposite.

Bishop Norbert Blanchet, undoubtedly distinguished himself by his eminently apostolic spirit, which had duly impressed the superior general just as it had the Congregation of the Propaganda at Rome. He had relinquished an assured position of honor at Quebec to plunge into the hazards of a faraway, dangerous, and very harsh ministry, and had displayed admirable courage and zeal in Oregon. However, he was a "headstrong man" [17] who, in addition, wanted to enforce rigidly a system that was inspired at one and the same time by the views of Bishop Luquet and by the crying needs of a mission burdened with heavy debts and almost entirely deprived of a secular clergy. Lacking financial means and personnel, he intended to take full charge of everything. To this end, he requested and obtained as his suffragans his own brother Magloire, whom he qualified as "eminently fit," [18] and Modeste Demers who had been his faithful co-laborer since 1838. As if the composition of this trinity were not enough to guarantee its unity, the archbishop further requested Rome to grant him "special powers" over the prelates he had chosen; lastly, he requested that Oregon, even though it had been provided with titular bishops, continue to be subject to the Congregation of the Propaganda. Thus the necessary intervention of the Holy See "in these faraway dioceses" would be assured, and all the more perfectly, since it would be exercized—as he termed it "directly"—through a personal delegation which he had managed to secure for himself.[19]

Bishop Norbert Blanchet, who made multiple statements of his devotion and attachment to the Holy See, was not showing inconsistency, still less dishonesty, in his pretensions to arrogate to himself the Holy See's authority. His logic, like that of methodical men, as well as his realism, admitted of startling eccentricities; at times that logic, out of urgent necessity, affected his principles, and at other times allowed itself to be carried away by utopian dreams. Wishing to set up an ideal organization immediately instead of proceeding gradually in proportion to the means at his disposal, the prelate devised one plan after another, which, like that of having eight suffragans, literally astonished Bishop Provencher and seemed completely ludicrous to Demers. In all good faith, he believed that he could serve the Holy See no better than by taking its place; in fact, the least suspicion of episcopalism cast upon his attitude and his principles would have astounded him more than it would have angered him. Undeniably, a firm and sustained direction was essential for coordinating efforts in this burgeoning part of Christendom. Because of his prestige, diplomacy, and prudence, Bishop Bourget, without being too obvious about it, had been highly successful in gradually molding the Canadian Church in accordance with his shrewd and well-balanced conceptions, by proceeding step by step. But Bishop Bourget had the right touch, and that touch was lacking in the archbishop of Oregon City, and his views were somewhat inconsistent and one-sided. Categorical in his ideas and imperious in his behavior, he believed that all that was necessary to settle every problem was to make an assertion and to assert one's authority. This intrepid, daring, courageous, and trenchant missionary, whom nothing fazed, was too unmindful of the fact that the administering and governing of a diocese called for a change in the method which had brought him undeniable success in an isolated ministry where all kinds of initiative were allowed and even required.

That he felt it was necessary to have a uniform administration within his metropolitan circumscription, and a concerted direction for the Catholic apostolate, would have merited nothing but praise for him, had he not concluded that this twofold objective would be impossible to achieve without his resorting to a series of measures which he declared were absolutely indispensable when he presented them to the Congregation of the Propaganda, and all of which were aimed at reinforcing his authority and that of the other bishops. It was only with reluctance that the metropolitan of Oregon had sought the help of the religious clergy; since they were under the double jurisdiction of their ordinaries and their religious superiors, the result was a *diminutio capitis* for the bishops, which weakened unity by limiting the bishops' power. Consequently, his logical ideas regarding the urgent need to form a native clergy were inspired solely by this major concern: "That is the only means," he wrote, "of assuring the bishop the support necessary for governing his diocese." His logic even prompted him to add:

Accordingly, the building of this first solid foundation of episcopal authority must be the main objective of the efforts of all the missionaries, to this extent, that the forming of religious novitiates must be temporarily suspended wherever this nucleus [of secular clergy] does not exist.

Finally, Bishop Blanchet went so far as to propose that, "toward this same end, and in order to conform to the essential principles of newly formed dioceses," "bishops" be given

complete authority over all missionaries indiscriminately, in such a way that the religious clergy, like the secular clergy, will be entirely and immediately subject to the ordinary in everything pertaining to the exercise of the public ministry and to the administration of temporal goods in the mission. For example, when it is a question of carrying out the orders of the Holy See or of undertaking such and such a work of the public ministry, is it not necessary that the missionaries obey the bishop immediately instead of suspending that obedience until they have received an answer from their superior general in Europe? [20]

Although the Congregation of the Propaganda consented to establish three dioceses and approved the promotion of the three prelates proposed by the vicar apostolic of Oregon, it disapproved the principles and measures he had submitted to it.[21] This did not stop the archbishop from enforcing his system; he likewise had it enforced by his brother who was entirely devoted to him, and by Bishop Demers, the Bishop of Vancouver (fortunately, the latter acted with more flexibility and moderation). As a result, there was friction with the Oblates and with the Jesuits;[22] Bishop de Mazenod became especially alarmed since the complaints of his sons brought to light the inadmissible pretensions of Bishop Blanchet; had he known, in 1846, of the *Mémoire* Bishop Blanchet sent to the Congregation of the Propaganda and had he harbored the least suspicion of what Guigues called the vicar apostolic's "extraordinary ideas" regarding religious orders,[23] the founder would never have granted Oregon the help of his missionaries. Now that it had been done, he wondered whether it would be possible to lessen the differences of opinion. The prelate realized that any attempt to come to an agreement on the matter of principles would very likely fail; the opinions of the two men were too radically opposed, and the superior general had no more intention than did the Jesuits of surrendering the rights belonging to religious. His efforts, therefore, were centered first of all upon practical attitudes so that, by bringing about a closer mutual understanding on both sides, he might ease relations between his Oblates and their archbishop. Hence his advice to Father Ricard who, he felt, was a bit too inflexible,[24] and, in 1857, his appointing the much more flexible Father Bermond as visitor extraordinary; hence also his recourse to Bishop Bourget, who prudently and gently hinted to Bishop Norbert Blanchet that he should strive for a reconciliation.[25] But all these attempts ended with the same negative result. The superior general urged his sons to practice the same patience he himself practiced, reminding them that trial, contradiction, and suffering enriched the fruitfulness of every apostolic work. However, since this forbearance remained ineffective and since the situation, far from improving, was becoming more strained each day, the founder decided to warn the Congregation of the Propaganda, enlisting the kind help of his friend Barnabo, the secretary of that Congregation. So that the Oblates might be free of a tyrannical jurisdiction, so that not only their rights but their religious life itself might be guaranteed, and so that the anticanonical and the unjust principles opposed to fairness and right order which Bishop Blanchet and his colleagues held might be counterbalanced, Bishop de Mazenod requested the Holy See to name Father Ricard either bishop or vicar apostolic of Nesqually, where his missionaries were already established.[26] This promotion seemed especially urgent to him since, during a gathering to which Bishop Blanchet and his two suffragans gave the name Provincial Council of Oregon, the three prelates voted to request that Bishop Magloire Blanchet's see be transferred to Nesqually; because of the chicanery of the Protestants, the latter's residing at Walla Walla was becoming impossible. Bishop Demers had even gone to Rome to support this request.

Naturally, the Congregation of the Propaganda was perplexed. Even though it saw the great advantages of Bishop de Mazenod's proposal, it felt it should not adopt the proposal. It was fully aware that even after rejecting two-thirds of Bishop Norbert Blanchet's colossal plan, it had still created too many dioceses in a country almost devoid of clergy. Adding a supplementary vicariate apostolic would only compound the error. Furthermore, Bishop Magloire Blanchet, who was being forced to leave Walla Walla, had to be given a suitable residence elsewhere,[27] and the problem was one of location. Thus, the Congregation of the Propaganda quite simply decided to transfer his see to Nesqually. Bishop de Mazenod respectfully expressed his disappointment and his forebodings to Cardinal Fransoni: "The transfer agreed upon has made it clear that my remarks were ineffectual." God grant that this transfer will not "result in trouble" for the poor missionaries who "have built a decent house with their own hands, and, so as not to die of hunger, have planted a garden at the cost of incredible labor." [28]

The three bishops of Oregon, who were seeking the right to forbid secular priests working in their dioceses to enter religious life, received an answer from the Congregation of the Propaganda, which they set about interpreting in their favor. The Congregation of the Propaganda, however, had simply invoked the general rule: *These priests cannot embrace the religious state without the permission of the Ordinary.*[29] The archbishop, nonetheless, concluded from this that he had the right to refuse it in any and every case; in fact, he made the Congregation of the Propaganda's rescript retroactive, by ordering Father Jayol, who had made his perpetual vows as an Oblate, to leave the society under penalty of suspension. When Father Jayol refused, Bishop Norbert Blanchet issued an interdict *a divinis* against him. On learning this, Bishop de Mazenod sharpened his finest quill and wrote to his friend, Cardinal Barnabo:

The bishops of Oregon haven't changed. It would take too long to tell you of their exorbitant claims. Imagine! this holy, and, I presume, this good archbishop, has declared that one of our religious who has been professed for more than a year, and perhaps two years, will be suspended even *a sacris,* unless he leaves our community and returns to him. I find it difficult to get along with prelates of this kind. . . . Evidently, these bishops are abusing the powers granted to them by the Sacred Congregation so that they might harass religious. They find nothing outrageous in wanting to give a retroactive effect to the prohibition of entering a religious congregation, even though a sufficiently proved vocation and probably a need to preserve himself from perils to his soul in those wide-open places induce a priest to seek a shelter.[30]

When Cardinal Fransoni requested an explanation from Bishop Blanchet, the latter, without making the least apology for what he had done, simply replied that the suspension he had imposed had not been put into effect, since the territory of Nesqually had, in the meantime, been transferred to the jurisdiction of his brother, Magloire.[31]

Unable to retrieve Father Jayol, Bishop Norbert Blanchet, who had no intention of accepting defeat, "then directed his attack against another priest who had already taken the Oblate habit, but who was still only a novice; he notified the priest to leave the novitiate and return to the post to which he had assigned him." This order was stiffened by the following assertion which wrongfully exceeded the principle invoked by the Congregation of the Propaganda: "It has pleased the Holy See to rule that in Oregon

there will be no more novitiates and no more entrances into religious orders for secular priests." [32]

Informed of this new offense, Bishop de Mazenod immediately sent an indignant protest to the cardinal-prefect himself:

If my missionaries have to submit to such procedures, then I have only
one course left, and that is to withdraw them from Oregon. What trust
can religious congregations be expected to have in bishops who treat
them in this way? . . . These bishops must have very little esteem
for religious societies and very little gratitude for the good they are
doing in their missions when they grieve them in this way, simply
because two simple priests, fearing the dangers of the ministry,
wanted to fortify themselves by practicing the evangelical counsels so
that they might do greater good, with more merit and with less danger
to themselves.[33]

In a less peppery vein, the Jesuit superior general, informed by his
fathers, proved to be no less categorical: "In short," he observed,
"they want the members of the Society of Jesus to become seculars
in order to be missionaries. No good religious can consent to such
a condition for becoming a missionary." [34]

The Propaganda was worried, particularly since complaints
had been pouring in from secular priests, who were on the verge
of abandoning Oregon. The Jesuits, for their part, were already
considering California. The departure of the Oblates would not
fail to hasten this general retreat. Bishop de Mazenod, therefore,
consented to suspend action; again, in 1852, at the urging of the
Congregation of the Propaganda, he agreed not to recall his fathers,
and at that time even made an attempt to reach an agreeable settlement with Bishop Magloire Blanchet regarding the financial and
material questions which had been the object of continual quarrels. Bishop Magloire fully accepted the arrangement proposed by
the founder, but in practice did as he had always done: "I do not
like these broad arrangements," he declared to Father d'Herbomez,
"and to put it briefly, I recognize none of them, big or small, old
or new." [35] During the Cayouse uprising in 1855–1856, the burning of the missions of Saint Joseph and Saint Anne by the Americans and the Indians created an intolerable situation for the Oblates. In 1858, therefore, Bishop de Mazenod decided to recall

them gradually to the diocese of Vancouver where Bishop Demers proved to be more understanding; with only three priests at his disposal for all the missions of British Columbia, he had been begging for the help of the Oblates.

Harsh as this experience had been, at least it had had a double advantage. First of all, at the cost of a slow and arduous detour, it led to a new and vast field of action for the Oblates among Indian tribes who were far more receptive to the Gospel message, more industrious, and more sound than those in Oregon—where, according to the judgment of the Oblate General Council, the establishments that had already been founded could "never be satisfactorily developed" even after peace was firmly established.[36] Thus, the failure which occurred in the southern region belonging to America resulted in a transfer similar to those which Bishop de Mazenod later effected in Africa and elsewhere in order to assure better returns from his limited effectives. The results at that juncture approximated what the bishop of Marseilles and the Oblate superior of the Oregon mission, Father d'Herbomez, had expected. The Oblates became established first of all at Esquimalt on Vancouver Island; they next launched into the evangelization of the Indians of British Columbia whose conversion Bishop Demers had entrusted to them through an agreement signed on September 1, 1860; they then pushed hundreds of miles northward, at the cost of fatigue and suffering, it is true, but they were generously rewarded by the fruitfulness of their ministry. Finally, in 1860, with designs on the future that were as apostolically wise as they were humanly shrewd, they settled opposite Vancouver Island in a spot where immigrants had begun to clear the virgin forest; this was the exact site of the future city of New Westminister, where they built two churches in the same year in which the founder died.

Advantageous as this first consequence of the setback in Oregon was, greater emphasis must be put upon the second, which was of a different nature, to be sure, but which was of far greater significance. That sad experience had convinced Bishop de Mazenod that the surest means of sparing his sons the disadvantages of a divided jurisdiction would be to organize their missions as vicariates or dioceses subject to an Oblate bishop, who would be their ordinary and their religious superior at one and the same time. When he had first sent his missionaries to Canada, he had placed complete trust in Bishop Bourget, assuring him that, by their very Rule, they were "bishops' men." Being motivated by this spirit was all that was necessary with prelates like his friend from Montreal and there was no need to specify the terms and conditions for a mutual understanding, since the latter had realized that he too had to treat them accordingly: that, in the words of the founder, he would have to be an "affectionate father to the missionaries and look upon the interests of the Congregation as though they were his own." [37] Advised by Bishop Bourget and following his example, the ordinaries of Canada had also, for the most part, acted in the same manner. However, it was too much to expect that equally broad views would be shared everywhere, particularly since, in the "19th century, bishops and missionaries in many newly organized mission territories were not as clearly informed regarding each other's rights and duties as are bishops and missionaries of our own day." [38]

A right to undetermined frontiers is all too conducive to mutual encroachments which provoke constant misunderstandings and even regrettable conflicts whenever there is a lack of reciprocal good will, pliability, balance, and tact. This was so well appreciated at Quebec, Montreal, Kingston, and Saint Boniface that the titulars of these sees confided the vicariate of Red River and the new diocese of Bytown to Oblate bishops. Although Bishop de Mazenod was grateful to the Canadian prelates for the sympathetic understanding they had shown his sons before entrusting these territories to them, the difficulties which were encountered in Oregon convinced him that these prelates had been wise in inaugurating this new system. In effect, it did away with the problems created by the convergence of episcopal and religious authority in unsettled portions of mission territories where the rights of one and the other were not clearly defined. Consequently, from that time on, the superior general of the Oblates used this argument with the Congregation of the Propaganda to induce it to place the missions entrusted to his religious under the jurisdiction of a member of their congregation, who would be at one and the same time their bishop and their religious superior. "Putting all authority in the same hand," he observed, "would give more consistency and unity to all their works," would give "a little stability to our missions,"

MISSIONS IN THE UNITED STATES

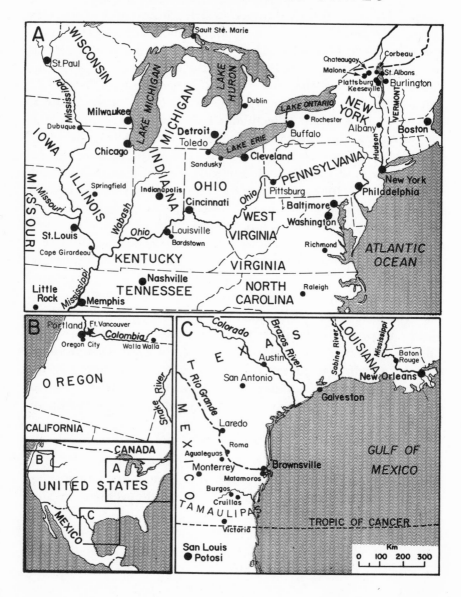

and would "spare our missionaries many harassing and disheartening annoyances." [39]

Other superiors of religious institutes, at the same period and for the same reasons, had come to similar conclusions and "perceived only one effective means of avoiding difficulties: the appointment of one of their religious missionaries to the office of vicar apostolic or of bishop." [40] Even the Jesuit fathers, who on principle originally refused the honor of the episcopacy, abandoned their initial intransigence "for the sake of assuring greater efficacy to their ministry." [41] Later on they perhaps regretted their having refused the vicariate apostolic of Oregon which the Council of Baltimore had offered them in 1843 and their having asked that Bishop Norbert Blanchet be substituted for one of their fathers. Would that young portion of Christianity have known happier and more fruitful beginnings had the views of the American bishops prevailed? Only hypothetical history can answer that question. Bishop de Mazenod was satisfied with learning a lesson from the painful experience that religious like Father de Smet and his Jesuit missionaries had undergone.

The steps Bishop de Mazenod took with Cardinal Barnabo from 1858 to 1860 to have the Congregation of the Propaganda detach British Columbia from Vancouver, form it as a vicariate apostolic, entrust it to the Oblates who were practically the only ones evangelizing it, and put an Oblate father at its head, did not succeed during his lifetime.[42] His wish was not granted until the end of 1863 when Father d'Herbomez was appointed vicar apostolic.

ABORTIVE ATTEMPTS IN THE NORTHEASTERN UNITED STATES

In spite of a poor beginning in Oregon whence the Oblates had to withdraw to British Columbia, the Oblate foundations in the United States, with varying fortunes, steadily increased until the death of Bishop de Mazenod. In those days, the American bishops, extremely in need of clergy and resources, urgently sought the help of the Oblates. So numerous were the appeals—we know of at least twenty—that it became absolutely impossible to give a favorable reply to all of them; even those which were heeded sometimes ended abortively for various reasons. Although the implanta-

tion of the Oblates in Canada was accomplished in three successive
and determined directions according to the plan conceived by
Bishop Bourget, their implantation in the American Republic
took place in a scattered fashion without any semblance of coordi-
nation in the initiatives of the prelates. These different circumstances do not permit an easy treatment of the subject. The best
method, it seems, would be to be guided by geographical divisions
and, in treating the foundations in the American Northeast and
South which at times took place simultaneously, to group them according to plans which were discarded and foundations which were
either attempted or which succeeded.

The requests that were not accepted might be omitted if they
did not amount to almost two-thirds of those which Bishop de
Mazenod received, and if it were not of interest to note his reasons
for refusing them. Their total amounts to twelve: Bardstown (Kentucky) in 1843; Dubuque (Iowa) in 1847; Rochester (New York) in
1850; Saint Alban's (Vermont) in 1854; Sandusky (Ohio) in 1855;
Philadelphia (Pennsylvania) and Chicago (Illinois) in 1856; To-
ledo (Ohio); Malone, Chateaugay, and Keeseville (New York) in
1857; and Sault Sainte Marie (Michigan) in 1860. Contrary to
what might be thought, in a certain number of these cases, it was
not the lack of missionaries which induced the founder to decline.
It is true that several times he pleaded the fewness of his effectives,
repeating the formula he used so often even with the Congregation
of the Propaganda: *ad impossibile nemo tenetur.* As a general rule,
however, other considerations prevailed which squared with his determination not to send just anyone, and to use the men at his disposal wisely and under conditions which would be most favorable
to their apostolate. What would be the good, for example, of accepting a college at Bardstown, Kentucky, since the Jesuit fathers
had already opened one nearby? It would be a useless duplication;
besides, the Oblates could not presume to compete with these master educators. At Sandusky, a town of German immigrants, a
knowledge of German would be necessary; at Saint Alban's, not
only was the parish laden with debt, but it was also an English-
speaking parish. At Philadelphia where it was a question of directing the seminary,[43] after enthusiastically agreeing to accept, the
bishop of Marseilles was obliged to go back on his word, since
Bishop Guigues refused to release Father Chevalier, the proposed

superior, and, at that moment, there was no other subject qualified to assume such a difficult task. The missions of Malone, Chateaugay, and Keeseville were too small and would have dissipated the missionaries' forces. Although the request of the diocese of Rochester was accepted at first, it was later refused in order to give preference to Buffalo where the future looked more promising.

Certain of the foundations undertaken by the congregation in the eastern part of America fared no better than those in Oregon. Some were even abandoned more quickly than they had been in the West where a few fathers still held on until 1878. An example of this quick withdrawal was Detroit, where, in 1851, the bishop had begged the Oblates to take charge of a parish and also of a college which enjoyed the privilege of a university. Father Santoni, the provincial, was not in favor of the idea, made many objections, and added delay upon delay. Only after a formal order from Tempier, who had completed arrangements during his canonical visit to Canada, were two priests sent to Bishop Lefebvre: Fathers Lagier and Grenier. They left Montreal on May 2, 1853, and were back there on the following June 27. When they arrived in Detroit, they both realized that the glowing picture the strapped prelate had painted for them hardly corresponded with the harsh reality. The church they were supposed to administer had been assigned to a secular priest before their arrival, and the college enjoying the privilege of a university was nothing but a "school for tots"; the land on which the congregation would have to build a dwelling for its members was laden with heavy mortgages. Two weeks later, Lagier and Grenier packed their bags.[44]

Four years earlier, Telmon had been only a little slower in leaving the Pittsburgh seminary where his term as superior lasted at least five months, from October 3, 1848, to March 12, 1849. It must be admitted that in the beginning he took his annoyances good-naturedly. Extremely colorful is the account he gave of his trip to Pittsburgh, during which he lost his traveling bag, and of his arriving there, covered with soot, after wondering for three days if "there was still a sun." [45] His description of the house where his lodgings were only temporary (he was expected to hand it over to the orphan society the following year) continues in the same vein. It was small and so low that Telmon was able to touch the ceiling with his hand. Its smallness corresponded to the num-

ber of its inhabitants: six seminarians and three maids, excluding
the vermin which overran the place since the maids, who were
lazy and wasteful, were so slovenly that poor Telmon did not dare
go into the kitchen for fear of losing his appetite. The condition
of the chapel was no better than that of the rest of the house:

For all the colors of the day, we have only one green chasuble, so
shabby, so filthy, and so tattered that it takes all our longing to say
Mass to put it on. . . . We have *one* amice and *one* purificator for all
of us. As you can see, there are no superfluities. And yet, why complain,
since the bishop puts up with this disgusting destitution and eats
and sleeps at the seminary. Besides he puts everyone at ease by his
simplicity; he refuses to be called "My Lord," and is satisfied with the
title "Bishop," stripped of everything that might wound the republican sensibilities of the country.[46]

Telmon knew through experience that on a foreign mission the
beginnings are always harsh. He also knew that Bishop de Mazenod was very happy that the Canadian province had been able to
accept Bishop O'Connor's offer which he had regretfully been
forced to decline in 1844. It involved an essential work, one which
was fundamental and would provide a diocese lacking in clergy
with native and well-trained priests. Furthermore, the bishop of
Marseilles had hopes that this foundation would lead to others
which would be equally advantageous to the congregation and to
America:

If we succeed at Pittsburgh, we shall soon have other establishments
in the United States. The Detroit seminary has already been offered
to us. With a third establishment, it would mean that we could form
a new province, and that is especially desirable since our fathers in the
United States are already finding it difficult to take orders from
Canada.[47]

Consequently, he encouraged Telmon; he was aware of the man's
generous impulses, but he was also aware of his need for activity
and change which made him somewhat unstable:

By founding the Pittsburgh house in the United States, you are casting
the foundations of a new province. However, you must act with
restraint, without prejudice and without excessive emotion, not falling

victim to undue optimism or yielding to pessimism, a detestable dis-
position which prevents anything or any good from being accomplished.[48]

The advice was timely, but it had little effect; Telmon became
discouraged, and the tone of his letters changed. In the beginning,
he had joked about his hardships, convinced that the material situation would gradually improve, as had happened elsewhere. But
the months rolled by without any noticeable improvement. Although the bishop had changed the seminary residence, the second
was no better than the first, and the poor superior, when not occupied with spiritual exercises, classes, and the spiritual direction
of his students, had to spend his time repairing and building: He
wrote on January 3, 1849:

What, then, have I been doing since my last letter? Alas! what I have
been doing since I first got here! I have been building, repairing the
roof, planing, sweeping, washing, getting covered with dust, ruining
myself, demeaning myself, ruining my clothes, all for the sake of
providing a suitable dwelling, that is, a place for sleeping and per-
forming our spiritual exercises. To become presentable, I would
have to be sent to the immigration center, be washed from head to
foot, have my hair fine-combed, since lice and dirt go together, and be
completely reconditioned. Sometimes the difficulties of our foundation
remind me of the foundation that took place five years ago at Bytown.[49]

At Bytown, however, the Oblates had been able to rely on Bishop
Bourget. The situation was totally different at Pittsburgh. Its
bishop, who was content to live in that sordid hovel and to eat his
meals prepared in that filthy kitchen, apparently considered this
disorderliness normal and was annoyingly impassive about it. He
"had prepared nothing for our arrival," observed Telmon;[50] nor
since Telmon's arrival had he done anything further to provide
acceptable living quarters for pupils and teachers. Telmon finally
lost patience; with one of those sudden decisions that were habitual
with him, and without consulting his Oblate superiors, he packed
his trunks and abandoned everything on March 12 after notifying
Bishop O'Connor of his departure. Bishop Bourget deeply regretted that Telmon, after only five months, had taken it upon
himself to disrupt everything:

Perhaps his ardent nature is not suited to American nonchalance. I confess that his failure at Pittsburgh grieves me, and I think it would have been more prudent on his part had he allowed the Bishops of Bytown and Pittsburgh to settle the differences which arose at the foundation.[51]

Some sort of arrangement would have been desirable, since Telmon himself admitted that he was not leaving "his students without sorrow; their progress in studies and in piety, and their docility and hearty cooperation had won" his affection.[52] It now remained to be seen whether there was any reasonable hope for a gradual improvement in the material situation which Telmon's confrère, Cauvin, also considered intolerable.[53] Cauvin did not think so, any more than did Telmon, in view of the indolence and indifference of the bishop, who had done nothing to assist in these difficulties and who was, in fact, less than cordial in his dealings with them.

Like his Montreal friend, Bishop de Mazenod would have insisted that a work whose undertaking had brought him so much joy and hope be carried on in spite of everything. He had written earlier to Telmon:

I am sure that, through your savoir faire, you will surmount the serious difficulties you are meeting. Those are the trials that beset the work of God. Only fainthearted souls lose confidence. When a person feels that the work is a good one and that he is divinely chosen to see it through, he falls back on his resources, takes courage, skirts difficulties, and ultimately conquers all obstacles.[54]

This exhortation to persevere, sent on June 1, 1849, arrived too late. Highly displeased by this sudden failure, the bishop of Marseilles was even more displeased that Telmon on his own authority had ended the undertaking so abruptly, thereby jeopardizing the implantation of the Oblates in the United States.

It was ten years before the Oblates accepted an establishment at Burlington, situated on Lake Champlain. Just as at Corbeau, Canada, they had given an excellent mission in Burlington in 1842, and, like the one at Corbeau, it was described in the press. But, unlike the Corbeau mission where a sharp controversy had resulted from the incident of Telmon's burning the Bibles, the mission at

Burlington earned nothing but praise in the *Gazette de Québec*.[55] At the time of the mission, however, the Oblates had no idea of settling there, in spite of the mission's undeniable success and in spite of the spiritual abandonment of

more than three-thousand Canadian Catholics living there; they had no one to preach the Gospel to them and they had been without confession for periods ranging from five to ten years, etc. . . . since there was not one French-speaking priest within a distance of more than seventy-five miles.[56]

Their apostolate among the emigrants deprived as they were of religious assistance was therefore a migratory one, similar to what they practiced at first, even in Canada. The scattered location of these emigrants and the lack of sufficient personnel prevented the Oblates from assuring continuous service to these people. For lack of anything better, itinerant preaching had to suffice.

Now, in 1844, Bishop Fitzpatrick, the coadjutor of Boston, with jurisdiction over Vermont, felt he could improve upon this initial step and prevailed upon the congregation to establish a community at Burlington. Once again, Bishop Bourget intervened to support a request which affected his compatriots and displaced diocesans: "I realize," he wrote to Bishop de Mazenod, "that I am taking unfair advantage of your kind heart to strip you of your best subjects." But, "there are thousands of lost sheep who have no shepherd and who are exposed to the full fury of the wolves." [57] Father Honorat also favored the plan. Nonetheless, the project did not materialize immediately. Without definitely refusing, the bishop of Marseilles, who wanted to give Red River priority, felt compelled to delay: "As for Burlington," he wrote to Guigues, "let us not think of that for the present. Time enough, later on, if God so wills it, to break into the United States. For a moment, Providence seems to be destining us for this other mission field." [58] Bishop Bourget received a similar answer which nonetheless gave him some hope since the *ad impossibile nemo tenetur* was now limited to an *ad tempus* and led to this encouraging conclusion: "However, we should not lose sight of this project." [59] Thus, it was simply a matter of postponement.

There was hope that the delay would not extend beyond a

few months, since the provincial Guigues, very anxious for the completion of the project, went to Burlington in August, 1845, to make arrangements for the fathers' establishment, and, on the following November 6, was given *carte blanche* by the Oblate General Council in Marseilles.[60] This authorization, however, was given only on the condition that he "continue as best he could with the personnel he had at his disposal in Canada"; hence, the provincial found he was not in a position to act. Where could he spare the few needed religious from his effectives whose numbers were insufficient and who were over-tired? He had planned to start the foundation in Burlington with reinforcements expected from the superior general. However, the latter had no intention of stripping himself any further: He wrote to Guigues:

I can understand why you still prize Burlington very highly. Certainly, I would ask nothing better than to begin in the United States in this way. However, your own soil must not become barren because of it. Why do we not receive more vocations from the dioceses like Quebec and Montreal? As you know, I have always hesitated to establish our men where there is no hope of recruiting vocations. That is why I postponed accepting the various proposals made to me in behalf of the United States.[61]

The first wave of enthusiasm which had stirred up so many excellent vocations in "those two regular dioceses" had now subsided and Bishop de Mazenod felt keenly disappointed by it. Overjoyed that requests were pouring in, but, at the same time, deeply grieved that he had to refuse so many of them, he was wont at times to remark that Canadians "outdo themselves in demanding Oblates, but are too neglectful of furnishing" him with any, adding: "If they were heeded, the whole Congregation would have to be moved to their country." In its own way, this typically Provençal sally revealed the high hopes he put in the generosity of that very Catholic country. But, here too, it would take time for the Gospel words *date, et dabitur vobis* to be verified; when they were, Canada would supply many more vocations than France. In his heart, the founder knew that; we can understand, however, why, restrained by the mathematical considerations constantly in his mind, his apostolic zeal burned to be free of these restrictions so that it might rush to the aid of abandoned souls without counting the cost.

The patient and tenacious Bishop Bourget held to his views, however, and, emboldened by Bishop de Mazenod's words "we should not lose sight of this project," presumed to refresh his friend's memory. Guigues, for his part, made sure that the matter which had been put in abeyance was taken out of the files from time to time, lest it be buried there. Finally, ten years after Bishop Fitzpatrick's offer was made, everything was again set in motion with Bishop Goesbriand's promotion to the episcopal see created at Burlington. The new bishop began the movement by having the Oblates preach a mission in the city; he then formally requested the new provincial, Father Santoni, to establish a house there. Santoni wasted no time complying. On July 28, 1854, he sent Bishop Goesbriand an encouraging reply; on August 4, the provincial council accepted the offer unanimously; on October 22, Father Gaudet was installed as pastor of Saint Joseph's church and appointed director of the community, with Father Cauvin as his assistant.

Both missionaries immediately set to work, since haste was essential to regain influence over the Canadians, more and more of whom were falling away. The quick success they achieved consoled the superior for being "nothing more and nothing less" than a pastor, an honor that had "always been repugnant to him." [62] It also recompensed the missionaries for the great hardships they had to endure in servicing the ten remote mission stations attached to Burlington, some of which were more than sixty miles away. Writing to Bishop Guigues, Father Gaudet enthused:

The good that can be accomplished in these outlying missions! It might almost be said that the good God and their guardian angels have told these people how sincerely we desire their welfare. They come to these mission stations to resume the religious practices which they have been neglecting for years for one reason or another. Others, who are twenty-five, thirty, and even forty years old, come to make their First Communion; mothers of families send their children whose ages range from fifteen to eighteen to study catechism, without which they would be irretrievably lost. In this diocese there are numerous places where Catholics abound, but the good bishop has only five priests, including us, to do all this work. Consequently, he is continually on the road, spending himself like a simple missionary.[63]

However, because of the dispersion of his confrères, who were always on the move, the superior soon had to recognize that there was no longer any community life. Each was being left to himself, working alone, and unable to acquire new spiritual strength through the regularity of religious life. As long as Father Santoni, who had taken the initiative for the foundation and had watched its progress, remained in charge, the abnormality of this situation in no way alarmed the provincial authorities. As early as 1856, however, a warning arrived at Marseilles, putting Bishop de Mazenod on the alert: "Father Leonard, in times past," wrote Honorat, "gave you, in connection with Burlington, a sample of what the provincial intends to do in matters of this kind when he acts alone." [64]

Did the founder give orders to Bishop Guigues after the latter had resumed the office of provincial which had been taken away from Santoni? Or did Guigues, apprised of the disadvantages pointed out above, act on his own? Whatever the case, on October 9, 1856, the provincial council decided to abandon Burlington where it was out of the question for the fathers to continue these missions since they were obliged to "live alone for the greater part of the year, and by that token, found themselves living contrary to the spirit and letter of our Rules." [65]

One can imagine the desolation of poor Bishop Goesbriand who would now be forced to evangelize the whole of Vermont with only a few priests. He tried hard to obtain a delay, since the immediate withdrawal of the fathers which came without any warning was leaving him almost entirely stripped of helpers. For his part, Bishop Bourget promised to write to Bishop de Mazenod "earnestly" to beseech his friend "not to suppress the Burlington establishment." [66] Nothing had any effect. On November 27, the bishop of Marseilles approved Bishop Guigues' decision; on December 4, when the matter was put before it, the Oblate General Council concluded: "We are convinced that this decision, although regrettable in many respects, was made in the interests of the Congregation." [67] On January 12, 1857, the Oblates left Burlington; they had stayed there only three years.

Contrary to what happened in other dioceses, the bishop was in no way accountable for this failure. The dispersion of the fathers, which destroyed their community life, was caused by the critical situation of his poor diocese. To limit the effects of this situation, he had reduced the number of missions entrusted to their care without correspondingly reducing their sources of income, since he left them the most lucrative places. The prelate avowed that he was prepared to make "any sacrifice" to retain co-workers whom he regarded as "a gift from Heaven." [68] His good will, his zeal, and his dire straits, it seems, deserved something better than the unyielding severity with which Bishop de Mazenod and Bishop Guigues brought things to an abrupt end. And yet, the uncompromising stand they took is explained by more than their determination to uphold the letter and spirit of the Oblate Rule which prohibits sending an Oblate alone into a mission. This prohibition was the reason which the provincial gave Bishop de Goesbriand, but there was another reason which carried as much, if not more, weight but which was carefully withheld from the bishop, since religious orders prefer to keep their family troubles secret. To clarify the prudently vague statement made by the General Council on December 4—viz. "We are convinced that this decision, although regrettable in many respects, was made in the interests of the congregation"—we must refer to a far more explicit letter from Bishop de Mazenod to Bishop Guigues:

There was no other course to take at Burlington than the one you took. In this case, I shall lay down the same principle which you cited in Father Honorat's case. Father Santoni had taken on an independence which is as blameworthy as it is preposterous. He regarded himself as a superior with unlimited authority in the province, whose rights he had to maintain against any and every one, even against the Superior General. Some sort of unbelievable aberration had blinded him to such an extent that he seriously advocated subversion. And what happened? On his own authority, and without consulting me, he set up those two establishments at Plattsburgh and Burlington. And lo and behold the words of Holy Scripture *hic, nisi Dominus aedificaverit* are verified for Burlington. Please God, it will not be the same for Plattsburgh! [69]

Thus, it was also a matter of maintaining discipline. The bishop of Marseilles had no intention of allowing the province and the fathers of Canada to act autonomously on the excuse that they were too far away, and he reacted all the more vigorously since some of Father Santoni's subordinates were imitating him. Moreover, Santoni had overly committed himself in accepting Burlington. It was only too easy to foresee that three or four fathers administering a city parish and ten widely scattered mission posts in Vermont would not be able to live a community life. It should be ascribed to Santoni's credit, however, that, in spite of the founder's gloomy premonitions, the Plattsburgh foundation which Santoni also accepted on his own authority, succeeded.

ESTABLISHMENTS AT PLATTSBURGH AND BUFFALO

In the State of New York, the Oblates were more fortunate on the western shore of Lake Champlain than they were on its eastern shore, since far more favorable conditions allowed them to develop and consolidate their work in Plattsburgh. The initiative of bringing them there came from the people themselves, and there was no cause to suspect that the population was seeking anything but spiritual help from them. This was not another Texas where a request had been made in the same manner but which intended solely to make a show of religion in order to dispel the rather shady reputation of unscrupulous traders and regain for their market a confidence that had been deservedly lost; in Plattsburgh, it was a case of a Canadian colony which had emigrated at the time of the great dislocation of 1837, and which was genuinely suffering from its spiritual abandonment. A recent mission preached by the fathers had proved not only that there were souls in need of spiritual help, but also that great things could be expected from such a well-disposed class of people. Years later, referring to this mission, Father Bernard recalled:

Never was there a more abundant harvest. Large sheaves were gathered in great numbers. Our threshing floor was a Protestant church which the Universalists rented to us for 100 dollars or 400 francs. In two weeks, the three hard-working Oblates heard nearly 1,600 confessions, and distributed an equal number of communions to the Canadians who had been hungering for spiritual food. Nearly forty marriages were blessed or validated and the baptisms numbered at least 250. It was always before or after dinner that we baptized the children; more than once we left the table to baptize children who had been brought to us from a distance of more than 25 miles. I, myself, baptized as many as twelve at one time.[70]

The French Canadians esteemed the fathers just as highly as the fathers esteemed them. Saddened by their departure, they hurriedly sent a delegation of twenty-five to Montreal to prevail upon the Oblates to return and establish a permanent residence in what they called their "American village." At the same time, petitions were sent to Bishop McCloskey, the Bishop of Albany, who strongly supported the request.

The provincial council favored the plan for several reasons: the need to help a large population which would grow steadily larger; the advantage of being located near Montreal which was within easy reach by railroad; the prospect of having the whole city entrusted to them on the death of the Irish priest who was in charge of a parish composed of his compatriots; lastly, the certainty of having a regular community life and sufficient work, thanks to their mission parish of Redford. A material and financial obstacle, however, stood in the way. Not only would the fathers have to be supported, but a church and rectory would have to be built. Where would the money come from? The Canadians were poor. Bishop McCloskey settled the matter by furnishing the needed guarantees through an agreement reached with the Oblates and approved by the officials of the local community.

On his arrival, August 26, 1853, with "plans for the church in his hand and nine piasters in his pocket," Father Bernard, who had preached the mission three months before, was welcomed enthusiastically. Before attending to his personal installation, he took possession of the land which the town officials had acquired for the Canadian colony and which was to be the site of the new church; then, with a thrust of the shovel, he "broke ground for the foundation work." Immediately "the purse-strings were loosened and each person made an offering proportionate to his faith and means." *Fervet opus* noted the Superior of the new residence.[71] Construction began; the missionaries, however, did not wait for its completion to organize and vitalize spiritually the parish which numbered

"600 families; 200 of these families, that is, 1,263 souls, lived in the village, and the other 400 families, that is, 1,860 souls, lived in country places within a radius of fifteen to sixteen miles." [72] Everything progressed smoothly until troubles of a financial nature arose with the town officials over the construction work for which the fathers had advanced considerable sums. The bishop of Albany vigorously upheld the missionaries and even threatened to take them away and place the parish under interdict. Fortunately, Bishop Guigues was able to settle everything, much to the satisfaction of Bishop de Mazenod who wrote:

I was delighted to learn what you told me of your visit to our Fathers in Plattsburgh. From all appearances, that establishment is on a rather solid footing. Our missionaries are doing good work there; they do not lack financial resources, and their material interests are guaranteed, as much as they can be in that country, thanks to the precautions you took to secure the sums owed them by mortgaging the property and to have the whole transaction approved by the board of trustees. As for the fathers in charge of the parish, an increase of personnel is certainly desirable so that this residence might become a regularly constituted house. However, I can't help wondering how we can take care of so many needs of this kind.[73]

Because of the sacrifices of the Oblate Congregation, and the generous allotments made by the Lyons Propagation of the Faith, it was possible to finish the church, and build a convent for the Grey Nuns who took over the education of girls and the care of the sick. The departure of the Irish priest who had been serving the Irish colony made it possible to entrust this flock to an Oblate from Ireland, Father Molony; this ended a distressing antagonism between two Christian communities which were at one and the same time sisters and rivals. Gradually the number of fathers increased; they built other churches and founded other parishes in the outskirts, and today, these parishes are flourishing. Bishop de Mazenod and Bishop Guigues had judged rightly by insisting that, despite the financial difficulties, it was necessary to retain this house which, for a brief time, had been in jeopardy as the others had been. "A money wound is not fatal." The Canadians, like the two prelates, understood this old French proverb. However, we should bear in mind that American bishops, in dioceses that were originally very poor, failed to be inspired by that proverb. Justice demands that, in giving the history of these foundations, this point be stressed, so that homage might be paid to the courage and faith of these two bishops.

Three years before there was any mention of Plattsburgh, the foundation in Buffalo at the western extremity of New York State was accepted in principle by Bishop de Mazenod himself; he had met Bishop Timon of Buffalo in the course of the latter's journey to Rome. On January 4, 1850, the Oblate General Council ratified the superior general's acceptance; it gave as reasons for its "full and entire" approval the "outstanding" advantages of the project: the location was "ideal for communicating with the ecclesiastical provinces of the United States and other parts of North America"; Buffalo was "only twenty-four hours from New York City" and equally distant from Montreal where the motherhouse of the Canadian communities was located; it was "only forty-eight hours from Bytown, the episcopal city of Bishop Guigues who is the vicar of our most illustrious Father-General in North America"; most of the great American highways converged on Buffalo, and plans "at that time called for a railroad to pass through that same city and go as far as Oregon beyond the Rocky Mountains"; lastly

the city's population, which now numbers about fifty thousand, will be double that number in a few years, according to Bishop Timon, and from then on, what an advantageous position! The venerable bishop has assured us of a small parish and a college, and is giving us the entire ownership of these establishments and whatever revenues accrue from them. For the present, he is content with obtaining three Oblates and promises to give them two priests to help them in directing and teaching the pupils.[74]

Thus, toward the end of July, Fathers Amisse, Pourret, and Molony arrived from France to run the college and the parish which the bishop of the diocese promised to entrust to them.

The beginnings of this foundation were certainly not auspicious; as soon as they had arrived, the Oblates realized that there had been a mistake, and, at the end of two weeks, they returned to Canada. Their reasons for decamping so quickly must have been valid since Bishop Guigues and the provincial council accepted them. Even the minutes of the deliberations conducted by the as-

sistants general in Marseilles mention the "awkward position" in
which Father Amisse and his colleagues were placed "by force of
circumstances" and through "a misunderstanding" between the
bishop of Buffalo and "our most reverend Superior General";
there could be no "thought of a college since the church from
which our fathers were to derive part of their revenue is now
administered by a Scottish priest who cannot be removed without
danger of schism." Although it fully approved the actions of the
Buffalo superior in abandoning such a poorly arranged undertaking, the General Council nonetheless tried to find a way to
make a second attempt succeed under more clearly defined conditions; "to avoid any further complications," the council commissioned Bishop Guigues "to conclude the business." [75] However, intricate maneuvering and cancelled meetings forestalled
the successful conclusion of the matter; it appeared that each side
was playing hide-and-seek. Wearied by these machinations and
delays, Bishop de Mazenod began to consider transferring the
priests who had been destined for Buffalo to Toronto: "What you
tell me about this country," he wrote to Bishop Guigues, "makes
me less regretful." [76]

In July 1851, during his trip to Canada as Visitor General,
Tempier ended the vacillation and concluded a clear-cut and
precise agreement with Bishop Timon. Under the terms of the
agreement, the Oblates would administer the "Catholic College
of Buffalo, which also served as the diocesan major seminary," and
would have charge of the "small wooden chapel which was situated
a short distance" from the episcopal palace; in return, they were
given guarantees which Bishop de Mazenod's delegate considered
completely solid.[77] It seemed, therefore, that every precaution
had been taken to prevent a repetition of the initial misunderstanding. Tempier, at least, was of this opinion, but certain members of the congregation in Canada, who felt they were better
acquainted with the Buffalo situation and the bishop's manner
of acting, deemed that Tempier had committed himself ill-advis-
edly. Once again, disagreeing with the general administration,
Santoni echoed their criticisms and took responsibility for them.
As he wrote to Father Aubert:

Confidentially and without consulting anyone, poor Tempier has made

a deal which has aroused the indignation of all the fathers. He is sending four fathers to Buffalo without any sure means of subsistence. They
will have to direct a college-seminary which will bring in nothing, and
the indications are that for years to come they will be able to live only
with funds either from the general administration or from the province
—and the province cannot give any help. This deal seems extremely
rash to me and probably the fathers will be obliged to come back
from there a second time. Father Tempier has discredited himself with
the fathers by this transaction. They are wrong to complain so
blatantly, but what they say is very true. Tempier is now biting his
nails, but he has pledged his word. It is too late to back out and the
fathers are leaving next Monday. What a tragedy! This is the fourth
establishment attempted in the United States, and it offers no more
hope of success than did the others.[78]

Unavoidably, this internal dissension soon compromised the future
of the foundation.

The bishop of Buffalo, who had asked for only three Oblates,
found his wishes more than gratified by receiving five. After arriving on August 19, Father Chevalier, the Superior, and his colleagues began the seminary and college classes on September 1,
1851, in a hastily improvised building. There were eleven seminarians and seventeen college students; seven of the latter were resident students and the other ten externs. Things began in a shabby
and destitute fashion, with a ramshackle building, few pupils, and,
consequently, few resources. However, this is usually the case with
a new undertaking. It was possible, therefore, to hope that, as time
went on, vocations and revenues would increase. In fact, in order
to provide more space, Bishop Timon purchased a large parcel of
land on Prospect Hill, on which stood a building formerly used
by the benevolent society as a refuge for the homeless poor and
for that reason called the "Poor House." The bishop transferred
the deed for the entire property to Father Chevalier for the sum
of $12,000 which he himself had paid for the property. In addition,
the prelate gave the Oblates title to another ten acres of land at
Blackrock, but, since this land carried a mortgage of $15,762, the
first debt of $12,000 was increased by an even larger one and les-
sened very little by an initial payment of $1,800.[79] In September,
1852, the seminary and college were established on Prospect Hill.
Undeniably, there was no lack of space, fresh air, and foliage, but

the buildings even with their coat of whitewash were not exactly impressive. The relatively few advantages of this relocation were hardly commensurate with the liabilities of a transaction which plunged the community, the provincial administration, and the general administration into grave financial difficulties. Eventually the deficit might have been eradicated if only the change in locale had brought about an increase in pupils; unfortunately, the name "Poor House," by which the place was known before its purchase, continued to be used in the area, in spite of its new purpose, and this deterred families from sending their sons there.

From the very outset, Santoni had been opposed to accepting the seminary-college of Buffalo, which, he felt sure, would inevitably fail; however, after a canonical visit to the establishment in April, 1852, he admitted that the fathers were doing very well:

So zealously and painstakingly have they performed the extremely difficult work assigned to them that, along with meriting the esteem of the congregation, they have also won the esteem and friendship of both clergy and laity who are in a good position to appreciate their manner of acting.[80]

But the college was making little progress, and this aggravated the problem that had to be solved if the house were to persevere. Consequently, the provincial council on several occasions in 1855 discussed abandoning the college, which had attracted few students, and keeping only the seminary. The general council, however, decided in favor of the *status quo*; Father Casimir Aubert informed the Canadian provincial that the council

hopes that this establishment, once it has surmounted the difficulties which always accompany an enterprise of this kind in its first years, will eventually prosper and become the source of true service in that country. It is necessary, therefore, to try to hoist all sails, in order to keep moving; the council reserves the right to take the step you propose, provided it is clear that the difficulty cannot be solved in any other way.[81]

The previous year, 1854, Bishop de Mazenod had expressed himself even more categorically; allowing for no discussion, he ordered that they hold on at any cost:

As for the discouragement of the fathers who comprise the Buffalo house, it is a cowardly attitude which I wish I could overlook. . . . Ask them what people think of soldiers who run away from the enemy. A man dies at his post; such is the code of honor. Should religion's code of honor be anything less? [82]

In 1855 new entreaties from Canada received a similar reply from Tempier, but in a less military style; Tempier defended his cause with reasons to support it: Bishop de Mazenod

does not think that you should give up the college and serve only the church and the major seminary which will probably be reduced to seven or eight pupils next year—or perhaps even more when the Bishop of Buffalo establishes his ecclesiastical school near his cathedral as he is planning to do, in order to use the seminarians for the service of the cathedral. If you were to give up the college, it seems to me that your status would be similar to that of a pastor of an ordinary parish. With patience and persevering effort, your college will grow since there has already been some progress and some increase in the number of pupils every year since you became established in Buffalo. Once the crisis ends, pupils will come.[83]

Two months later, the founder delegated Father Santoni to go to Buffalo, to encourage the fathers, and to straighten out the temporal affairs in such a way that they might be able to persevere materially and morally until the next vacation: "By that time," he instructed Santoni, "we shall have had all the time needed to examine what will have to be done subsequently and to come to a definite decision regarding our establishment." [84]

Santoni followed all these instructions except the last part, that is, to hold out until the next vacation. On June 19, after holding a meeting, Santoni's council wrote to Father Chevalier, instructing him to inform the pupils that the date of reopening of classes could not be settled since it was not known whether the Oblates would be able to continue directing the college; a month later, on July 27, Santoni notified Bishop Timon that dire necessity forced the fathers to give up a work which could not be carried on under such precarious living conditions and in such an unsuitable location. A new building would be necessary—and how could that be dreamed of, "drained" as they were by the "heavy expenditures we had to incur in order to pay singlehandedly for a part of the establishment"?[85]

This sudden notice was given without any prior consultation with Bishop de Mazenod, in spite of the fact that he had reserved the final decision to himself. Father Santoni had a reputation for giving up foundations too hastily, even cheerfully, and for closing them down unceremoniously on his own authority, as was the case with Saguenay, Orignal, South Gloucester, and Detroit; that Bytown and Quebec did not suffer the same fate was no fault of his. However, it must be granted that at that particular juncture very serious reasons required an immediate withdrawal, since the provincial council, meeting on September 23, agreed that the measure he had taken was one of urgent necessity. The minutes of the council's deliberations, however, do not specify the nature of those serious reasons. Those which Santoni officially included in his letter to Bishop Timon undoubtedly played some part in the matter, but, as Guigues later admitted, these "initial difficulties had been partly surmounted": the enrollment was growing, the preceding year had realized a profit, considerable expenses had made the house more comfortable, and the strides which had already been made justified the hope that, with time and patience, others would follow.[86] A subsequent document reveals that the prime motive lay elsewhere, and, by its very nature, suffices to explain why the provincial and his councilors preferred to keep it *in petto*, without entering it into the official record. In effect, a letter from Father Chevalier to Cardinal Barnabo put the blame on the bishop of Buffalo and offered precise information and details justifying the action of the Oblates: when, "on finding himself in extreme need," Father Chevalier reminded Bishop Timon that, through an agreement the latter had signed, he had contracted to pay a certain sum for the college grounds which the congregation had purchased, the prelate called him "insolent"; not only did the bishop fail to keep his word, but he was guilty of behavior which, to say the least, displayed a complete disregard of even the most elementary demands of courtesy. A simple admission of his helplessness to pay by arousing pity would certainly have straightened out matters far more favorably than did the awkward manner he assumed in trying to avoid payment. "It was mainly for the refusal I have just mentioned," Chevalier assured the cardinal, "that our provincial decided to discontinue the college."[87]

Thoroughly annoyed as he was, Bishop de Mazenod did not deem it possible to reverse Santoni's decision. He wrote to Santoni:

It is true that the matter has been practically settled, in fact terminated, because of the decision you felt obliged to make to abandon the work of the college, and above all, because of the communication of this decision to both Bishop Timon and Father Chevalier. You must have judged the difficulties very grave and this solution imperative to have concluded the matter in this way. Now, as things stand, since the Bishop of Bytown, after consultation with you, has announced that he favors the provincial council's decision, what course can we take here? Obviously, that of accepting the situation.[88]

Tempier was even more peeved by the abandonment of a project which he had accepted in spite of Santoni's criticism and opposition: "I cannot see how this measure will be satisfactory in any respect nor can I see any necessity for it," he wrote to Father Chevalier. "I still think it is extreme. It is a step backward, an about-face, a semi-retreat not too unlike a full retreat."[89]

The retreat was not as full as the first assistant had feared. Undoubtedly he showed keen insight in predicting that once the Oblates left the college they would lose the major seminary where vocations would lapse. Actually, the Oblates continued for a while to direct the major seminary which had become independent of the college, but since the number of seminarians soon diminished, Bishop Timon deemed it wiser to entrust the training of his clerics to a neighboring seminary. Even so, the community did not leave; on the contrary, relieved of all teaching, it began intensifying and broadening its ministry not only in the parish assigned to it, but throughout eastern America where they preached numerous missions.

At first, the parish was not impressive. Its place of worship was merely a wooden chapel of about 30 square feet, pretentiously referred to as the "basilica." This cramped building had to be abandoned in 1852 when the Oblates moved to the "Poor House," and there they made use of a shed which was as dingy as the "basilica," but much larger. It was given the name Holy Angels.

It, too, proved inadequate for the flock which had been suffering from extreme spiritual destitution and was deeply appreciative of the apostolic zeal of Oblates who had come to its aid. They then began thinking of building a church, but, here again, financial difficulties stood in the way; the land purchased for the now-abandoned college had burdened the mission with a heavy debt without furnishing any of the revenue needed for its upkeep. The provincial treasury was depleted, as was that of the general administration. Bishop de Mazenod then took out a loan of 11,000 francs, as did Father Honorat; because of this double contribution, the community which had been thinking of dissolving was able to continue.

Once the community was assured of its livelihood, a drive was started for funds to build a new Holy Angels Church, an extremely harder task. The first funds collected made it possible to begin the foundation work in 1855. This work was suspended for eighteen months so that all available funds might be used for the construction of a school to be run by the Grey Nuns. It was then resumed and progressed in proportion to the flow of resources. When these were exhausted, a generous response to an appeal made to the Lyons Propagation of the Faith and a loan granted by the Honourable Hudson's Bay Company made it possible to complete the nave in 1859. However, work on the transept and apse had to stop temporarily, and it was not until 1874 that they were completed. On the other hand, the lack of funds did not prevent the completion of the interior decoration, thanks to Father Lux, who gave generously of his time and his artistry with the paintbrush. Inspired by the thought of God's infinity, he painted an immense tableau depicting the Eternal Father "sixteen feet high" while the Son, equal to His Father, was given the stature of an "imposing giant." [90] The work of spiritual regeneration went on apace with the growing parish. As Father Fabre noted with gratification, the Oblates of Buffalo were achieving the twofold purpose of the foundation:

first, to have a residence and church in the episcopal city which will enable us to minister to Catholics, especially the poor, and, secondly, with every available means for doing good, to strive to bring back to the Catholic faith poor souls who have gone astray into the thousand different sects of American protestantism.[91]

Although the parish was essentially missionary in the modern sense of the word, Father Chevalier and his colleagues did not devote their zealous efforts exclusively to evangelizing it. Conforming to their vocation and the spirit of their institute, they preached eighty-three missions properly so called in the Buffalo diocese and its neighboring dioceses from 1856 to 1861; the missions lasted from one to three weeks. "All the Catholics in these localities," wrote Father Chevalier in 1861, "received the Sacraments"; sometimes there were a few exceptions, but these amounted to no more than "four or five people"; most of the time, however, there was not a single one who did not take advantage of the grace of the mission.

This does not mean that we are working in the midst of a devout population. Generally, the greater part of these poor Catholics . . . have not been to the Sacraments for ten or twenty years. A large number of them reach the age of twenty and twenty-five without having made their First Communion and without knowing a thing in the catechism. Unfortunately, all too many of those we meet are half-Protestant. . . . I may be under an illusion and I may be exaggerating, but I am convinced that were it not for the missions half the Catholic population would be lost.[92]

These apostolic triumphs, unfortunately, were not the general rule. In certain settlements, the greeting they received in no way cheered the preachers. For example, at Carron-Brook (known today as Dublin in the Province of Ontario), Father Chevalier was forced to take his meals in a cabin where, he wrote, "my constant companions were two dogs, two pigs, a cat, and three hens. One dog on my right, the other on my left; the two pigs under the table, the cat on my shoulders and the two hens wandering all over the place pecking at the crumbs." [93] Such discomfort could be excused on the grounds of poverty. However, there were times when open hostility forced the Oblates to retrace their steps without attempting anything, since these people were not Canadians, but pioneers—in fact, free-booters, without any religion

and without allegiance to any government. At times, the missionaries also met violent opposition from Protestants who had been
aroused against the Papists; evidently, not all of them were as
liberal-minded as the Protestants of Hammondsport, New York.
There they lent the missionaries their comfortable church benches
which the latter then used in the sorry barn where they preached
their sermons.[94] Lastly, it seems that the undeniable—and considerable—success of Father Chevalier and his colleagues was
limited to Catholics whose fervor and practice of religion were
revived and whose dangerous veering toward Protestantism was
halted. Did the missionaries make inroads on the rest of the population? One would like to be able to say so. Their letters, it is
true, report individual conversions among the Protestants or improvements in good will and understanding. But there is no
evidence to show that the missionaries had any general impact
upon the very mixed elements which were then flowing into the
country to exploit it and which were concerned with neither
religion nor the most basic morality.

THE TEXAS MISSION

    The Texas foundation was similar in certain respects to those
previously mentioned: like Pittsburgh, a decision was reached
without authorization from Bishop de Mazenod; like Buffalo, after
an abortive beginning, it succeeded after the second attempt; like
Plattsburgh, it was founded in response to an appeal from immigrants, and, after having included the work of directing a college-
seminary, in addition to its parish and missionary work, it eventually reduced its activity to include only the two last-named
ministries; like Oregon, it was undertaken in a territory recently
annexed by the United States; lastly, like all of them, it encountered
financial problems. But the enormous demographic growth of the
country, the wars with Mexico, the dangers resulting from proximity to this anti-clerical republic constantly in a state of revolution, the law of the jungle which prevailed in certain areas, the
mixture and antagonism of races, the fevers and epidemics which
resulted from an enervating climate, and finally the Civil War in
the United States: all these factors demanded more courage and
effort from the Oblates than elsewhere—demanded, in fact, the

sacrifice of their lives. Well might Bishop de Mazenod write: "Cruel mission of Texas!"

Before annexing Texas in December, 1845, the United States had peaceably invaded it through a systematically organized immigration, and then, through war, helped it to gain its independence from Mexico; it had been Mexican territory since the revolution in that country which freed her from Spanish colonization. The influx of Protestant Americans, the almost constant skirmishes or battles between more or less regular troops, the settling of accounts between private individuals, and the political disorders stemming from general lawlessness: all these resulted in worsening a religious situation which had never been particularly stable. In 1838, the Vincentian Father Timon had been sent there to investigate and on the basis of this investigation to try to find a remedy; in that whole territory, he found only two priests. The founding of the diocese of Galveston which two years later (in 1847) was entrusted to the Vincentian Fathers, marked the first step in reorganizing this portion of the Church which had been almost totally abandoned. However, at the time of its founding in 1845, its first ordinary, Bishop Odin, had at his disposal only three Vincentians and six secular priests. Although four years later the clergy numbered twelve, the insufficiency of its numbers was becoming all the more acute because of the increasing number of Americans who came seeking wealth. The disproportion between effectives and needs became even more apparent when the treaty of Guadalupe Hidalgo, signed after twelve years of war, pushed the Texas frontier back to the Rio Grande and joined a territory larger than the whole of France to Bishop Odin's diocese. It is true that the prelate inherited a certain number of pastors who took care of 30 parishes and 6,000 Mexican Catholics, now American citizens. However, his remarks about their priestly life suggests that it was preferable to replace them than to utilize them.[95]

Searching for priests to assist him, Bishop Odin, who was on his way to the Council of Baltimore, met Father Telmon in Montreal; the latter had not been reassigned to any particular work since the failure of his major seminary at Pittsburgh. Moved by the prelate's distress, and influenced even more by the pleas of the people who were begging for priests, Telmon, who never hesitated to forge ahead, volunteered his help, and it was immediately accepted; he felt empowered to take this initiative by virtue of a general delegation which Bishop de Mazenod had granted him for the United States; he committed himself without seeking approval of any kind from the superior general, and set out immediately, taking with him Father Gaudet, his companion in misfortune at Pittsburgh, Father Soulerin, a scholastic, Brother Gelot, and a lay brother. After leaving Father Gaudet and Brother Gelot at Galveston, he went on to Brownsville, a frontier town on the Rio Grande, and established his residence there. Naturally, this spur-of-the-moment foundation upset—in fact, irritated—Bishop de Mazenod. Writing in his *Journal,* on November 10, 1849, he complained:

What is happening in Canada is outrageous. Here we have Father Telmon accepting the mission of Texas on his own authority, acting on the faculties I had granted him when he was at Pittsburgh. He goes off and takes with him subjects of his own choosing, one of whom is Brother Gelot, the same brother who was admitted to vows without the approval of the general council; furthermore, I had expressly told the Bishop of Bytown not to allow him to be ordained without my approval and now the Bishop of Bytown writes me that he has learned through the newspaper that he has been ordained subdeacon. This is a monstrous and unbelievable state of affairs! Father Telmon surely must have received my letter in which it was very clearly pointed out to him that he had been officially put back under the jurisdiction of the Canadian Provincial; and he gave no heed to it, evidently because he was too deeply committed to the Bishop of Texas who was waiting for him at Cincinnati or someplace else. What is worse, however, is that, when writing, he does not seek to legitimize what he has done by requesting posterior authorization. Moreover, the Bishop of Bytown felt so fortunate in being able to rid himself of the only subject who dared to defy him that he made no objection, and, worse still, made a deal with Telmon, giving him Brother Gelot in exchange for Father Bayle who was more suitable for his Bytown establishments. Truthfully, I don't know who is more culpable, the bishop or Father Telmon. Enough of this! It would take reams to write down everything that is happening in those far-off places.

This first reaction was immediately followed by another. After letting off steam, he suddenly quieted down and concluded that his fathers deserved a vote of confidence: "However, judging from what they say, I have no reason to be disturbed. They are all doing fine work." [96]

The welcome Telmon and his confrères received at Brownsville was warm but not very promising. During a gathering arranged in their honor there was no lack of exhuberant handshakes and lusty votes of thanks, but the missionaries quickly perceived that the enthusiasm of the very diversified group was by no means inspired by pious feelings. A quick glance at a number of jailbird faces sufficed to show that there were scoundrels in that boisterous and obviously irreligious mob. Moreover, a whitebearded orator, without beating about the bush, made it clear to the fathers that they had not been brought there for spiriual purposes: "We should be deeply grateful for the presence of the missionaries in our growing city, not because it will be of any spiritual advantage to incorrigible men like ourselves but because it will be of advantage to our children." [97] Quite plainly it was a matter of securing a moral guarantee for the success of their business affairs; the Brownsville traders needed a respectable guise for their commercial operations. The appeal that had been sent to the missionaries had no other aim but to restore their commercial credit which was in a very bad state.[98]

In spite of these unpromising beginnings, Telmon and his assistants bravely set to work; their sheep, however, were as indifferent to the lodgings of the missionaries as they were to their own conversions. At first, the fathers had to set up temporary quarters in a wretched shed "where spiders and rats live a community life." [99] They utilized a store for their chapel, and used its counter as an altar. Few people attended services; only one man had the courage to attend Mass. Four changes of living quarters in as many months made very little improvement in their living conditions. The Oblates were finally able to purchase a piece of land, and in two months built themselves a wooden church and rectory. Thus, temporary arrangements came to an end, and the work of evangelizing the people began. Although they were unreceptive to the spiritual, the American colonists admired Father Telmon's dash, his initiative, and his unique character. By earning the reputation of being a "smart man," he made a deep impression on them. This resourceful improvisor, who had a knack for resolving any kind of difficulty, also appealed to them by the direct and blunt manner in which he did away with objections; for, in conversing with the people as well as in preaching to them, he enjoyed launching into controversies, either in Spanish or in English. The oratorical feats performed by this champion, who was never caught off-guard, attracted even the infidels who appreciated juridical contests in a field other than that of ideas, dogma, and morality.[100] Thus, a movement took shape, whereby grace gradually began to operate through the uniqueness of the pastoral program. In spite of what the white-bearded old orator had assured Telmon and his colleagues when he welcomed them and voiced the general determination that there would be no amendment, some conversions were effected.

In a letter to Bishop de Mazenod, Bishop Odin declared that the influence being exerted upon priestly circles delighted him even more than did the first results which the missionaries achieved with the faithful:

I deem myself truly fortunate that Providence sent me these good fathers for that part of the diocese. Not only were zealous and exemplary workers needed there, but also men of proven and solid virtue. The Rio Grande separates us from Mexico and the clergy in the bordering towns of that unfortunate country are very lax, not to say depraved and dissolute. The exemplary conduct of the two fathers is a very happy contrast to the disorderly life of the priests on the opposite shore and has already had a most favorable effect upon the minds of the people. I hope that the missionaries will succeed in becoming solidly established there and that later their community will be asked to effect a salutary reform within the Mexican clergy and to instruct the Mexican people; these people have great faith, but they are uneducated and unpolished.[101]

Unfortunately, summer withered the hopes which a few months of apostolic toil had been nurturing; the Oblates could not withstand the tropical heat which was all the more oppressive because of the food they had to eat and the unsanitary conditions they had to endure in that region of the country. Bishop de Mazenod then decided to send Fathers Soulerin and Gaudet back to Canada; they were exhausted. But this did not mean a general retreat; Father Telmon was allowed to remain along with Brother Gelot "but would have to assume full responsibility for the work there." [102] Telmon made a valiant effort to continue but, three months after his companions left, he returned to Canada, and, on January 22, 1851, he sailed for France, his health ruined by the frightful climate of Texas.

Are the all-too-valid reasons which Bishop de Mazenod cited the sole explanation for his decision to recall Soulerin and Gaudet? Did his dissatisfaction with the foundation which had been accepted without his authorization induce him to deal severely with a mission into which Telmon had rushed without previous permission? Did the founder take that opportunity to teach a stern lesson he deemed necessary to the leader who lacked sufficient regard for his superiors, by depriving him of the co-workers he had chosen on his own authority? Whatever the answer may be to all these questions, one thing seems certain: Bishop de Mazenod did not intend to abandon Texas since he left Telmon there as a sort of foundation stone, which meant continuing the work with whatever means were available. In addition, it seems that, although the founder was somewhat severe with Telmon because of the breezy manner in which he dashed into ventures on his own initiative and then abandoned them without any warning, he had to admit in all justice that at Brownsville, under extremely difficult conditions, this missionary had shown a zeal that was equally courageous and skillful. Bishop de Mazenod esteemed this apostolic religious very highly and gave many proofs of his affection for him. More than once he took occasion to justify him before his confrères who found it difficult to get along with him.[103] Individualistic, eccentric, reckless, and possessing a forceful personality, Telmon had little taste for discreet timidity; his very zeal made him unusually severe on those who could not appreciate his impulses. But the bishop of Marseilles, who also possessed a fiery temper, knew that eminent qualities must of necessity be accompanied by defects. The finest homage paid to the talents of the zealous Telmon came from Bishop Odin who had seen him at work; in 1851, when arrangements were being made to resume the suspended foundation, the bishop of Galveston urgently requested that the Oblates again send him this dauntless missionary whose personality was so suitable to Texas. Unfortunately, much to the prelate's disappointment, Telmon's poor health made it impossible to grant this wish.[104]

Telmon's departure had been felt all the more keenly by the bishop of Galveston since it was added to twenty-three others. Of the thirty-five priests whose help he had secured, noted the secretary of the Propagation of the Faith, "ten died of fatigue and hardships; eleven others, Vincentians and Oblates, were recalled by their major superiors, and two seculars returned to their native dioceses." Thus, all that remained were "twelve colleagues for a population of 40,000 Catholics." [105]

To replenish his steadily dwindling effectives, Bishop Odin therefore went to Europe and, while passing through Marseilles, succeeded in persuading Bishop de Mazenod to dispatch a new contingent of Oblates from France. This one was even larger than the first, and, according to an agreement signed by the superior general and Bishop Odin, was to form two communities; one would provide "religious service" at Galveston and the other at Brownsville. The latter would also evangelize the "adjacent populations in the county of which Brownsville was the county seat." Each community was to found and direct a college "in the city of its residence." Lastly, the two communities "would be expected to teach theology to the diocesan seminarians." To guarantee an establishment for the fathers, the bishop ceded parcels of land to them and agreed to pay their traveling expenses.[106] Never in the history of the congregation had Bishop de Mazenod sent so many of his sons at one time to the same place; furthermore, he was determined to choose elite troops for Texas. Five of the best scholastics were chosen and were immediately ordained to the priesthood. Under the leadership of the newly appointed superior, Father Verdet, they embarked in March, 1852, and arrived at Galveston on May 14, 1852.

Instead of sending three Oblates to Brownsville where they were intended to resume Father Telmon's work, Bishop Odin kept all six with him at Galveston. This was an immediate violation of the agreement reached with Bishop de Mazenod. But the reasons which Bishop Odin gave seemed so valid to the bishop of Marseilles that he offered no objection to the delay his colleague had put upon the departure of the fathers for the Rio Grande: the Carvajal revolution on the Mexican border made such a journey too dangerous; the fathers, especially the younger ones, had to be initiated into a rather unique ministry and had to improve their English and Spanish; lastly, wisdom demanded that, before anything else was done, the first foundation and the seminary in particular, a work that was essential to the future of the diocese, should be firmly established under the direct supervision of the bishop and through the combined efforts of everyone.[107] To gain the superior general's consent to delay installing his religious at Brownsville in favor of the seminary, all Bishop Odin would have had to say was that he wished to give the seminary priority. We know, as a matter of fact, that the bishop of Marseilles considered the training of a native clergy one of the principal objectives of the missionary apostolate.

His ideas, however, as to how to achieve this objective differed from those of Bishop Odin. Although they agreed that the major seminary required special organization to assure theological studies and to provide immediate preparation for holy orders, the two prelates differed about the minor seminary which provided a classical education and cultivated both vocations and minds at one and the same time. The bishop of Marseilles believed that the minor seminary should accept only aspirants to the priesthood and should constitute a separate house. Unable in his *de facto* situation to realize an ideal upon which Bishop de Mazenod with his French viewpoint proved to be unyielding and absolute, the bishop of Galveston felt he had to start off with more adaptability; he had neither the teaching staff nor the resources which a distinct establishment demanded; even if he did have the teachers, buildings and needed funds, it would have seemed unreasonable to devote them exclusively to about ten adolescents and children. Only one solution seemed workable to him; join a college to the seminary. Economizing on professors and money in this way would provide the added advantage of assuring a Catholic education to the young men of the area.

The fact of the matter was that Bishop Odin did not want to restrict himself to a missionary apostolate. To regenerate his diocese, which was in a very pitiful state, he felt it was indispensable that the new generation of girls and boys be given a Christian education—hence a vast program which included the establishment of educational institutions to be entrusted to religious congregations of men and women. In his opinion, the fathers sent by Bishop de Mazenod could utilize their zeal in no better way than by extending it also to students who were not seminarians. With a little effort, the same course of studies and the same building would serve two purposes. Did he honestly believe that Father Verdet and his Oblate colleagues shared his ideas to the extent of wanting such an extension of their apostolate? Whether he did or not, he wrote to the Lyons Propagation of the Faith: "I have decided to form my own seminary, and I am entrusting its direction to the Oblate Fathers. Not only will young clerics be admitted, but all the children to whom the fathers wish to give a more rounded education." [108] A month later, his vicar general wrote more explicitly to the Lyons Propagation:

The Oblates have taken over the direction of the seminary-college under the leadership of Father Baudrand who arrived a short time ago from Canada. Soon they will have a new field of action opened to their zeal. While instructing our Protestant young men in the humanities, they will be able to instill the fear of God and love for virtue in their minds; this is the only means we have for regenerating modern society.[109]

Now, the Oblates, who held the same views as those of their founder, were simply enduring a temporary arrangement which, unknown to them, concealed a radical misunderstanding. The ambiguity of the bishop's words to the Propagation gave way to a clear-cut formula under the pen of the vicar general who explicitly called the establishment a "seminary-college"; as time went on, a third formula appeared: a college-seminary; by reversing the terms it clearly stressed that the essential end which Bishop de Mazenod had envisaged was being changed.

Bishop de Mazenod was, of course, deeply conscious of the importance of a Christian education, as was proved by the role he played in France during the debates about the freedom of Catholic education. But, as he pointed out, the Oblates were not founded for educational work; this work had been completely excluded from their ministry by the original constitutions. By no means did their own training in the seminary give them the competency needed for the teaching profession. Other orders whose members had been duly prepared specialized in this form of the ministry—to each man his charisma and his task. He wrote to the superior, Father Verdet:

I can understand how your zeal induced you to want to help those poor souls who have been so neglected, but there was no need to do so much at one time. I read your letter to the Council and it was unanimously agreed that your mission was never intended to form a college (in the meaning you give it) whose care would absorb all our forces in Texas. We are sending missionaries to convert souls and not to establish colleges in competition with those formed elsewhere and firmly established. Who are we to pretend that we can compete in this type of work with a society so rich in subjects as the Jesuits? Here you are, all together at Galveston, when half of you were intended for the missions, and you now ask for helpers, and even designate those you want sent to you . . . ! It must be clearly understood that our Congregation is not a teaching order like the Jesuits. We were instituted to preach missions, etc. . . . Our family is too young in the Church and too few in numbers to be able to divert a large number of subjects from our special vocation and assign them to colleges. For that work, they would have to apply themselves to studies different from those to which missionaries must devote themselves if they are to fulfill their ministry worthily. It was only by way of exception, therefore, that we took charge of a college in the United States, and precisely because we do have one, we cannot have a second with all the equipment that is needed for assuring the success of such an establishment.[110]

The superior general also reminded Verdet that he had contracted with Bishop Odin to found a seminary and only a seminary.

As a result of this letter, Bishop Odin finally decided to send to Brownsville the three fathers he had been detaining at Galveston. The three who remained behind, however, continued to direct the seminary-college under the same conditions.

As categorical as he had been, Bishop de Mazenod nevertheless allowed the experiment to continue although it was entirely different from the project he had outlined with Bishop Odin. The beginnings of the seminary-college were rather discouraging. Its first director, Father Baudrand, who was sent from Canada in May, 1853, died of yellow fever a few months after his arrival, during an epidemic which claimed 335 lives; among these victims were four young secular priests who had recently arrived in the diocese. The loss of Father Baudrand was a severe one, since this holy and learned religious had been expressly chosen by his superiors and had been warmly welcomed by his confrères. He would have been ideally suited for the task. Because of the bishop's lack of funds, construction work on the buildings he had begun was suspended. The pupils were unruly, lazy, and even insolent; the parents took no interest either in the children's class-work or in their conduct. But gradually things improved. With a subsidy from the Oblates and the considerable sums collected by Father Parisot from Louisiana plantation owners, the walls were built, the rest of the work was speeded up, and the furnishings completed; on January 1, 1855, the new building was opened for occupancy. Discipline as well as studies benefited from it; the fathers' devotion to duty did the rest, and the college took on new life. Bishop Odin expressed his delight to Bishop de Mazenod over the thriving situation: "It numbers from 90 to 95 pupils," he wrote; "it has gained the confidence of the parents and promises to become one of the great schools in the country." [111] As a matter of fact, an act of the House of Representatives of the State of Texas, dated July 26, 1856, officially confirmed the high caliber of its teaching by conferring upon the college the title Saint Mary's University, "with full power to confer diplomas and degrees. It was the first charter of its kind ever granted by the Texas State Legislature." [112]

Rather than making them more eager to pursue the work, this title disturbed the Oblates, since it emphasized more forcibly how far the institution had deviated from its original purpose. Bishop de Mazenod discovered for himself that Bishop Odin no longer referred to it as a seminary but purely and simply as a college; what his sons reported to him verified this change of name only too well, since the only seminarians Bishop Odin kept at Galveston were those who had almost completed their studies, and he kept them there not for the sake of completing their seminary training but to serve as professors. All the other seminarians were sent to the Vincentian seminary at Sainte-Marie des Barrens (known today as Cape Girardeau, Missouri). Thus, what had originally been an end was changed to a means. All that remained of the seminary were the elements capable of serving the college by filling in the gaps in hard-to-find teaching personnel.

And yet, when Father Gaudet, writing to Bishop de Mazenod, pointed out the bad position the Oblates were in and proposed that this school—really a "grade school" and which was "scarcely suited to their vocation as missionary priests" [113]—be given over to the Christian Brothers, the founder replied by urging him to be patient: they would have to complete the year and wait until the next vacation period; it would then be easier to make "new arrangements" with Bishop Odin, whereby the Fathers would be assigned to work more in accord with their vocation.[114] Father Gaudet, however, was in no mood to be patient; several fathers had been demanding that they be changed to the active ministry.

The bishop of Galveston who had an inkling of these complaints and requests tried in vain to avert the blow threatening his college. Writing to Bishop de Mazenod on May 15, 1857, he declared:

The more I reflect, the less I can understand what motive could induce you to discontinue this excellent work which is of such advantage to religion. What will become of these many children who will now be deprived of a Christian education, and will have to enroll in the public schools where they will imbibe the poison of infidelity? So important is the education of young people in our missions that all the religious communities here are endeavoring to open educational institutions.[115]

Bishop de Mazenod felt he could not grant Bishop Odin's wishes since he believed the time had come to give the college, which was unsuited to the ends of his congregation, to one of the religious communities which specialized in teaching and education. Although unswerving in his decision, he revealed a touching delicacy when it came time to make that decision known to a prelate whom he esteemed very highly, and whom he was now obliged to disappoint:

Your letter of May 15, which I received a few days ago, places me in a real quandary. It informs me that you will be displeased should our Fathers no longer be in charge of the college at Galveston. On the other hand, I find it will be impossible for them to continue this work under present conditions. It is not that they have the least complaint about Your Grace; on the contrary, they are the first to acknowledge the kindness with which you have always treated them, and the generosity you have always shown them in helping them with every means, pecuniary or otherwise, to make the college of Galveston a success. I am very glad of the opportunity to let you know their feelings toward you; they are feelings of respectful affection and sincere gratitude for all your kindness to them, feelings which I try to instill in all my sons and which should characterize the Oblates of Mary wherever God may send them and wherever the bishops may confidently call them. The difficulty, however, does not lie there. Unfortunately, it stems from a cause beyond anyone's control, one which neither you nor the Fathers can obviate. The difficulty lies in the very nature of the work that is being done by the Oblates stationed in your episcopal city. It appears that the college of Galveston is at present, and for a long time will be, simply a business school in which students of Latin, particularly those destined for the priesthood, are few in number. Now, to conduct ordinary classes in such an institution, there is no need to employ priests whose zeal could be put to better use serving souls in a country where the Lord's vineyard lacks workers. A religious congregation of teaching brothers would suffice for the college. It is not surprising that, faced with such a situation, our Fathers conceived the idea of withdrawing from the school, and finally decided to do so with the intention of seeking a ministry more in keeping with their vocation; for I feel sure, Your Grace, that you are aware that education, even of ecclesiastics, is but a secondary end of the institute of the Oblates of Mary Immaculate, and that the instruction of lay students in the humanities is entirely foreign to their work. . . .

And so, that is how things stand. In such a situation, I think that nothing further can be done except to arrange that the coming transfer will be effected with the least possible inconvenience for the college of Galveston. Even though you bring other teachers into the school— for example, the Christian Brothers—to run it at their own risk and under their own responsibility, you may, if need be, insist on your right to keep one or two priests there to serve the religious needs of the house or even to take care of the overall direction of the whole establishment. And to prove our good will I am willing to allow two of our Fathers to remain there temporarily for that purpose, one to be engaged specifically in that work, the other to be his companion and at the same time to be at your disposal for different little services he might render you in the city or its environs. The other Fathers who are now at Galveston will go to Brownsville to join their confrères and thereby build up that community, enabling it further to increase its apostolic work.

You can see, Your Grace, that, although I am forced to give up your college, I am taking every means to avoid any disastrous consequences that might result from this step, and, on the other hand, to guarantee that this step will have a useful result for your diocese since it will mean a greater number of workers for the sacred ministry. My wish to lessen the distress you might suffer from this measure also motivates me to make no claim for the expenses the Congregation had to incur since undertaking the college; I leave all compensation or financial indemnity entirely to your sense of justice and generosity, relinquishing to you all the sums we had obtained from the Propagation of the Faith for the college buildings.[116]

This long letter merits being quoted in its entirety since it characterizes the manner the bishop adopted in his later years: his temperament was still that of a leader, but he allowed his heart to speak with touching kindness without losing any of its firmness. In years past, his youthful rigorism and his trenchant and impulsive pen brought about a lack of appreciation of his best qualities. In the serenity of his twilight years, the depths of his warm and human soul which had been purified and softened by trial, grace, and virtue were revealed under a gentler light. Abandoning Galveston in 1857 made it possible for the Texas Oblates to concentrate all their efforts on Brownsville where Fathers Olivier, Keralum, and Gaye had founded an establishment in October, 1852.

These three had gauged the amplitude and the difficult nature of their mission as soon as they arrived in Brownsville after a long and arduous journey of 300 miles through the cactus and the mesquite which cover the border region of the Rio Grande. Not only were they faced with the problem of evangelizing an immense territory of 100 by 150 miles in size—the size of Belgium or Holland—but they also had to face an extremely complicated situation which seems to have nonplused Father Verdet at the very outset when he came to Brownsville to install the missionaries sent to resume Father Telmon's work. Summarizing his impressions, he wrote: "Strange country!" [117] Having no police force, Brownsville was ruled by the law of "might makes right"; a good musket-shot took the place of law and order; assassins had a particularly free hand since, if they wanted to take cover in Mexico, they had only to cross the Rio Grande. By virtue of the "lynch law," since there was no officially organized system of law, individuals or groups took the law into their own hands, hanging criminals without any pretense of fair trial. Passions, grudges, hatreds, and jealousies naturally came into play in these summary executions, and offenses that were not really crimes were punished with death; there were occasions when community leaders considered some insignificant offense deserving of the fate of the worst criminals. What is recounted about this sad subject in the *Journal* of Father Domenech,[118] who took care of the Brownsville parish for a short time after Telmon's departure, agrees with the reports of the missionaries in their letters to the Propagation of the Faith.

The racial and commercial rivalry which pitted the immigrants, especially the Americans, against the natives contributed even more to their recourse to these summary executions, which were judged to be normal—in fact, lawful—by reason of local ways and customs. Although they numbered only a few hundred, the Yankees strove mightily to monopolize trade, and the Mexicans of Texas were more resentful of their wish to dominate the country economically than they were of any conquest by arms. Before they were finally settled, the problems of assimilation posed by the treaty which pushed the frontier back to the Rio Grande caused constant tension throughout the 19th century. The very proximity of Mexico provided the Mexicans of Brownsville with support from gangs on the other side of the river who crossed over to assist them.

The religious situation reflected all this. A Protestant minister, the Rev. William Passmore, felt he could best describe it with a reference to a historical precedent, which, for him, epitomized the abomination of desolation: "I found Brownsville such a place as I suppose the French cities were when Reason was the goddess of the French." [119] The Protestant immigrants had so little fervor that on his arrival the Reverend Passmore counted only four parishioners. This very indifference, however, made the Protestants more tolerant toward the Oblates. Here, unlike Canada and Oregon, the missionaries were not frustrated in their efforts by the opposition of the ministers; in fact they benefited from their kindness. To balance the scales, however, an apathy on the part of Catholics similar to that found in the earlier settlements paralyzed the ministry of the Oblates. When they first undertook that ministry, "it was a rare occasion if thirty or forty people attended Sunday services; the Sacraments were completely forsaken." [120]

On the other hand, although few people went to church, the priest had many visitors at his rectory and was treated as a friend. Faith was there, but it was poorly enlightened and very ineffective. Sunday was no different from any other day except that the bars, poolrooms, and gambling houses were more crowded, and there was more widespread drinking, carousing, cursing, quarreling, and fighting.[121]

In the eight counties which comprised the Brownsville parish and which were beset with similar problems, evangelization was even more difficult because of the wide scattering of the population. With the exception of Brownsville, a few more or less populated centers in the rich region of the Rio Grande, and two or three villages in the arid coastal region, most of the settled population lived on the *ranchos,* immense tracts of land granted gratuitously to *señors* by the King of Spain after 1746, and purchased for almost nothing by Americans. Scattered over these isolated and immense farms, each under the supervision of a master or overseer, were settlements of laborers called *rancheros* who lived in semi-serfdom. Except for the fertile valley along the Rio Grande, which produced sugar cane, cotton, corn, beans, and melons, there was little agriculture; instead, there were vast prairies, broken at rare intervals by clumps of trees, and over these plains roamed large herds of cattle and flocks of sheep and goats, marked with the owner's brand, and wild horses which were roped by the cowboys and domesticated. Other Mexican families, even poorer than the *rancheros,* led a nomad existence and traveled from place to place to earn their living, carrying all their belongings on their backs, with the ever-present *santitos* and picture of Our Lady of Guadalupe. One can surmise the problem posed for the Oblates by this scattering of their flock. Although the *rancheros,* as well as the nomads, were extremely hospitable to the missionaries and showed them marks of the deepest respect, their religion unfortunately consisted of only an instinctive and vague faith, and a strong devotion to the Blessed Virgin. Catechizing them would have required frequent visits—in fact, extended stays with them. But the missionaries could make only brief visits during their journeys which covered hundreds of miles. They had become such excellent horsemen that, throughout that region, the small detachment of these apostolic cowboys was nicknamed the "Cavalry of

Christ." With all their great zeal, however, the task was beyond their means.

To lessen the constant moving from place to place in the southwest, the Oblates acceded to Bishop Odin's request and in 1853 established a residence at Roma, a small town of 1,000 inhabitants, situated on the American side of the Rio Grande and midway between Laredo and Brownsville; from this central point, the two missionaries assigned there were able to reach the surrounding missions more easily. (One of them, Father Keralum, built a stone chapel with his own hands.) However, at the end of two years, even though the mission at Roma promised to become a fruitful one, Father Verdet requested Bishop Odin to replace the two missionaries with a secular priest since the isolation of the two Oblates was endangering their religious regularity; moreover, Brownsville needed reinforcement. Thus, in June, 1856, the two Oblates left Roma, where they were succeeded by a diocesan priest, Father Planchet.

Actually, progress had been taking place at Brownsville. The number of churchgoers was increasing, and conversions were being effected. Telmon's chapel, which, at first, had been adequate, was becoming too small for the steadily growing attendance. This meant that a church had to be built. Keralum, who had been an architect by profession before he entered the congregation, was needed to draw up the plans and direct the work; manpower was also needed. Lastly, the over-burdened ministry demanded an increase of helpers. This did not mean that the *ranchos* were being neglected, but before the work of evangelization could become more effective, the fathers had to wait for the arrival of their confrères from the now-abandoned college of Galveston and for a more methodical arrangement of the work. Father Gaudet wrote:

Until my arrival at Brownsville, our Fathers had ministered to the *ranchos* rather regularly, in spite of their small numbers. However, a different Father would be sent to them on each visit. To me, this system seemed poorly suited for making any progress. Now it is always the same one who visits a set district. The people have expressed their approval of this system; they have grown accustomed to "their" Father and have finally heeded his voice, while the Fathers themselves have grown fonder of their respective posts. These outside mission posts are divided up among three districts. The first district, north of

the river and comprising about thirty *ranchos* spread over a distance
of 87 miles, has been assigned to Father Olivier; the central district,
comprising about fifteen *ranchos* and spread over a distance of 50 to
75 miles, has been assigned to Father Keralum; the district south of
the river as far as the Gulf comprises about 12 *ranchos* scattered over
a distance of 30 miles, and has been assigned to Father Parisot.[122]

The results achieved gave just cause for satisfaction:

Our population seems to be rising out of its torpor. God is beginning
to reward our Fathers' patience and labors, which had been unfruitful
for so long. Lenten confessions and communions were never so numerous as they were this year.[123]

The new church at Brownsville was solemnly blessed on June 12,
1859, and was attended by a large gathering of people drawn from
a fifty-mile area. The missionaries felt it advisable to decline the
services of musicians who had come from Matamoros in Mexico
"to present a melodious" concert. Father Gaudet wrote:

I felt too great a repugnance to allow people who are so often the life
of diabolical gatherings to take part in a religious ceremony. Besides,
the purpose of the celebration was striking enough by itself to attract
both Protestants and Catholics—which is what happened. The French
parishioners of Brownsville sang the Bordeaux Mass with fine precision. . . . Now we can breathe easily. It was about time that we left
our venerable little chapel; it was a real furnace in the summer and an
iceberg in the winter.[124]

Delighted as he was to have a much larger and more comfortable
church, Gaudet was even more delighted with the vast improvement evidenced in the Brownsville mission during the following
months; confessions became frequent and things augured well for
the future.[125]

All this apostolic success, however, exacted a heavy toll. In
the five years from 1853 to 1858, five of the Texas community
lost their lives: Father Baudrand in 1853; Father Duperray in
1855; in 1858, Father Lustrac and Brother Garcia died of the yellow fever, and the community's first superior, Father Verdet, was
drowned in the wreck of the *Nautilus* while on his way to New
Orleans to collect funds sent by the Propagation of the Faith.

These repeated losses wrung a "cry of anguish" from Bishop de Mazenod: He wrote on November 26, 1858:

What a thunder-bolt! my dear sons, to learn that Father Gaudet is also seriously ill. I am not cut out for this kind of misfortune and I don't think I ever will be. Losing dear Father Lustrac and good Brother Garcia was too much as it was. Until your next letter arrives, I shall be bowed down by the ominous threat to Father Gaudet's life. He was not even convalescent the day he took the pains to add a few lines to Father Parisot's letter, hoping to lighten the blow he knew I would suffer because of his sickness. How has he been since then? Please let me know at the earliest possible moment. How long these days of waiting will be! In God's name, reassure me as soon as possible. The hours seem like days and the days like weeks. Cruel mission of Texas! What frightful wounds you inflict on me! You have already devoured your fifth victim! And again, I ask, what of the sixth whom you have struck with your fierce blows? Dear God, pardon this cry of anguish. I do not mean to murmur against your providential will. I know—it is more than trust—I am sure that those you have taken from us have been called to heaven only that you might reward them with eternal happiness. But is it not permissible for this sensitive and tender heart which you gave me to be torn by such an unexpected bereavement? Then, too, how can the task you have assigned us be carried out if you take away the instruments I am using to procure both your glory and the salvation of the souls you have entrusted to our ministry? You too, my dear sons, forgive my weakness. Perhaps I should be more selfless and more courageous in bearing the greatest cross which the good God could send me. If it were only a question of myself, I think that it would not be too great a sacrifice, but I cannot help but moan when those whom God has given me are taken away in the very thick of the fight; I would almost be tempted to say before their time, were it not that such a remark would offend God who, I must acknowledge, is the master of our lives and of events.

Consequently, I would rebuke myself for my cry of anguish if I did not have the example of our Divine Saviour in the Garden of Olives begging His heavenly Father to remove the chalice He was being given to drink.[126]

Shortly afterwards, the bishop of Marseilles was informed that the Texas mission, decimated by so many losses, was in a critical situation: "We are in the midst of a civil war," wrote Father Gaudet on October 3, 1859. The United States Government withdrew all the troops it had garrisoned on the border since the invasion of Texas. Mexican bandits took advantage of this to swoop down on Brownsville. Led by an outlaw, Cortina, a troop of cavalry crossed the river and fell upon the city with shouts of: *Long live Mexico! Death to the Americans!* They broke open the prisons, massacred the Yankees and public officials, and then drew back beyond the river under cover of artillery fire from the Mexican National Guard. While help was being awaited, the streets were barricaded; we keep watch night and day for fear of new raids, since the bandits have camped only a few miles away and have been devastating the nearby *ranchos*. The Fathers cannot leave Brownsville to visit their mission stations. In Brownsville itself, where the population is in a state of panic, their ministry has come to a halt and their church deserted. There go all our hopes.[127]

Troops sent by the United States fortunately put an end to the depredations of Cortina and his bands of outlaws. Soon, however, the Mexican revolution and later the American Civil War created a crisis far more serious than the raids by the bandits: Wrote Father Gaudet who was growing more and more pessimistic:

Nothing can be planned at this time. Here we are, cut off from the great American Union. All our troops have gone up North; for a while, they were replaced by volunteers, and later by regular troops of the State of Texas. I don't know how things will turn out for us; everything now depends on chance. What will the future reveal? Only God knows! [128]

Bishop de Mazenod, whose days were then numbered, was not discouraged by all that. Far from forsaking this unpromising and hazardous mission, he actually increased its effectives, sending it two fathers in 1859, and three more in 1861, the very year in which he died. He even planned to extend its activity into Mexico in spite of the political troubles and religious persecutions destroying that unfortunate country. It would be the last bold undertaking of the old patriarch who was still at heart the dauntless missionary of his young days. From the very beginning, he looked upon Brownsville as but a springboard for new apostolic conquests. In spite of all the obstacles, he kept forging ahead to the very end.

THE APOSTOLATE IN MEXICO

The gaining of its independence which freed Mexico from Spanish rule had given rise to an internal crisis of extreme gravity. Once victory was achieved, those who had joined forces against the foreigner became such impassioned and violent opponents that, not content with restricting their opposition to the political arena, they took up arms against each other. Civil wars were followed by more civil wars, revolutions by revolutions, and the Church was involved in all of them. The nationalist movement had combined some very heterogeneous elements; some of these intended only to put an end to the exploitation and enslavement resulting from colonialism, and among them were good Christians —in fact a certain number of priests like Hidalgo and Morelos. But there were others who aimed to destroy, with a single blow, the ecclesiastical system modeled upon that of Spain, the champion of Catholicism. The alliance of these two groups was based upon a misunderstanding and was broken when it became a question of orienting the government of the liberated country. The liberals then claimed to be the only patriots, and all those who refused to adopt their program even for reasons of conscience were branded as bad citizens—in fact, as foreign agents. To this effect, the liberals exploited the Holy See's condemnation of the insurrection against Spain, and her refusal to grant the revolutionaries the same honors and privileges she had accorded the King of Spain, particularly the right to submit names for bishoprics and major benefices. They likewise exploited the opposition which existed between the upper and lower segments of the clergy, and for the same reason that it had been done in France toward the end of the 18th century. Once in control, the liberals, who for the most part were Freemasons, waged an aggressive campaign of anticlericalism, and, like the Jacobins of 1789, began by confiscating church property. In 1857, when the Oblates from Galveston arrived in Brownsville, the liberals published and enforced the famous *leyes de reforma* which decreed the suppression of religious orders, wrested all educational institutions from the Church and, in fact, even her right to own property. An attempt was even made to establish an independent Mexican Church, and bishops and priests who refused to take the oath of allegiance to the new constitution were imprisoned or sent into exile.

Catholic resistance in the northern region of Mexico remained weak and sporadic. The people as a whole disapproved of the antireligious attitude of their leaders, but did nothing more than bemoan it; what the Oblates reported regarding Tamaulipas, bordering the Rio Grande, gives a clear picture of general passivity.[129] In the southern region, however, defense of the rights of the Church was supported by armed insurrections of conservatives who were accused of being backed by Spain and by those governments favoring colonial expansion, to the greater profit of the enemies of national independence. In every region, the liberals, striving to disunite their opponents, excelled in exploiting the breach between the high and the low clergy mentioned above, and the scandal given by certain priests who were either ardent revolutionists or corrupt counter-revolutionists. For propaganda purposes they made use of the press—something the Catholics lacked—and they benefited from the help given by the United States and by the secret societies which were as active as they were highly organized.

The Oblates, however, did not hesitate to venture upon this dangerous ground and sought more helpers for their difficult campaign. Writing to the founder, Father Gaudet pleaded:

Please! dear Father, it is imperative that we be provided with two more fathers and a coadjutor-brother to work in Matamoros next autumn. Don't let these deaths discourage you! Look what happens when your sons die! They go straight to heaven. Should we not have brothers up above? After all, is it not God who calls them to Himself? Let the thought of the abandoned souls in Mexico touch your heart and move you to come to their assistance in spite of the fewness of your cherished troops! Now that I have survived the test of the climate, I feel doubly attached to our Rio Grande mission and doubly encouraged; and, if the means are available, I am determined to give every possible help to our Mexican neighbors who are so deserving of compassion. And so, grant our wishes! [130]

In sending this fervent appeal, Father Gaudet knew that his wishes were those of the founder himself; the latter was as eager as Father Gaudet, if not more so, to see the Oblates settled beyond the Rio Grande. Only a few months previously, he had asked Gaudet what plans he was making for the foundation, adding that if the Texas superior had been allowed a more than sufficient community at Brownsville, it was with the hope that this Mexican foundation would be established.[131] Gaudet likewise knew that he was furthering the plans of Bishop Barajas, the Bishop of Saint Luis Potosí, who had taken refuge in the Brownsville community after his expulsion from Mexico; the Mexican prelate had urgently requested that he be given missionaries as soon as conditions improved. In his aforementioned letter to the founder, Father Gaudet had written:

I derived great satisfaction from all my conversations with this zealous prelate. He is surprisingly vigorous in spite of his sixty-three years; his devotion and energy in defending the rights of the Church make him a real confessor of the faith. He has never yielded to or been afraid of the revolutionists. He has told me over and over again: "Father, rest assured that as soon as the political situation has straightened out I shall send for you to establish a major seminary in my episcopal city. I already have the building for it and certain funds set aside for that purpose. Furthermore, I want to give you a church and a good-sized parish only a short distance from the city." Bishop Barajas wants at least twelve priests for all this work, but for the first year he will be content with six so that they might begin the major seminary and provide certain services in the city. And so, dear Father, if I should receive a letter one of these days from this good bishop, asking me to arrange for this foundation, I promise you I will not hesitate to do so, hoping that you will support me and not allow such a fine opportunity to become established in the third largest city of Mexico to escape; Saint Luis ranks after Mexico City and Guadalajara in size. Let us keep on hoping. With perseverance, sooner or later we will be in Mexico.[132]

It would have been very much later rather than sooner, had the Oblates waited for the political situation to straighten out, as Bishop Barajas had proposed, since peace was not to come to the country for a long time. They began with missions into Mexico, facilitated by their location on the border town of Brownsville. The Rio Grande served them as a means both of entering Mexico and, if necessary, of escape from the liberals.

We have no precise information regarding these first thrusts. However, the successful results they achieved at Matamoros, where they found relative security, must have induced the missionaries to establish a beachhead on the other side of the river—since, in 1858, two of them were working continuously in that Mexican city.[133] Father Gaudet, on his own initiative, had taken a chance on this foundation at Matamoros; the proscribed bishop of Monterrey who was in hiding in his diocese could not be reached and the Brownsville superior had been unable to consult his superior general before accepting the foundation. Before proceeding any further, however, he wanted to obtain proper authorization from either one or the other. When Bishop de Mazenod learned of Gaudet's initiative, he warmly approved it, and, to reinforce the mission at Matamoros which he termed "permanent," directed that two fathers be kept there.[134] The pastor of Matamoros, Don Musquiz, to whom the bishop of Monterrey had delegated the jurisdiction of his diocese by making him vicar general, not only welcomed the Oblates very cordially, but, having grown old and exhausted, wanted to give them his difficult parish which their zealous ministry was beginning to revitalize. He even urged them to begin evangelizing the entire province of Monterrey. He wrote a long letter on March 14, 1858, to the bishop of Marseilles, picturing the sad religious plight of that province, and earnestly begged the superior general to grant the apostolic laborers so urgently needed there.[135]

Because of the new legislation in Mexico which had suppressed religious orders, it was deemed inadvisable to cede the pastorate of Matamoros to the Oblates; that would have been too openly acknowledging the community's presence in the city and would have brought about their expulsion. It was better not to open the eyes of the local authorities too wide; until then, they pretended to see nothing. Don Musquiz, however, gave the Oblates an entirely free hand in the parish of which he was officially the pastor. Since he was unable to give them his own church, he entrusted another to them, the shrine of Our Lady of Refuge at Agualegas, where they took up residence. This shrine had the double advantage of being free of official regulations and of attracting much larger numbers of the faithful, since the Mexicans of the surrounding country, with their great devotion to the

Blessed Virgin, preferred this shrine to their parish church. Thus the missionaries were able to reach a greater number of souls and ran less risk of attracting the attention of a government which had been granting them a very precarious sufferance.[136]

Bishop de Mazenod felt impelled to express his gratitude personally to Don Musquiz:

First of all, I must thank you for all the kindness you have shown our Oblate missionaries since they settled in Brownsville. From what they have told me of your treatment of them, I feel sure that you are a true friend and a benefactor of our society. I am equally sure that you are a priest according to God's own heart, one who appreciates what it means to be pastor of souls, and who zealously seeks every means of bringing them spiritual help. I rejoice that through the province of God, you have chosen our Oblate Fathers of Mary to exercise their zealous and Christlike ministry not only in your own church at Mata- moros, but also in several other parishes over which the Bishop of Monterrey has delegated jurisdiction to you.

The founder nonetheless pointed out that

to do solid and more extensive good in that part of Mexico, our con- gregation would need some assurance of stability in Mexico by way of a suitable establishment founded upon solid bases. I am sure that you yourself have this in mind and that you have already begun to effect it. I hope therefore that you will continue to further this idea, and I feel confident that, with your cooperation, it will eventually be realized.[137]

Without waiting for this guarantee of stability which the troubled situation in Mexico rendered impossible, Bishop de Mazenod im- mediately sent two fathers who brought his letter to the pastor of Matamoros. This concrete help proved his gratitude to the vicar general far more effectively than anything he could have written.

Shortly afterwards, in November, 1859, with his bishop's ap- proval, Don Musquiz offered a second parish to the Oblates— that of Victoria, the capital of the State of Tamaulipas. This offer delighted Father Gaudet since it would "open the doors of Mexico to us," [138] and he knew that the fathers would find greater response in that region than on the banks of the Rio Grande where the people were far less favorably disposed. It was decided therefore to take this new place on a trial basis. The first impressions were excellent. Father Sivi wrote:

On one of the first days of our arrival, I was impressed by the religious attitude of Victoria. I was bringing Holy Viaticum to a dying person. Never have I seen such a display of pomp on an occasion of this kind. It was like a procession at a king's coronation. A band led the procession; two long lines of men carrying torches formed a guard of honor for the Blessed Sacrament; the canopy was carried by the leading men of the city while others walked in the procession followed by more than 200 women; almost everyone was carrying lighted candles. The streets were strewn with flowers and, at spaced intervals, decorated arches had been erected.

Sivi continued his letter by describing with equal enthusiasm the Holy Week processions, in which, conforming to Spanish custom, the statue of Christ was borne along, surrounded by Judas, the Pharisees, and the centurion on a black horse, the whole group followed by a thousand men carrying candles.[139] The solemn reception of First Communion which took place a few weeks later was, however, a French innovation: "It was the first time" that this touching ceremony was held at Victoria;

consequently, it made a deep impression; we made it as colorful as possible: renewal of the baptismal promises, solemn procession, and, when the procession returned to the Church, consecration to the Blessed Virgin in the midst of a splendid illumination. The good Mexican people were enraptured. They went into ecstasy at the sight of the flags, the banners, the decorated arches and the Blessed Virgin's throne which had been richly adorned with flowers and drapery. The parents were particularly moved; many mothers wept with joy and some of the fathers, envying the happiness of their children, knelt before the priest and cleared their consciences which had been laden with sin for many years.[140]

The conversion of these fathers proves that religion was not merely show at Victoria. For several days during Holy Week, the confessionals were crowded with people from the *ranchos* who had traveled great distances; this, along with the communions of several hundred men, was an added proof of it. Unfortunately, on December 21, 1860, in spite of public protests, the Oblates, who were succeeding too well, were forcibly expelled by the liberal prefect of police.[141] Grieved as he was by their eviction, Father Gaudet was not disheartened: "I am not at all discouraged," he wrote on March 12, 1861, to Father Fabre.

The authority which our beloved Father General invested in me . . . will enable me to reconstitute the house as soon as circumstances seem favorable to me. The arrival of the new Fathers will facilitate all these arrangements.[142]

The reinforcements sent by Bishop de Mazenod in the very last months of his long life were, in fact, already on their way to Texas and Mexico. There was hope that, with increased resources, they could become re-established at Victoria, as soon as the political climate ameliorated. Even in the worst days, the frequently shifting situation, which never guaranteed lasting stability, by its very reversals made it possible to hope for better times.

The steady work of the Oblates at Our Lady of Refuge Shrine in Victoria was duplicated by another which was even dearer to them, since it was better suited to their vocation than the parochial ministry: the work of preaching missions. Texas, where there were few large centers of population and where the population as a whole lived scattered among the ranches, did not lend itself to this type of apostolate. The situation was entirely different in Mexico. There, where cities were more numerous, the fathers were able to devote themselves to the preferred work of their congregation and to apply its traditional methods. Besides, Don Musquiz, acting in behalf of his bishop, had urged them to extend this work of their ministry to the entire State of Tamaulipas;[143] in his opinion, nothing could be more effective in reviving the faith and quickening Christian life. The detailed information that has come down to us regarding the two most important of these missions—i.e., Cruillas and Burgos, about 135 miles southwest of Matamoros—proves that the fathers were not deluded in thinking that the people of the interior would be more favorably disposed; as Parisot wrote:

We have seen that there is a vast difference between the Mexicans of the interior and those on the border, many of whom are fugitives from justice. The missions we preached, especially the last two, were unqualified successes. Enthusiasm was at its peak and even the surrounding populations within a radius of more than 100 miles had an ardent desire for the grace of the mission. The marvels which the good God wrought through the ministry of two poor missionaries, who have but an imperfect grasp of the language, prove that much easy and lasting good is waiting to be done among the Mexicans.[144]

Crowds flocked to the mission instructions, since "hearing the word of God was a new experience" for these uninstructed Catholics;[145] "The Mexican pastors do not preach sermons except now and then on a few solemn occasions." The "clear and simple explanation of the catechism," to which the missionaries restricted themselves, became a veritable revelation for "these simple people." Speaking of these instructions, these people exclaimed: "The missionaries are teaching us many things we had never known before. . . . Their religion is much more beautiful than ours!" [146] However, although they were all eyes and ears so as not to miss anything of the instructions, they showed no eagerness to receive the Sacrament of Penance. At Cruillas, "it was a question of who would begin. We went for almost two weeks without hearing a single confession." [147] It took a thorough preparation and a whole series of sermons to get them moving. At Burgos, the most difficult one to pry loose was the sacristan. However, after yielding, he made up for his stubborn resistance with a demonstration of joy that surprised Father Parisot somewhat:

He was so happy, that, after receiving holy communion, he told his son to go fetch his guitar. The boy came to the chancel where I happened to be at that moment, and his father said to him: "My son, your father has just received the good God. Play the most beautiful tunes you know while I make my thanksgiving." Whereupon the young guitarist gave out with waltzes, dances, and quadrilles. I didn't know whether to laugh or cry or flee from the place. On second thought, however, I stayed there out of respect for such simple piety.

On another occasion, without benefit of music or guitar, a young man of 23 was content with giving forth cries of joy and embracing the missionary. His confession, however, had required "three sessions that had lasted at least four hours." [148]

Understandably, therefore, Parisot concluded:

You see, it takes many strokes of the chisel to make something slightly resembling a statue out of this rough stone. However, one good thing about it is that the Mexican people are docile and pliable, and if the missionary is true to his vocation, he will have much work to do; his progress will be slow, but he can be sure that his labor will result in great fruit. We have seen many miracles of grace. It would take too long to enumerate them.[149]

Rather than enumerate them, Parisot simply stated that "during these missions, the majority of the men went to confession, whereas, at Brownsville and Matamoros, out of a population of about 20,000 souls, hardly fifty men made their Easter duty." [150] He added:

But once again it must be stressed that painstaking effort and devotion are necessary. God grant that we gain a foothold in Mexico. A thorough reform is in the offing, at least among the people we have seen so far. The pastor of Matamoros said to us: "You have seen the people of Cruillas; all the other people of Tamaulipas are just like them." [151]

Parisot's restrictive "at least" had to be inserted, for in addition to the two general constants—viz., ignorance of religion (the great scourge of the country,[152] and the immensity of the work that had to be done—there was another consideration; not all the Mexicans were equally receptive to having their faith enlightened and their Christian life quickened. Nonetheless, in the less amenable zone, that of the border, the future was to verify the confident predictions of Bishop de Mazenod. At Matamoros, for example, no more than 15 to 20 Easter communions were recorded in 1858; in 1866 their number totaled 4,000. In that same period, the Oblates recorded more than 7,000 baptisms and 2,000 marriages.[153]

The bishop of Marseilles died without the consolation of witnessing this progress. On the contrary, at the end of his life, the position of the Oblates in Mexico, as well as in Texas, had become untenable because of the political crisis. The fathers at

Victoria had to flee before the "revolutionary turmoil." [154] Those at Matamoros "had barely enough time to escape." Brownsville was threatened with an attack by sea, since the "fleet from the North was swarming over the Gulf and, for some time, had been keeping close watch with a heavy warship at the mouth of the Rio Grande." [155] The Indian tribes of Mexico "were able to take great advantage of the situation by avenging all the many injustices and cruelties that had been inflicted upon them." [156] "I don't know what we are coming to," wrote Father Gaudet. "What will the future reveal? Only God knows. Pray for us so that we might get through this crisis without too much suffering." [157]

The crisis was a long and terrible one. However, the future proved that the daring with which the founder had sent his Oblates upon that shifting and volcanic terrain was fundamentally supernatural and confidently discerning. The frightening moments which this dramatic foundation had caused him, and the cries of anguish which the death of five of his sons had wrung from him, were simply a preparation, by way of suffering and faith, for the harvest of the future.

CEYLON

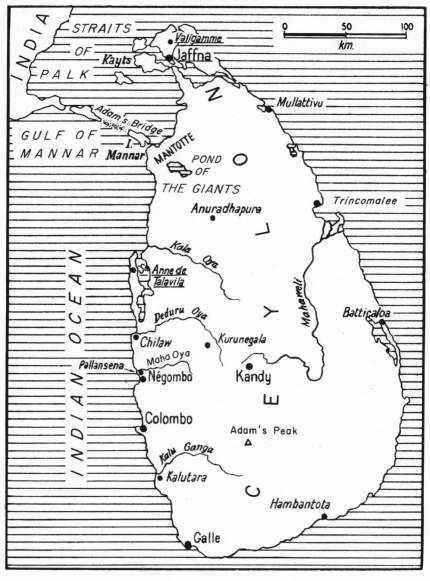

INDIA

STRAITS
OF
PALK

Valigamme
Jaffna

Kayts

0   50   100
km.

Mullattivu

Adam's Bridge

GULF OF
MANNAR

I.
Mannar

MANTOTTE

POND
OF
THE GIANTS

Anuradhapura

Trincomalee

Kala Oya

Sᵗᵉ Anne de
Talavila

Mahaweli

Batticaloa

Deduru Oya

Chilaw

Kurunegala

Maha Oya

Pallansena

Négomba

Kandy

INDIAN OCEAN

Colombo

Adam's Peak
△

Kalu Ganga

Kalutara

Hambantota

Galle

N O L Y E C

Chapter Four

Ceylon and South Africa

ENTHUSIASTIC ACCEPTANCE OF JAFFNA FOUNDATION

Bishop de Mazenod was highly enthusiastic about accepting a foundation at Jaffna in 1847 at the request of Bishop Bettachini, coadjutor to the vicar apostolic of Colombo. On August 12, he wrote to Father Vincens:

His Excellency, the coadjutor to the vicar apostolic of Ceylon, has just spent two days with me. Our conversations were prolonged until after eleven o'clock at night. What a field is opening up to us! A million-and-a-half gentiles to convert and in the most beautiful country in the world! One hundred fifty thousand Christians to instruct! All this immense population, in its innate goodness and fondness for religion, disposed to listen docilely to God's envoys when they arrive to preach the gospel to them! But Protestantism must be counteracted right at the very moment when it is planning to establish headquarters in that beautiful land. How can one not be swayed by such powerful motives to yield to the plea for cooperation in this great work. I therefore accepted this new mission, one of the most beautiful on earth, and I predict that one day this large island will be given over to our congregation and that our congregation will make the whole island holy.[1]

There can be no doubt that once again, and with very sure insight, Bishop de Mazenod had looked far beyond the feasibility of the present to envision the realizations of the future. It does not seem so certain, however, that he had a clear appreciation of the odd and complicated situation which existed in what the first Oblate superior would soon call a "strange country," and which would discourage his sons as well as himself. Had his informer been as objective as he was experienced, the two days of conversation "prolonged far into the night" might have enlightened him about the multiple paradoxes the Oblates would have to consider in order to proceed moderately and prudently. The Colombo coadjutor's objectivity, however, did not match his experience. Well-informed as he was regarding persons and things, he was too involved in local dissensions and rivalries not to project the light more or less consciously according to his own preferences, and there resulted a faulty play of lights and shadows and a contrast that was either too sharp or too vague. That his overly one-sided and somewhat partisan views distorted the picture is undeniable.

Bishop de Mazenod's letter, which has just been quoted, merely reiterated the two major arguments put forth by his guest to support his request: the mass of gentiles to be converted, and the Protestant propaganda to be counteracted. Both were as much *ad rem* as they were *ad hominem*: they proved the urgent need of evangelizing the Buddhists who had hitherto been too neglected and of counteracting the ministers sent from England; they also touched the apostolic heart of the Bishop of Marseilles. Other, supplementary documents, however, reveal that, in order to inveigle a favorable decision, Bishop Bettachini tipped the scales by citing the peril of schism which was threatening the Catholic population. Actually, it is doubtful whether a real schism[2] was contained in the Goanese opposition to Gregory XVI's bull, *Multae praeclare,* which removed a number of territories—one of which was the island of Ceylon—from the jurisdiction of the Archbishop of Goa and established them as vicariates apostolic. The fact remains, however, that this opposition sadly complicated the religious situation of a country where bishops, priests, and faithful were all too prone to factions and antagonisms. It is within this context—which is as muddled as it could be—that we must place ourselves in order to understand, in addition to Bishop Bettachini's presentation of the situation, his personal behavior, the obstacles which the Oblates had to surmount or avoid, and the faulty manner in which arrangements were made for the assumption of the mission.

The pontifical decision concerning Ceylon was justified by a concern not only of furthering the religious interests of that island, but also of harmonizing the new situation with the political conditions. Although Ceylon had been colonized and evangelized by the Portuguese, it had been English territory since 1815, and it would have been incongruous to maintain its dependence on a metropolis subject to Lisbon and to sustain the right of patronage of the king of Portugal who had exercised no sovereignty there since the seventeenth century. On the contrary, it would be advantageous to establish friendly terms with the court of London which, after expelling the Dutch persecutors, had been granting the Church a benevolent freedom. Then too, this part of the Church, which had been shaken by two centuries of trial, needed a resident bishop who would re-establish a tight control over it. However, great pressure was exerted by the king of Portugal and the clergy of Goa in demanding the inalienable rights conferred upon them by the bulls of Pope Paul III. To make this necessary but disagreeable amputation less painful, Rome, in her wisdom, took the precaution therefore of choosing Oratorians of the Archdiocese of Goa as the first vicars apostolic of Ceylon.[3]

This was Rome's way of appeasing the local clergy and of justly rewarding the Goanese priests who, at peril to their lives, had preserved the faith during the dark days when Protestant Holland claimed its conquest of Ceylon would eliminate Catholicism. Now, this meant avoiding Charybdis only to fall on Scylla, since the "burghers" of Colombo and the Europeans of the island, mortified at finding themselves under the spiritual jurisdiction of an Indian bishop, protested vehemently. Skilled in the art of *conciliazione* and *combinazione,* the Holy See then tempered that appointment of the vicar apostolic by appointing an Italian coadjutor, Bettachini,[4] bishop *in partibus* of Toron; he had been acting as chaplain at the Colombo garrison, after having served as a missionary in the province of Kandy. But the native priests of Goa, in turn, protested, and thus, whether the two prelates intended it or not, they represented two factions. This unfortunate situation was worsened by personal animosities. By no means delighted that an eventual successor had been forced upon him, Bishop Gaetano fell under the influence of his secretary, who fed his displeasure, and of Father Sylvestrin Bravi, a Benedictine, whom Bettachini later accused of spiteful double-dealing because he had not been appointed coadjutor. Bravi tried to induce Bettachini to deal rigorously with the schismatics in order to make them even more antagonistic to the coadjutor.[5]

In such ticklish circumstances, Bishop Bettachini would have needed consummate prudence, but prudence was not his outstanding virtue; he was zealous, certainly, but he was also impulsive and outspoken. Things were further complicated by the fact that the papal bulls gave him charge of Jaffna and made him accountable to the vicar apostolic of Colombo. The Goanese clergy of Jaffna received him very cooly, refused to recognize his authority, and admitted no authority other than that of the vicar apostolic of Colombo. This further strengthened the anti-Goanese attitude adopted by Bettachini and intensified his conflict with Bishop Gaetano. The obstruction he faced "induced him to go to Rome to obtain independent jurisdiction over the northern part of the island, no matter what the cost might be." [6]

The Holy See yielded to his arguments all the more readily inasmuch as the Congregation of the Propaganda had been planning since 1845 to divide Ceylon into two vicariates. The size of the island, the difficulty of communication, and the difference in race and mentality between the Tamils and Cingalese were all considered; but another factor had come into play: Bishop Louquet, who favored a native clergy. It was decided therefore that the North would be given over to European missionaries under the jurisdiction of a European prelate; the South would be reserved for the Goanese Oratorians who would maintain jurisdiction over it and recruit a native clergy. Cardinal Fransoni, prefect of the Propaganda, and the Congregation itself agreed. The division was then made in principle. Bravi, however, feeling that this plan was inspired by theories which were impractical in the actual situation, had opposed them. Rome, therefore, judged it wiser to stay proceedings. The appointment of Bettachini, residing at Jaffna, as Bishop Gaetano's coadjutor, would be an intermediary step. In 1847 his *ad limina* visit to Rome and his entreaties induced Pius IX to carry out the plan of 1845 which had been kept in abeyance and to create a second vicariate in the North.[7]

Scoring this first point, however, did not mean that the match was completely won: Bettachini had to make sure that he had missionaries to help him. He was intent on recruiting Italians for his vicariate since there were already three Lombards in the Jaffna clergy, and he fondly hoped to achieve perfect harmony by selecting his collaborators from among his compatriots. However, in Italy, save for an Oratorian cleric, Guidi, no one volunteered to help him. In desperation, therefore, while passing through Marseilles, the prelate appealed to Bishop de Mazenod. The conditions the founder put upon his acceptance, after Bettachini had won his confidence, show that the vicar apostolic of Jaffna had cited the danger of schism, had prejudiced him against Bishop Gaetano as showing favoritism to the Goanese, and had pictured himself as the champion of unity. According to the terms of the contract, the Oblates would remain under the exclusive control of the "saintly bishop of Toron," who would act as the founder's *alter ego,* and they would not be subject "to the whims of the Goanese." [8] This clause, which was supposed to guarantee security for the fathers, was to earn them the distrust of the Colombo vicar apostolic, to say the least, and thereby plant the seeds of future difficulties. Moreover, Bishop de Mazenod would soon become aware that in Bishop Bettachini his sons did not have a second Bishop Bourget. However, all apostolic undertakings involve some risks and although, in his daring, the Bishop of Marseilles did not hesitate to incur them, it must be appreciated that, dealing with such a strange country from such a distance, and relying on incomplete information, he had not realized the extent of these risks.

He felt that he could at least lessen the risks by choosing "excellent subjects" for Jaffna, subjects who would be particularly suited to furthering the needed harmony. Three of them were Italians: Father Semeria from Piedmont, Father Ciamin from Nice, and Brother de Steffanis from Genoa; this corresponded with the desires of the coadjutor and would insure better relations with the other Italian missionaries of the vicariate. The fourth member of the group, the Irishman Father Keating, would establish other relations because of his knowledge of English of which his confreres had little or no grasp and because of "his angelic face and manner." Lastly, although the superior, Father Semeria at thirty-four, was still young, he had already "matured in virtue and in all the religious qualifications" and had proved his mettle in Corsica; his kindness and zeal had effected marvelous conversions there and had achieved "spectacular reconciliations; even bandits had come to him seeking absolution." Undoubtedly, the Bishop of Ajaccio would resent his transfer, but it was important to put such a man "at the head of our little colony." All four Oblates chosen joyfully accepted the assignment the superior general gave them and expressed their willingness even to sacrifice their lives in order to sanctify the Christians and convert the pagans of Ceylon.[9]

Their generosity, zeal, and selflessness however did not solve the initial problem, a purely material one: where to find the funds to take care of their traveling expenses? Bishop de Mazenod was unable to obtain free passage to Alexandria from the French government. Because of the economic crisis which was seriously affecting its collections, the French Propagation of the Faith lacked funds. For the same reason, the Congregation of the Propaganda in Rome also declined, though it eagerly approved the foundation and was granting the title and privileges of missionaries apostolic to the fathers. Without mincing words, the Bishop of Marseilles observed in a letter to Cardinal Fransoni that the funds lavished on a certain *poltrone* Macario would be better used to pay for the missionaries' transportation,[10] but it was of no avail; Rome still granted him no money. No help could be expected from the vicar apostolic of Colombo who was on very poor terms with Bishop Bettachini because the latter had arranged everything without consulting him; furthermore, he was not favorably disposed towards the Oblates since they had been carefully put beyond reach of his jurisdiction. As for Bishop Bettachini, he was in very straitened circumstances. Bishop de Mazenod actually reached the point of fearing that the project would have to be postponed for lack of money. Ultimately, the Lyons Propagation of the Faith strained its resources and the missionaries were able to embark October 21, 1847.

INITIAL DIFFICULTIES UNDER BISHOP BETTACHINI'S EPISCOPATE

Bishop de Mazenod was sure that Bishop Bettachini would reserve the island's central province of Kandy to his sons and this plan appealed to him, since living in a separate sector offered a double advantage: on the one hand, it would keep them together in one group and thereby benefit their community life; on the other, in restricting them to their own territory, it would spare them the frictions which would inevitably result from laboring together with sensitive European and Goanese priests. But when Semeria and his companions disembarked at Ceylon, Kandy had been returned by the Propaganda to the direct authority of Bishop Gaetano and had been in his jurisdiction since September 17; before that date it had been taken away from him and given to the coadjutor residing in Jaffna. Semeria, who had intended to settle in Kandy and had been "given orders to that effect" by the Bishop of Marseilles,[11] found himself obliged to go in an entirely different direction. What made this new orientation all the more difficult was the fact that the terrain in this unknown country seemed strewn with snares, and the people untrustworthy. The charitable but not too altruistic advice he received from Father Reinaud, a former member of the congregation, who had come to evangelize the island, served but to put him on his guard not only against the European missionaries but even against the counselor himself: "Trust no one; be as aloof as the English are. Don't let anyone suspect that you belong to a religious congregation,"[12] otherwise they will think that the Institute plans to monopolize the whole of Ceylon.

Semeria, who had no intention of engendering distrust by concealing his status as a member of a religious order since this open secret would soon be discovered by everyone, deduced from this warning that, while treating everyone "politely, honestly, and simply," he would have to be extremely wary.[13] Moreover, he had seen "from the very outset that everything ahead of us would not be easy." By warning him, Reinaud actually did him a favor since it put him on his guard against the latter's own scheme to lure him into the Province of Kandy where he had ambitious dreams of forming a vicariate apostolic for himself. Semeria, whose alert watchfulness and innate shrewdness enabled him to discover the game being played by the sly Reinaud, then entrenched himself behind the express orders of the Bishop of Marseilles. Going to Kandy would be putting himself and his confreres under the jurisdiction of Bishop Gaetano; now, his instructions called for his remaining under the exclusive jurisdiction of Bishop Bettachini, to whom the superior general had "specifically" confided the Oblates.[14]

Bishop de Mazenod fully approved the decision Semeria made. Although he was more compassionate than he had been in the days when he called anyone who left his Order an "apostate," he nonetheless pointed out the secret motives of "that poor child," Reinaud. Evidently, he wrote,

having left us with the mania for becoming a bishop, [he] would have readily used us as a stepping-stone for that goal. After his hopes were dashed at Bagdad, he felt that he had a good chance at Ceylon by way of the arrangement he has suggested.[15]

The Bishop of Marseilles also approved Semeria's determination not to follow Reinaud's advice concerning his identity as a religious. "It is not necessary to capitalize on it or to boast about it unnecessarily. But to conceal it—never! Anyway, it would be like trying to hide behind your finger." In the same letter, knowing the Jaffna superior's "innate goodness," he drew from his own experience in order to forewarn him against any unexpected development:

Don't be deceived by appearances and think that men are any better than they are. I love the simplicity of the dove, but I never like to separate it from the wisdom of the serpent.[16]

Such wisdom advised maintaining the greatest reserve with individuals, and the greatest caution. Semeria especially appreciated this since he was somewhat slow in acting and extremely patient; even his style of writing was easy-going and meandering, as is revealed in his *Journal* which abounds in marginal notes and supplements. Others would have demanded a cleary defined situation immediately, even if it meant upsetting everything in order to renew it; Semeria, however, was content with an undecided situation for the present. He knew nothing definite about the task Bishop Bettachini was going to assign the Oblates. He perhaps surmised that the latter was not too sure himself what it would be and, with little freedom to make any moves, he hesitated, groped, and weighed the pros and cons. The very enthusiastic welcome Bettachini had given the missionaries from Marseilles and the instructions he had received from the founder, advised leaving everything to the pro-vicar apostolic who was lodging them. Moreover, the Oblates could undertake no missionary work without first learning the difficult language of the Tamils. This delay could not but offer advantages, for it enabled them to prepare for the future and, to gain a clear knowledge of people and things. The superior, in particular, benefitted from it by learning something of the complexities of the country, since Bishop Bettachini was using him as his secretary, taking him with him on his pastoral rounds, and had even assigned him the task of composing a pastoral letter. Thus, little by little, he became acquainted with things, formed his own ideas, and worked out a plan of action. With his gift for viewing things clearly, he devised a well-defined program and submitted it to the vicar apostolic: the Oblates would open a house at Jaffna where they would live as a community; they would not be in charge of any fixed place, but would always be at the disposal of the bishop; as in France, they would preach missions and conduct retreats in the various Christian settlements in order to instruct the people in religion and revive Christian practice along with faith; they would open a seminary at Jaffna to prepare catechists and to train a native clergy. Semeria pointed out, however, that in view of the lax, languid, and secretive temperament of the natives, it would be necessary to test the future priests by first using them as catechists and to allow them to become Oblates so that their perseverance might be assured. Under these conditions, the Oblates would be willing to take charge of the seminary; they would make no objection, however, if the vicar apostolic wanted to invite the Jesuits to establish a college. Bettachini approved all these proposals, declared that he had no intention of putting the Jesuits in charge of any educational establishment, and even requested Semeria to ask Bishop de Mazenod to send two more Oblates for the seminary; the founder granted them immediately.[17]

There seemed to be agreement, therefore, on the matter of methodical and concrete action. Actually, however, the plan agreed upon was to remain a dead issue, since Bishop Bettachini, who was incapable of mastering the situation, allowed himself to be hindered by momentary difficulties. He lacked the broadmindedness to ignore them and the energy to impose an over-all direction. Consequently, the Propaganda which had evaluated him, considered him, according to what Bishop de Mazenod said, "a virtuous man, no doubt, but extremely mediocre." [18]

The total number of foreign missionaries serving the Jaffna vicariate posed two difficult problems. On the one hand, the clergy was lamentably insufficient in number and had to be supplemented; of the six Goanese priests who had been stationed in the northern part of the island, five had left to go to Colombo where Bishop Gaetano acted more favorably toward the Indian clergy; the sixth one had fallen into schism. Bishop Bettachini was left, therefore, with only two Spaniards, both Benedictines, who had been more or less secularized, and three Lombards. The arrival of an Oratorian and the three Oblates priests did not fill the gaps. Where to find the urgently needed helpers? On the other hand, the few workers he did have were of very dissimilar temperaments. There was need to maintain fraternal unity among them and to coordinate their apostolate. Now, although the departure of the Goanese had put an end to frictions between the Orientals and the Europeans, a new antipathy arose within the latter group. Although Semeria was a native of Piedmont and Ciamin a native of Nice, they belonged to a French congregation, and the Lombards, like Bettachini himself, would have preferred the vicariate of Jaffna to remain a purely Italian fief; their Spanish colleagues were even more prejudiced against the newcomers. Thus the reception they received was more than cool, causing Semeria to write in his *Journal*, "I began . . . to suspect that we would not be looked upon kindly." [19] Lastly, the religious status of the Oblates which he refused to keep secret gave rise to the prediction that his congregation would not be satisfied with the role of vanguard, and that, once it became established in Ceylon, would gradually reinforce its effectives with the aim of taking over the entire island. A full-size intrigue was therefore evolving to prevail upon the bishop to bring in the Jesuits; this seemed the surest means of keeping the undesirables from Marseilles in the background, of reducing their influence, and, in fact, of forcing them to leave the country.

It is no easy task to give a clear picture of this regrettable affair which resulted from a complicated situation and from a misunderstanding, and which seems to have taken on undue proportions; there are contradictory charges and denials, and the threads of the plot are further tangled by what we read in the *Memoirs* of poor Semeria, who was so affected by the whole affair that he was unable to sleep and walked the floor of his room throughout the night, trying to unsnarl everything. One thing is certain: Bettachini had been striving for a long time to obtain the help of the Jesuits.[20] Although the superior of Jaffna knew nothing of the transactions made before his arrival, at least he was acquainted with the later steps undertaken by the prelate, since, as Bettachini's secretary, he had drafted the prelate's letters urging the Jesuits to accept a mission in Ceylon because of the wholesale defection of the Goanese priests. Semeria even affirmed that he had readily approved the idea without any feeling of "mistrust" toward these religious, though the presence of two congregations on the same field might result in a "few misunderstandings." [21] What is more, he had personally spoken to the Jesuit provincial and renewed Bettachini's proposal while on a trip to India to collect funds sent by the Propagation of the Faith and to inquire about the teaching methods employed by the Jesuits in their colleges.[22] Semeria, therefore, could not have been surprised, much less offended, that, during his absence, preparations for the installation of the Jesuits had been completed and some of them had been sent from India to study the situation.

At first, Semeria had no thought of complaining about the Jesuit Father Castanier whom the Jesuit Bishop Canoz had granted to Bettachini to accompany him on his episcopal rounds, and whom Canoz had commissioned to settle matters with the vicar apostolic of Jaffna. At first, too, he felt nothing but satisfaction with an English Jesuit, Father Strickland, who had lavished care upon him when he became gravely ill following his return from India; Strickland had called in a British doctor and had been so solicitous of him that "one would think he was one of us." [23] Once he was on his feet again, however, Semeria learned that the good Samaritan had taken advantage of the Oblate superior's trip to India to weave a plot against the Oblates and had been aided and abetted by the Benedictine Garcia who had been hostile to them from the outset. Both intriguers advised Bettachini to go over the head of Bishop Canoz and appeal directly to the general of the

Jesuits, who, they assured him, would grant a certain number of subjects expelled from Italy and as yet unassigned. They therefore put pressure upon Bettachini to have the departure of the new Oblates whom Bishop de Mazenod had promised cancelled, since there would no longer be any need of them. Lastly, Strickland planned to found a college at Jaffna and, in order to get rid of Semeria who insisted upon his seminary, the English Jesuit urged the vicar apostolic to send the undesirable to some mission in the center of the island.

At least, that is what Semeria claims he had discovered. Not everything is imaginary in the lengthy account of this "storm" which he gave in his *Journal*. In fact, Bettachini personally admitted to the superior that

he had been advised to write to the Bishop of Marseilles and urge him not to send the new missionaries who had been requested several months previously either for the minor seminary or for the missions;

he added that he rejected this ungracious suggestion in view of the great service the founder had done him by coming to his aid in a critical hour.[24] Nonetheless, one gets the impression that Semeria was over-dramatizing things if one reads the anguished and minutely detailed pages in which the poor Jaffna superior relates how he untangled the skeins of the nefarious plot.[25] In his eyes, the work of his congregation was in danger; quite simply, this was a plot to eliminate the Oblates. Semeria was level-headed and had the patience of a Job, but, unconsciously, he was inclined to dramatize this Ceylonese intrigue since he was sensitive, timid, thorough, bothered by petty details which others would have scorned, uncommunicative for fear of making rash statements, tense because of his lack of sleep, and depressed by an atmosphere of mistrust. Because he had excessively repressed his feelings, his reaction became all the more spirited, and this in turn started a chain reaction. His manner of protesting to Bishop Canoz earned him a cold and curt reply from the Jesuit prelate. Bishop de Mazenod, who put trust in his statements, raged and fumed, called the English Jesuit's conduct "horrible," [26] and then, taking his sharpest quill, wrote to Father Roothaan to denounce Strickland's machinations.[27] Obviously, Strickland was not entirely guiltless since the Jesuit superior general felt obliged to make apologies; he agreed that Strickland's moves were "of a repulsive nature," declared that he was "distressed beyond words," and inferred that he had acted "not as a Jesuit but as an Englishman." Father Roothaan readily acknowledged that for several years there had been talk of "forming an establishment of the society" at Jaffna, but that Bishop Bettachini had not informed him that the Oblates of Mary had already been installed there and that they too were planning to open an "educational establishment." He could not understand why, regarding this matter, the prelate had maintained a silence which was creating such an unfortunate situation.[28] In his turn, the vicar apostolic barely escaped a sharp rebuke from the Bishop of Marseilles; fortunately, the latter held back the first redaction "written peevishly" and in its stead sent a second, considerably more conciliatory.[29] Eventually the storm blew over. While passing through Marseilles, Father Strickland visited Bishop de Mazenod and begged his pardon; the prelate received him with open arms and forgave him. In accord with the prelate, who instructed Semeria to welcome them without any resentment, four Jesuits came to the aid of Jaffna by temporarily accepting the missions in the islands of Mannar and Kayts. From then on there was no more talk of a college. Relations between the members of each society were to be as excellent as they had been in Oregon. With the affair finally settled, poor Semeria breathed more easily. Not that he was yet free from worry; in Ceylon, troubles not only succeeded one another, they were piled one upon the other and became entangled when they took on unexpected proportions. Once one problem was solved, another arose to throw everything back into confusion. Crowning it all, just when a trustful collaboration between Bettachini and Semeria might have helped, at least relatively, to resolve these problems, the shameful plot devised by the Spanish ex-Benedictine and the Jesuit Strickland created a bad atmosphere which was to grow steadily worse.

In ordinary circumstances, the arrival of the three new Oblates on May 13, 1849, would have dispelled this uneasy atmosphere since, on the one hand, Bishop Bettachini, to his credit, had refused to cancel their arrival despite the urgings of Father Garcia and the English Jesuit, and on the other hand, Bishop de Mazenod had kept his promise despite the grave incident that had occurred and the observations Semeria had sent him. Unfortunately, such was not the case. Instead of assigning the new arrivals to establish the seminary for which they had been requested and granted, Bishop Bettachini assigned them to missionary work. Thus a dissension until then hidden, broke out into the open between Semeria and Bettachini on the matter of utilizing the subjects sent by the founder. Semeria understood why Bettachini, because of his dire financial straits and the extreme shortage of clergy, immediately sent the meagre reinforcements from Marseilles to the front; but he also expected that, instead of becoming an established practice, this *modus operandi* would be merely temporary. Nor would he allow his religious to be subjected to the same regimen imposed on secular priests scattered over the thirteen districts belonging to the vicariate; these districts were as large as dioceses and most of them numbered from twenty to fifty Christian settlements which were often widely separated. Shortly after his installation at Jaffna, Semeria had notified Bettachini of his intention to keep his confreres together in that city so that they might be reserved for parochial missions, and Bettachini agreed. This, however, did not prevent Bettachini from going back on his word almost immediately by assigning Ciamin to Mantotte. Although he fully opposed this assignment on the grounds that the Rule forbade leaving a religious isolated, Semeria did not feel at that time that he was obliged to forbid it since the bishop had given Ciamin his own catechist and there was an urgent need to provide a priest for this region which had been without attention.[30] Even Bishop de Mazenod, after the move was made, had allowed this waiving of principles, provided contact and control were maintained.[31] Nevertheless, they were starting out on a path leading to a dispersion. After the Oblates arrived in May, 1849, to direct the seminary, Semeria again resigned himself to their being immediately utilized in those areas which lacked priests, since the establishment of the seminary was not possible at that time; it seemed only reasonable to assign them to the ministry in the meantime and to attend to the most pressing things first. Thus a situation resulted which suited Bettachini perfectly, but which the superior merely tolerated. As fast as effectives were replenished, the new arrivals were sent to various mission posts. It is true that the constitutions were not being violated since the missionaries were sent two by two, but it remained just as true that, instead of forming a religious community at Jaffna and devoting themselves to parish missions as Semeria wanted, and as the pro-vicar Apostolic had agreed, they were placed in charge of parishes, no different from seculars appointed by the bishop, and consequently bound by the common regulation. In addition, every year or two, Bettachini transferred the missionaries to new posts, and these constant changes prevented continuity of action.

Semeria, whose conception of organizing the work differed radically from that of Bettachini, continually criticized the disadvantages of the latter's system, but nonetheless exercised forbearance and drew inspiration from the principle he repeatedly cited: "In these foreign countries, the first virtue a missionary must have is patience, the second is patience, and the third is patience." [32] Besides, how could an ideal ecclesiastical organization be realized immediately when the effectives of the vicariate were limited to a few priests? Semeria's program could be put into effect only gradually in proportion to the growth of a native clergy and the number of the reinforcements sent by Bishop de Mazenod. For the time being, Bishop Bettachini could not be blamed for striving to shift his few available men over his immense chessboard so that he might cover the blank spots; but the Oblate superior had just cause to complain that the pro-vicar, accustomed to playing this type of game, was not concerned about making any long-term plans for a future solution and was satisfied with settling problems as they arose.

In Marseilles, Bishop de Mazenod found it very difficult to grasp the exact picture of such a complex and delicate situation, though Semeria had been sending him very lengthy and detailed reports; these reports, however, seemed all the less clear to him since they were worded so guardedly. The founder, therefore, kept asking for supplementary and precise information and complained that Semeria was being vague. Thus, he sent questions to which the Jaffna superior had to give a yes or no answer, little realizing that Oriental logic, which is by no means Cartesian, is poorly suited to categorical assertions. The analysis of the Ceylonese psychology and of the social conditions which Semeria, a careful and shrewd observer, sent to him, could not but baffle him.

In cases of sporadic schisms, the single word "schism" caught his eye and he resorted to the strongest expressions to stigmatize the Goanese as *veri carnefici dell'anime,*[33] though the latter claimed that they were still in communion with the pope since, although they fully challenged the vicar apostolic's authority, they nonetheless recognized that of the supreme pontiff. Furthermore, how could the Bishop of Marseilles not attribute to diabolical malice the many attempts to secede which were caused by what he termed trifles: at Jaffna, for example, a door in the Church which Bettachini ordered to be opened, the prelate's disputed possession of a garden, or a crib erected in a parish in defiance of the main parish of the city which, from time immemorial, had held exclusive rights to it, all resulted in threats of secession. Thus the threat of schism became blackmail to which recourse was made on the least provocation whenever there was a disagreement with the bishop. Their blind attachment to customs, their rivalries, their touchiness, and their resentments always prevailed over considerations inspired by faith, as much for the purpose of tearing away from the faith as being reconciled to it. The observation made by a Protestant who had hit upon an argument *ad absurdum* was all that was needed to stop the Jaffna schism: "How could you," he asked the fishermen, "entrust the people of another caste with bringing priests from Goa here in a boat?" [34]

Semeria, who adopted a severe attitude toward the priests of Goa, usually terming them "black sheep," proved on the contrary, very understanding towards those who favored them for silly reasons, since what appears silly to a Westerner takes on extraordinary importance at Ceylon. After relating the incident of the crib, the Jaffna superior wrote:

All that I have just said, and a few other particulars . . . have convinced me more than ever that we cannot, we must not, act in these lands as we would in Europe. The missionary must have great prudence as well as a good dose of patience. Otherwise he would destroy with one hand what he is building with the other. As yet, our Christians do not have the true religion of Jesus Christ; they don't know it. How could they? Until now, at least the majority of them have had only the externals, the outer wrappings. Consequently, until they are well instructed, there can be little hope of doing them much good. If too much were attempted at one time, there would be danger of doing much damage. We must have the patience to take people as they are and to strive to make them gradually become what we want them to be. For some time to come, it will be useless to try to change their customs. They hold these customs too sacred, though they are of very little importance in themselves. But, precisely because certain things are of a small importance, the missionary, without approving them or disapproving them, must allow them since the Christians are so attached to them. Once the Christians become better instructed, once they become more aware of the sanctity of the sacraments and receive them more frequently, they themselves will discard certain of their customs, and that is precisely how the prudent missionary will bring these poor Christians to ask that a custom be changed or allowed. He will thus avoid the harm that can be caused, at least indirectly, by a thoughtless zeal. And almost imperceptibly, good, great good, will be accomplished.[35]

Two conclusions follow from these wise reflections: first, European missionaries had to make allowances for the local mentality and psychology in order to avoid regrettable incidents leading to schism; instead of trying to crush the schism by irritating and humiliating excommunications, public penances, appeals to the courts and the police, diplomacy and artfulness should be used. Secondly, the missionaries had to devote themselves to basic work and provide a sound Christian education for a population left for too long a time without any instruction. Hence the need to train catechists and establish schools. At one and the same time, this was stressing the lack of cohesion paralyzing the efforts of an incompatible clergy, it was stressing the blunders of Bettachini who was awkward and impulsive in dealing with the faithful and always ready to take offence, and above all, it was stressing the latter's mistake of continuing to govern the vicariate haphazardly and without any guiding principle.

Although Bishop de Mazenod was bewildered—and for good reason—by the labyrinth of Ceylonese castes, customs, and subtleties, at least he clearly perceived that the apostolic efficiency of his missionaries, who were opposed by their secular confreres and poorly utilized by a shortsighted bishop, was not commensurate with their devoted efforts. The prelate gathered from Semeria's reports that these efforts were being wasted by being scattered, at a time when they should have been concentrated on fixed and broad objectives. In the first place, he could not agree to the system in use, in which the evangelization of the Catholics was absorbing the activity of the missionaries at the expense of the 30,000 pagans who remained unconverted. With a superabundance of repetitions which emphasized his impatience, his letters kept reminding Semeria that the Oblates were committed first and foremost to the most abandoned souls: "When will you begin winning over infidels? There in your island, aren't you merely pastors of people who have been Christians for a long time?" [36] There might be some good if the latter were true Christians, but they are fallen away Christians. The founder, therefore, asked whether it was worthwhile traveling so far to devote one's ministry to them when an abundance of such Christians could be found without going outside France and Europe. He stated that if he were sure that his sons would be assigned the task of "battling idolatry and infidelity," he would be willing to make any sacrifice and would send many of his missionaries to Ceylon, but he was entirely unwilling to have "so much zeal and devotion result in merely keeping that sorry, feeble, and decayed Christianity" alive. "New Christians cast in a different mold are what I want." [37]

As for the mold in which the degenerate Christians of the island had been cast, it, too, had to be changed. In fact, the Christians had to be completely re-educated and, in certain respects, this task would be more difficult than the conversion of the pagans, since it would mean correcting false ideas and deep-rooted habits. Since, obviously, there was no hope for a total metamorphosis of the older generations, the major effort had to be devoted to the children and young people. Thus, like Semeria, Bishop de Mazenod put stress upon the work to be done through catechism classes and schools and upon the house which would prepare catechists, teachers, and a native clergy, that is, the seminary, for which he had sent the two Oblates whom Bettachini had assigned to the missions.

All these projects presupposed financial means. Now, in the vicariate of Jaffna, which was less favored than the much richer vicariate of Colombo, these financial resources were by no means abundant. Moreover, what resources Bettachini did have, were, in the founder's opinion, being apportioned very poorly. The mystery surrounding Bettachini's budget and financial reports left the Bishop of Marseilles deeply perplexed. The prelate's honesty, of course, was above suspicion, but his management was unreliable. Each time the founder granted him Oblates, a great argument arose over their travel expenses. Bettachini, of course, received financial help from the Propagation of the Faith, but he had no intention of using any of it to defray the cost of travel. Bishop de Mazenod was obliged to argue with him and with the Lyons Propagation about the matter and often found it necessary either to advance the money himself or to take out loans;[38] in fact, there were times when the superior general had to economize and send his sons by sailboat on an interminable and exhausting journey through the Cape of Good Hope in order to avoid the costly fares on steamships and the transfer from Alexandria to the Red Sea upon which the English had levied a very high tax.[39] It is understandable why he was indignant and irritated when he was informed that Bettachini, who claimed to be too short of funds to pay for the passage of the missionaries, had indulged in the luxury of purchasing expensive chandeliers in Paris[40] and vestments in Lyons,[41] and hired some music teachers in Italy, bringing them to Ceylon at his expense by the most direct and most comfortable route.[42]

The Bishop of Marseilles was, therefore, convinced that it was imperative to place his sons in a position where they could work more effectively, more enterprisingly, and more methodically. When they had first arrived in Ceylon, the difficulties created by the opposition of the European missionaries and the intrigues of Father Garcia had led him to propose having a distinct part of the vicariate reserved for them, thereby avoiding a thorny collaboration and leaving them a free field.[43] It soon became apparent, however, that this initial solution was inadequate; he then felt that the entire vicariate of Jaffna should be entrusted to them under the direction of an Oblate bishop. Reams of pages could be filled quoting all the letters in which, for several years, he pointed out to his friend, Bishop Barnabo, the secretary of the Propaganda, the urgent need to appoint Semeria as Bettachini's coadjutor. Justly singing the praises of the Jaffna superior, he stated that he would be ideal for the position and would atone for the prelate's shortcomings, the lining sometimes being stronger than the outer material; he would lay the groundwork for reorganizing the vicariate and, once he became the titular, would put his wise and judicious plan into operation. It seems, wrote Bishop de Mazenod, that in this way

great good could be accomplished in that vicariate since it would prosper for having a unified discipline and a oneness of views. The faith could then be propagated more extensively, and educational establishments could be founded, and, perhaps a seminary as well. These things, which could be achieved by a religious congregation would be much more difficult for isolated priests working separately.[44]

Confident that, under these conditions, his sons would be fully utilized, he would gladly grant numerous missionaries, even if it meant passing up other foundations which the Propaganda had been offering him. He even hinted that if the *status quo* were to be maintained, he was ready to recall the Oblates from Ceylon where the results were not worth the effort. Why sacrifice such worthy subjects to an unstable present and an uncertain future?

The Propaganda finally yielded to his arguments and, in 1851, wrote to Bettachini, proposing that he formally request Father Semeria as his coadjutor in order to further the development and success of the vicariate. Bettachini flatly refused to do so. He felt he was still young enough to shoulder the whole burden by himself; sharing the burden would for all practical purposes result in his being permanently shunted aside.

Although today it is felt that two mitres are needed for the good of the vicariate, scarcely will there be two of them when it will begin to be seen that only one is needed [for the good of this diocese]; the older one will then begin to be useless and then become a burden."[45]

He therefore concluded that it would be impossible to subscribe to such a premature and troublesome plan. Bishop de Mazenod happened to be at Rome when this extremely sharp and somewhat cavalier reply arrived there. Informed of it by Bishop Barnabo, who did not feel he had the authority to force Bettachini's hand, the founder then decided, with the approval of the Propaganda, to appeal personally to Bettachini to try to convince him. In a letter to Father Semeria, he informed the latter: "The good bishop is looking at the matter only from a personal standpoint; I, myself, see it in an entirely different way." [46] A letter sent to Semeria some weeks later, was even more explicit: "He has yielded to self-interest." [47] For his own part, the founder was motivated by general interests; Semeria's coadjutorship would be just as advantageous to the vicariate as it would be to the Oblate congregation, since the future of the vicariate would be assured by the guarantees furnished to the members of the congregation which had made, and was still ready to make, such great sacrifices for Jaffna. Assuredly, the plan could be postponed, but the days of the Bishop of Marseilles were numbered, and he wanted to see the situation of his sons settled during his lifetime. Although Bishop Bettachini was still young, he was also mortal, and what would become of the religious confided to his paternal care by the superior general, if he should die? [48]

Dodging the essential part of the problem so that he might insert personalities into it again, Bettachini replied with bitter sarcasm and rather questionable taste. Bishop de Mazenod wrote:

I was not too edified by his letter. His little joke about one less *minchione* in this world if he should die struck me as being coarse. It ignores the point I justly made to him, and that point still holds. I have been definitely assured at the Propaganda—I tell you this in strict secrecy—that I have no cause to worry, that the whole island is being reserved for us; however, I am too old to wait for that day.[49]

Still not discouraged, the Bishop of Marseilles felt he had to pursue the dialogue and it must be admitted that he made an extremely heartfelt appeal in his next reply. However, it was a dialogue between deaf people. For months, and even years, no solution was reached. Bishop de Mazenod continued to send urgent pleas to Bettachini, and Bettachini continued to send complaints to the Curia regarding the tactlessness of his colleague who was wearing him down with his inopportune sermonizing. At times, the tone grew angrier on both sides. Writing to Semeria about the vicar apostolic, the founder exclaimed: "Did he take me for a puppet, set to move only when he pulled the strings?" [50] Bettachini, who had no intention of allowing himself to be supplanted, made a formal complaint to Rome that the Oblates were striving to take over everything in the island. They are excellent religious, but even though it is natural for them to want their own coadjutor, when they do have him, it will be natural for them to want to hold the reins of the vicariate.[51]

In 1855, however, Bettachini began thinking it would be wise to propose a *combinazione*; this would limit the damage by granting the Oblates partial satisfaction; he proposed to leave them the spiritual and temporal direction of the northern and eastern districts, but he insisted on retaining episcopal jurisdiction over them. He instructed the Propaganda not to send any remarks regarding his administrative methods for the purpose of gaining anything further. His letter deserves to be quoted:

If Your Eminence is definitely set on giving me a coadjutor, if you cannot get out of it because of the Bishop of Marseilles, *fiat voluntas tua*. All I ask is that you do not cite my incompetency or try to convince me with stronger reasons that I am stupid and imbecile, for I find it too painful to be accounted as such.[52]

In 1856, worthier motives induced him to accept another mitre alongside his own: his health, prematurely impaired by the climate and his apostolic labors, was failing. After gaining his consent, Pius IX, on May 25, named Father Semeria Bishop of Olympia *in partibus infidelium* and coadjutor to the vicar apostolic of Jaffna with the right of succession. The Oblate superior did not have to wait long to receive that succession; summoned to Marseilles for the general chapter of the Oblates, he was consecrated bishop on August 17, 1856, by Bishop de Mazenod, assisted by Bishop Guibert of Viviers and Bishop Guigues of Ottawa. On July 26, 1857, five months after the new coadjutor's return to Ceylon, Bishop Bettachini died at the age of forty-seven.

THE VICARIATE-APOSTOLIC UNDER BISHOP SEMERIA

Bishop Semeria was now free to organize the vicariate according to his ideas and to carry out his plan methodically. In spite of his predecessor's obstinacy in pursuing a system of day-to-day improvizing without any concerted or long-range views, the Oblates, even with their scattered fields of action, had nonetheless put forth much zeal in their individual sections during those ten years and had been relatively successful. But, in 1850, their superior had admitted that he could give "only rambling and disjointed information" about their work;[53] in the years after 1850, his annual reports to the Bishop of Marseilles, meticulous as they were, furnished only fragmentary data concerning their different missions. While asserting that a great improvement was evident "in several respects," Semeria admitted that good was being accomplished "very slowly and almost imperceptibly." There was progress in the practice of religion; this was particularly true of Jaffna, where "there was a much more pious observance of Sunday: work on that day was almost entirely suspended"; whereas previously, only one Mass had been sufficient for the city, two have now become necessary, and "the large church, which holds more than fifteen hundred people, is almost filled"; this represented four times the number who had formerly attended Mass there. An improvement was also noted in the reception of the sacraments; hitherto, they had been seldom received due to the excessive rigorism of the Goanese priests who followed the principle: *melius est sacramenta negare dignis quam dare indignis*; only the fervent Christians received communion at Easter time; "the great majority marry, grow old, live their whole lives, and even embark on their journey to eternity without having once received the Holy Eucharist." After 1850, however, a certain increase in the number of communions was noted, not only on great feast days, "but almost daily." [54] Moreover, great effort had been expended in remedying religious ignorance. Semeria taught catechism to the children on Sundays and Thursdays, and gathered them together three times a week; their parents, who often accompanied them, also derived profit from his instructions. Unlawful marriages were validated, morals were purged, and drunkenness decreased noticeably. The other Oblates noted similar results in their mission stations, although the vastness of the districts they served and the difficulty of communication complicated their task; for this reason they trained catechists to assist them and substitute for them.

Efficacious as it was, this sort of ministry nonetheless remained that of dispersed and more or less itinerant pastors. What was needed was an organized vanguard; in place of disjointed action, there was need for concerted action to launch a general movement;

apathy was great and it was a case at one and the same time of changing an entire mentality, and of combatting schism, Protestant propaganda, and superstitious practices which at times amounted to witchcraft. The people, who were in some ways puzzling to Westerners were, however, likeable and friendly. The main problem consisted in arousing them from their apathy; the numerous conversions brought about during the cholera epidemics, during which Bettachini had risked his life and the Oblates had exhausted themselves, proved that a hold had been gained over the population; even some Buddhists had been won over. In short, although those first ten years of an embattled and thankless apostolate had shown no spectacular success, they had been far from fruitless. Their very gropings and trials had enabled Semeria and his confreres to acquaint themselves with the situation, to gain experience, to give their ideas mature deliberation, and, through suffering and even death, to fertilize the difficult terrain where eventually the good seed was to spring up and bear fruit. Three of them died of cholera or of dysentery: Leydier in 1851, Ciamin in 1853, and Lacombe in 1855; certainly Semeria was not exaggerating when he wrote to Bishop de Mazenod: "My real journey to Calvary began with my arrival in Ceylon." [55]

His appointment to the episcopacy did not mark the end of that sorrowful journey. Although setbacks and difficulties continued to abound, the new vicar apostolic now had the authority to coordinate efforts and focus them on measures which had seemed essential to him since 1847. In fact, he proved consistent in his views: in 1857, his *Journal* stated with simple humility that, after ten years, these views were still the same. Assuredly, there was nothing brilliant about him, nor anything trenchant; his judgment, which was a sound one, was never erratic nor were his actions. *Chi va piano va sano.* Unobtrusively, slowly, and quietly, he persisted in the course which, in all wisdom and conscience, he felt was the only good one. His quiet perseverance had never faltered. Thus, after the long delays which for ten years had put his virtue and shrewdness to the test without, however, irritating him, Semeria now embarked upon the course which Bettachini had been unable to take and he went forward progressively with as much resolution as prudence. During his episcopate, his unpretentious work was to consist above all in guaranteeing firm bases upon which his successors could continue to build and perfect the spiritual edifice of Ceylon.

On July 2, 1852, highly displeased by the reception afforded his sons by Bishop Bravi, the coadjutor of Colombo, Bishop de Mazenod had written: "Jaffna is the place where [this spiritual edifice] must be started." Writing to the then Father Semeria, who had estimated that twenty-five priests would be needed for that "vicariate alone," the Bishop of Marseilles remarked: "Undoubtedly, it is a large number, but if the vicariate belonged to us, we would strive to satisfy that need, even if we had to let some other missions wait." [56] As soon as this condition was fulfilled, the founder no longer measured the sacrifices. Ten additional Oblates were sent successively into the northern part of Ceylon to reinforce the ranks or to fill the void, for, in ten years (from 1851 to 1861), five Oblates were to die from the epidemics or from exhaustion. Thus, after adequately providing for the mission stations in the different sections of the vicariate, Semeria, who had now become the titular, decided to use part of these reinforcements to form a preaching band which, including himself, would engage in preaching missions "properly so called" in the style practiced by his religious Congregation. He felt that "in the present wretched state of this vicariate," these mission exercises were "perhaps the only means we can and should employ in spiritually regenerating our Christians." Certain of his confreres, however, were somewhat skeptical that such an apostolate which had had such notable success in Europe would achieve any similar results in Ceylon. Quite a few doubted whether their flocks, who were overly fond of external displays, would support "a series of sermons lasting several weeks." But convinced "that God attaches a special grace to this type of ministry practiced by the fathers of our beloved congregation, since it is the principal work for which we have been especially approved by the Church," Semeria decided that "it had to begin soon . . . , were it only an experiment." [57]

The results proved him right. Assuredly, this prudent man went about nothing haphazardly. He was careful to choose the most capable missionaries to help him, and was equally careful in choosing his field of action. Jaffna was not given the honor of being first. Knowing the city's inhabitants only too well, he felt it would be much wiser to assure himself resounding success elsewhere and wait until his episcopal city expressed a desire for the mission. A man gains more by making people want him than by forcing himself upon them. He therefore chose the island of Kayts as the first place, since it was especially troubled by schism; the traditional methods proved as fruitful there as they had been in France during the Restoration. The success of the mission was appreciated all the more since—not to mention the other vices— the spirit of dissension which pitted caste against caste, and, within these individual castes, the higher against the lower, had been fostering religious separatism. The women, even the most devout, were actually more stirred up than their fathers, husbands, or brothers. In fact, they "became so brazen that, claiming to be acting in the name of the queen, they formed a mob near the church doors to prevent the missionary from entering the church." [58] The mission ended in triumph, however, and "the ringleaders had to admit defeat." [59] After Kayts came Trincomalee and Batticaloa and, finally, Jaffna. There, also, the mission succeeded magnificently. To the vicar apostolic, however, the lasting after-effects were far more appreciable than the enthusiasm which marked the mission:

I will say nothing about the truly edifying eagerness of our Christians to make the mission. . . . All that will be read with the keenest interest in the account which Father Bonjean has written of it. . . . I will simply add that the immense salutary fruits produced by God's grace during that wonderful mission were not of short duration. As I write these lines, several months after the closing of the mission, I can attest to the great changes wrought at Jaffna: a much more assiduous frequenting of the sacraments; a more exact observance of Sundays and holy days; eagerness of a great number to hear the word of God; edifying conduct of many people, especially the members of the two confraternities established in honor of the Immaculate Conception and Saint John the Baptist; frequent visits to the Blessed Sacrament and to the mission cross. . . . All these are so many proofs which speak volumes for the gratifying fruits of the mission. In addition, during the holy season of Lent and the paschal season which came shortly after the closing of the mission, almost all of us were constantly in the confessional. It might almost be said that although the preaching had ceased, the mission still went on, so strong and powerful was the holy impression left by our pious exercises. . . .[60]

This glad news delighted Bishop de Mazenod. Bishop Semeria's reports not only caused him to relive with emotion the thrilling days of his Provençal missions, but they also showed him that the form of the apostolate which had been assigned as the primary purpose of his newly formed congregation still retained all its excellence and that its effectiveness was not limited to one era or one country. The old bishop had been somewhat saddened when he saw that this form of the ministry, which had been highly favored during the Restoration, had taken on a certain discredit on the soil of France; he was consoled therefore by this proof that the preaching of missions had lost none of its vigor and that it was even achieving a universal appeal. Remembering his own experiences, however, he cautioned the vicar apostolic, reminding him that the feats of valor the Provençal de Mazenod had performed when he was thirty years of age should not be too closely imitated, especially in that tropical region with its enervating climate. Thus he gave the same advice to Semeria which he had received from his uncle Fortuné who had become disturbed by his nephew's excesses—advice, incidentally, which he had very seldom followed: "Don't overtire yourself. Always rest between one mission and the other." [61]

In spite of his personal preference for the ministry to which the Oblate Congregation had been especially dedicated, Semeria remained convinced that to bear full fruit it had to be an integral part of a continuous process. At Ceylon he verified what had been proven so often in Provence and elsewhere, namely, that before this intense period of sowing the seed—and even more afterwards—the ground had to be cultivated to guarantee the productiveness of the planted seed; a comparison between the results achieved at Jaffna and those achieved in places less regularly served gave further proof of this.

Obviously, this continuous process required an increase of missionaries. Bishop de Mazenod did grant generous reinforcements, but they were still insufficient. The vicar apostolic realized how important it was to recruit native priests, but, since the formation of a native clergy involved such long and exacting efforts, the prelate decided to proceed gradually.

His school program would, in effect, prepare Christian laymen who would make their homes solidly Christian, then lay apostles who would assist the missionaries, and finally, what would take the longest time, aspirants for the priesthood. What is contained in his *Journal* about the boarding school to be set up in Jaffna shows the gradual procedure he planned to follow:

In this school, our Catholic children will finally be able to receive a solidly Christian education; that is what they need most of all and that is what we want to give them most of all. . . . As we progress, we shall try to provide [the boarding school] with the needed improvements, insofar as the Lord will furnish us with the means for doing so; these, naturally, will be suggested to us through experience. In our view, this boarding school must also serve as a preparatory school for catechists and perhaps also the beginning of a seminary; from it we shall be able to obtain a few good catechists and—who knows?—a few good native priests. As I have already pointed out—in fact, during the first year of our arrival on this island—if we realize how absolutely necessary a native clergy is for the future welfare of religion in this country, by no means are we blind to the great difficulties we shall encounter at the outset in choosing candidates for the priesthood and in deciding the type of education most suitable for them . . . , their spiritual training, and the positions they will have to occupy. . . . In brief, all the precautions suggested by consummate prudence and a thorough knowledge of the country and by the experience of the vicariates of India should not seem excessive; on the contrary, they must be employed wisely to insure the success of such an important work as that of forming a native clergy. I shall say no more of that. . . . One can see what I wrote about that twelve years ago. . . . Unfortunately, during all this time, it has not been possible for us to put [these ideas] into practice, even experimentally.[62]

This boarding school of Jaffna, which marked the beginning of a great achievement, presented the bishop with two problems which were not easy to solve: matériel and personnel. There was a building in Jaffna, of course, but it was inadequate. Semeria adapted it as best he could and planned to enlarge it. Unfortunately, he lacked finances. Now, although Semeria had a reputation in the congregation of being as poor a financier as Bishop Grandin, Bishop de Mazenod, rather than restraining him, encouraged him in this venture: "You will have rendered a great service to the vicariate when you have established Catholic schools for both sexes," he wrote to Semeria. The first important step was to acquire the land. Thus, when the vicar apostolic, out of excessive prudence, deferred buying a site that suited him, the founder reprimanded him for it: "You acted unwisely. . . . One often rues having missed a good opportunity." Unable, however, to advance the necessary funds, the Bishop of Marseilles referred Bishop Semeria to the Holy Childhood Society, explaining why he could not appeal personally to that Society:

For the simple reason that, with the exception of the Archbishop of Lyons, I am the only bishop who has not allowed the society into his diocese. I had to act that way to avoid displeasing the Propagation of the Faith which is our only source of help. Don't be hesitant about insisting. . . . Be sure to tell them that you are laboring for the conversion of the Buddhists, and that you are baptizing their children whom you will one day have to instruct and preserve from Protestant propaganda.[63]

Bishop de Mazenod was as unable to furnish Jaffna with the needed professors as he was to finance the buildings and the purchase of land. The vicar apostolic, however, continued to stress how urgently they were needed. He pointed out that for lack of qualified personnel he was being forced to hire a Protestant as principal of his boarding school at the very moment when he wanted to give Catholic youngsters the means of receiving a Christian education in a country where only Protestant educational establishments existed. The Bishop of Marseilles had only missionaries at his disposal; their seminary training was not intended to prepare the Oblates for teaching, and, furthermore, the missionaries felt that this was not their vocation. Then too, in spite of the founder's instructions, the study of English was not being given sufficient attention in the scholasticate, and classes in Ceylon were conducted in that language. Semeria, who was aware of this state of affairs simply asked, therefore, that he be given "a few scholastics once they had been initiated by the Christian Brothers into their method of teaching in primary schools." This solution seemed possible because of the newly formed province of Great Britain. Conforming to his plan—"in proportion to our progress, we shall try to provide the needed improvements"—Semeria now judged it essential to raise the level of studies in his boarding-school so that it might not be inferior to Protestant establishments. When the higher standards brought an increase of requests, Bishop de Mazenod, forced to change his plans, admitted his dilemma:

Here they are, talking to me about trigonometry, physics, and even the humanities. It's enough to baffle us. Even in France, it would be difficult for us to find teachers for a school of that kind; why expect that they can be found in England? However, I have written this very day both to Father Provincial and to Father Boisramé, the Master of Novices. I presume that you also have written to further the request. I am even proposing that a good missionary be recalled from Dublin; he comes from Belgium but he knows English well. No doubt, numerous objections will be offered but I think I'll be able to handle them. You can see that I am constantly concerned with the needs of your mission. However, work on this principle: we do not have the members to comply entirely with your views.[64]

That word "entirely" left hope for a relative satisfaction. And as a matter of fact, it was possible to spare three English scholastics who very satisfactorily assumed the direction of the Jaffna boarding school. As for the "young girls," Bishop Semeria was equally concerned about building a school for them as well as a house for the sisters who would supervise their education. The problem was to find a congregation of nuns which would supply the necessary sisters. Since the Holy Family Sisters had become affiliated with the Oblates in 1858, Semeria was inclined to choose them. However, since he feared that recourse to the Holy Family Sisters would entail long delays, he planned to search elsewhere; on learning this, Bishop de Mazenod wrote to him, urging him to be patient and assuring him that his request would be granted and that the sisters would give priority to Ceylon.[65]

With his usual quiet tenacity, the vicar apostolic strove to carry out his program, in spite of the numerous difficulties he encountered in equipping his schools and particularly in purchasing land for the sisters, "a complicated affair." [66] To insure success, he devoted his talents in 1860 to changing public opinion.

Since his efforts had to be sustained by those of the clergy and the faithful, he published a pastoral letter and then a circular letter to the missionaries. It was a question of appealing for generous donations on behalf of an essential work and of imbuing everyone with his firm conviction: "The basic regeneration of our Christians must begin with education." [67] For his part, Father Bonjean, aware of the value of publicity, used modern means of propaganda in pleading the cause of Catholic education in the press and through brochures. He pleaded his case so effectively that one Protestant newspaper in Colombo, *The Examiner,* made its columns available to him, and a compilation of his different writings went into several editions.

Bishop de Mazenod did not hesitate to notify Cardinal Barnabo of the fruitful results of this campaign which the vicar apostolic had waged so skillfully and so vigorously:

I have just received Bishop Semeria's pastoral letter printed in both Tamil and English. It is an excellent piece of work, and I imagine the prelate has sent a copy of it to Your Eminence. In it you will see proof of the enlightened zeal of this outstanding bishop. He was almost taken away from all those who love and admire him because of the grave illness he contracted during his apostolic visits to some terribly unhealthy regions of his Jaffna vicariate. For the love of God, take him away from there. If he remains in that vicariate, he will die and it would be no easy matter to find another of his worth. Not that we do not have missionaries of the highest caliber in that mission field; one such is Father Bonjean, who was the most outstanding subject from the diocese of Clermont, both in ability and in virtue. He has just published a pamphlet in English, one of the six or seven languages he knows perfectly. A copy of it must have been sent to Your Eminence. This pamphlet was deemed necessary for remedying the negligence of Bishop Bravi in the matter of Catholic education. It has made the most favorable impression, and, it is hoped, will effect some very happy results. If Your Eminence decides to transfer Bishop Semeria to Colombo (and I shall continue to urge Your Eminence to do so), Father Bonjean would then have an opportunity to do boundless good in that truly dead vicariate . . . with its present system of quietude which lets everyone wallow in ignorance and wretchedness of every kind.[68]

By justly extolling the merits of Bishop Semeria and his best missionary in this letter, one of the last which he was to send to the prefect of Propaganda, the Bishop of Marseilles hoped to obtain what he had long been proposing to the Holy See. Convinced that only a concerted direction would permit harmonizing and vitalizing the evangelization of all Ceylon, he had been seeking to have the entire island of Ceylon entrusted to the members of his congregation; as he saw it, the vicariate of Colombo was prevented from making any progress because of that "system of quietude" which let "everyone wallow in ignorance and misery," and because of the erroneous principles which Bishop Bravi had insisted on following.

PAINFUL BEGINNINGS AT COLOMBO

From the very outset, Bishop de Mazenod had been under no illusions regarding the grave difficulties his sons would encounter in the South of Ceylon where it was made all too obvious that they were not wanted. On this point, the Colombo vicar apostolic, Bishop Gaetano Musulce, and his coadjutor, Bishop Bravi, both of whom merely tolerated the other and criticized him at Rome, were in agreement for a change. Bishop Gaetano, whom his coadjutor called "the old man," had no desire to share his authority with his future successor; however, because of his lack of personnel, he had given Bravi *carte blanche* to recruit the needed missionaries wherever he could find them, and thereby keep the Oblates out of Colombo. Both prelates feared that if they were unable by themselves to escape their predicament, they would be forced to accept the Oblates who were now working in the northern part of the island. Since the island had been divided into the two vicariates, a rather bitter rivalry had been growing between the Colombo and the newly independent Jaffna; bringing into their vicariate a religious congregation which had been implanted in Bettachini's vicariate would put them in danger of being controlled by subordinates. Added to this truly regrettable concern for prestige were more sober reasons which Bishop Bravi soon undertook to stress with Cardinal Fransoni in order to justify his coolness toward the Oblates and the stand he had taken against them:

Bear in mind, Your Eminence, that our vicariate is totally different from that of Jaffna in climate, customs, language, economy, and politics. The way in which we believe missionaries should behave here is contrary to the one followed by those in Jaffna. The policy which I have adopted and from which I cannot swerve in any manner at the present time, has, in the past two years, restored peace, unity, and harmony to a vicariate that had been entirely controlled by the Goanese priests whose hearts are blacker than their skin. As a result of that policy, the arrival of five European missionaries has in no way disturbed the outward tranquillity of the vicariate, and I am hoping that, with God's help, that same policy will let the Goanese, the present masters of the vicariate, die in peace and leave everything to us without schisms, dissensions, and scandals. That is the greatest blessing I think I can obtain for the time being. You know how the vicariate of Jaffna was erected, not only by force, but against the will of the Goanese. This created such an antipathy toward everything comprising it, that here the Goanese not only detest and abhor everything belonging to that vicariate, but everything that has any dealings with it as well. That was the great objection to the entrance of our Oblates.[69]

Evidently, Bravi feared that the arrival of the Oblate Fathers would mean an abusive encroachment on Jaffna's part and would introduce methods from the North which he deemed harmful to peace in an entirely different and extremely delicate situation.[70] Furthermore, he felt that it would be impossible to count on their willingness to conform to the directives of the vicar apostolic and his coadjutor when, as religious, they would be subject to a superior who had completely different viewpoints from theirs and who knew nothing of the terrain.

Rather than diminishing the "great obstacle," Bishop Bravi had, on the contrary, striven to enlarge it in order to serve his own prejudices and choose according to his personal preferences. Being a Sylvestrian himself, as was his secretary and adviser, Father Cingolani, he would have preferred first to obtain a few members of his own order. However, that "small order" had so few members that there were "barely enough to form their insignificant communities" in Rome;[71] since none of these were available, he had then written to various congregations and clergy of his own country to assure himself Italian helpers. Again he failed. Then he had even resigned himself to seeking recruits from other European congregations, provided they were not French, but his advances and urgings brought only refusals. In desperation, he had to fall back on the Oblates—"a last resort," remarked Bishop de Mazenod, who was not taken in by this scheming.[72] Was he forced to accept the Oblates, as the Bishop of Marseilles affirmed? Or by force of necessity, did Bravi, who was determined to find help, appeal personally to the Propaganda to put pressure upon the founder, since the latter's feeling toward Bravi seemed somewhat unfavorable and since Bravi's request included conditions likely to antagonize the superior general, one of which was the demand that the Oblates sent to him be not of French but of Italian origin? Naturally, the Propaganda pointed out to him that such a demand would compromise everything, and even termed the request "strange and ridiculous"; nonetheless, it forwarded the demand to Bishop de Mazenod. The founder had good reason to be offended by Bravi's not writing directly to him, and even greater reason to be offended by the "uncomplimentary" insinuation regarding the French, "who had as great a reputation for zeal as any other nationality." [73] However, since "the glory of God and the salvation of souls" were at stake, he ignored such a lack of propriety, and even such patent lack of tact, and decided to send four fathers to Colombo as soon as possible, making it very clear to Semeria, however, that he was to be their superior as he was for those in Jaffna.[74] Evidently, the Bishop of Marseilles felt no optimism regarding the welcome and the fate awaiting his sons, and he even admitted to Cardinal Barnabo that he felt pessimistic about this foundation.[75] But he was thinking more of the future than of the rather unpromising present. To him, introducing his sons into the South of Ceylon seemed indispensable for realizing later the desirable uniformity of action throughout the whole island when it would be placed under their direction and for putting an end to the shameful rivalry and discord between the two vicars apostolic to the detriment of God's work. With the opportunity presenting itself, he seized it as he had seized all others he had deemed providential. The beginnings would be harsh, but it was necessary to look beyond them and anticipate the hour when the Oblates, finally "free to pursue their work zealously," would accomplish great things on the island. He had been assured by the Propaganda that Colombo was being reserved for the congregation. He himself would not see this come about, but, "although he was too old to await that day," he was determined "to see the beginning of the plan carried out before he died." [76]

Contrary to Bishop de Mazenod's expectations, Bishop Bravi afforded an effusive reception to the four Oblates who arrived at their destination July 25, 1851, and he assured them that he would be like a second father to them. But the four missionaries quickly perceived that the prelate intended to practice this touching paternity in his own fashion, by cutting them off from their religious family so that he might substitute himself as their regular superior and impose his own ideas upon them. In this, he was acting in agreement with old Bishop Gaetano who was equally opposed to the authority which Semeria would exercise over the missionaries under his jurisdiction. Semeria was preparing to join the new arrivals to give them his instructions, as he had been ordered to do by Bishop de Mazenod, when a letter from Bravi casually informed him that he had already arranged everything with his confreres, that his coming would be "a faux pas" and that he had assured the four fathers:

Semeria and I will work together secretly, but in no way must grounds be given for believing that there is a coalition with the fathers in the North; otherwise, a conflagration would break out. I shall look upon them as my sons; you need have no fears.[77]

A second letter specified that the two communities should act as though they "had no more to do with each other than did the canons of Genoa with the canons of Ancona. Do anything you wish with the Oblates here, but let it be a secret among them, you, and me," added the prelate; a few lines further on, he limited the meaning of the "anything you wish," and ended by voiding it. Prevented from going to Colombo personally, Semeria wanted to dispatch Father Mouchel there as superior, substituting him for one of the fathers who had arrived from France, who would then come to Jaffna to replace him. Bravi, however, was opposed to this, invoking the authority of Bishop de Mazenod himself who had sent the four missionaries exclusively for Colombo. He wrote once again:

Set your mind at ease regarding the situation of all our missionaries. Bear in mind that they are in the hands of a man of honor who will do all he can and must, without taking away an iota of your authority.[78]

Less than reassured, Semeria had intended to react in a manner which, after he was better informed, he found would have been too forceful. In effect, he had intended to notify Bishop Bravi that he was summoning the four Oblates in Colombo to Jaffna and would keep them there until Bishop de Mazenod reached a decision in their regard, since, as superior, he could not countenance the coadjutor's injunction that they forgo "one of our most beautiful titles to glory" by concealing "their status as members of the Oblate Congregation." [79] On reflection, however, he deemed it wiser to postpone such a radical step and one so fraught with consequences. It was fortunate that he did, since a *combinazione* of Bravi's devising allowed Father Mouchel, though he was barred from becoming superior, to go to the South of Ceylon to improve his supposedly impaired health; this enabled him to avoid appearing as though he were carrying out an official assignment. After he arrived in Colombo, Father Mouchel noted that the situation of the Oblates there did not seem "as bad" as might be imagined by someone looking at things from a distance. He declared that their situation was "even better" than that of his Jaffna confreres. Allowances had to be made for the precautions the vicar apostolic was forced to take in dealing with the Goanese priests in order to convince them that the newly arrived French missionaries did not intend to "supplant them, and that they would be allowed to die in peace" at their posts. Mouchel observed that Bravi was acting for the best; nothing was being placed in the way of the Fathers' "living according to our Holy Rule as faithfully as our Jaffna missionaries." "It is true," he conceded, "that outwardly, your dealings" with them "will not be as free and open as they are in the North," but basically, there is "no great difference. At Jaffna, we see each other only once a year." Mouchel's report added that Bishop Bravi would offer no objection if Semeria or one of his delegates made "an appearance in the South," using health or travel as a pretext. The following conclusion was gathered from Mouchel's report: "Don't rush anything; be patiently resigned to indispensable accommodations." [80]

Had Mouchel allowed himself to be brainwashed by Bravi

who was well known as a trickster? Semeria had every reason to fear so since the very delicate situation in which Bravi found himself was only too conducive to his cunning maneuvering. The Jaffna superior was entirely reassured only when he received Bishop de Mazenod's instructions which were completely in line with the moderation recommended by Father Mouchel:

What can you expect? Everyone has his pet idea. [Bishop Bravi] has taken it into his head that all would be lost if it were learned in his vicariate, and especially in the city of Colombo, that his missionaries depend on those of Jaffna. This kind of pride is understandable. He has kept within due bounds by assuring you that they would always be obedient and submissive to you. Our fathers will never fail to conform to that. Don't become too worked up, therefore, over poor Bishop Bravi; he is trying hard to appear kind and paternal; he even flatters himself that he *a non esser padre meno amoroso inferiore al padre de Marsiglia*. As you say, it will be difficult, but we must be grateful to him for his good will and remain on friendly terms with him. I do not know how things will turn out, but patience in everything is needed.[81]

Things were solved by appointing a vice-superior from among the four Oblates who had arrived from France. He was appointed to deal immediately with the vicar apostolic and to refer matters to Semeria who was to remain the titular superior. Semeria, therefore, delegated his authority to Father Pulicani and felt that, at last, he could relax: "And so now," he wrote, "this matter is settled for a while! God be praised!" [82] Unfortunately, it was a case of a one-sided settlement; proud of winning the first round, Bravi soon after strengthened his gains, and the situation became increasingly strained, and deteriorated.

There would be no end to the account if all the disputes which the good Semeria recorded in his *Journal* were to be related. It is really necessary therefore to mention only the major difficulties which determined the attitudes assumed by Bishops Gaetano and Bravi and by the Oblates in the South. The two Colombo prelates had been striving in the main to prevent the type of incidents which the local mentality and its prejudices provoked only too frequently, and, being well acquainted with the people and their temperament, they had good reasons for practicing prudence: they had to cope with Christians quick to take offense and often more devoted to their traditions, ceremonials, and privileges than to the genuine principles of Catholicism, and with a Protestant bloc which controlled wealth and business; their clergy was reduced in number, poorly organized, and, consequently, difficult to manage; the Goanese priests who had immigrated into the South, where they fared better materially and enjoyed greater toleration, greatly exploited the fear of schism—which terrified their superiors—in order to insure the independence they jealously guarded; the Italian priests and the too-few Sylvestrians who were available had to make themselves acceptable to the native clergy and behaved accordingly by remaining in the background. There is no doubt that, although they did not achieve harmony among these groups, by their scheming and by what Bravi proudly called his "policy," he and Gaetano did succeed in maintaining the peace.

Fathers who had been sent to Colombo by Bishop de Mazenod soon became aware that from a religious point of view, the so-called "policy," which was a wholly negative one and had been pushed to extremes, was causing a deplorable stagnation. Young, eager, and zealous, they intended to push ahead, to take initiatives, and, as Bishop de Mazenod had instructed them, to bring back fallen-away Catholics, win over Protestants, and convert Buddhists. They lacked experience and the ability to adapt to a complicated milieu where many things escaped them, and these very things are sometimes all the more important for natives when they seem the more futile and insignificant to foreigners; prudence would have been particularly needed since they were to encounter malevolence.

Thus, at times, they made mistakes which were immediately criticized, and Bravi used these mistakes to justify his complaints to the superior general and to speak ill of his missionaries, not only on the island but even in Rome where he had secret dealings in the offices of the Propaganda.

Although he had put little stock in the coadjutor's touching assurances that he would be a second father to his sons, the founder, from the very outset, had proved to be accommodating: he had agreed that his religious would not be officially subject to the Jaffna superior, and, in spite of his indignation that Bravi had forbidden his sons to wear the Oblate cross (Bravi himself had discontinued wearing his pectoral cross to avoid offending the

Protestants), had finally consented that in the Colombo vicariate they would wear the cross beneath their cassocks when they were outside the mission house. He honestly admitted that his missionaries could have erred and were "not as blameless as he attempted to make them appear when writing to the Sacred Congregation";[83] yet, though he freely admitted that they did not always act as prudently as possible, he defended them without reservation in regard to fundamentals. Of course, since he was so far away and in an entirely different kind of world, it was impossible for him to appreciate fully the unique situation in Ceylon. However, although he was aware that precautions were necessary and that Bravi was not always wrong, he became more and more firmly convinced that the precious "policy" on which the coadjutor prided himself was completely anti-apostolic in its excesses, deliberate concessions, self-effacement, and accommodativeness. The kingdom of God was not founded without effort, contradiction, and risk. The Lord's words "sleep now and take your rest" were by no means a command; they were, in fact, a reprimand; but the words "let down your nets and cast out into the deep" were a resounding command. Thus, as the divergence in the viewpoints of the coadjutor and those of the Oblates became more obvious, the founder strove more energetically to make the Oblate concept prevail since it was the only one capable of spreading the kingdom of God.

Events, moreover, intervened to stiffen his attitude and at the same time to toughen his orders. Everything began with a "riot" in the mission station of Pallansena to which Father Lallement had been assigned. He had refused to go to give Extreme Unction to a sick person across the Maha Oya River, the border line of the two vicariates, since he possessed no faculties for that territory which belonged to Jaffna. His refusal was a convenient excuse for the population to make a violent demonstration and to threaten to seek the services of a schismatic priest. The Christians on the Jaffna bank of the river were of the same caste as those in Pallansena and, before Ceylon had been divided into the two vicariates, had belonged to the Pallansena mission. Now, the vicar apostolic of Colombo, Bishop Gaetano, felt obliged to agree with the rioters and ordered Father Lallement to "administer Extreme Unction as it had formerly been done" to the faithful across the river and to bless their marriages, even though they resided on territory assigned to the northern vicariate. Thus, the poor missionary found himself "betwixt and between." To obey, without faculties, would be exercising his ministry invalidly; to disobey would be exposing himself to the danger of an "uproar" and a "scandal" and might even put him under interdict. Undoubtedly, Bishop Gaetano had on his side reasons of a sociological nature which, in our day, seem more valid than those based on mere geographical boundaries; from a canonical standpoint, however, Father Lallement's holding to the established circumscription was unassailable. When Father Semeria complained, Bishop Gaetano agreed that he had gone beyond his rights and he then revoked his decision.[84]

Although this first "squabble," which resulted from a popular riot, was rather quickly settled, the "storm" that resulted in 1852 from the pronouncements of the Goanese priests regarding the frequent reception of the sacraments was prolonged for years and had repercussions even at the Roman Curia. As soon as the Oblates had succeeded in learning the Cingalese language spoken in that region, they made it their first endeavor to catechize the children and give them a solid spiritual formation. Since they all but despaired of bringing the adults back on the right path, they felt that the surest way to regenerate the mission stations was to prepare new Christian generations. To give a "liking for piety" to them while they were still amenable to the frequent reception of the Eucharist, the essential source of grace, the young people had to be oriented from the time they reached the age of reason. The pastoral program of the Oblates concerning these two points contrasted with customs that had arisen from the passivity and lack of zeal of the local clergy of that time; for, until the Oblates arrived, that same clergy had bothered little about teaching dogma and moral and they preferred to postpone First Communion, using the excuse that they wanted to guarantee that necessary dispositions were present; as a result, very often First Communion was received at a very late time in life, in fact, sometimes only as viaticum. Allowing ten- or twelve-year-olds to receive Communion, therefore, was certain to be something of a sensation and, at one and the same time, would oppose the principles of the native clergy and the mentality of their sheep who were hostile to any changes whatsoever and too little instructed not to include very questionable elements—some of which were incompatible with the genuine tradition of the Church—in their religious traditions which they were determined to preserve to the least detail. But instead of proceeding individually and in simple fashion so as to spare local sensibilities, Fathers Lallement and Duffo, aware that the Ceylonese were very impressed by "externals," and eager to "attract the adults," organized solemn First Communion ceremonies for the children patterned after those conducted in France and containing approximately one hundred boys and girls. Denunciations and "false reports" immediately flowed into the vicariate apostolic. It was claimed that the majority of the children were not instructed, and could not be, because of the poor knowledge the two Fathers had of the language; it was even assured that some of the children had not gone to confession and that they had taken something to eat and drink beforehand. Greatly upset by the complaints of the Goanese priests, Bishop Gaetano then ordered the Oblates to conform to the customs of the country and even forbade Father Duffo to "allow any children to make their First Communion, stating that it amounted to sacrilege." Bishop Bravi entered the controversy as well on June 15 and took the same stand, but being more astute, he ignored the theological implications and simply pointed out what "horrible consequences" the intemperate zeal of the fathers would have: "The Goanese priests would sing hosannah!" He added:

I believe that these servants of God have a sense of duty. Now, the first and greatest duty they have is obedience. And it is great because their superiors have made it so. . . . . If [the fathers] were to persist, we would be ruined.[85]

After being informed, Semeria upheld Father Lallement and his colleague on basic points. They could not be reproached for allowing properly instructed children to make their First Communion, and, in spite of what had been reported, they had sufficient grasp of the Cingalese tongue to catechize these children. And therefore they should judge in each case whether a particular child has the requisite dispositions, for the general rule of the Church and that of their congregation prescribe that every Christian, when he has reached the age of reason, should receive the Eucharist at

least once a year, and this rule must prevail over the customs of this
"blissful country." The superior conceded, however, that to effect
the necessary change-over in this regard, it would be advisable for
the time being if the fathers dispense with the ceremonies connected with a general and solemn First Communion and confine
themselves to private First Communions. Bishop Bravi concurred.[86]

This did not mean the end of the debate; the Goanese priests
continued to agitate and to denounce not only solemn and general
First Communions, but also those in which both children and
adults took part. Bishop Gaetano, therefore, in August, 1854, went
so far as to impose a radical rule under pain of suspension and, to
make it look more legal, notified the Oblates of it in Latin:

Cum Oblati sint valde propensi ad dandam primam communionem
pueris ac puellis, et ex his non pauci recipiant sacram communionem
sine sensu quid sit illud, quia recipiunt sacrilege, ne in posterum fiant
tanta sacrilegia, primam communionem prohibeo ne fiat sine mea
expressa facultate sub poena suspensionis a divinis.[87]

The poor bishop had placed himself in a very bad predicament
and it was all too easy to exploit such an inadmissable act of authority. Father Semeria excused him for making this strange decision.
"He is becoming very old," he wrote, "and his mind is not always
clear, as I could perceive during my recent trip to the South." [88]
At first, the Jaffna superior tried to persuade the prelate to agree
to a lenient and acceptable interpretation of the impossible
decree. However, when Semeria received a vague and evasive reply
from the latter who was unwilling to face the issue, he therefore
decided to have recourse to the Holy See, the court of last appeal.
A long letter to Cardinal Fransoni then informed the prefect of
the Propaganda of the difficult situation of the Colombo Oblates;
it referred Gaetano's prohibition to the Holy See as well as the
interdict imposed by the vicar apostolic, quoted it verbatim in its
Latin form, complained indignantly of the methods followed by
the Goanese clergy and the rigoristic principles they invoked to
postpone communion: *Melius est communionem negare dignis*
quam dare indignis; and it requested the prefect of the Propaganda, in view of the circumstances, to suggest a line of conduct
that could be followed by the fathers who were fully disposed to

obey.[89] Bishop de Mazenod was then at Rome for the definition of the dogma of the Immaculate Conception and he, too, intervened personally with Cardinal Fransoni to inform him of "many other things" apt to enlighten him and to counteract the maneuvers of Bravi who had informants in the offices of the Propaganda. The result was what Bishop de Mazenod had hoped it would be. He wrote to Semeria:

I hasten to tell you, that you need have no fears in regard to the Propaganda. Your work and that of our fathers are known and appreciated there. There is unanimous agreement in that regard. They have already written to Bishop Bravi disapproving the prohibition that was placed upon our fathers in the matter of First Communions. They expressly enjoined him to treat the Oblates in his vicariate with more consideration. Moreover, they informed me that the Sacred Congregation was going to ask me for a certain number of Oblate missionaries for the vicariate of Colombo.[90]

CONFLICTS BETWEEN THE TWO VICARIATES

In addition to this regrettable affair there was another which pitted the vicar apostolic of Jaffna against the vicar apostolic of Colombo, the former demanding that he be given a more equitable distribution of territory and financial resources. Now, under the circumstances, the Oblates of Colombo, along with their Jaffna confreres, agreed with Bishop Bettachini, thereby making themselves even more undesirable to Bishop Bravi. From the time the island had been divided into the two vicariates mainly for financial reasons, the jurisdiction of the pilgrimage shrine of Saint Anne of Talavila had been a bone of contention between Bishop Gaetano and Bishop Bettachini. Bettachini justly pleaded his extreme poverty by pointing out that Bishop Gaetano did not need the income from the shrine since he was well supported in a very wealthy region where Christians were numerous, whereas, his own missionary territory, with its small flock and its materially deprived provinces, could not survive without that income. What was an overabundance for Colombo was a vital necessity for Jaffna. But Gaetano had no intention of allowing himself to be robbed of what he by no means considered an overabundance, and, in 1848, after numerous disputes, the Propaganda allowed Gaetano to keep

Saint Anne's shrine "temporarily." [91] However, far from giving Bettachini cause for hope in regard to the future disposal of the shrine, this prudent "temporarily," was, in his opinion, an arrangement inspired by his cunning colleague of Colombo so that, in time and without commotion, a permanent and *de facto* annexation would result. Determined not to allow his rights to be invalidated by prescription, Bettachini increased his protests to the Propaganda and enlisted Semeria's support; he, in turn, brought Bishop de Mazenod into the controversy. Gaetano and Bravi, who were not without support in the Curia, did not limit themselves to defending their interests. Encouraged by their first victory, they strove to push their advantage and, under pretext of saving the Goanese of the South from suffering, they also demanded the mission of Chilaw.

The Sacred Congregation, which had hesitated to solve the problem, then decided to settle the difficulty by obtaining mutual concessions. It proposed giving Saint Anne's to Jaffna, but, by way of compensation, allot one-third of the revenues from the shrine to Colombo and, in addition, award Colombo the mission of Chilaw. These proposals of Cardinal Fransoni, which reached Bettachini at the beginning on May, 1853,[92] literally astonished him. By stripping him of Chilaw, they were depriving him of his best, healthiest, and richest mission, which numbered 12,000 Christians,[93] and were leaving him with only two-thirds of the revenue from Saint Anne's. He therefore sent a letter to the Prefect of the Propaganda, pointing out to Fransoni that the apportionment in question would strike a "fatal blow" at the already mistreated vicariate and requesting that before making any decision, the Sacred Congregation send a "visitor-apostolic" to Ceylon, "to examine everything with the most scrupulous attention and impartiality." [94] On June 6, Semeria, as spokesman for the Oblates, composed a lengthy report[95] which Bishop de Mazenod personally handed to Fransoni while vigorously supporting it. Lastly, Bettachini decided to leave for Rome to defend his cause personally.

Gaetano and Bravi, on the other hand, had approved the line of demarcation proposed by the Propaganda—in fact they had inspired it; accordingly, they drew up some maps and, in order to insure their victory, ordered all the priests of their vicariate to sign a document accepting the proposed plan. Now, two of the

Colombo Oblates refused to sign. Bravi then denounced them again to Cardinal Fransoni as being disobedient and accused them of forming an *imperium in imperio* and of disturbing the peace by exasperating the Goanese. Bravi wrote:

From the kind of protest which Fathers Lallement and Duffo added to their statement, Your Eminence will see what sort of asses they are, not only because of their Latin, but also because of the reasons they give for refusing to sign.[96]

Bishop de Mazenod could not foresee that Bravi would go so far as to call the poor fathers "asses" because they were incapable of handling the Ciceronian tongue with Gaetano's dexterity; he had no doubt, however, that Gaetano would, under the circumstances, draw up a formal indictment against them and would picture things to suit himself. After duly apologizing for what appeared to be meddling in the affairs of the Propaganda, Bishop de Mazenod undertook the vindication of his sons by giving the Cardinal-Prefect an entirely different picture:

Our poor missionary Oblates are fully aware that their refusal to yield to the wishes of the vicar apostolic will very likely result in their disfavor, but they were unable to overcome their repugnance to doing what they feel is wrong. They refused to sign because their conscience forbade them to approve what they knew was not only contrary to truth and harmful to the welfare of religion, but even contrary to justice. One of them, in a letter regarding this matter, employed the strongest terms to explain his refusal to sign Bishop Bravi's circular. He says that he wants to save his soul, and that, in all conscience, he cannot make himself guilty of falsehood and injustice for the sake of gratifying the vicar apostolic. They all agree that the Colombo vicariate is rich while that of Jaffna is truly poor, and that, to take Saint Anne's away from Jaffna would be to rob it of its livelihood; they even think that the proposed measure would promote schism. The vicar apostolic [Bravi] will denounce them to you, but I think that Your Eminence will justly appreciate the tender consciences of these missionaries who do not wish to endanger their souls at any price, and for that I cannot blame them.[97]

This letter resulted in convincing the Sacred Propaganda that only an investigation conducted on the scene by an official representative of that Congregation would enable it to come to a clear decision with full knowledge of the facts. The Propaganda, therefore approved Bettachini's proposal and sent a visitor-apostolic to Ceylon; he was instructed to gather on-the-spot information, listen to the parties involved, and compile a report; chosen for this delicate mission was Bishop Bonnand, the vicar apostolic of Pondichery. Bravi made no secret of his disappointment. When Semeria was commissioned by the Holy See to represent Bettachini, who had been detained in Rome by sickness, Bravi wrote to Semeria concerning the latter, with bitter sarcasm:

I thought that, by going to Rome, Bishop Bettachini had *providentially* removed the difficulty, and that the plan [for a visitor] had flown to Emmaus where the Lord, out of mercy for this island, would keep it buried. Through you, I see that this plan is still alive and I am truly surprised at the one they have chosen as visitor. Please God that the one who conceived this idea will not have to weep over the scandal that results from it. Enough! God seems to be doing strange things in Ceylon.[98]

Bishop Gaetano and his coadjutor strove to get the Propaganda to countermand the order, then to challenge Bishop Bonnand, and finally to have the investigation delayed. The Sacred Congregation did not even deign to answer them, and they were forced to submit to the investigation as well as to the choice of investigator. The conclave opened at Negombo on April 20, 1854, with Bishop Bonnand presiding; taking part in it were Father Semeria and the two Colombo prelates assisted by some native priests; in view of the circumstances, therefore, there was little cause for optimism. The two sides could not reach any agreement about Chilaw or Saint Anne's.[99] The apostolic representative had to abandon any hope for mutual concessions which would have made a friendly settlement possible; but, at least he could leave sufficiently informed concerning the actual situation and the persons involved. His report was very explicit: he proposed giving Chilaw and Saint Anne's to Jaffna, stated that he could not approve Bishop Bravi's attitude towards the Oblates, and acknowledged that they were excellent missionaries. On April 2, 1855, concurring with these views, the Sacred Propaganda decided that Jaffna was to retain Chilaw and would be given Saint Anne's shrine, but that one-fifth of the annual revenues from the shrine would be allotted to the southern vicariate; lastly, it decided that since the Sylvestrians, who were few in number, were unable to supply Colombo with missionaries, the southern vicariate's ranks would be increased with Missionary Oblates, "with an eye to giving that mission field eventually to that congregation to which the Jaffna vicariate had already been assigned." [100]

Although the aged Bishop Gaetano, who was becoming more and more senile, gave up the fight after this grave setback, Bishop Bravi, who would succeed Gaetano in 1857 when the latter died, refused to submit. Holding stubbornly to his aims, wily in his methods—Bishop de Mazenod even termed him dishonest—, he never ceased scheming to make his plan succeed, a plan that was entirely contrary to that of the Sacred Propaganda and of the Bishop of Marseilles. Did he deliberately set out to make things unbearable for the Oblates of Colombo, as the superior general assured Cardinal Barnabo? One could think so, after reading the founder's letters and what Semeria relates in his *Journal*; in these documents, one sees what use Bravi made of the smallest incidents, which were embellished and distorted, so that he might discredit the French missionaries. The malicious accusations of the Goanese priests, who were constantly attempting to trap them, were readily accepted and immediately exploited. Thus, his vaunted peace policy, which made every concession to the Protestants and the Ceylonese clergy, turned into a spiteful war of attrition against the Oblates whom he wanted to eliminate; whenever incidents arose involving the fathers, rather than trying to quell the disturbances, the prelate increased them; he gave credence to the calumnies without verifying the accusations, and, in 1855, Semeria was obliged to devote eight full pages in order to relate the true facts.[101] Bravi assigned only the poorest missions to Pulicani and his confreres, and, disposing of the funds from the Propagation of the Faith to his own liking, allowed the Oblates no share of them. With all their resources limited to their Mass stipends, they were materially and morally destitute; everything was done to demoralize them. In his lengthy and numerous letters to the Propaganda, Bishop de Mazenod continually and tirelessly recounted these abuses while at the same time praising the tenacity and selfless zeal of his sons, who, under the most thankless conditions, were laboring unremittingly for the spread of the kingdom of God. As time went on, the prelate even threw all caution aside and "began to speak frankly and without mincing words," and even went so far as to imply to the Propaganda that it was badly misinformed: "It is possible," he admitted to Semeria, "that this way of acting, to which they are not accustomed, somewhat startled them, at least that is the impression I have judging from the answers I get." [102] However he had to write in a strong tone to be sure of gaining a hearing, since he was unable to go to Rome to plead his case because his cardinalate was "still undecided." [103]

The prelate, who was feeling his years, wanted to see some progress, and was growing rather impatient because for years the Propaganda had been deferring the application of the plan decided upon in 1855. Delay was added to delay, and this was giving the advantage to Bishop Bravi, who, by his war of attrition, hoped that as time went on, he would emerge victorious. He, at least, was not sleeping, and was continuing his intrigues. Having lost Chilaw, which he had wanted to annex to his Vicariate, he shortly afterwards put in a claim for Kurunegala under the pretext that the Christians of that mission station were natives of the South. Once again, Bishop de Mazenod blocked his path. He wrote to Cardinal Barnabo:

I am truly disgusted about our Ceylon mission. I wish that a little more consideration would be shown to saintly Bishop Semeria and his missionaries who are doing so much good in their wretched vicariate. They do not complain of the excessive work caused by the distance of their missions and by the poverty of the country, but it grieves them to see one claim after another coming from Colombo and always to their disadvantage. . . . I cannot tell you how greatly our missionaries are disheartened by the latest demand that Kurunegala be taken away from them. From the way things are going, I predict that instead of evangelizing the whole island as we had predicted the Congregation of the Oblates of Mary will have to be withdrawn, leaving the field free to the favorites of those on whom Your Eminence has to rely because of the excessive work connected with your supreme office.[104]

With the partiality of the Roman *Monsignori* working as secretaries in the Propaganda now clearly involved, the Sacred Congregation decided to resort to an investigation of Kurunegala by Bishop Bonnand, as it had done for Chilaw. Now, exactly as before, Bishop Bonnand decided in favor of Jaffna. Kurunegala was kept within the northern vicariate, and Bishop Bravi once again found his claim rejected.[105] At the same time as he was attempting to extend his jurisdiction, Bravi had been taking many steps to recruit missionaries of his own liking so that he might dispense with the Oblates. In 1856, Father Lallement, one of the four missionaries sent to Colombo by Bishop de Mazenod, had been forced to return to France for reasons of health. Bravi had refused to accept any replacement, and it was obvious that if the other three were likewise to become exhausted, the vicar apostolic would not consent to any relief. Meanwhile, the number of the Goanese priests had been diminishing steadily, and the dead, the aged, and the infirm had to be replaced. Bravi, who wanted to prevent any compulsory replacements, undertook to enlighten the Propaganda regarding those he wished excluded and those he preferred:

As things now stand, I cannot in any way whatsoever accept any more Oblates from Marseilles. . . . Do everything possible to send me a few [missionaries] immediately. It matters little whether they are very learned; it suffices that they be good priests, that they be sincerely willing to obey and be of but one mind and one heart with all the others, and that for the present they be exclusively Italian.[106]

In view of these conditions, the Propaganda, which had decided to reserve Colombo for the Oblates, offered him no one. The Sylvestrians, whom the Vicar-Apostolic had alerted since he wanted the direction of the vicariate reserved to his own Order, lacked personnel. Thus he found himself forced to look elsewhere, even in Australia. In his own words, it was a case of "winning" the match.[107]

These intrigues had not escaped the Bishop of Marseilles. He was fully aware that Bravi was making "desperate efforts to prevent more missionary Oblates from being sent to Colombo." Now, the Bishop of Marseilles pointed out to Cardinal Barnabo that, on the contrary, the latter would have to be "brought little by little into the Colombo vicariate, which was a much more impor-

tant vicariate than that of Jaffna, so that, in due time, the whole
island might be evangelized by the same congregation." Thus,
would end a deplorable rivalry which was causing so much opposition between the two parts of this unfortunate portion of Christendom; it would then be easier to minister to the Christians and
"to convert the numerous infidels who filled the country." [108]

Reasons of health made it even more necessary that new posts
in the South be assigned to his religious. The northern part of the
island was extremely unhealthy. Almost all the fathers, including
Semeria, had contracted fever there; four had died, and all hope
was abandoned for a fifth. In the opinion of the doctors, the only
chance of curing him "would be a change of air and a temporary
sojourn in a healthier climate." The congregation, therefore,
would have to be assured of two or three houses on the salubrious
territory of Colombo; through an exchange between the communities of the two vicariates, the fathers of the North could go there
to recover. Since this was a "matter of life or death," urgent measures would have to be taken. Undoubtedly, these measures would
be opposed by the obstinacy and ill-will of Bishop Bravi, but, with
his heart condition and his "enormous obesity" which kept him
inactive, there would be sufficient reasons to prompt him to retire
to Italy, leaving his vicariate free for Bishop Semeria to transfer to
it. Under these conditions, the Bishop of Marseilles assured Cardinal Barnabo, he would not hesitate to send considerable reinforcements to Ceylon. But why agree to sacrifice his sons in vain in
a country where they were dying and where they were being prevented from doing good? [109] If no solution were forthcoming, the
superior general would even feel obliged to recall his sons. Appeals
for their services were coming in from all sides; what was the
sense of squandering his manpower on such a thankless field when
they could be more effectively employed elsewhere, treated more
considerately, and work more happily! [110]

In truth, the prelate was using this threat only for the purpose of getting action from the Propaganda, which, he knew, was
unable to replace them. In fact, he counseled Semeria, who was
increasing his complaints, to continue at any price; evacuating
the island would be playing into the hands of the vicar apostolic
who had been constantly scheming to achieve this very result.
Now that they had gained a foothold in Colombo the fathers had

to stay there so that they might assure the future. Bravi would not live forever. It was merely a question of time. Once he disappeared, an Oblate would succeed him.

Now, far from laying aside his arms and planning to retire to the center of Christendom, the vicar apostolic of Colombo left for Rome to organize a counteroffensive. Bishop de Mazenod, aware that Bravi was supported by highly placed advocates and fearing his intrigues, then played the trump card he had been holding in reserve. Apologizing for writing in French so that he might "better control" his pen in the complaints he was forced to lodge regarding Bishop Bravi and his supporters in the offices of the Propaganda, he revealed to Cardinal Barnabo that there was "a certain man" in his Propaganda office "who was devoted to the interests or rather the pretentions" of Bishop Bravi, even to the extent of "betrayal."

I have proof that one of the secretaries employed in your dicastery has revealed to Bishop Bravi the correspondence I had with Your Eminence, the opinions I expressed regarding this prelate, the plans I confided to Your Eminence, and among others, the opinion I expressed in strict confidence when I wrote to you of having the two vicariates eventually entrusted to the devoted zeal of the Missionary Oblates of Mary.

After furnishing proof of this "official betrayal," the Bishop of Marseilles wrote a lengthy indictment summarizing what he had many times stated concerning the intrigues of "that jealous and dishonest individual," who opposes truly apostolic men, while he defends against any and everyone priests who do nothing for the salvation of souls and who "wrongly bear the name missionaries." What was worse was that, emboldened by some supporters, who, undoubtedly, did not suspect that they were abetting a vice, he had been boasting "that he was supported and approved by the Sacred Propaganda." The Congregation's good name, therefore, was being "compromised as much as was the welfare of religion in Ceylon." [111]

Cardinal Barnabo defended his department. This was no surprise to Bishop de Mazenod:

Naturally, they do not want to admit the breach of trust on the part of the employees who made the contents of my letters known to the other side. But they now know that we are keeping our eyes open.

This was sure to be of advantage later. Furthermore, this letter was no longer necessary as far as Bravi was concerned, since he had died suddenly during his voyage to Rome. On learning this, Bishop de Mazenod admitted that he had been "very hard on poor Bishop Bravi." Consequently, he offered Mass for the deceased prelate the very next day. However, although he expressed regrets about the language he used, he had no regrets about intervening with the Propaganda: "I was speaking to his superior. I felt no scruples about making him known such as his actions showed him to be." Convinced that he had held to the truth, he did not alter his basic judgment and even composed an obituary which, in truth, was in rather poor taste.

Now he is dead, and all his plans for recrimination are swallowed up in the sea! His traveling companion will be able to carry them out, but it will never be with the shrewdness, finesse and talent of that poor dead man, whose conduct was always so blameworthy and so harmful to the vicariate of the South.[112]

With the situation thus clarified, the superior general felt sure that his plan, which conformed to that of the Propaganda, would be realized. During the last year of his life—even during his last illness—he kept urging that his long-standing project be realized before he died. On March 2, 1861, physically unable to write his thanks to Cardinal Barnabo for sending him the Pope's blessing, he instructed Bishop Jeancard to remind His Eminence of his "wish that Bishop Semeria be transferred from Jaffna to Colombo" and urgently recommended "this favor" to the "benevolent and well-proven solicitude" of the Prince of the Church.[113] On the following April 6, profiting from an improvement in his health, he himself wrote to the Cardinal to inform His Eminence of it and added this brief postscript, which concluded all his correspondence relative to Ceylon with a moving supplication: "For the love of God, do not forget Ceylon or our excellent Bishop Semeria." [114] The Bishop of Marseilles rendered his soul to God without the consolation of seeing his desires fulfilled. Had the Propaganda hesitated to strip the Sylvestrians of their only mission

in Ceylon? Did the Sacred Congregation want to make one last
attempt to preserve it for the members of that Order before resorting to the plan decided upon in 1855? [115] Whatever the case, after
there had been much discussion and a vacancy of two years, the
Colombo vicariate was assigned to the Sylvestrian, Sillani. It was
not until 1883 that it was transferred to the Oblates. Bishop Bonjean then inaugurated a brilliant and fruitful episcopate in the
South of the island.

AN ILL-STARRED ATTEMPT IN ALGERIA

Although the serious difficulties encountered in Ceylon were
finally overcome, it was an entirely different story in Africa where,
during Bishop de Mazenod's lifetime, two successive foundations
failed, the first permanently in Algiers, and the second, in Natal,
but only temporarily; in Natal, it was merely a wrong beginning.
And yet, it was this continent, the nearest one to France, where
the prelate had first considered extending the work of his religious family to foreign missions, and thus realize his great apostolic plan which, for lack of means, had remained dormant until
then. With the taking of Algiers, the opportunity to go forth
seemed to be offering itself, and under the most favorable conditions. Sending Oblates into France's new possession could not
but profit from the enthusiasm aroused in Marseilles by the victory of the French armies. Although the motives for this enthusiasm were not altruistic in a city where commercial profit counted
above all others, it nonetheless caused the people of Marseilles to
favor the idea of the fathers' of Provence going beyond the Mediterranean to spread the kingdom of God. Undoubtedly, the government of "good King Charles X" [116] was willing to accept their
services which had been volunteered by their superior general,
an ardent supporter of the legitimate monarchy. The steps that
had already been taken with the Grand Aumônerie toward this
end warranted hope for government support. "If the government
had not been overthrown at that very time," [117] the plan would
very likely have been carried out. The Revolution of 1830, however, doomed it to failure, since Louis-Philippe had no intention
of promoting the evangelization of the Arabs, much less of entrusting it to a congregation whose founder was considered an

enemy of his government. The Holy See, therefore, turned a deaf ear to the repeated offers of Bishop de Mazenod. Even after the prelate's reconciliation with King Louis-Philippe, it gave preference to the Vincentians. The advent of the Second Republic, which was free of the political prejudices of the preceding regime, made it possible to hope for the Algerian foundation which, against his wishes, the Bishop of Marseilles had had to defer until then. Although Africa would no longer be the first foreign foundation, as he had hoped it would be, he still held it closest to his heart.[118] A journey he made to Bône in 1842, for the transfer of the relics of Saint Augustine, had made him all the more desirous to Christianize the Arabs, although a fleeting contact with the country misled him regarding the eventual results. Judging prematurely, he blamed the failure of the clergy's initiatives there on their lack of zeal, their lack of confidence in divine grace, and their ignorance of the language. "As if it were easier to convert the Chinese!" he noted in his *Journal*. ". . . That they should despair of seeing their efforts succeed in due time, that I could not tolerate, and I told them so." [119] He himself had no doubt that the Oblates would succeed where others, refusing to admit their deficiency, claimed that failure was inevitable. Consequently, he wrote with as much joy as assurance on July 18, 1848: "Algeria calls us. We were destined for this mission." [120] Bishop Pavy, the Bishop of Algiers, had indeed asked him for the help of his sons. He granted it immediately with the provision that they be able to "live a community life in accord with their rule so that they might maintain their regularity and fervor, and be of mutual help to one another in fulfilling all their duties." [121] Although he considered the conversion of the Arabs the prime objective, the prelate nonetheless allowed Bishop Pavy to be the sole judge of the time when the Oblates would undertake that task. He simply asked Pavy that, in the meantime, they be given a "humble ministry" among the "most abandoned souls" rather than "be put into a cathedral pulpit to give Lenten courses." [122]

Everything began inauspiciously with an establishment at Blida where, under the terms of a contract, the fathers were supposed to administer the parish and the hospital. In reality they were forced to settle just outside the city and were ordered to close their chapel to the faithful and devote themselves exclusively to caring for seven villages which were from three to six miles away and which had no churches. This resulted in serious dissensions between the fathers and the bishop, none of which were settled by the flare-ups which occurred. "Cut to the quick" [123] by the offensive letters he had been receiving from Bishop Pavy, Bishop de Mazenod had difficulty controlling his pen; he nonetheless recommended moderation and patience to his sons. "If we can hold on at Blida, truly the right place for us, it is only a short distance from Algiers and is within reach of Atlas through which, subsequently, we shall have to make our way in laboring for the conversion of the Arabs." [124] With this in view, the missionaries applied themselves to learning the language for their apostolate among the natives while devoting themselves to the Europeans whose religious condition left much to be desired. They soon had to stop with that, for, before two years had passed, Bishop de Mazenod had recalled them.

One might think that the Oblates' withdrawal would have been avoided and their shaky position stabilized by a second foundation in Algeria at Philippeville at the end of November, 1849. Quite to the contrary, it was this foundation which decided the withdrawal. As chance would have it, one of the fathers sent to Philippeville, Father Bellanger, complicated matters completely by ingratiating himself with Bishop Pavy and espoused his cause, even to the point of divulging what his confreres had written to the Bishop of Marseilles. He was a venturesome and heedless individual, plunging into constructions, expenditures, and financial transactions which culminated in a crash. Thus, Bellanger, whom Bishop de Mazenod termed a Judas and a liar, had to be expelled from the congregation. Actually, it had been a mistake from the very beginning to allow him to make his religious profession and to receive Holy Orders since his imbalance should have excluded him from these steps. Some objections had been raised against him, as is evidenced by the reports and deliberations of the house councils, on the grounds that he was not of the soundest mind and that his over-active imagination could not but cause certain misgivings. However, within the restricted and somewhat unnatural surroundings of novitiates and scholasticates, insufficient judgment is less discernible than it is in real life. Much enthusiasm, fervor, generosity, and zeal can sufficiently conceal this defect and at the same time compensate for the different quirks that are noticed, so that there is hope that later on, thanks to the lessons learned from experience, only the best will remain. The decision of Bellanger's superiors who declared that they were dubious about him, was balanced in his favor by his good qualities.[125] Besides, the man was skilled in prevarication. Before the affair with Bishop Pavy, even Bishop de Mazenod had

allowed myself to be taken in many times before I knew him thoroughly; unfortunately, this happened too late. . . . When a man who is not suspected of being an inveterate liar, tells you of things he says he has seen with his own eyes, things, in fact, in which he claims to have taken an important part, it is only natural to believe him. I was amazed, and necessarily so—I will say almost stupefied—when I learned there was not a word of truth in all his stories.[126]

When Martin Bruneau, the vicar general of Mans, expelled Bellanger from the Mans diocesan seminary, he knew the true story regarding the individual's idiosyncrasy and his unhealthy irresponsibility. He wrote to Tempier in 1850:

This idiosyncrasy of poor Bellanger is a very deplorable one. Perhaps he is not fully aware of his actions. However the victims of his lies are no less to be pitied, and it is important to know what he is and that he cannot be trusted.[127]

In that era, however, psychiatrists had not yet clearly diagnosed or accurately classified such a character trait which is so patently incompatible with the priesthood or the religious life.

Bellanger's wild spending resulted in making the position of the Oblates in Algeria still more difficult. The wronged creditors bombarded them with claims and complaints, informed the Bishop of Algiers and even the ministry of cults. Added to this was the misfortune suffered by Father Eymère, who had been sent to Algeria "to replace the Judas who had betrayed both the congregation and the Church. Even before he reached his destination," Eymère was the victim of a very serious accident. The horses which were bringing him to Blida had "bolted," and he had jumped down from the coach and was fatally injured. "Mission of Algiers," mourned Bishop de Mazenod, "how dearly you are costing us!" [128] In view of such harsh trials and such heavy sacrifices, results seemed all the more meagre. The question then arose whether to put an end to such an unfortunate experience or to continue it in hopes of a better future. The Bishop of Marseilles was hesitating between these two alternatives when a letter from Cardinal Barnabo made him decide to recall the Oblates from Algeria. The Holy See wanted to create a new vicariate apostolic in Natal, South Africa, and was offering it to the Oblates. The superior general's first impulse was to refuse, stating, as had the Jesuits and the Holy Ghost Fathers, that his lack of men made it impossible for him to accept. However, he quickly perceived that such an unexpected proposal was providential. "None of us had dreamed of such a thing," he noted in his *Journal*; "it came to us through the official voice of the Church. . . . Undeniably, this call comes from God." For that reason, it had to be accepted. The problem was to decide what other mission could spare the men that were needed. An immediate solution was hit upon: "Aha! I think I see a way to answer that," he noted immediately, after asking himself the question. That way consisted in resorting once again to the method of transferral he had used in Oregon; he would transfer the Oblates in Algeria to South Africa and thus avoid squandering his effectives in a fruitless mission, and utilize them instead on a more promising terrain where the fathers would have a ministry more in conformity with their vocation and where they would be able to exercise it in full accord with the views of their hierarchical superiors. At Blida and Philippeville they had been merely pastors of very small villages where scarcely any good could be accomplished and were taking care of Europeans instead of devoting themselves to the conversion of the Arabs; now they would be stationed among the Zulus. Furthermore, since the Propaganda was offering the vicariate apostolic to one of their own, there would be no danger of conflict with the conceptions of a secular bishop. Only a half-page of reflections was needed for Bishop de Mazenod to weigh motives, make a decision, and decide what course to take. In fact, he decided then and there on the candidate to be proposed for the office of vicar apostolic, and, as usual, striking while the iron was hot, sent his reply letter to Cardinal Barnabo immediately, accepting "the mission offered to us" and giving the Propaganda the name of the one suited "to head this mission," Father Bellon.[129]

In spite of Bishop Pavy's recriminations, the Algerian mission was immediately abandoned. The Oblates of Blida and Philippeville were recalled on June 20, 1850, and arrived back in France in July. Their apostolate in Algeria had not lasted for even two years.

THE NATAL MISSION IN SOUTH AFRICA

Bishop de Mazenod had made an ideal choice in Father Bellon; he was a fervent and zealous religious, an excellent theologian, and, through his stay in England, was familiar with British ways and customs—an important asset in a colony of the United Kingdom. Gifted in languages, speaking English, German and Italian fluently, he was therefore ideally suited to direct the new foundation. However, he excused himself for reasons of health, and these reasons were so valid that the superior-general had to accede. With few to choose from the founder then decided on Father Allard; in a letter to Cardinal Barnabo, Bishop de Mazenod spoke highly of Allard's record of service and stressed that the nominee was regarded everywhere

as the embodiment of priestly and religious perfection. I esteem him as worthy of the sacred character to which a vicar apostolic must be raised; he will admirably fulfill the ministry which the Holy See will confide to him.[130]

Relying on the judgment of the Bishop of Marseilles, the Propaganda appointed him without the least objection.

But objections came from other sources, principally from the candidate himself. And yet Bishop de Mazenod had clearly notified him that a refusal was out of the question since it was a case of a "formal command," emanating from the Head of the Church. Bishop de Mazenod, therefore, commanded him to obey without any discussion, and to set out immediately for France.[131] But in spite of the imperative nature of this summons, Father Allard still declined. He expressed his full willingness "to go to Natal as

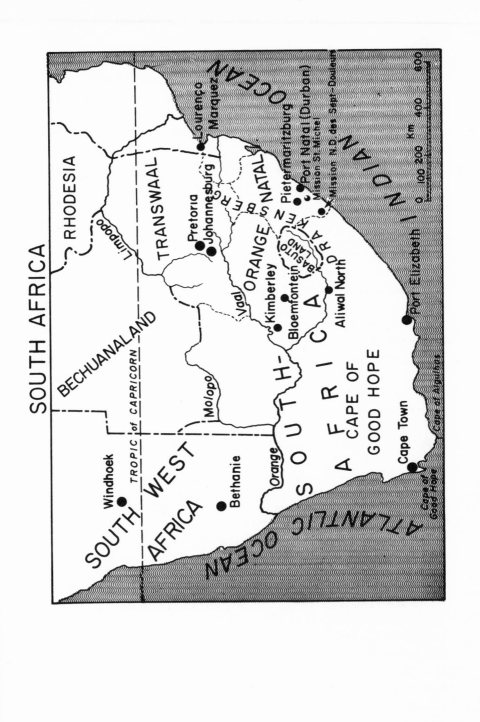

a simple missionary," but, as for being promoted to the episcopacy, certain "reasons he believed legitimate," prevented him from consenting to it. He therefore asked that another be chosen as vicar apostolic, whereupon he would strive with all his heart to evangelize the Zulus.[132]

What were these "legitimate reasons"? Bishop de Mazenod spoke of them in the plural, but confided only one of them to Father Baudrand—the modesty of the father.[133] However, although we no longer possess Allard's reply to Bishop de Mazenod, which would make it possible to enumerate all the others, all the correspondence gives at least a hint of the most determining one. Allard wanted to retreat from a position for which he felt he was unsuited. This was also the feeling of the Oblates in Canada who were equally startled by a nomination which they deemed unfortunate because of Allard's too rigorous virtue. Bishop Guigues of Bytown who shared this opinion hinted to Bishop de Mazenod that his choice was giving rise to criticism. He had cause to rue it, for the founder replied:

Understand clearly that the observations you made regarding our future vicar apostolic are superfluous. . . . He has been ·named by the pope. What is there to say after that? From now on, my conscience is perfectly clear. . . . He will make up for what you think he lacks. . . . Console him as best you can and do not make things more difficult for him. I am as little bothered by what might be said or thought, either by the Canadian clergy or by our own fathers as I was on the occasion of your own election. Would that each and everyone of them had the virtues and qualities of the one they presume to criticize. Father Allard must have received my directive by now; it is *sub gravi*. Have him conform to it and leave immediately on a safe ship.[134]

Naturally, poor Father Allard was aware of the strong disapproval provoked by his nomination, and it further convinced him that he was not the man for the position. However, he was wasting his time enumerating his "legitimate reasons" for refusing; Bishop de Mazenod would not even consider discussing them and, to force the candidate to accept, he simply placed him under obedience. Moreover, it was impossible to understand how such a scrupulous and strict religious could be guilty of such inconsistency. Although he would not tolerate the least infraction in matters of obedience, he had sent only "a piece of paper" [135] instead of obeying immediately and setting out for Marseilles. Since, instead of submitting, Father Allard continued his pleading, the founder referred the matter to the Propaganda and then appealed directly to Pius IX. After first pointing out, as the Propaganda had done, that the founder "had the authority to order Father Allard," the Pope agreed to make a personal pronouncement.[136] Thus, Allard finally had to yield to the Holy Father's orders, and, on July 13, 1851, was consecrated bishop by his superior general. Naturally, the Bishop of Marseilles brought out the splendors of the ceremony on that occasion, but in a letter to Bishop Guigues for the benefit of the Oblates he put stress on what had determined his choice and what he felt should do away with all criticism:

the admirable way in which the new bishop observed the Oblate rules. He is staying at the Calvaire. I have purposely not insisted that he stay at my place where he is free to come whenever he wishes. . . . However, I foresaw how deeply the community there would be edified by his example. He is always first at all the exercises and he pursues perfection to such a degree that he seeks the superior's permission before entering a sick father's room, just as he asked me for permission to give a few holy pictures to his parents. His foreign mission and all its hardships do not disturb him any more than if he were going from Marseilles to Aix.[137]

Whether Bishop Guigues' apprehensions regarding the vicar apostolic's general qualifications were banished by the reading of this complete fidelity to the Rule and this highly praised indifference to hardship, we do not know. At any rate, he learned soon after that there was nothing groundless about his initial fears.

On March 15, 1852, Bishop Allard arrived in Durban with two priests, one scholastic brother, and one lay brother; he was spared the local rivalries which were then paralysing the work of the Oblates in Ceylon. From the very outset, his dealings with the other two vicars apostolic of South Africa were trustful and cordial. There were no disputes with his immediate neighbor, Bishop Devereux, about territories belonging to their jurisdiction. As a matter of fact, feeling that his territory was far too extensive, Bishop Devereux had himself taken the initiative to have it divided, and although the Propaganda, lacking complete data, had left the boundaries of their circumscription undecided at certain spots, neither party had any thought of using this to his own advantage. To assure the validity of the ministry in those undecided places, the two prelates even delegated their powers to each other. Moreover, the newly arrived vicar apostolic sought the advice of his colleagues regarding pastoral problems affecting the European population in order to harmonize his method of procedure with theirs and to settle problems of conscience as they did.[138] More fortunate than their brother Oblates who had arrived in Canada in the dead of winter with all its snow, the missionaries found the climate in Natal both inviting and pleasant.[139] Lastly, the people were congenial. Their newspaper *The Colonist* gladly welcomed the arrival of the missionaries who had come "to take up their excellent apostolic work." The Catholics of the vicariate, who had been without the services of any priest, rejoiced that their abandonment had come to an end; most of the Protestants, for their part, evidenced no hostility. There was only one isolated case in which a Protestant minister urged his parishoners "to throw the Roman envoys back into the sea." [140]

Bishop Allard and his Oblate confreres spent two weeks at Durban, at that time a town of about two thousand inhabitants; the town included only twelve or fifteen flimsy thatch-roofed houses and was still visited by lions, leopards, and snakes. The rest of the population lived in huts.[141] The missionaries immediately rented one of these rather makeshift dwellings, one room of which they turned into an oratory, and then set out in search of Catholics. They numbered no more than one hundred, and there were many mixed marriages and unbaptized children among them. The vicar apostolic decided that they should be given a mission so that their faith might be renewed. For a very good reason, no doubt, he did not elaborate on the success of the mission which he had assigned to Father Dunne, the only one of the missionaries with a suitable knowledge of English. Nor did he remain very long in Durban, leaving there on April 1, and taking up residence at Pietermaritzburg, the most important and the most centrally located town of the vicariate and the seat of the colonial government.

Pietermaritzburg, as well, contained about two thousand inhabitants including those in the garrison; the house in which the vicar apostolic took up residence had to serve both as a dwelling and a place of worship. They therefore set about the task of building a chapel and thus became masons; however, zeal is no substitute for ability and, much as they wanted to build, they discovered to their grief that the bricks they had made could not be used. Besides this manual labor they made apostolic journeys to contact Catholics who were scattered over a vast territory. This involved trips of from 25 to 40 miles, and they had to be made on foot since carriages were out of the question; in fact, there were not even enough funds to rent horses.

As soon as the missionaries returned from these exhausting and rather fruitless journeys, they were subjected to the severest kind of schedule by the vicar apostolic who had no intention whatsoever of allowing them any relaxation. Their poverty was extreme, on principle no doubt, but also by necessity. All they had were a few pieces of frayed linen, some shabby clothing, and meals reduced to a minimum and poorly prepared; as for the domestic comforts inside the episcopal palace, they defied all description.

If Bishop Allard forced his missionaries to live impecuniously, it was because he himself was suffering from a grave lack of funds. Before the vicariate had been erected, Bishop Devereux had sent Father Murphy into Natal on an inspection tour to gather data to support his proposal for the erection of a new vicariate. At that time, Father Murphy felt justified in reporting that the Catholics of that very rich area would be able to provide a livelihood for the missionaries. On the strength of that report the Propaganda felt dispensed from any unneeded generosity. Now, shortly afterwards, wars between the Zulu tribes within the colony caused an exodus of many colonists to the gold mines of Australia. Those who remained behind, instead of cultivating the land, which would have been very profitable, preferred to engage in commerce, a far less laborious field. As a result, there was a surplus of merchants which greatly reduced the business and earnings of each one. Since methods of communication were indirect and slow, it would take time for the Propaganda to be notified and informed of the need of funds, and for the money allotted to arrive at its destination. Being in dire straits, Bishop Allard, who was never prone to take risks in money matters, simply regulated his budget according to the meagre funds he had on hand.

Very strict with himself, the prelate, who did not stir from his residence, accommodated himself to a harsh regulation which was entirely unsuited to his exhausted fathers when they returned from their arduous journeys. Having been a master of novices for a long time, he still held to habits and methods which he had cultivated in that former position and which he felt should be retained for the sanctification of his colleagues. In entirely different surroundings, under entirely different conditions, and dealing with men of entirely different ages, the prelate, therefore, treated his missionaries exactly as he had treated the novices he had trained for the religious life, subjecting them to the same mortifications and the same ordeals. Highly esteemed by Bishop de Mazenod because he was the embodiment of the Rule, Allard intended to fashion his subjects to his own image, constantly making them observe every detail of the Rule, frequently reprimanding them, and forbidding them to do anything without his express permission. Lastly, there was nothing cheerful in living with this saintly man who was always serious and stern. All this, therefore, brought on such tension that very soon his missionaries could stand it no longer, and two of his companions, Father Dunne and Brother Compin, deserted him. Thus were verified the fears of Bishop Guigues and those of the Canadian Oblates.

With half his effectives gone, the bishop, consequently, had only one priest, since Brother Logegaray was still only a deacon. Bishop de Mazenod immediately sent him reinforcements of one priest, a scholastic deacon, and a lay-brother, but they would not arrive until January 21, 1854; they had been granted free passage on the warship *Belle Poule* and had to wait for it to get under way; since the ship, without touching Africa, had sailed to Bourbon Island, they were detained there for two months before they could find a ship to take them to Durban.

In the meantime, Bishop Allard had to station his extremely reduced personnel as best he could to minister to the three main centers of Catholics, Pietermaritzburg, Durban, and Bloemfontein. He had to rely upon Father Hoenderwangers who had been loaned to him by Bishop Devereux when the vicariate had been erected, to take care of Bloemfontein. The town, which was a two-week journey from Pietermaritzburg, contained, at the most, "100 Catholics," 45 of whom were soldiers.[142] The prelate remained in charge of Pietermaritzburg, assisted by Father Loge-garay who was ordained a priest in December, 1852, and who would also defect, in August, 1856. Father Sabon was assigned to Durban.

In addition to devoting their time to the ministry, at Pieter-maritzburg, the Oblates undertook the construction of a chapel on a plot of land given to them by the colonial government. Blancheton, the consul, took the initiative by opening a subscrip-tion in the Cape province and by obtaining financial assistance from the Protestants; this helped the missionaries somewhat to pay for the construction work. However, the efforts that had to be made to reach the scattered faithful were far from easy. If they had been concentrated in one place, one priest would have been enough to serve the whole vicariate since there were barely five hundred of them;[143] instead, the missionaries had to travel for miles and miles to come into contact with these tiny settlements. The very meagre results they achieved amounted, therefore, to only a tiny flock which, until then, had been neglected. Then too, only the Europeans, both military and colonial, were being served. But it was principally to minister to the Zulus that Bishop de Mazenod had sent the Oblates, and he constantly reminded Bishop Allard of that fact; the vicar apostolic was instructed, therefore, to concentrate on the evangelization of the pagans instead of allow-ing his efforts to be monopolized by a minority of more or less fallen-away Catholics.

Allard made no attempt at this until 1855; the reinforce-ments which arrived in January, 1854, and which were intended for the Zulu missions could not be used for that work until they perfected their English and learned the local dialects. Now, these dialects presented extreme difficulties of pronunciation for the Europeans, and, at that time, could only be learned orally since there were no dictionaries or grammars in existence. To begin learning these dialects, the fathers had to rely on the English-speaking Zulus and, since most of these were employed by Protes-tant missionaries who forbade them to act as interpreters for Catholic priests, the Oblates had great difficulty obtaining their indispensable help. Because of this lack of special facilities, there-fore, progress in learning the language could only be painful and slow. As for speaking the language, Bishop Allard never became a skilled polyglot. Although he composed a Sesuto vocabulary in Basutoland for his own use, he never excelled in teaching catechism in that dialect. As for his English, Father Barret serves as our authority regarding what the vicar apostolic accomplished in that direction:

I accompanied His Excellency during his visits among my Catholics whom he wanted to meet. Good Lord! What a torture it was! . . . On Confirmation day, he insisted on preaching for almost three quarters of an hour. Naturally, no one understood him. It was pitiful! [144]

Fortunately, one of his missionaries, Father Gerard, finally succeeded in mastering the local dialects, and as soon as he had a grasp of the rudiments, it was decided to go into action.

The main problem was "where to begin" in the vast field open to them in Natal. In a letter to Bishop de Mazenod, Bishop Allard admitted his quandary since, of three possible solutions, all of which were unsatisfactory, he was forced to find the least unsatisfactory:

At the extreme end of the colony—that is, in the kingdom of Panda —Protestant missionaries have already established mission stations; west of the colony there are some communities governed by the Boers, who have always been openly hostile to the Catholic religion; south of the colony are the tribes which are at war with England. Which of these three localities will we choose? . . . We, ourselves, have no answer to that. That is why we continually pray God to direct us.[145]

Eventually, Bishop Allard chose a spot sixty miles from Pietermaritzburg "which had not yet been infected by heresy" and was located in a valley belonging to Chief Dumisa. Fathers Barret and Gerard then set out on February 27, 1855, with an African as their guide. "The chief gave [our two envoys] a friendly reception," the vicar apostolic wrote in a report to the Lyons Propagation of the Faith;

he allowed them to select a place on his land which would be most suitable for an establishment, and this place, finally chosen as the first of our mission stations among the Zulus, . . . was placed under the protection of Saint Michael.[146]

The two missionaries began by building "a small circular hut, eight feet in diameter," which served as a lodging and oratory, and which they opened for worship on September 2, 1855. Although this oratory was very simple it made a deep impression on the local people who had come to the opening out of curiosity. In a letter to his parents, Father Gerard wrote:

It would be very difficult to give you a description of this gathering of black people. They looked wide-eyed at the priestly vestments and the pictures hanging on the posts. They were enraptured by everything. To them our sorry little chapel was greater than a magnificent cathedral.[147]

Unfortunately, the missionaries were soon forced to admit that the effect produced upon the Zulus was only one of admiration. Although they agreed to come to listen to the missionaries' instructions and even to sing the *Veni Creator* with them, repeating it immediately afterwards from memory, nothing could lift them out of their indifference. Protestant pastors, with all their years of preaching and the financial means at their disposal, had not converted any of them. The Oblates, in their turn, met the same difficulties. Bishop Allard, after stressing the principal moral difficulty, polygamy, put special emphasis on the difficulties which sprang "from the nature of the people": "These people are proud and haughty," and while they readily welcome the white missionaries solely for the advantages they hope to gain from them, they do not at any price intend to adopt what those missionaries call their "civilization." They are perfectly resigned to grant the white man three things: to hire themselves out to him, to pay him taxes, and to attend his religious services each Sunday. "But," they add, "let there be no talk of changing our customs and habits!" Furthermore, and this is the most serious obstacle, they are completely lacking in any desire for religion. The vicar apostolic even reached a point of regretting that they had no idols to be overthrown. Idolatry would be better "than this indifference with which they look upon Christianity." As for any religion, they "have only a vague idea of the Divinity and pay Him no formal homage." [148] Long and patient effort among these poor people would have been necessary to make them receptive to the mysterious realities of faith. But only fifteen months after the arrival of the Oblates, the Zulus of Saint Michael were forced to flee before the army of chief Dumisa who had originally welcomed the fathers, but who now claimed ownership of the whole valley.[149] On July 23, 1856, Bishop Allard decided to abandon the mission station.[150]

Bishop de Mazenod was sorely disappointed by the failure of the Saint Michael mission:

There is reason to be grieved about the failure of your mission among the Zulus. There are few examples of such unproductiveness. Think of it! Not a single one of those poor infidels to whom you were sent has yet opened his eyes to the light you are bringing them! It is difficult for me to find any consolation, for you were not sent [to Africa] to minister to the few heretics who people your town, but to the Africans, and it is their conversion that the Church expects from the sacred mission she intrusted to you. Therefore, all your attention must be given to them and all your plans must be made for their benefit. It is imperative that all our missionaries realize this and that they be convinced of it.

Bishop de Mazenod cautioned the vicar apostolic not to be discouraged by the failure of this first attempt and suggested that, before he make a second attempt, it might be advantageous for him to consider a change in his approach to his mission—"I would be very pleased if you were to make a survey of your vicariate. A missionary bishop should not remain within his episcopal residence. You should mingle with the people to whom you were especially sent" [151]—and in the treatment of his confreres. Bishop de Mazenod who had been deeply grieved by the defections of Father Dunne and Brother Compin in 1852 was no doubt aware that the responsibility for them was not unilateral. Since that time, Father Sabon had become discouraged and had been requesting that he be recalled. Moreover, in August, 1856, Father Logegaray had withdrawn on his own[152] after some "odd behavior" which was astonishing, coming as it did from a young missionary for whom the superior general had had such great hopes.[153] To add to it all, Father Barret was beginning to feel a "distaste" for his work. Bishop de Mazenod was willing to overlook the fact that Barret "should feel a repugnance toward teaching" since "that is not our vocation." Although in certain cases it is necessary to adapt oneself to it, that does not warrant attributing his aversion "to his wounded vanity," as Bishop Allard had done. "Aren't you a bit harsh in judging him that way?" asked Bishop de Mazenod.

Personally, I can excuse such repugnance in a missionary who was sent to convert infidels, but I cannot excuse his lack of zeal for the conversion of the Africans. That is his special mission. He was sent for that, just as others of his brother Oblates were sent for the conversion of Indian tribes in Canada, while others were sent for the conversion of the orientals in India. *Euntes Praedicate!* I say that I cannot excuse it, but I can understand it, in view of the obstinate indifference of those poor infidels.

This lesson in understanding given without severity, led to another: "I cannot recommend too strongly, my dear Bishop, that you be a kind father to all of them and at all times. You realize, I am sure, that these dear sons have only you to comfort them in affliction." [154]

The comparisons which Bishop de Mazenod saw between the negative results of the Natal missions and the apostolic success his sons had achieved elsewhere, prevented him from viewing the situation as it was. Therefore, a few months later, there came a new reprimand, even more severe than the others:

"I must confess, my dear Bishop, that your letters are always distressing. Until now, your mission has been a failure. Frankly, a vicar apostolic and a sizable number of missionaries were not sent to care for a few scattered dwellings of former Catholics. . . . The vicariate, obviously, was established in that district only for the evangelization of the Zulus. Now, we have been on the scene for several years and you have been busy with something entirely different. . . . What is especially distressing is that you make so many complaints about your co-workers. With God as your witness, ask yourself whether you should not act a little differently in dealing with them and in directing them. There has never been such disaffection. They all admire your virtues, but you lack something that will cause them to combine with their admiration that affection which makes it easier to be obedient and docile. It is frightening to see so many defections from your vicariate. . . .

As long as I am stating some distressing facts, please allow me to add that I feel you are acting a little too much like a European bishop;

that is, that you are abstaining a little too much from the active ministry in order to concentrate on administration. I see vicars apostolic
elsewhere putting a hand to the plow like any other missionary. . . .
In order to carry out the functions proper to their office, they learn
the languages of the countries they are in, however arduous that study
might be. In brief, they are in command of everything which zeal for
the salvation of infidels might demand. It seems to me that you are
not acting this way, and the failure of your mission up to now may be
due to the system you follow. . . . As for the difficulty which causes
you to think that it will be several years before you succeed, that difficulty is no greater than it is in other places where the work was begun
immediately. It took our Ceylon missionaries only six months to learn
the Cingalese tongue, and yet it, too, was very difficult. The same thing
holds true of Oregon. Why does it take more than a year to be fluent
in the African language? . . . For that, however, a sense of duty is
needed as a stimulant and an aid for overcoming difficulties. Please
tell that to our fathers. But, I repeat, you yourself must set the example, since you, too, have been sent to lead the Africans to the knowledge of the truth.

I urgently beg you, my dear Bishop, not to be displeased by these
remarks. I make them only for the sake of doing good and of fulfilling
an obligation of conscience. Rest assured that I appreciate your good
intentions. No one knows better than I how difficult it is to govern
men. And it is my long experience which prompts me to suggest that
you do not try to fashion everyone in the same mold and that you try
to get as much as you can from each one with gentleness and graciousness. God be with you, my dear Bishop; I send you my warmest re-
gards.[155]

Although Bishop de Mazenod found it difficult to understand
how the obstacles in Africa could be so different from those which
his Oblates had so successfully surmounted elsewhere—as is
evidenced by what he wrote about the Zulu dialects—at least, he
was aware from then on that, in spite of Allard's virtues, the vicar
apostolic he himself had chosen did not know how to adapt himself to a situation or how to handle confreres demoralized by his
severity.

Bishop Allard was the type of man who knows how to accept
reproval, and, instead of becoming disheartened by his setbacks,
humbly pursues his task. Although he lacked initiative and sure-
sightedness, he remained an exemplary religious in discharging

his episcopal duties, humbly submissive not only to the orders but even to the simple suggestions of his superior general. Confined until then within his residence, where he had been leading the cloistered life of a religious with scrupulous punctuality, the prelate decided to "make a survey" of his vicariate, and, in March, 1858, went to join Fathers Gerard and Bompart who were attempting to re-establish the Saint Michael mission. The bishop had obtained a grant of 500 acres from the English government, and these adjoined 6,000 acres which had been specifically declared a mission reserve. At least there was no longer fear of any attack by Chief Dumisa in that location since the reserve was under the protection of the British government. The prelate certainly deserved great credit for acting against his own preferences in this way and for changing a daily routine so carefully regulated by the clock. This holy bishop was anything but an outdoors man and yet, because of his lack of money and his spirit of poverty, "he made practically the entire journey on foot and under a burning sun"; Father Gerard wrote:

he arrived here, completely exhausted, hardly able to stand up. I think that Monseigneur should go a bit easier on himself. These journeys are too long and too arduous for elderly people, especially when they are made on foot.[156]

At least the prelate had a place in which to rest, since the two priests had, inside of a month, built a hut; not without difficulty, however, inasmuch as their only tools were two small hatchets and two sickles. They still had to build a chapel, and this involved much toil since all the needed materials had to be hauled by hand from a distance of six miles. Although he had no special talent for this kind of work, Bishop Allard did his share, just as he shared the chores of cooking, cleaning, and finding food supplies, with all the humility and simplicity of a novice. By July, 1859, they were finally able to open the new chapel with a pontifical Mass. Then came the first disappointment: although the missionaries had visited the surrounding villages to invite the Zulus to the ceremony, only "between 80 and 100" accepted the invitation. To make matters worse, the village chiefs who were present looked "entirely downcast" and "the congregation shared their gloom." [157] Thenceforth, the people who wanted to attend were brought together every Sunday; during the week, Bishop Allard and his fathers went out in search of those in the country-sides, exhausting themselves in the effort to attract them. The people merely listened to them respectfully, but no one wanted to be converted. The most the missionaries were able to accomplish was to baptize dying children, under the guise of curing them by washing them from head to foot. Months passed and the poor vicar apostolic found himself repeating the same sad reports. The morale of the missionaries worsened, and Father Gerard even reached the point of concluding "All seems hopeless in this district. The natives are becoming more and more obdurate." [158]

Far from giving up, the poor vicar general went in search of more promising territory in the Évète valley on the northern bank of the Umzimkulu river, 20 miles from its mouth, and in 1860, made a third attempt in Zulu country.[159] It is understandable that he named this mission Our Lady of Sorrows. What Father Gerard wrote to Bishop de Mazenod concerning it is equally as gloomy as the reports the vicar apostolic sent the founder concerning the preceding foundations:

Reverend Father: how sad all this is. I know that always hearing such distressing news must be very painful for you who are so wholeheartedly and zealously devoted to the interests of our Lord. It is also heartbreaking for us to witness the obstinacy and refusal that persist day after day. Why should we not weep when we think of the eternal abyss into which these infidels will be hurled as they continue to laugh, dance, and indulge in sinful pleasures. Every day is a feast. In the space of only two months, they have slaughtered more than thirty cows or oxen to gorge themselves and to honor and placate the spirits of their ancestors. Consequently, I cannot help but look upon each village as a villa of the ancient Romans. There are just as many pleasures here, less refined, of course, but still equally effective in keeping these souls out of the kingdom of God.[160]

Bishop de Mazenod died without the consolation of knowing that, after so many disappointments, the mission of South Africa began to have a little success. On August 23, 1861, Bishop Allard and his confreres abandoned the mission of Our Lady of Sorrows where, "just as at Saint Michel, the Africans refused the divine seed we wanted to plant in their hearts." [161] They then crossed the mountains to evangelize Basutoland, and it was there, through an abundant harvest, that they reaped a reward for work which had been fruitless for a time but which they had carried on for seven years. Before he died, Bishop de Mazenod had predicted:

The moment will come when the merciful grace of God will effect a sort of explosion and your African Church will take shape. For that to happen, perhaps you will have to go a little deeper into the territory of these peoples. If you find some who have not already been won over to heresy and who have not had any dealings with white people, you will very likely win over the greater number of them.[162]

FRANCE

ENGLISH CHANNEL

0 50 100 150 km.

PARIS

Nancy
+N.D.de Sion

Quimper

Orléans

Angers Blois N.D.
de Cléry

Autun

ATLANTIC

Loire

Seine

OCEAN

Limoges

Vienne

Lyon

N.D.
de l'Osier

Parménie

Isère

Rhône

Valence

Grenoble

Bordeaux Talence

Allier

Romans

Gap

Largentière

Ardèche

Rhône

N.D.
de Laus

FRANCE

N.D. de +
Bon Secours

N.D. des Lumières

Durance

Garonne

Avignon
Cavaillon

Apt

Aix

Fréjus

MEDITERRANEAN

Bastia

Vico
Ajaccio

Marseille
le Calvaire, Montolivet
N.D. de la Garde

MEDITERRANEAN

Chapter Five

The Oblate Congregation (1837–1861)

GROWTH OF THE CONGREGATION IN FRANCE

As these foreign missions multiplied, the Oblate Congregation itself expanded steadily. Until it undertook this work, its numbers had increased very little. Even the promotion of its founder to the see of Marseilles had not effected any appreciable gains. In fact, only 5 made their perpetual profession in 1837, 4 in 1838, 4 in 1839, 6 in 1840, and 4 in 1841. In that year, those in perpetual vows numbered only 59.

In 1841, however, vocations increased dramatically when the founder broadened the congregation's field of activity by sending the first group of missionaries to Canada. This was God's reward for the founder's apostolic daring and for the supernatural spirit which had induced him to offer assistance to Bishop Bourget in spite of the small size of his community. He firmly believed that any work willed by God would be providentially supplied with the necessary means for that work, and in point of fact, on the day the founder died, his congregation numbered 6 bishops, 267 priests, 53 scholastics, and 89 coadjutor brothers, a total of 415 professed Oblates; in twenty years, therefore, its ranks had increased sevenfold;[1] during the same period, the number of houses similarly increased from 8 in 1837 to 54 in 1861. This rapid progress was, no doubt, aided by the missionary impetus which Pope Gregory XVI transmitted to the Church and which characterized the nineteenth century, but it was also the result of the broadening of the congregation which had ceased to be regional and had branched out from the South, first to the whole of France and then to other nations. In fact, by 1861 the congregation numbered among its members 20 priests, 19 coadjutor brothers, and 13 professed scholastics of English or Irish nationality; 15 priests and 4 coadjutor brothers of Italian nationality; 9 priests, 3 brothers, and 2 professed scholastics from Canada; 4 priests and 1 scholastic from Belgium; 2 priests and 2 brothers from Switzerland; 1 Spanish priest, 1 German, 1 Hollander, 1 Luxemburger, and a coadjutor brother from the New York diocese.

It is rather interesting to note that the initiative for creating the congregation's recruitment program outside the southern provinces of France came from Canada; the initiator, a Father Leonard Baveux. Originally a Sulpician and a pastor of Montreal, he had seen in the Oblates an ideal consonant with his aspirations and, in 1843, had become a professed Oblate. Accustomed to doing things with dispatch, he could not resign himself to his religious family's sending missionaries in numbers so completely disproportionate to the demands of the vast expanses of the New World.

From the moment he entered the congregation, he was thoroughly convinced that Oblate vocations in France were few in number because the Oblates were not sufficiently known. This conviction constantly preoccupied him and gave birth to the idea of going back to France . . . and recruiting subjects who were sorely needed in America. He then made his plan known. Numerous objections were made. . . . Finally, he was pointedly reminded that several others smarter than he had made similar attempts and had failed. . . . With his customary good humor, he replied that he would succeed where the smart ones had failed, precisely because he was less intelligent than they.[2]

Eventually, Father Guigues yielded to his urgings and, in October, 1846, he sailed to France to begin his campaign.

His initial conquest was of the founder himself. Rather skeptical at first about the results Baveux hoped to achieve,[3] the prelate was intrigued by the zeal, enthusiasm, and cheerfulness of this recruiter whom he had not chosen and who had forced himself upon him. In fact, instead of restricting Baveux's field of action to the territory he had chosen the superior general decided that he should visit every seminary and college not only in France, but in Savoy and Belgium as well. With this encouragement, Baveux worked feverishly and succeeded beyond all expectations: within four months, twenty-four applicants had entered the novitiate. The superior general wrote to him:

Dear Father Leonard,

What sort of man are you? You break through every door and storm every fortress. Nothing stops you; and if, by chance, a bishop wants to retain his subjects, he has to forbid you to speak to them, like the good archbishop of Chambery did (I thought he was more generous than that). The bishop of Annecy made up for it by being doubly generous. Did you ever meet anyone kinder, more zealous, more unselfish and more church-minded? And his priests are just like him and follow in his footsteps. Why, even missionary societies are letting you have some of their members! It is unbelievable! You see how right I am in wanting you to visit every diocese. Father Burfin gave you wrong advice when he dissuaded you from doing at Grenoble what you have been doing everywhere else. Carry out your mission and don't worry about the opinion of this one or that one. Always keep me informed about your schedule so that I'll know where to write you; and don't forget to tell of your successes, or even your setbacks, if you have any.[4]

A few months later, rather than checking the missionary's zeal— as he was being advised to do—the prelate encouraged him:

As I have told you, no matter how efficient the postal service is, there is no way of keeping up with you. You go from conquest to conquest, and the houses which are to receive your recruits now have to be enlarged completely. Let me assure you that the trouble your success is causing us does not make me shed any tears. I chuckle over the concern which our good Father Tempier feels; he keeps telling me: "Stop this bully who has us in desperate straits; he'll be the ruination of us!" I assure you, I simply laugh in his face when he wipes his brow. He always ends up by laughing himself and by agreeing that you have taken him at his word.[5]

Tempier was not the only one wiping his brow. Father Vincens, the novice-master, who no longer knew where to find room for the newcomers, was also worried and wanted to see the flow halted. Bishop de Mazenod refused; he wrote to Baveux:

No! I am not the least frightened by your miraculous draught of fishes. Keep on casting your nets. Remember the widow in the days of

Eliseus . . . *Stetitque oleum.* I fear this *Stetitque oleum.* That is the reason why I want always *auferre vasa* and never to say, "That's enough!" This is a time of grace and we must take advantage of it.[6]

A second novitiate was opened at Nancy. Caring for 67 postulants, however, created financial problems that seemed insurmountable. The superior general therefore decided to interrupt the drive for recruits. On October 27, he wrote to Baveux:

There is no longer any room for newcomers. There is no money to feed them. The flag must be lowered, in spite of our courage. And so, *flens dico,* halt your very fine work. I swear no sacrifice has ever cost me more than this one. To be forced to reject help from God and to divert the rich spring which would have so abundantly supplied all our missions—that is harsh! It is heartbreaking! and it happens precisely at the moment when our heavenly Father's field of harvest is opening to us. Oh well, an end to regrets! We cannot do the impossible. Let us wait with resignation. Perhaps God will provide later. Halt your journeying since God has disposed things in this way.[7]

The prelate soon changed his mind, however. Less than two weeks later, he wrote to Father Baveux:

Sufficient for the day is the evil thereof. The thought of how poor we are is what caused me to write to you to tell you to suspend your drive for recruits. But lo and behold! I have just learned that another recruiter, as skilled as yourself, is about to visit all the dioceses of France to enlist any ecclesiastic who might be willing to join the society in whose behalf he is preaching. We cannot afford to delay. It would be useless to visit any place in which he has been; it is important, therefore, to get the jump on him. And so, my dear Father Leonard, put on your walking shoes, or, to put it better, take up your cross and go out in search of the vocations God has destined for us. . . . Go then! God be with you! May the Lord bless your undertaking! I feel confident that He will furnish us with whatever we need to take care of those vocations.[8]

Nothing further was needed for the missionary to resume his miraculous draught of fishes. During 1847 and 1848, a total of 115 received the habit in the two novitiates; progress was finally being made in France. Understandably, it did not maintain the same rhythm since the 52 professions made in 1848 marked a ceiling for that period and was not reached again during Bishop de Mazenod's superiority. However, from 1849 to 1861, with a total of 326 oblations, that is, 267 priests and 59 coadjutor brothers, an average of 25 a year was maintained.

From then on, 43 dioceses furnished recruits. The southern and southeastern dioceses led the rest: Grenoble took the lead with 24 priests and 22 brothers, followed by Valence (23 and 5), Viviers (13 and 6), Fréjus and Avignon (14 and 1 each), Le Puy (13 and 1), Ajaccio (11 and 3) Marseilles (11 and 1); the last diocese gave an average of only one vocation a year; as for Aix, the birthplace of the congregation, its diocese furnished only 4 priests. On the other hand, progress in the West was quite noticeable: Quimper (16), Le Mans (10), Laval (8), Vannes (7), and Rennes (7). The same was true for the East: Nancy (20), Saint Die (14), Metz (8), Lyons (8), and Cambrai (8); all of this marked a hopeful beginning. Moreover, this increase of recruits was matched by the increase in the number of the congregation's houses in its native land. Until 1840, it numbered only 8 communities: Aix (1816), Notre Dame du Laus (1818), the Calvaire at Marseilles (1821), Marseilles' major seminary (1827), Notre Dame de l'Osier (1834), Notre Dame des Lumières (1837), Ajaccio seminary in Corsica (1834), and Vico (1836). From 1841 to 1860, 15 new foundations were established: Parménie (1842), Notre Dame de Bon Secours (1846), Limoges and Nancy (1847), Notre Dame de la Garde and Notre Dame de Sion (1850), Fréjus major seminary and Notre Dame de Talence (1851), Valence major seminary at Romans (1853), Notre Dame de Cléry (1854), Montolivet scholasticate (1854), Quimper major seminary (1856), Autun (1858) and Paris and Angers (1860).

THE MAJOR SEMINARIES AT QUIMPER AND ROMANS

Three of these were only temporary foundations: Parménie, the Romans major seminary, and the Quimper major seminary.

In 1842, Bishop de Mazenod reluctantly accepted the shrine at Parménie where pilgrimages to our Lady had been restored by a former constitutional priest, Father Marion, who, after joining the *Little Church*, had fallen into Messianism, a forerunner of the form taught by Vintras. The founder quickly realized that this residence, atop an uninhabited hill where the missionaries were left isolated during the entire winter, was better suited to hermits than to missionaries. He felt that instead of maintaining a house which offered no prospects for the future and which was only about twelve and one-half miles from Notre Dame de l'Osier, it would be more advantageous to have his fathers settle in a new section where they would be able to do useful work and find vocations. He therefore abandoned Notre Dame de Parménie without the least regret.

But he was extremely distressed, in fact offended, by the double setback he suffered at the major seminaries of Quimper and Romans which his congregation was forced to relinquish almost simultaneously. In 1856, Bishop Sergent, the bishop of Quimper, proposed to Bishop de Mazenod that the direction of major seminary there be entrusted to the Oblates, a proposal the founder immediately accepted because he wanted to involve his sons more and more in the essential work of the training of clergy, and because he felt it would offer them access to pious Brittany where they would find vocations for their institute. Thus, without specifying any conditions, he gave Bishop Sergent *carte blanche* "to decide what would be suitable," [9] feeling confident that whatever he decided would be agreeable to both of them. Besides, he could not afford to be too demanding, since, for a time he was limited to sending only the superior and another Oblate, Fathers Lagier and Bellon. He planned to complete the professorial staff as soon as possible, at which time the formal contract would be signed. Until then the diocesan priests who had been teaching there would remain in charge, and the former treasurer would supervise financial affairs.

In spite of the disadvantages connected with such a temporary and poorly defined arrangement, and in spite of the delicate problems posed by the collaboration of the new arrivals with the former professors, both sides were delighted with the way things were proceeding. Father Lagier and Father Bellon had nothing but praise for the fine welcome they had received from the bishop, the vicars general, the seminary staff, and the students; Bishop de Mazenod thanked Bishop Sergent in behalf of his fathers who, he assured him, "were repaying him in devotion for the favors you have done for them." [10] On December 9, he wrote enthusiastically to Father Soullier that the Quimper house was "going along beautifully," and that "bishop, clergy, and seminarians are delighted with it and are proving their delight in word and action." [11] On January 8, 1857, the prelate took advantage of the peace and quiet he was enjoying at Montolivet to express his gratitude once again to his Quimper colleague for

the many acts of kindness you shower upon my good Fathers Lagier and Bellon. They are forever telling me about them and expressing their heartfelt gratitude. Please accept my own gratitude for what concerns me personally. You will always find me ready to cooperate with you wholeheartedly. We both have but one aim: the greater glory of God and the salvation of souls. How then could we not agree? It seems to me that I would retreat only in the face of the absolute impossible. There are some things which appear to be weak only in the beginning, but they improve as time goes on. I know that from daily experience.[12]

In February, the Bishop of Marseilles and the Bishop of Quimper met in Paris and made plans to sign the final contract. Bishop Sergent even urged the founder to send the rest of the Oblates needed to replace all the diocesan priests who were still teaching at the seminary. The two prelates made an appointment to meet again in July to sign the final agreement, and agreed that during his return trip from England, Bishop de Mazenod would again go through Brittany and visit a Marian shrine near the town of Saint Pol-de-Léon which Bishop Sergent had offered him and which Father Lagier had been urging him to accept.[13] Finally, in May, the Oblate General Council approved the appointment of Fathers Boisrame, Rambert, and Viviers to the Quimper seminary for the opening of classes the following October.[14] The temporary would then give way to the permanent.

The Bishop of Marseilles was sorely surprised, therefore, on the following August 1, while he was in Scotland, when he received a letter from Bishop Sergent, notifying him of his decision not to sign the prearranged contract and to restore the direction of his major seminary to his diocesan priests. A few difficulties had arisen it is true, regarding the contract, but Bishop de Mazenod had already conceded in the matter of a clause which Bishop Sergent had found offensive and he had every hope for agreement on all the others, since the contract, modeled on those of the Sulpicians, differed in no way from the standard contract adopted by other dioceses. The prelate had been particularly confident of being able to settle everything since Bishop Sergent on a visit to Tours that same month, far from betraying the slightest uncertainty, had been enthusiastic in his praise of the Oblates to Archbishop Guibert and "had seemed delighted that he had requested their help." [15] The reason given by Bishop Sergent to justify such an unexpected and sudden decision stung Bishop de Mazenod to the quick, and he considered it groundless and less than honest. Bishop Sergent's letter had stated: "As you know, we began with the intention of making an experiment, without considering ourselves committed to anything." [16] This *we* literally made Bishop de Mazenod's blood boil, since it very gratuitously ascribed to the Oblate Superior General an intention which he had in no way shared, and which, had it been expressed in words by his colleague, would have elicited an immediate refusal. The founder deemed it a blatant breach of trust masquerading as an initial misunderstanding. His spirited reply, therefore, blazed with indignation:

What interpretation can I put upon this inexplicable step? [You write] that "it was an experiment which did not succeed." To begin with, it was no experiment! It was a determination made in good faith by both parties. How could anyone even consider consenting to an experiment capable of such disastrous consequences? You invited the Congregation of the Missionary Oblates to your seminary because you had confidence in it, and that confidence was inspired by the congregation's experience in this work and by the blessings God has bestowed upon its work in the seminaries it has been directing for so many years. The congregation took the matter seriously and gave you some of its most outstanding members who had already proven themselves in other seminaries; they are men of learning and virtue, who have devoted themselves, heart and soul, to serving you and who have never given any cause for complaint during the year that has just ended. Furthermore, why claim that this "supposed experiment" did not succeed? I find proof to the contrary, not only in the letters you did me the honor to write, but also in the kind words you have spoken on this matter and in your frequent requests that I complete the number of directors and professors you had the right to demand; the only reason for the delay in their arrival was that you felt it wiser not to bring them to the seminary until the end of the school year. Everything had been settled about the request you again made to me in Paris last month, namely that the philosophy professor with whom you were satisfied be allowed to remain at the seminary, and this was immediately acceptable.

As for the clauses under consideration, they were no different, "radically and essentially from those you would have proposed" since they were merely the usual stipulations found in contracts which have been approved for the direction of all seminaries, and it has never entered my mind to force conditions on you.

The prelate then appealed to Bishop Sergent's sense of justice, urging him

not to take a step I consider disastrous and defamatory to the congregation at whose head the Church has placed me. No, let it not be the hand of a bishop, especially one such as you, which will leave this indelible stain upon a religious family trustfully and firmly devoted to your service. And do not say that the failure to come to an agreement has resulted from the conditions of the contract. First of all, as far as I am concerned, I cannot say so since I would be lying if I did. And even were I willing to make myself look ridiculous in the eyes of the Church because I was unable to come to an agreement with you in such a simple matter—a foolishness, the like of which could not be found in any diocese of France—it would be the same as wanting to look like a dottering old man who demands things that no one could reasonably accept, and thereby wanting the doors of every diocese closed to my congregation. No, Your Excellency, no other interpretation would be put upon it and it would soon be known all over France and in Rome that the Oblate Congregation to which, as everyone knows, the Quimper seminary had been entrusted, has been ignominiously expelled from it.

Bishop de Mazenod concluded his letter by begging the bishop of Quimper "in Christ-like compassion," to listen only to his heart, to rely only on his own judgment, and to extricate the Bishop of Marseilles from the

bizarre position I am in. What will I look like? At my age, should I expect such humiliation? Will I be able to find any consolation in knowing that the humiliation comes from you, Your Excellency, whom I had come to regard as a friend, and whose friendship I have been returning with unbounded esteem and affection? Let me know! I shall await your answer at Paris; I shall be there the day after the Assumption.[17]

In spite of these arguments and entreaties, Bishop Sergent held to his "calamitous decision"; Bishop de Mazenod, therefore, wrote to him, making a formal protest which his office as bishop obliged him to make;

but this protest will be made quietly and privately, since it is addressed to the same tribunal to which I had appealed so confidently before: your conscience. Now then, Your Excellency, before that tribunal and in the sight of God, without malice or animosity and, for that reason, without losing my esteem for you, to satisfy my own conscience and with that frankness demanded by our episcopal character, I have no hesitation in saying that you have allowed yourself to be swayed by a prejudice which has caused you to act unjustly.

After reviewing point by point what he had already stated on the matter of the supposed experiment which his colleague had regarded as temporary and unsuccessful, the prelate then made a retort to an added criticism Bishop Sergent had made; he denied

with all the vehemence of a calumniated man the treacherous and dishonest insinuations which were sent to you and which made such a strong impression on your mind. Would to God that my age, my seniority, and my feelings which I made known to you with my characteristic sincerity had inspired you sufficiently to confide in me. If you had only deemed it necessary to send for those rash detractors who certainly cannot have weighed the consequences of their assertions, I should have had no trouble disproving them entirely. If you had only taken enough time to become better acquainted with me, you would have been convinced that there is no one with a higher regard for the episcopate nor one who has defended its prerogatives more than I. . . . And yet I am the one who is supposed to influence my sons to encroach upon episcopal authority! Why, that is the most horrible calumny that could be leveled against our religious family and its head, since, as I told you at the beginning of this letter, our Oblates are essentially bishops' men, are of but one mind with them, and have no fathers other than the bishops whose sacred authority they must uphold and to whom they must bring back those who, repudiating that authority either through excess or lack of principles, have turned away from the respect and obedience due them.[18]

This second letter had no more effect than the first. In fact, the bishop of Quimper's reply was "extremely cold." [19] Bishop Sergent wrote:

Neither you, Your Excellency, nor your pious congregation will suffer any damage from my decision to cancel our agreement. Your virtues, which are highly esteemed in Rome and in France, and your long and glorious episcopate, put you above the judgment of men. If anyone must fear such judgment, it is I, whose failings and inexperience can give rise to harsh appraisals. Still I feel it impossible for me to proceed any further. I thank you for what you did so willingly.[20]

The truth of the matter was that Bishop Sergent wanted to take advantage of the fact that the agreement had not been signed and use it as an excuse for ending an experiment he deemed unfortunate. He wrote to the bishop of Nantes the following October:

I had assigned my major seminary to the Oblates of Marseilles. They are excellent religious. Nonetheless, it was an impossible situation. For many reasons, I realized that we would be bringing very serious trouble on ourselves by continuing it. Since we were only in the experimental stage, since there were only two of these gentlemen at the seminary, and since there was no signed agreement, I invoked a planned agreement, which Bishop de Mazenod had submitted and which was completely ruinous and unacceptable to me, as a reason for backing out. It would have been the same as allowing not only our seminary but the whole diocese as well to be carried off to Provence. The saintly and venerable bishop made so many objections to abandoning this conquest that I am thankful I did not wait two or three years more. A triple umbilical cord would have been harder to cut. I did not dare seek the help of another religious congregation for fear of offending the one I was dismissing, and for fear of succeeding no better with a second than I had with the first.[21]

Although Bishop Sergent alleged that there were "many reasons" for canceling the agreement, he gave only one in this letter: the tendency on the part of Bishop de Mazenod and his sons to steal vocations from the seminary. As a matter of fact, five of the Quimper seminarians had entered the Oblate novitiate from September, 1856, to May, 1857, and these joined nine others who had been attracted during Father Baveux's recruitment campaign. Perhaps Bishop Sergent felt that the exodus would continue and increase; whatever the case, he could not make an issue of it without seeming to be opposed to religious vocations within his clergy. Then too, he may have been encouraged to withdraw from the arrangement because of what he had learned of the Bishop of Valence's intentions. On August 6, 1857, the Bishop of Nevers had written to Bishop Sergent:

The poor bishop of Valence told me last year that he had decided to dismiss the Oblates from his seminary. It is impossible to come to terms with the bishop of Marseilles; he wants the whole blanket for himself.[22]

Bishop Sergent was well aware that his colleague in Marseilles would have difficulty supplying him with the teaching staff he needed since he had to be satisfied temporarily with two Oblate Fathers, and the Bishop of Ajaccio had taken it upon himself to put Bishop Sergent on his guard:

I had cause for nothing but rejoicing over the subjects which the bishop of Marseilles provided for my seminary during those first years. Would that I could say as much for those who were later sent to me, although I must say that I never had any cause for reproaching them in regard to their behavior. The frequent and continual changing of personnel had a noticeable effect on their teaching and in their direction of the seminary. I put the blame for these changes principally on the inordinate extension of this newly founded congregation; by that I mean the large number of foundations and missions it undertook in several places at one and the same time—even in the New World —in spite of the congregation's limited membership. What makes it still more regrettable is that in recent years death has robbed the Oblate Congregation of its most distinguished members.[23]

In spite of this warning, the Bishop of Quimper had proceeded with his plan to bring the Oblates into his seminary, and had not allowed himself to be deterred by the criticisms of his clergy who were opposed to the training of the diocesan seminarians by a religious congregation. It seems very likely, therefore, that in all good conscience, having gone too far to retreat, he had decided to make the experiment in spite of the risks pointed out to him. Thus a false situation was created, and the only way of preventing it would have been a frank understanding. However, knowing the bishop of Marseilles, Bishop Sergent could not very well have said to him: "We have some misgivings about seeking the help of your Oblates. If they do not measure up, we shall send them back to you." For his part, Bishop de Mazenod, who was very eager to have his Oblates assume the direction of the Quimper seminary, had agreed a little too hastily without waiting for definite commitments to be made by both parties. This bad beginning compromised everything. Now, instead of attempting to reach a frank understanding, Bishop Sergent made things more difficult for himself by nurturing the illusions of his Marseilles colleague with the high praise he showered upon Fathers Lagier and Bellon. To dispel the misunderstanding, the poor bishop extricated himself as best he could, but he went about it in the wrong way. Hence Bishop de Mazenod's indignation and typically Provençal reaction in his letter to Father Lagier:

You have been dismissed almost as though you were lackeys who had proved unsatisfactory, and this, after being eulogized up to the last minute. The alleged reasons are worthless. Quite simply, they are pretexts which are being used to justify a rank injustice. And to complete this shameful behavior which would not be expected even in dealing with worldly people, you are deceived by dishonesty and trickery up to the moment of firing when there was no time left to ward off the blow. It is staggering! For myself, whenever I think of it, I imagine I am dreaming. . . . As I told you, it was not a case of a contract broken arbitrarily by one of the parties; rather it was simply a case of throwing flunkies out of the house.[24]

This distressing setback was almost immediately made more painful by a second, felt even more sorely by Bishop de Mazenod. Under what conditions did the Jesuit Fathers succeed the Oblates at the Valence diocesan major seminary which the Oblates had taken over in 1853? Did the Jesuits themselves take the initiative or did they simply accept the offer Bishop Lyonnet made to them in seeking their help? We have two versions regarding this matter; one offered by Father Burnichon in his *Histoire de la Compagnie de Jésus en France*, and the other which emerges from the documents preserved in the Oblate archives. The versions differ, and the contradictory statements of Bishop Lyonnet, Bishop Chatrousse's successor as Bishop of Valence, only heighten the confusion.

Admittedly, things had not been proceeding well at the seminary. The handling of finances had given rise to complaints on both sides. Bishop Chatrousse felt that the superior, Father Bellon, was incurring unauthorized expenses and, as a consequence, refused to pay the salaries to which the professors were entitled. Moreover, he forced them to pay all the living expenses of the missionary house connected with the seminary, thereby putting an added strain upon the seminary budget. On the other side, the superior and bursar were at odds with each other, and the bursar ultimately left the congregation; this merited Father Bellon a severe rebuke from Bishop de Mazenod and an official order to demand that his authority be better respected by his religious subjects. Bellon took this order so literally that the seminarians nicknamed him "top-sergeant," [25] and he had to be relieved of his duties. This change, coming after so many others, justified the complaints of Bishop Chatrousse, who had been demanding more stability and competence in the professorial staff which was constantly being changed and always of an improvised nature. Lastly, the situation prevailing in the diocese helped to strain relations between Bishop Chatrousse and the Oblates, since a group of the clergy had undertaken a leaflet campaign against the autocracy of the old and ailing bishop who retaliated with suspensions, causing the suspended priests to denounce him to the State Council for abuse of authority.[26] Now, Bishop Chatrousse's administration believed that, instead of supporting it, certain Oblates at the seminary were espousing the cause of the rebels. When Bishop Chatrousse's reign was terminated by this distressing situation, Canon Craisson, who thereby received broader powers, took advantage of those powers to close the missionary house whose support the seminary was unwilling to assume. It was under these particularly difficult conditions that Father Lancenay succeeded Father Bellon to become the superior at the seminary. Determined to "lie low," Lancenay hoped that the coming of the new bishop, Bishop Lyonnet, would prove favorable to "poor religious congregations which are forever being abused by everyone." [27] This hope seemed all the more justified since the prelate, who was anxious to restore peace to the diocese, adopted a policy diametrically opposed to that of his predecessor, dismissed the preceding administration, reinstated the suspended priests, appeared to be fatherly and conciliatory, and displayed considerable confidence in the Oblates. On the basis of all this, Father Lancenay concluded that the Oblates in their turn would profit from this "turn of the tide. Our worst enemies," he wrote to Father Vincens, "those who seemed determined to destroy our work, are now completely overthrown and have been reduced to nothing." [28] A week later, however, his optimistic forecast was abruptly belied, for, on October 10, Bishop de Mazenod notified Bishop Lyonnet that he was withdrawing his fathers from the Valence seminary.

What, then, had happened? Through what Bishop Lyonnet himself has written we know that a vicar general of Valence, who had come to Saint Flour to pay his respects to the new bishop, had expressed his opinion of the Valence major seminary in very unfavorable terms and had assured Bishop Lyonnet that the seminary "had failed to meet his revered predecessor's expectations." As for that, Bishop Lyonnet assured Bishop de Mazenod:

I replied that, for the time being, I was leaving things as they were and that I had no intention of making any changes either in the personnel or the affairs of the house until I saw for myself whether or not the charges were well-founded.[29]

This would therefore explain the "affectionate tone of the welcome the good bishop" extended to Father Lancenay at Lyons on September 22, and "the unreserved confidence" he showed him. In his letter to Bishop de Mazenod, Lancenay wrote confidently and cheerfully: "The three hours he spent telling me of his fondest hopes were not long enough to suit him." [30]

Lancenay's astonishment, therefore, was extreme when, at the beginning of October, he learned from some Valence priests, who heard it from the Jesuits, that their order expected to succeed the Oblates in the administration of the major seminary. On hearing this rumor, he immediately rushed to Lyons to have it confirmed. Bishop Lyonnet admitted that he had had some discussions at Lyons on this matter with some members of the Society of Jesus; in fact, he even furnished Father Lancenay with precise details which the latter afterwards transmitted to Bishop de Mazenod. Bishop Lyonnet told Father Lancenay:

Look here! I'll tell you exactly what happened. A few days ago, I had dinner at the archiepiscopal palace with Father de Jocas and a few other Jesuit priests. Father Jocas said:

"Well, Your Excellency, it's fortunate that we did not go to Saint Flour, now that you're leaving that diocese."

"What difference does that make? You were going to Saint Flour not for the bishop but to do good there."

"Oh!" said Father de Jocas, "we could still do it in your new diocese where, so they say, you plan to dismiss the Oblates."

Lyonnet evidently deemed it wise not to say anything further to Lancenay about that particular conversation, but what the bishop went on to say proves that there had been more to it than that:

A few days later the Jesuit provincial came to see me here at Fourvière [the Jesuit house where he was making a retreat], and told me he was happy to inform me that he was writing to Rome to ask his Father General to appoint a professorial staff for the Valence major seminary which was to be assigned to them.

Bishop Lyonnet then became hazy as though he wanted to mislead the Oblate superior, but he, wishing to know precisely what to believe, suggested that the bishop deny these rumors by some positive statement. Bishop Lyonnet then lost his temper, said that he was free to do as he pleased. . . . The superior bowed and left.[31]

As soon as he returned to the seminary, Father Lancenay immediately notified Bishop de Mazenod; in view of Bishop Lyonnet's clear-cut statements, the founder attributed the sudden change that had taken place to the advances made by the Jesuit Fathers, and, on October 10, bristling with indignation, wrote to Bishop Lyonnet:

I have just received an account from Father Lancenay of the conversation he had with you; from it, I gather that you felt it advisable to take preparatory steps with the Jesuit Fathers for assigning your major seminary to them. This implies a more or less imminent dismissal of the Oblates whom your predecessor had engaged to direct that seminary. As a consequence, I had no other recourse but to recall these fathers; it would have been unfitting for them to remain in a community which had been informed of their impending dismissal and over which they would have been unable to exercise the least authority. I hereby inform you of this measure so that you might take steps accordingly. The Jesuit Fathers are quite numerous and will have no difficulty in providing you with the qualified personnel on whom you were relying after the advances that were made to you by the Father Provincial.[32]

Two days later, the bishop of Marseilles wrote to the superior general of the Jesuits to inform him of "the way your fathers transact business in these parts. I will simply give you the facts, though they unquestionably justify my adding complaints." After enumerating the facts and relating verbatim Bishop Lyonnet's conversation with Father Lancenay, and then notifying the Jesuit General, Father Beckx, of his decision to withdraw his Oblates from the Valence major seminary, Bishop de Mazenod added:

Now that his mind is at ease regarding the arrangements he made with your fathers, the bishop *"has complied with the will of God."* Such were the edifying words he used in his reply to my letter. . . . I must be too old to understand the way things are being done these days in modern society. I am simply pointing them out, fully determined never to treat anyone the same way. Please excuse the haste of my letter. I do not have time to reread it. However, I am forwarding it to you, not by way of complaint, but simply to inform you.[33]

Eventually, the prelate admitted that the Jesuit Fathers had not offered their services at that time to supplant the Oblates. The Jesuit provincial had hurried from Lyons to Marseilles to convince him of this; however, as he wrote to Bishop de Mazenod, he had left Marseilles

without the comforting assurance that I had completely dispelled the regrettable suspicions which some inaccurate reports had created in Your Excellency's mind about our conduct in the matter of the Valence major seminary. I feel sure that my explanations altered your judgment, but not sufficiently it seems. I have written, therefore, to Bishop Lyonnet, and I venture to hope that the assurances he will give Your Excellency will completely exonerate us in your eyes of a wrong which we should never have wanted to commit.[34]

The Jesuit historian, Father Burnichon,[35] writes:

After the provincial, Father Gautrelet, appealed to him, Bishop Lyonnet complied with complete honesty by writing to Bishop de Mazenod: "You know only too well how things happened to believe that the Jesuit Fathers had anything to do with the decision I have just made. . . . Consequently, great was my astonishment when, on the eve of the beginning of classes, Your Excellency notified me that you had just withdrawn your subjects. . . . Under such circumstances, I had no other choice but to look for help elsewhere, and, out of preference, I appealed to the Jesuits for whom I have the greatest esteem and affection." [36]

Father Burnichon then comments:
"That should have been sufficient to satisfy an impartial judge, but the Bishop of Marseilles was a founder and a father." [37] In all truth, the founder and father had every reason to be upset by Bishop Lyonnet's later assertions which he found so inconsistent with the explicit statements of the Bishop of Valence to Father Lancenay when he begged the prelate to deny the current rumors regarding the replacement of the Oblates by the Jesuits at the Valence seminary. Between Lyonnet's contradictory statements and the concordant and unchanging assurances of the Jesuit provincial and the Jesuit superior general, the balance manifestly was in favor of the Jesuits; why put faith in the assertions of the bishop who, at first, attributed the initiative to the Jesuits and then gave his assurance that they had no hand in his decision?

Bishop de Mazenod, who was exasperated by any kind of subterfuge, then wrote to the Lyons provincial and admitted that he had been wrong, giving reasons for his mistake in terms that were quite unflattering to Bishop Lyonnet:

Nothing suits me better than to be convinced that you did not offer your services and thereby provoke the shameful step which the bishop of Valence has just taken against the Oblates of Mary Immaculate. It would have been too painful for me who, long before any of you were born, loved your society, perhaps even more than you yourselves love it, and who, throughout my entire life, have proved my esteem and affection for it, even to the extent of compromising myself several times; I repeat, it would have been too painful for me to believe that you were capable of such dishonorable behavior. I gave you the exact account of Bishop Lyonnet's conversation with Father Lancenay, and Father is willing to affirm under oath what he related of it. What the bishop said at that time does not agree with what you affirm. I prefer to believe that you are telling the truth. A prelate with such questionable principles of justice and equity may well have very elastic ones when it comes to honesty and sincerity. I therefore admit that I was wrong and I gladly exonerate you of such a shameful initiative; such a thing would have made you the vilest of men in the eyes of anyone with a sense of delicacy and honor.

Although Bishop de Mazenod fully accepted the version given by the Jesuit General and the Lyons provincial, he still took offence at the way in which the Oblates were ousted from the Valence seminary, and bluntly said so to the Lyons provincial:

This does not mean that I exempt you of all wrong. The alacrity with which you espoused the views of a bishop who judged and condemned a religious congregation before giving it a hearing makes you guilty of collusion in this injustice. . . . How was it possible for you to accept such an arrangement? In your opinion, was this not supplanting a congregation which, admittedly, is only an atom compared to your society, but which, nonetheless, has some right to prevent any appreciable damage to its reputation? And it must be entitled to its reputation if it is to do the good which the Church has commissioned it to do for her. No, I cannot condone what you have done, and I can tell you plainly that all those who have been hearing of this incident have spoken their minds in terms that I could not repeat. I do not know what benefit you will derive from this encroachment, but it saddens me to foresee that you will suffer a great loss of esteem because of it. As for myself, I had to do what I did as soon as I perceived the underhanded tactics of the bishop of Valence. I preferred to withdraw my Oblates before they were publicly expelled and I left the field clear to you. That is my manner of acting. I always act honestly and above board. Frankness and honorableness are my distinguishing marks. I have a horror of duplicity no matter where I find it, but especially in places where one least expects to find it. And so, since I did what I had to do, let come what may! I am resigned to whatever God allows and I pray for whoever acts wrongly toward me.[38]

The Bishop of Marseilles felt that the Jesuit General should also know his "opinion about the tactless disregard of your society for the Oblates of Mary Immaculate of whom I am the Superior General." For that reason, he wrote to Father Beckx:

I cannot do otherwise than send you a copy of the letter I sent to the reverend provincial in answer to the one he felt obliged to write to me to explain his conduct. From now on, I shall say nothing further of this affair which has stirred up so much criticism of your society on all sides. I could not begin to tell you how distasteful it is to me to be forced to repress within my heart the esteem and affection I have always had, and still have, for your society; the most elementary fitness demands that I cease to manifest my well-known fondness for your society, and grant it only what is strictly demanded by charity.[39]

As evidence that he would no longer manifest his fondness for the Jesuits, the Bishop of Marseilles restricted the faculties he had granted the superior of the Jesuit community in Marseilles. He lost the right to delegate faculties to the members of his community, and, from then on, they were obliged to apply individually and directly to the chancery for permission to exercise the sacred ministry in the diocese.[40] As for Bishop Lyonnet, Bishop de Mazenod chose not to send a personal acknowledgment of the letter in which the Bishop of Valence attempted to explain his behavior and at the same time exonerate the Society of Jesus, leaving it to Father Vincens, the Oblate provincial, to explain his silence. Vincens wrote:

The transactions which forced our Most Reverend Superior General to close our house at Romans have so affected him that, not feeling equal to the task of answering Your Excellency's letters, he has commissioned me to do so.[41]

It should be added that although Bishop de Mazenod continued to believe the denials made by the Jesuit General and provincial, the Oblates, as a whole, preferred to believe that the Lyons Jesuits had volunteered their services to Bishop Lyonnet during the retreat he made at their house before assuming the see of Valence, since his presence there would have afforded them an opportunity to add the Valence major seminary to those of Montauban, Aire, and Mende which they were then directing in the province of Toulouse.

The Jesuit General, Father Beckx, "brought out the moral of the story" in a letter to the Lyons provincial, Father Gautrelet:[42]

It is always troublesome to take the place of others when they are loathe to yield it. Now that the matter has been settled, nothing more can be done except to ask God to bless the work and to urge our fathers never to criticize their predecessors at the major seminary, either in front of the seminarians or the clergy or anyone else.[43]

For his part, Bishop de Mazenod was worried about the consequences that his congregation could suffer from what Father Tortel called "the dreadful thunderbolt" at Romans,[44] at a time when he was orienting the congregation toward the training of the secular clergy. At the General Chapter of 1850, Bishop de Mazenod had, in effect, made the direction of major seminaries one of the principal works of the congregation by indicating "the principal points" which the proposed additions to the Constitutions would have to consider if the Constitutions were "to be brought into harmony with the spread" of the congregation and "with its future state."[45] After two paragraphs pertaining to the missions ("the principal end of the Institute"), two others were then proposed, discussed, and approved, the first article of which assigned another end to the Congregation of the Oblates which was qualified as *praestantior: directio seminariorum in quibus clerici, pro sua idonea institutione, versantur,* since it would be "useless" for the missionaries to labor for the conversion of sinners if the parochial clergy were not men filled with the Holy Spirit, earnestly following in the "footsteps of the Divine Shepherd and feeding with watchful and constant care the sheep that have been brought back to Him." Next there was a series of requisites governing the choice and preparation of prospective seminary directors, specifying that in addition to the intelligence, maturity, sound judgment, regularity, and piety required for such a delicate ministry, the seminary directors should possess the needed proficiency in teaching—two years of supplementary study "under a learned and experienced seminary director" would therefore be necessary; only rarely and for exceptional reasons would the seminary directors be reassigned since it takes long experience to acquire what is demanded by this work, namely, "profound knowledge of the sacred sciences, a prudent method of giving spiritual direction, and, in order to discern minds and form souls into the image of Christ the Divine Model, a wisdom acquired through prayer and experience." All the regulations were patterned on those traditionally followed at Saint Sulpice, among them, attendance at all spiritual exercises and prohibition of all outside work except during vacation periods. Great stress was put upon loyalty to the bishop and to the Sovereign Pontiff, and upon reverence for the priesthood of Christ in anyone who has received it.[46]

In his original plan, Bishop de Mazenod had foreseen no other aim for his institute than the preaching of parish missions; thus, like Saint Vincent de Paul and, before him Father Olier, he had come to realize that such a purely apostolic work required another of deeper, though of less immediate import, that of the seminaries. The same experiences of his predecessors in the seventeenth century had induced him to broaden the objectives of his congregation; salutary as it was for the moment, the influence of his Oblates in that work was of short duration because of a lack of due preparation but especially because of the lack of support from pastors animated by a genuine zeal. Now, "the dreadful thunderbolt" at Romans, following that of·Quimper, endangered the reputation of the Oblates who might be considered undesirable by bishops seeking religious to direct their seminaries. And, as a matter of fact, in 1858 and 1859, the bishops of Arras and of Saint Breuc declined the offers of Bishop de Mazenod when he volunteered the services of his sons.

SHRINES AND PARISH MISSIONS

With the exception of the failures at the Quimper and Valence seminaries, the foundations in France from 1842 to 1860, far from giving rise to disputes with the bishops, all benefited from their cooperation; the bishops either asked for the help of the Oblates or gratefully accepted the offers of their superior general. The plan of this biography, however, makes it impractical to review the history of each house. The ones that can only be mentioned, therefore, are the following: 1) the scholasticate opened at Montolivet in 1854 for the Oblate students of philosophy and theology who, from then on, no longer pursued their studies at the Marseilles major seminary; 2) the major seminary at Fréjus, which was under the direction of the Congregation from 1851 until the expulsion of religious orders in 1903; 3) the juniorate at Notre Dame de Lumières which was re-established in 1859 after abortive attempts from 1840 to 1847 and was the inspiration for Father de Foresta's *Ecoles Apostoliques*. Nonetheless, it is important to describe certain distinctive features of some other foundations which were then broadening the apostolic activity of the Oblates, in particular, those which supervised the pilgrimage shrines (Notre Dame de la Garde, Notre Dame de Bon Secours, Notre Dame de Sion, Notre Dame de Talence, and Notre Dame de Cléry) and those which had been established in cities and towns and were devoted to the preaching of missions (Limoges, Nancy, Autun, and Angers). The first group was devoted exclusively to shrines of the Blessed Virgin, thus continuing a tradition inaugurated at Notre Dame du Laus in 1818 [47] and continued at Notre Dame de l'Osier in 1834 and at Notre Dame de Lumières in 1837. Although this type of ministry seemed inconsonant with the essential end of the newly formed society, Bishop de Mazenod accepted it for his sons, recognizing in the pilgrimage the opportunity for an "on-the-spot mission" which would permit evangelizing among the faithful attracted to these shrines by their devotion to Mary and by the solemn celebrations organized in her honor. Moreover, the prelate foresaw that by establishing friendly relationships with the diocesan priests and giving them a cordial reception at these shrines, his fathers would be able to improve the morale and sanctification of the neighboring clergy.[48]

The importance he attached to this form of the apostolate explains why, in spite of these principles, he allowed the superiors of Cléry and Talence to be pastors as well. Both these places provided the Oblates with a rectory and church in good condition.

The same was not the case, however, at Notre Dame de Bon Secours in the Ardèche department; Bishop Guibert had hastily given the members of his congregation charge of this shrine so that they might "give a new start" to a place that was too lifeless to suit his taste. The Oblates assigned there were required to build a house and acquire ownership of the former college where they invited the Sisters of Saint Joseph, to establish a suitable house to accommodate women pilgrims and to make it possible to begin retreat work; the fathers also had to rebuild the church which was too small and in poor condition, and then "furnish it with beautiful altars and huge statues." The steady increase of pilgrims and their generosity ended the material problems, for, by 1862, "almost 100,000 people" were visiting the shrine every year. Spiritual progress kept pace accordingly: "500 communions each week, between five and six thousand" on one day alone, that of the patronal feast, "and a fifth of these were received by men and boys." [49]

At Notre Dame de la Garde, there was no need to rekindle fervor since the Marseillais had always been deeply attached to "la bonne Mère"; nonetheless, the means and space needed for the development of that fervor were lacking. The first thing to be done was to provide continuous service at the chapel which, until the Oblates took charge, had been served by a single chaplain who locked the chapel and left each morning after he had said Mass there. Thus, in 1833, Bishop Fortuné de Mazenod replaced this chaplain with the Oblates from the Calvaire church, and they kept it open all day. Father Semeria, the future vicar apostolic of Jaffna, inaugurated this ministry; Fathers Martin and Bernard, who succeeded him, "did much to increase the attendance and devotion of the faithful at the shrine." [50] But the distance from the Calvaire to the shrine was so great, and the hill so difficult to climb, particularly in mistral weather, that, in 1850, the founder decided to have his Oblates live at the shrine in a house bought by the Congregation. They then began enlarging the chapel, which was becoming more and more inadequate, by adding a side nave to it. This did not improve symmetry but it was the best they could do since the chapel was located within the confines of the fortress and the military authorities would allow construction only on top of the cistern. The founder considered this awkward and unattractive addition merely temporary since he was fully determined to erect a monument worthy of "la bonne Mère" and Marseilles at the top of the hill which dominated the city and its port. Such a project, however, necessitated long, involved negotiations to obtain the needed land for the military engineers were reluctant to cede land they considered indispensable for the defense of the fort. Only through the intervention of Marshal Niel was everything finally settled, and, in 1853, construction began. A financial problem now arose which was equally difficult to solve since the prelate visualized things on a grand scale. Besides his own contribution and those of the chapter, clergy, and faithful, there were proceeds from a lottery sanctioned by the government. Progress was slow and could be made only as the necessary funds became available. Bishop de Mazenod did not live to see the completion of the shrine, the plans of which were drawn by the architect Espérandieu, for it was not until 1864 that the new Notre Dame de la Garde was opened.[51]

At Sion, another "holy hill," there was no building problem since there was a church as well as an immense monastery there for the convenience of the pilgrims. The monastery was built in 1626 by two Dukes of Lorraine, Francis II and Charles IV, for the monks of the Third Order of Saint Francis (called Tiercelins), and the monks had been assigned the care of the pilgrim shrine which was deeply revered by the pious people of Lorraine. The main problem at Notre Dame de Sion was to end a schism provoked by the rebellion of three priests who were also brothers, the Fathers Baillard, who had fallen into the false mysticism of the neo-prophet Vintras. Before their rebellion, one of them, Leopold, a pastor at Favières, had been appointed by the bishop of Nancy as superior of the Brothers of Christian Doctrine, founded around 1817 by Dom Joseph Frechard and disbanded in 1830; Leopold accepted the appointment only on the condition that he be allowed to transfer the headquarters of the congregation to Sion, and that he be given permission to take up a public collection to defray the expenses of the installation. He then purchased the buildings formerly used by the Tiercelins, established the Brothers' novitiate there, opened another novitiate for the Sisters of Mattaincourt, and joined to all this a school of agriculture, arts, and crafts. It was an ambitious undertaking, even with the help of his two brothers, François and Quirin. The episcopal administration soon became worried over the independent attitude of the Baillards who acted like feudal lords and tended to exempt the church at Sion from the jurisdiction of the administrator of Chaouilley; all this provoked incidents worthy of Boileau's *Lutrin* with the administrator of Chaouilley and with the mayor of Saxon, about the vestibule which protected the shrine from drafts. Bishop Menjaud became even more concerned about the enormous expenses incurred by Leopold and his two assistants when it was rumored that they were deeply in debt. The prelate demanded an accounting and when they refused to comply suspended them and put the chapel under interdict. At first all three submitted, in February, 1848. In 1849, however, Leopold made a retreat at Bosserville and, during the retreat, an illumined Carthusian, Dom Magloire, revealed to him that the hour foretold by the neo-prophet Vintras was near at hand when the Church would be regenerated in tribulation; the enraptured Leopold then rushed to Tilly to consult Vintras, the *Oracle of the New Revelation.* He returned from Tilly, an initiate of the *Oeuvre de la Miséricorde,* a group whose aim was to prepare for the coming of the new Christian society which would succeed the Church, just as the Church had succeeded the synagogue. Declaring that Jesus Christ Himself had invested him with the plenitude of the priesthood so that he might accomplish his providential mission, Vintras consecrated the three brothers bishops: Leopold was named Pontiff of Adoration; François the Pontiff of Wisdom; and Quirin, the Pontiff of Order. Thenceforth Leopold was to be called Phréheptaël, or Divine Light, François Ephretaël and Quirin became Boephtaël. One of the nuns at Sion, Sister Thérèse, who claimed she had been favored with visions, was consecrated superioress of "The Free and Most Pious Ladies of the Merciful Love of the Divine Heart of Jesus."

One can imagine the bewilderment of the pilgrims and the parishioners of Saxon when Leopold, the new Pontiff of Adoration, vested in his new robes, revealed these absurdities to them on September 8, 1850. As a matter of fact, a schoolmaster named Morizot interrupted the pontiff, exclaiming: "Father Superior, you're crazy!" The bishop of Nancy, knowing that the bishop of Bayeux and the Council of Paris had condemned Vintraism, believed he could put a stop to this foolishness by resorting to canonical measures; the three brothers were temporarily suspended and summoned to the diocesan court. Unfortunately, they remained obdurate, meanwhile attracting about forty parishioners of Saxon to their aberration, most of whom were sodality women and girls. The Baillards discontinued their public ministry in the church, secluding themselves in the private chapel of the monastery where they celebrated their Vintrasian rites.

Faced with this very delicate situation, Bishop Menjaud appealed to the Oblates whom he had allowed earlier to open a house in Nancy at the suggestion of the founder who was eager to extend their ministry into the eastern part of France. In effect, this permission was an acknowledgment of Menjaud's gratitude to Bishop de Mazenod for having recommended him for coadjutor of Nancy after Bishop de Janson had made it impossible for him to remain in his diocese. Bishop Menjaud then appointed Father Dassy administrator of Sion and begged him to allow one of his community to reside at Saxon. Father Dassy, who had only four fathers in his community, chose Father Soulier, a future superior general, for this difficult mission. Bishop de Mazenod immediately reprimanded him for allowing his zeal to get the better of him; writing to Father Dassy, he complained:

What a disadvantage to send our young fathers to that disturbed place all alone! Had I been in your place, I should have declined such a delicate trust. You had an excellent reason for refusing, namely, that our fathers must always work in pairs, and that your community is not numerous enough to have two members taken from it.[52]

Father Dassy, however, felt that he could not refuse the help Bishop Menjaud had sought under such grave circumstances. To do away with the very real "difficulty" which was disturbing his superior general, he so arranged things that each month an alternate would be sent to relieve the missionary isolated at Saxon and living in such materially hazardous, and, what was worse, morally debilitating conditions. This system of alternating between Father

Soulier and Father Conrard continued until June 30, 1851. During that time, pilgrimages to the shrine were resumed, order restored to the parish, and minds put at ease. It was then possible for the Oblates to withdraw and to entrust the task of carrying on their work to the pastor of Vaudémont.

Meanwhile, entrenched within the monastery of the Tiercelins, the Baillards continued to defy the anathemas of their bishop and those of Rome which had likewise condemned them. They were soon forced to sell the buildings, however, in order to pay their creditors, and, in October, 1851, the new owner, Marie Lhuillier, served an eviction notice on them, and they were obliged to move. The bishop of Nancy then established the village of Saxon as a subsidiary parish, and the church of Sion was made the parish church. The Oblates of Nancy were assigned to the new parish, and Father Conrard took possession of it in September, 1853. He gradually succeeded in instilling new life into the pilgrim center, restored the dilapidated shrine, and extinguished the schism, in spite of the fact that the Baillards were still in the vicinity. In July, 1856, Bishop de Mazenod officiated at a forty hours' devotion attended by 2,000 faithful who had traveled there from the surrounding towns.

In 1868, Bishop Foulon repurchased the monastery, and the Oblates returned there the following year. Leopold and Quirin Baillard made deathbed repentances, but François refused to retract and died impenitent. Maurice Barrès, in his *Colline inspirée,* gave a magnificent tribute to the work accomplished by the Oblates of whom he made Father Aubry the prototype. At the summit of the high place, "where the Holy Spirit breathes," the energetic labors of these religious, their patience, and their sufferings had made the true spirit which breathes through the Church triumphant over an extravagant and false mysticism.[53]

The Oblate communities of Bon Secours, Sion, Talence, and Cléry, besides assuming the duties of preaching at these various shrines, devoted themselves to missions as such, but the communities at Angers, Autun, Limoges, and Nancy, devoted themselves exclusively to that form of ministry for which their congregation had been founded. The very incomplete information we possess regarding their success with these missions substantiates what we have already concluded about the religious state of other regions they evangelized: in places which had remained Christian, missions were successful, and in places where Christianity had been de-emphasized, much less so.

Father Martin points out that the successful missions in the Ardèche department in 1861 rivaled those "of time past." He noted, however, that although at Burzet, "a large village of more than three thousand souls" nestled in the mountain, the population was "very religious," the opposite was true of the people of Chomérac, which was located at "the intersection of all the main highways—these people were too concerned with business matters." At Vivarais, the missionaries were not forced to

contend with any great spirit of indifference and impiety so common elsewhere. However, although faith and piety prevail in these districts, our ministry often encounters other obstacles which are no less formidable. Familiarity with holy things often results in routine and an indifference toward the sacraments which is extremely dangerous to souls. Consequently, our ministry is probably more necessary and more fruitful among believers than it is in less religious sections. We noticed this in the last campaign when our missions reanimated so many persons who were becoming lax in their religion and corrected a thousand different faults which had crept into the reception of the sacraments.[54]

In the department of Maine-et-Loire, the missions wrought "miracles of grace and salvation. This year we have been working continually in the diocese of Angers," wrote Father Roux in 1862 . . .

We introduced the practice of having regular missions, a practice which until now has not been observed. We showed these Catholic towns the splendor of our beautiful ceremonies; the few days required for a retreat would not have been long enough to do that. The things that I could tell you! The pious rapture on the faces of these people when they attended our superb devotions! . . . The many sinners who made a sincere return to God after neglecting their religious duties for many years! As a rule, it is the leading people of a district who set the example for the rest of the people in faithfully attending all the exercises; often they are eager to help defray the necessary expenses of the mission. Several times, in spite of their high position, they asked us to allow them to carry the mission cross which they themselves had donated.[55]

In the department of Saône-et-Loire, everything varied according to the locality. In the Anost parish in the Morvan mountain region, "we witnessed one of those stirring demonstrations which live forever in the memory of a missionary: 1,200 men went in a body to the altar rail to receive Holy Communion from the hands of the bishop of Autun. His Excellency and the missionaries were deeply moved while they watched this imposing scene. "Two months after that fine mission," however, "results were decidedly less noticeable at the other extremity of the vast diocese of Autun, in a region where lack of faith and lack of religious practice seemed widespread, and the region itself impervious to any religious impression"; the mission report did observe, however, that "there were seeds of conversion which would need only a shower of grace to germinate and bear abundant and salutary fruit."[56]

In the region around Bordeaux, "it was especially difficult to give Lenten courses, retreats, and missions in towns where there was great material prosperity." In the village of Saint-Terre, "Fathers Eymère and Duclos encountered great obstacles. . . . Through self-denial, patience, and devotion, these two fathers were able to succeed, and their preaching proved surprisingly fruitful." At Villandreau, "a very materialistic region," the mission made "an agreeable impression." At Sauveterre,

the zeal of Fathers Soullier and Génin was put to a severe test. Neither of them knew anything about the problems confronting the missions of Gironde, and they had to grope their way. But the good God did not permit a work undertaken for His glory to go unrewarded. Although the Fathers returned home somewhat discouraged with the results of their labors since they had not found there the same enthusiasm as in other areas, the pastor expressed great satisfaction.

At Lafosse, "attendance at the instructions was always gratifying," but most of the inveterate sinners had turned a deaf ear to the appeal of the pastor and had stayed away from the mission."[57]

In the diocese of Orléans, which Bishop Dupanloup had

found to be "in a frightful state" when he took possession of that see, the religious situation was such that the Oblate Fathers had to discard their traditional style of mission. In 1863, Father de l'Hermite wrote to Father Fabre, the superior-general:

I need not tell you what difficulties the Orléans missions present. Seeing the religious indifference of certain localities would lead one to believe that they are completely pagan. Consequently, the ordinary weapons and traditional assaults are completely useless against such resistance. You would greatly embarrass me by asking what method we follow in these evangelical jousts. The battle plan is devised only at the moment when we are facing the enemy; more than one missionary, after arriving with nothing but a breviary, has been astounded by the gratifying success of a strategy which changes from day to day. What Bossuet said of a cadaver might well be said of this strategy: *it is a something which hasn't any name in any language.* Sometimes it is no small sacrifice to remain alone for an entire winter in towns where the Word of God merely trickles like the slow dripping of water which gradually will make an impression on the rock, and to stand alone, subjected to disapproving looks and disdainful attitudes which seem to reproach you for coming there and disturbing the peace. Consequently, when the missionary sees the distant church steeple of the modest village where he is going to catechize souls, and realizes that they will probably flee from him and that he will be unable to reach them, his eyes sometimes dim with tears and, momentarily dismayed, he yearns to be back in the bosom of his community where he is assured of finding love and encouragement. Once this feeling passes, he resolutely takes up his ardous task, gathers the children around him, gives them holy pictures and medals, and urges them to bring their parents to him; he goes in search of these lost sheep and, in this way, forms a small congregation which finally consents to listen to the Word of God. Those of our fathers who have worked on these hard missions appreciate, I am sure, the picture I have painted here and they will not accuse me of exaggeration, just as they will agree with me that everywhere in these difficult places these unconventional missions breed Christians and gradually regenerate souls.[58]

Sully was a happy exception, but Father de l'Hermite did concede that:

this parish is one of the best in the diocese, and consequently you must understand why it was easier for me to derive these consolations.

In spite of these hardships, the Oblates did not slacken their efforts to evangelize a region where their "task was not to promote the faith, but to establish it." They hoped that, through their zeal, their apostolic preaching, "which Bishop Dupanloup considered one of the principal factors in the renovation of his diocese," would eventually bear fruit and effect a genuine religious revival.[59] In fact, in her work dealing with the Dupanloup episcopate Mme Marcilhacy, after citing statistics to prove the degree to which le Loiret had been deChristianized by 1850, indicates that there was a progressive recovery which reached its peak in 1865—a recovery which, unfortunately, did not continue.[60]

In the Haute-Vienne department, there were three missions preached at the start of 1856; two of them in the southwestern part of the Limoges diocese, at Flavignac and les Cars, succeeded beyond the hopes of the missionaries since "ignorance . . . had withered any consciousness of Christian duties in the hearts of most of the people." At Flavignac, the women set the example, and communions totaled 900, 400 of which were received by men. At les Cars, "an equally unpromising parish, 500 communions were recorded for a total population of 900, and of these communions almost half were received by men. However, at Mézières, in the northwestern section of the department, the missionary soon realized that it would be useless to make

an eloquent appeal for a mission in the strict sense of the word. Consequently, he wisely limited it to some simple announcements and a small number of exercises each week. . . . That was all—in fact it was quite enough since attendance was very light, although we gave our sermons in the form of dialogues in order to attract more people. For a short time, I thought that this method of fighting singly and, so to speak, like skirmishers would be successful. That first experiment disillusioned me for good.

Father Bise, who gave the above account, understandably entitles it, "Excursion to Mézières."

La Creuse, which was under the jurisdiction of the Bishop of Limoges, had become even more deChristianized. In his report about Saint Maurice, Father Chauliac wrote:

Almost half the men of that parish work for nine months of the year in Paris or in some other city of France, and these migrations to the large cities are very harmful to the practice of religion in this region. . . . Consequently, it would have been rash to attempt to carry out any set program there at the very outset. That is the reason why I was sent alone to Saint Maurice to experiment rather than to accomplish anything specific. The population, numbering 2,000 souls, is unfortunate rather than evil; almost all the women made their Easter duty and, although only about 40 of the men were expected to make theirs, I managed to attract more than 200 of them to the altar rail on Easter Sunday.

At Saint Sulpice-les-Champs, the beginning was inauspicious. During the house visits they made to encourage the people to attend the mission, the missionaries were given "a cool and uncordial reception, and the success of that first step may be considered negligible." During the mission

the attendance was lowest on the days when we had no special ceremony scheduled and, I confess, a little of the zeal of good Saint Francis de Sales was needed to keep me from sending those who did come away without instruction. The small number of women who received communion on their appointed day made it clear to us that we would have to redouble our efforts if we were to attract even a few men. The arrival of bad weather, however, was in part responsible for our discouragement.

But the missionary was somewhat consoled by the thought that the elevation of the mission cross "in as impressive a ceremony as possible" would prepare the way for their return to a region where their ministry was so badly needed.

At Gentioux, the mission given by Fathers Coste and Bretange in 1854, "at a time of the year when most of the men were away working in other cities," had not reached "those who most needed to be led back to God." In 1856, a retreat intended to fill that gap failed, for its scheduled time coincided with a carnival then in progress. As a result, services were poorly attended, and only about twenty men received communion each day. Since that time, however, the numbers had increased and the pastor expressed his delight in seeing "almost 400 men receive communion at Easter— a very high number in comparison to that of other years." At

Peyrat-la-Nonière, on the other hand, Fathers Coste and Séjalon reported "rather consoling results: from a population of 1,700, 1,000 received communion—600 women and 400 men." The missionaries attributed this success, which contrasted so greatly with failures elsewhere, to "the influence of a zealous and able pastor" who, "in the course of his twelve years there, has successfully instructed his parish." [61] Thus, in his mission report of 1862, Father Coste drew this conclusion: "Some parishes have been so neglected, and by that very token, have fallon so low, that it is morally impossible to raise them to a Christian level in a month of preaching." [62] This substantiates what Father Bise wrote after his unfortunate experience at Mézières for it generalizes the judgment which he made about the pastor of Mézières who, as he remarked, could not pass as a model "evangelizer of all time. That remark, which is true of all districts, is especially true of this diocese where the clergy are generally in danger of becoming as apathetic as the ordinary faithful." [63]

The Oblates had had no intention of preaching missions immediately in Paris when they settled there in 1859, only to establish a very temporary residence there. And Bishop de Mazenod regarded as very provisory the modest dwelling in which Father Vincens, the provincial of northern France, lived with his two companions; the house was situated on a "small street unknown to carriage drivers and hidden away in the Batignolles quarter." When giving Father Magnan his obedience, the founder had promised him: "You will be stationed at the gates of Paris and you will enter [the city] as soon as they open." Nor did he lose any time in seeing to it that the fathers passed through the gates. During his stay in Paris at the time of the 1860 session of the senate, after visiting several areas of the city, the founder chose the quarter near the Place de l'Europe, bought a large plot of land on the rue de Saint-Petersbourg, and construction soon began.[64] Did he foresee that with his passing his congregation, which had long since ceased to be exclusively Provençal, would have every advantage in establishing its headquarters in the center of the capital which radiated to the whole of France, even to the whole world? Perhaps. In any case, without knowing it and without intending it, the prelate had prepared a providential refuge for the General Administration which was forced to leave

Marseilles after his death, in the face of the retaliatory measures taken in that city against the Oblates who were judged to have been too encroaching during the episcopate of their founder and father.

Although Bishop de Mazenod's religious family, which was exclusively French at first, had spread into Canada, the United States, Ceylon, and Africa before his death, it failed to penetrate the European continent until after his death. The house at Billens, in Switzerland, which had been opened as a place of refuge after the 1830 revolution, lasted but a short time. Of all the countries of the West, still called the Old World, England, which was so tightly circumscribed and so antipapist, was the only one to welcome the Oblate missionaries. The missionaries themselves stressed their surprise at such a favorable reception, and the Bishop of Marseilles, for his part, termed as providential the circumstances which had induced him to open a new field of missionary endeavor in Great Britain to the zeal of his sons.

Two visits, which were as accidental as that made by Bishop Bourget in 1841 on behalf of Canada, impressed the superior general as precursory signs of an apostolic experiment which would have to be tried. The first of these visits, in February, 1837, was that of a young Irishman, 22 years of age, who came to the Calvaire house, "as though he had been sent from heaven" the founder wrote.[65] Father Richard relates the circumstances as follows:

One Sunday, on his way to Rome to study for the priesthood, the young traveler stopped in Marseilles; learning that there was a priest at the Calvaire who could hear confessions in English, he went there and talked with Father Aubert; the latter then invited him to spend the day at our house. God arranged things so well that our visitor, gifted with a colorful and lively imagination, was completely captivated, and resolved then and there to join our Society; he began his novitiate immediately. . . . This young man was Father Daly.[66]

After making his solemn profession on February 17, 1838, the new Oblate then successfully pursued his philosophical and theo-

BRITISH ISLES

logical studies at the Marseilles major seminary; during those years, as Bishop de Mazenod wrote in his *Journal,*

he fed within his soul a flaming fire of charity and an unquenchable zeal for the conversion of English heretics in England and elsewhere. He had no sooner become a deacon than he began devising ways and means for creating some kind of establishment which would help our congregation to achieve its great work. He requested my permission to write to Ireland to appeal for subjects who would be suitable for our type of ministry. He received some replies which nurtured his hopes of succeeding in this venture.[67]

The second visit was no less unexpected; "about this same time," continued Bishop de Mazenod in his *Journal*:

a young man, whose face mirrored his guileless soul, called at the Calvaire, for what reason I do not know. He had a reservation on the boat sailing for Rome the next day. Father Casimir Aubert happened to enter the sacristy while the young man was explaining in Latin why he was there. From his pronunciation of the Latin, Father Aubert presumed he was English and spoke to him in that language. Delighted to find someone who could speak his language, the young stranger stated his business to Father Aubert; in the course of the conversation, he revealed that he had left Ireland to become a missionary. He felt that here was a fine opportunity to achieve his desire since he was in a missionary house and was undoubtedly speaking to the superior. That was all he needed to make up his mind, and he asked to be admitted. His reservation was canceled and he entered the community; Brother Daly, who was summoned in order to explain things more clearly to him, saw here a new proof that God wanted him to pursue his undertaking.[68]

The young man's name was Naughten; he was a native of Ennis, in the county of Claire, where the renowned Daniel O'Connell was born, and took the holy habit on October 31, 1840. Bishop de Mazenod continues:

the story does not end there; lo and behold! by the strangest coincidence, Brother Daly, who usually had no connections with outsiders, became acquainted with a Protestant Englishman just as he was about to make a trip to England with his family. A few days after they met, this Englishman offered to take Brother Daly along with him and to pay for his transportation as far as Liverpool. I am still astounded by this stroke of Divine Providence. I was reluctant to think of it as such and did so only on the day he sailed. However, won over by the confidence of this fine Daly boy, who had settled the whole matter with the Englishman in a single conversation, I hurried things up so that he might be ordained a priest. The day after his ordination, he left for England in God's keeping, for God had manifested His power and goodness very strikingly as a reward for the simple faith and trust of His young and faithful servant. This voyage, therefore, is being taken to make an on-the-spot study of the possibility of establishing a house for our missionaries in England so that they might labor for the conversion of English heretics and, if necessary and if the number of new vocations is sufficient, branch out into England's colonies or her new acquisitions in America, or any other part of the world.[69]

Thus, Father Daly was ordained a priest on May 2, 1841 and left Marseilles for England the next day. Once again, Bishop de Mazenod had seized an unforeseen opportunity to launch out into a new mission field, and looked upon it as a sign from Divine Providence. A few weeks later, he did the same thing by answering another appeal which took him equally by surprise: that of Bishop Bourget, who came seeking the help of the Oblates for the diocese of Montreal and the vast expanses of Canada.

When he decided to send the young Irish priest across the English Channel, the Bishop of Marseilles had three ends in view: first, to collaborate in the religious revival which was attracting Anglicans to the Roman Catholic Church through the twin efforts of the Oxford Movement in Protestant circles and of Bishop Wiseman in Catholic circles; secondly, to recruit English-speaking subjects for his congregation; and thirdly, to inaugurate a foreign mission field for his congregation in the British colonies, a project he was passionately eager to undertake. The third objective was the most remote, but the first two could succeed immediately if the circumstances were favorable. Although the departure of the first Oblates he sent to Montreal a few months later made it possible for him to extend the missionary apostolate of his sons to the New World, and although he had to exhaust his resources to send this vanguard of six professed Oblates to New France, he nonetheless persisted in his plans for the British

Isles. But, before definitely committing himself on his own initiative to a land which appealed to his zeal, but from which he had received no call, he wanted to wait until he had received the reports from Father Daly, and these reports justified all his expectations. Both Bishop Wiseman, who was coadjutor to Bishop Walsh, the vicar apostolic of the London area, and the Assembly of Bishops in Ireland proved kind and encouraging. The drive for vocations was showing promise, since, by that time, two postulants had arrived at the novitiate of Notre Dame de l'Osier. The founder had no intention, however, of relying solely on the judgment of such a young father, or especially of allowing a religious, barely out of the scholasticate, to remain there by himself; in July, 1842, therefore, he decided to send Father Aubert, who was reliable and experienced, to England.

Aubert planned to begin in Ireland where, he felt, he had a greater chance of success among Father Daly's compatriots, and this success appeared all the more certain because of the encouragement he received from Daniel O'Connell who gave him a cordial welcome at his Merrion Square residence, and from the Archbishop of Dublin who had been convinced by the Canadian Bishop of Halifax after his praise of the very meritorious work of the Oblates in the Montreal diocese. As a matter of fact, however, he failed with Bishop Murphy, the bishop of Cork, who had been warned by his clergy against this foreign congregation, and at Tullow where he wanted to incorporate the Brothers of Saint Patrick into his Institute. This unsuccessful beginning, later deemed providential, had the fortunate result of turning him toward England which he originally had planned to visit very much later. An Irish priest, Father Young, who was trying to bring help to his much-neglected countrymen in England and who was himself desirous of becoming a religious, sought Aubert's help at Penzance in Cornwall where he was in the process of building a church. Thus, in the summer of 1843, Father Aubert joined Father Daly in England. A year later, Bishop de Mazenod thoroughly delighted by what he had learned from Father Daly, wrote to Father Aubert who by that time had returned to France:

He is doing wonders there. He is very pleased with his delightful mission. He tells me that there is nothing more consoling than the sight of our beautiful church filled with people every Sunday. There are always between three and four hundred Protestants of every sect coming to hear sermons on the sacred truths of the Catholic religion. The Protestant churches are practically empty while ours is always filled, even in the worst weather. These Protestants, who come out of curiosity, always leave edified and very satisfied; they always behave reverently in church; they admire our ceremonies and doctrines, and they conclude from them that the Catholic religion is good. He adds that there is a very notable leaning at this time toward our holy religion, that minds are changing and are searching for the truth with extraordinary eagerness, or, to use his own words which I am merely copying, with an "indescribable eagerness." [70]

These extremely encouraging results earned the Oblates a fine reputation, and soon, foundations followed one after the other: Grace-Dieu in 1845, Evringham in 1847, Aldenham in 1848, Maryvale and Manchester in 1849, Liverpool in 1850, Leeds in 1851, Sicklinghall in 1852. Scotland came next, with a foundation at Galashiels in 1852 and one at Leith in 1860. In Ireland, which originally had been selected as the starting point, the Oblates became established only in 1856 with a house at Inchicore; in 1859, they took charge of Glencree penitentiary, and in 1860 opened a novitiate at Glen-Mary. [71]

This simple catalogue would be adequate enough to show the spread of their work, but it does not begin to explain the rapid strides made in that work, nor the contrasts to be considered in giving an accurate assessment of it. The work of the Oblates in this territory was strictly among the common people—and it suited the motto of their Congregation: *Evangelizare pauperibus misit me*—since there was widespread poverty in the British Isles, a consequence of Manchester's industrialization and liberalism. The most unfortunate among these poor were the Irish immigrants who had come to England seeking work; they were forced to accept miserable wages and were lodged in the slums of the large cities. Submerged by Protestant populations, these Irish Catholics were deprived of any religious attention, and, with no places of worship and no priests, they practiced their religion intermittently or not at all. It was they who made up a large part of the listeners to whom the Oblates preached in make-shift buildings or hastily constructed churches; where there were no such places, the Oblates preached in the streets or on public squares. Joining in these gatherings were Anglicans, some of whom came out of mere curiosity and others because of a more or less conscious desire for enlightenment as a result of the impetus given by the Oxford Movement; some of them were converted. The numbers of those attending these missions, which were held more and more frequently, were increased through the use made of the public press and through the newspaper *The Catholic Citizen*, published at Liverpool in 1851. Lastly, when chapels were added to the fathers' residences, they made it possible to carry on a continuous program of action in one place.

This great endeavor would not have been possible, however, without some very important patronage. On the spiritual and moral side, the support given by the bishops, and of Bishop Wiseman in particular, must be singled out before all others. The prelates encouraged and furthered the missionaries' efforts, and through their reputations and recommendations, gained benefactors for the Oblates who provided for their material needs. Their apostolate which was devoted so exclusively to the poor class had its own Maecenases, recruited from among the aristocracy; people such as Phillipps de Lisle at Grace-Dieu, William Maxwell at Everingham, the Acton family at Aldenham, the Norfolks, the Shrewsburys, and the descendants of Sir Walter Scott in Scotland. Within the stately castles of these people, the Oblates made contacts with highly placed persons who encouraged their ministry: Lord Granville, Lord Canning, the relatives of Lord Palmerston. They also made the acquaintance of Newman and other converts from Oxford University. Some of them, such as Doctor Crawley, a former Anglican minister, even joined the Oblate Congregation, and they were indeed valuable recruits because of their purely English culture which gained for them an access to the intellectual circles of England. Although the fathers from France were not of the "gentleman" class and, because of their poor dress and austere manner of living, felt out of place in these sumptuous gatherings, at least these places afforded them the opportunity to become acquainted with the religious problems of a country where a work of hopeful renewal was taking place.

Small wonder, therefore, that in 1845, after being informed by his sons, and with full knowledge of the situation, Bishop de Mazenod wholeheartedly answered the appeal which Bishop Wiseman sent to the bishops, asking the prayers of their people in behalf of England. A long pastoral letter which the bishop of Marseilles addressed to his clergy and faithful explained why they were obliged to beg God for the return of the British Isles to a union with the Church. Admittedly, Bishop de Mazenod used the argument generally employed at that time by the French clergy, in contrast to Bishop Wiseman who, in his own circular letter, showed great consideration in speaking about his Anglican compatriots; in fact, he showed a delicate sympathy for them. Nonetheless, to his credit, the Bishop of Marseilles spoke understandingly of the Oxford Movement and marked out, step by step, the route followed by "upright and sincere" men whose minds were open to the truth:

They began by examining the monuments of tradition and found there what we Catholics hold to be true. They listened to the voices of the ancient Doctors of the Church and discovered that these Fathers taught what we teach; the first ages of the Church loomed before minds qualified to understand them and proved to them that we, and only we, Catholics have preserved the teachings of the apostles in all their purity and integrity. Then they began to read our ancient liturgical books; our ritual seemed almost divine to them; the beauty, grandeur and glorious symbolism of our majestic ceremonies made a deep impression on them; they felt a yearning to adopt our sacred rites; they drew closer to them and thereby drew closer to the doctrines symbolized by those rites. Some drew even closer and discovered all the reality hidden beneath the symbols, and they wanted to conform completely to the holy and venerable practices of antiquity, to pray and believe as the primitive Church did, and they immediately prayed essentially as we pray and believed what we believe. They had become Catholic. It was unavoidable. Once they had entered this path which was deserving of their enlightened minds and their attachment to Christianity, they needed only to follow it perseveringly, and the majestic and imperishable edifice of our Church opened its doors to welcome them into the faith and charity of God. This final and happy result of their spiritual quest was inevitable for such solid and logical minds; it was the prize awaiting them at the end of the path, the reward for their love of truth. They were the pathfinders, the vanguard for their brothers. My dear brethren, let us pray that they bring all the others into the Church with them. That would be a world-shaking event. What an impact it would have on the welfare of souls! Catholic England! In our eyes, it is a great part of the universe. One might even say, it is the whole universe. At least it comprises the immense British possessions, in so many corners of the globe which would be one with us in the same holy unity. Who among us would not thrill at the thought of such a happening? Who would not wish it? Who would not welcome it from afar just as the patriarchs and prophets prayed for and welcomed the coming of the Lord? It would then be acknowledged that the special genius which has made England such a great sea power and which has extended her empire so mightily into far distant countries was given to her by Divine Providence, just as Rome's conquering genius was given to her so that she might prepare the way for the peaceful conquests of the Gospel.[72]

This was a very exact and charming way of tracing the spiritual odyssey of Newman who had come into the Catholic Church on the preceding October 8. The Bishop of Marseilles had clearly perceived the slow but sure steps of that conversion and had grasped its full import. From then on, he always spoke admiringly and affectionately of that illustrious and brilliant convert, as well as of all those who, at the cost of painful renunciations, imitated his example. Some years after his pastoral letter, he gave tangible proof of his affection by associating his clergy and faithful with the drive for funds to cover the expenses resulting from a libel suit brought against the founder of the English Oratory by an Italian priest named Achilli.[73]

In 1849, the bishop of Marseilles therefore rejoiced on learning that, because of the initiative taken by Bishop Ullathorne, an Oblate novitiate was being established at Maryvale in the college where Newman and his disciples had begun to practice the Rule of Saint Philip Neri before moving their community to Birmingham. The prelate keenly realized, however, that the high spiritual and intellectual level of those who preceded his sons at Maryvale would be a difficult challenge for them:

It is a burdensome heritage. It is no easy thing to replace so many men famed for their knowledge and sanctity. I feel that the eyes of all

England are on you and that great examples of virtue are expected to come from this place which has been sanctified by the Milners, the Newmans, etc. . . . I am still astounded at seeing you settled there and I am still thanking God from the depths of my heart.[74]

It was impossible to demand the same style of work from the Oblates as that which had been carried on by the doctors from Oxford. Their task was entirely different. However, to acquit themselves worthily of that task and to bring God's blessing upon it, they were still expected to realize the ideal of the religious life according to the mind of their institute. It was essential that the new recruits from England, in spite of their different nationality, language, and customs, be given the solid, intensive, and traditional training of the congregation. In the beginning, a few postulants were brought over to France so that they might come into direct contact with the original source. But, this first experiment was not a successful one. Not only did the young novices feel like exiles, but, accustomed to heavy fogs, they suffered from the extreme heat of the southern climate. Finding it difficult to understand why they were not becoming acclimated Bishop de Mazenod wrote:

They persist in claiming that it is too warm here, and this year especially, when the heat is felt only in the sun. In fact, the mornings and evenings are too cool and the days are not particularly warm. But they make this objection to me when I speak of having the novices you are preparing for us come here. However, some decision will have to be made. I shall go to Marseilles this evening and tomorrow I shall discuss this matter and a few others with the fathers there.[75]

We do not know whether that discussion resulted in an agreement that the founder's defense of his beloved Provence would be able to convince any native Britisher. Actually, its effectiveness was rather doubtful. However, Bishop de Mazenod's firm determination to overrule a valid objection to this transplanting is explained by his concern for a more complete assimilation. In effect, he had been disturbed for a long time by the "English manners" which certain of his fathers across the Channel were adopting, and as early as 1851, he accused Father Daly of becoming too "fashionable." [76] In 1853, a lengthy rebuke containing particularly severe expressions dwelled on the same subject:

Guard against thinking too much like those who try to persuade you that you must be content with being a religious only when you are indoors, and that it is not fitting to be different from other gentlemen when you are outdoors. That is a disastrous way of acting and, rather than attracting people to us, will keep men called to a life of religious perfection from coming to us. I do not say that the cassock is to be worn in places where it is forbidden, but, for that very reason, care must be taken to avoid dressing like worldly men in all their studied refinements. Instead, do as the Passionists do. Do you think that they have drawn so many distinguished men to their order by dressing fashionably? They are not afraid of being known for what they are. . . . Personally, I think that we shall see vocations come to us when it becomes known that you live a truly religious life, that you have trampled vanity underfoot, and that there is a great difference between you and the seculars.[77]

Bishop de Mazenod believed, therefore, that in order to preserve the character, regularity, and spirit of the congregation, which was in danger of becoming anglicized, the French effectives would have to be reinforced, since, in his eyes, character, regularity, and spirit were all one and the same thing.

Father Daly's unfortunate financial operations made the founder still more aware of possible deviations and perilous insubordination, and caused him to insist upon strict obedience and to point out that anyone who falls prey to the "fashionable" eventually undertakes dangerous initiatives in other directions. Originally, Bishop de Mazenod had never tired of showering praises upon this Irish Oblate—justly deserved praises, too, since it was mainly through Daly's efforts that the Oblates had first come into England and that their first missions there had succeeded. Now, in his eagerness the young priest, without the founder's permission, had rashly acquired a property in Ashbourn (Derbyshire) worth 200,000 francs and intended for a new foundation. Sued by the seller whom he could not pay, Father Daly was forced to cede the Penzance house to him, a house which had been acquired in his name, but had been paid for by the congregation. Penzance then had to be abandoned. One can well imagine the founder's indignation since it was a question not only of "enormous stupidity" which "bankrupts us and endangers our reputation," but also of a grave violation of the prescriptions of the rule, and an inexcusable breach of obedience. "The hare-brained" Daly was then "expelled." [78]

Two trips which the bishop of Marseilles made across the English Channel dispelled the clouds: the first trip, in 1850, was limited to England since the Oblates had not by that time established any communities in Scotland or Ireland; the second, in 1857, brought him to Dublin and Edinburgh. Both trips left "indelible marks" in his heart.[79] What discoveries and surprises awaited him in England, a country of which he knew so little! Some of these had nothing to do with religious matters and yet they impressed him deeply, if we can judge from the spontaneous manner in which he described them and from the comparisons which they prompted him to make, comparisons scarcely flattering to France. The "wonderful railroads" amazed him with their speed, which averages a mile a minute, "that is, twenty leagues" an hour.[80] Moreover, they were so comfortable that a person could travel 150 miles "without being any more exhausted than if he had been in his armchair." The London means of transportation afforded him the pleasure of sailing down the Thames "for one or two pennies," or of climbing *incognito* to the upper deck of omnibuses of which there must be "literally thousands." It was impossible to imagine the "perpetual motion" of the capital.[81] "It is like a giant anthill of men and women all moving about in every direction at the same time." And "the number of travelers one meets" on the English roads, "is incredible. It is countless. We in France are the only ones making no progress." [82] The countryside, which he viewed under a magnificent sun entranced Bishop de Mazenod without, however, causing him to lose any of his appreciation for the poetic serenity of his native Provence. On the other hand, his letters contain little mention of English art and architecture, although some members of the nobility had arranged a visit to the Tower of London and Westminster Abbey, had made it possible for him to attend a session of Her Majesty's Parliament, and had opened their ancient castles to him where princely receptions awaited.

Although it was less astonishing to him than England's bustling activity and technological superiority, the welcome he was accorded by the bishops and the aristocracy delighted him, for the bishops had showered their French colleague with kindness and attentiveness. With a keen sense of protocol, the Bishop of Marseilles gave appreciative details about the cordial reception of the archbishop of Dublin who had even stepped out of his carriage first so that he might lend a hand to Bishop de Mazenod when he alighted. In Leeds, at the dedication of the Oblate church, Cardinal Wiseman accorded him the honor of celebrating the pontifical Mass, though he retained the privilege of preaching the homily;[83] and that evening, Doctor Manning preached at Solemn Vespers over which the superior general presided. In every city where the prelate stopped, the residing bishop came to meet him at the railroad station and to offer him hospitality.

The prejudices against foreign religious which, in the beginning, had caused the Irish hierarchy to adopt a distant attitude toward the French Oblates, had now completely disappeared. Their arrival was now considered providential, since at that time destitution was forcing thousands of Irish to emigrate to the large cities of England where the clergy, much too few in number, was unable to provide spiritual care for them. The influx of these emigrants posed a great problem of pastoral equipment, requiring places of worship and priests to staff them. The Oblates, however, had demonstrated their ability to inspire generous donations for the construction of churches, and certain of these donations had come from the heirs of Catholic families who saw in Bishop de Mazenod not only a successor of the apostles but also a man of noble birth. While regretfully recalling the bygone traditions of the French aristocracy, the prelate readily acknowledged that these rich English heirs, who had not been robbed of their riches and property by an egalitarian revolution, had shown much greater generosity than did the bourgeois businessmen of Marseilles, and that they were carrying on the tradition of utilizing their riches for the founding of parishes. He was of the opinion, however, that certain of these benefactors might have apportioned their generous gifts more sensibly and he made a point of saying so in referring to "the magnificent Gothic church which Lord Shrewsbury had built *in a village*, and which had cost him at least a million francs— a sort of folly I find impossible to admire." [84] Bishop de Mazenod declared that he was much more deeply impressed when he celebrated Mass at London in a much less pretentious church, "built by an emigré priest who had endowed it on his death-bed." [85] He was even more deeply moved at the sight of the church some good Irish people had built in a week; writing to Cardinal Barnabo, he remarked that it was truly a simple build-ing but its real value lay in the labor that had been put into it—that was the only wealth of these people, and it had been poured out eagerly, piously, and lovingly. [86]

The Bishop of Marseilles acknowledged that the religious situ-ation in England was much more hopeful than he had thought. Undoubtedly, he had fully appreciated the grandeur, spread, and importance of the Oxford Movement but in view of his prej-udices against the established religion of the British Kingdom— which he knew mostly through incomplete reports—the prelate had seen nothing more in the sudden shifting of course than the triumph of orthodoxy over heresy. Relying solely on what he knew of Henry VIII, Queen Elizabeth, the misfortune of Mary Stewart, and the persecutions of the Catholics, he had failed to realize what Newman and his disciples owed to Anglican-ism from which they had derived their spiritual life and in which they had found their inspiration. In a letter postmarked Liverpool, he candidly admitted how very impressed he was by the chanting of the Divine Office in a church of the "Catholic Apostolics," that is, the Irvingites:

It was evening and we could attend only their vespers; they were chanted very solemnly and were presided over by two priests vested in surplice and stole; the chanters and choir boys also wore surplices. At times they knelt and at other times stood; at the *Gloria Patri* they bowed towards the altar and again whenever the sacred name of Jesus was pronounced; the priest used the salutation, *Dominus vobiscum,* but everything else was sung in very clear English. Their psalmody and especially their prayers took so long that we left, after I noticed that Father Aubert had fallen asleep, and, as a consequence, I was unable to witness the incensing they perform at the altar during the *Magnificat*. The sacristan told us that, as a preparation for Sunday, they anticipate matins on Saturdays; judging from the length of their vespers, I should say that their matins must be frightfully long. Twice during the week and on Sundays, they say Mass with Gothic vestments exactly like ours.

Worthy of quote is the remark which he addressed to the French canons regarding the example of "those poor misguided Irvingites who have strayed from the path leading to eternal life":

From what I have been observing in the places I have been visiting, I have come to the conclusion that it is shameful to hurry the recitation of the official prayers of the Church, as is done in our chapters. One must watch these poor heretics at prayer to see with what solemnity and with what tone of supplication God's creatures should address Him when they invoke His aid.[87]

The prelate's conversations with Manning and Newman, which, unfortunately, he did not record, helped to enlighten him further.

Lastly, he was taken completely by surprise when he received a cordial, and at times enthusiastic, reception from a population which he had expected to find indifferent and even hostile, and he was only too glad to admit his error. In a letter to Cardinal Barnabo, he wrote:

It was astonishing; I can truthfully say that my trip to that heretical country was one long triumph. Not a single scowl did I see, nor even the slightest sign of resentment on the faces of these heretics, and among the Catholics, there was the most lively expression of their regard; nothing could restrain it. It was the same at Liverpool and at Leeds, and at Dublin: enthusiastic cheers and *Vivats* in their own language as soon as they saw me. I am not speaking here of the official greetings at receptions; they were always favorable to our holy Catholic religion and were made without any concern for what the heretics might think. It is truly amazing that such broadmindedness has not provoked the least reprisal or produced any bad effect. On the contrary, crowds of non-Catholics and countless ministers filled our churches, listening to the instructions given by our fathers and reverently attending our services and ceremonies.[88]

Understandably, the prelate could not remain indifferent to this triumph in which the episcopacy of his era took such great delight. But he looked beyond the honors that were paid to his person and saw the increasing marks of homage that were being paid to the Church which he represented and the approval given by the public to the work accomplished by his Oblate sons across the Channel. Afterwards, he wrote to Father Noble:

I recall with genuine happiness the few days I spent in those very interesting countries in connection with the implanting there of the true faith which is flourishing because of your devotion and zeal and because of the good example of those excellent Christian families who will one day enrich that soil with worshipers of Jesus Christ in spirit and in truth. . . . Consider only the good wrought by our congregation—is that not sufficient reason to offer profuse thanks to God? I sometimes return in spirit to our different establishments and I am struck with admiration. I take in the past, present, and future all at the same time, and I would think that I was dreaming did I not know that all this is real, that I have seen these things with my own eyes, and that what now exists is but a preparation for what will be done later.[89]

While he fully appreciated what his sons owed to the Catholic aristocrats, those models of Christian living who patronized their foundations, the Bishop of Marseilles was particularly delighted that the apostolate of his Oblates in England was being devoted to the poor and the destitute, as the spirit of their institute required. Moreover, in England, the dazzling façade of bustling activity, progress, and wealth had not blinded him to the widespread poverty there. In fact, through Father Aubert, who served as his guide there, we know that, after visiting the historical places in the British capital, the prelate insisted on venturing into the dark and filthy alleys between the Tower of London and the docks where the spiritually and materially destitute Irish were crowded in among a wretched and degraded population. "That," he declared, "is where an Oblate house should be established." He held fast to this plan, and although it could not be realized until after his death, at least it proves that, while he remained completely loyal to the apostolic ideal of his youth, the old bishop still had his sights set far into the future.[90]

CONGREGATION DIVIDED INTO PROVINCES; HOLY FAMILY SOCIETY
AFFILIATED WITH THE OBLATES

This expansion of the Oblate Congregation, which extended its geographical boundaries and introduced new forms of apostolic activity not originally envisaged prompted the Chapter of 1850 to bring the Constitutions and Rules drafted in 1826 into harmony with the new situation and with situations that were to arise later.[91] "Since it would now be difficult for the superior general to supervise everything connected with the different houses of the congregation—their superiors, their members and their business affairs"—it was decided that the congregation would henceforth be divided "into provinces and vicariates," and that there would be a separate organization for the home and foreign missions. A province would require at least three established houses and be assured of a revenue sufficient for its administration. A vicariate, on the other hand, would include only residences with a limited number of subjects and would be allowed a special type of administration in keeping with the difficulties arising from distances and places.

The decentralization, which had become necessary, did not, however, lessen the monarchical character which the founder had willed for his congregation and which he fully intended to maintain: only the superior general, with the consent of his council, had the power to establish provinces, assign provincials, remove them when he saw fit, and choose the members of their councils and their admonitors. Provincials would have no power to erect or suppress a house, or to appoint or remove a local superior without the approval of the superior general; they would be required to submit a report to the superior general four times a year, and local superiors an annual report. Every member of the congregation, however far away he might be, would still be free to have direct recourse to the superior general "for the purpose of revealing his conscience to him, and seeking his advice and direction." Only the superior general would be able to transfer professed members and novices from one province to another, should the good of the society or the individual demand it. Provincials were obliged to obtain the superior general's authorization to incur an expense above 10,000 francs, and provincial bursars required to submit financial reports to the bursar general of the congregation. More latitude, naturally, would be allowed vicars of missions, but the superior general would still have the right to choose the two members who comprise the vicar's council, as well as the right to choose his admonitor. Vicars of missions would be entitled to administer their own finances "through mandate of the superior general," but they would be required, to submit a financial report twice a year and would have no power to transfer ownership of the society's property without express authorization.[92]

This creation of provinces also entailed changes in the format of the General Chapter. Each province or vicariate would be entitled to representation by the provincial or vicar and by one delegate; the delegates would be elected by provincial or vicariate chapters to which each community would send a representative who in turn would be elected by the members of his individual community. Since the General Chapter would still be the supreme authority of the congregation, to which even the superior general is subject, the provincial chapters had authority only to name delegates to the General Chapter without any right of deliberation, except on those questions the superior general would propose to it in writing, "should such a case arise." However, the fathers would be allowed, either by open or sealed letter, or by spoken word, under the seal of secrecy or not, to confide their viewpoints to the provincial, the vicar of missions, or to the delegate; this last clause was a compromise measure to satisfy certain members of the 1850 Chapter who urged that the provincial chapter be given the right to express its wishes and discuss them.[93]

That same Chapter also discussed certain forms of the apostolate which had not been foreseen and had even been excluded by the original constitutions; these primitive constitutions had been formulated for a society which had been intended primarily for parish missions, and which was not to be deterred from that objective by any other work. Now, with the expansion of the congregation, circumstances in various places had intervened to prompt the fathers to broaden their objectives. In principle, directing parishes, schools, colleges, and minor seminaries was tolerated only on condition that the superior general authorize a special waiver. But directing major seminaries had been officially recognized as one of the principal ends of the institute, and numerous articles on this subject, were incorporated into the rules.

The Chapter of 1850 voted unanimously on all these points; such, however, was not the case in the matter of the founding and direction of communities of nuns. One delegate demanded, in effect, that the prohibition imposed by the constitutions be obeyed, and to support this demand, reminded the chapter of "the reasons for which the rule had wisely deterred the fathers from such a ministry; perfectly praiseworthy as it was in itself, it could distract us from the principal end of our vocation." The delegates readily agreed that it "would not be necessary to bring the Congregation back to the strict observance" of the article concerning the spiritual direction of religious communities of women; that the "prohibition which [the rule] ordained on this matter had not been overlooked when, by way of exception, it had been thought advisable to accept this form of ministry in one of our houses, for reasons of evident necessity and with the consent and, at times, even the formal order of the superior general." Still, there were some "long and spirited" arguments about the founding of communities of nuns; the delegate who had demanded obedience to the general principle was actually criticizing the particular, personal initiative Father Guigues had taken at Notre Dame de l'Osier before he became bishop of Ottawa. While he was superior at l'Osier, Guigues had, in fact, formed a congregation of women religious whose purpose was to greet the pilgrims and "supervise the material needs of the pious women who wanted to renew their fervor" by making retreats at the Virgin's shrine. Moreover, Guigues had given these women religious the name of Oblate Sisters of Mary Immaculate.[94]

The delegates, somewhat embarrassed, then made a distinction between "the prohibition of founding any community of religious women not connected with the Oblates and that of founding others which bear our name and are affiliated with us." The first case presented no difficulty as long as the superior general would give his consent to that decision, but the second "deserved every consideration" since it involved a "serious matter." Opinions

about the decision to be made were very much divided, and
the arguments, though heated, did not result in any agreement,
and the outcome of the voting appeared uncertain. But after a
"few of the more esteemed members of the chapter had expressed
the opinion that it would be advisable to leave things as they
were and to rely upon the wisdom of the superior general who
would be responsible for whatever resulted from Guigues' undertaking, and after the superior general had declared that nothing
had been done without proper authorization, the chapter unanimously agreed that Guigues' society be allowed to continue un-
disturbed in the work it had begun." Thus, after all the lengthy
arguments, only the particular case of l'Osier had been discussed,
and matters were left to the discretion of Bishop de Mazenod
without any specific decision about the general principle.[95]

The chapter, evidently, had not wanted to censure the bishop
of Ottawa who was personally involved in the case. While
avoiding the fundamental problem, it had decided to allow
for a simple waiver, a waiver which could, however, set a
precedent for others. In fact, certain of the fathers fully realized
that the initial perspectives of the congregation bore the stamp
of a particular era and were suited to the limited means at the
disposal of the newly formed congregation and to a conception
of the word "mission" which now required broadening. Without in any way sacrificing what, under the Restoration, was the
institute's essential purpose in Provence, the congregation could
not afford to refuse apostolic initiatives of a different nature
which general or local interests might demand. Moreover, with
its recruitment assured, the congregation no longer needed to
concentrate its efforts in a form of apostolate which was still
indispensable but no longer exercised in France under the same
conditions as those of 1818. In fact, by sending his Oblates into
all paths open to them, including the direction of pilgrim shrines
and major seminaries, Bishop de Mazenod had given his own
interpretation to the prohibitions contained in his rule. He was
therefore given a free hand regarding communities of women
religious.

At that time and without foreseeing it, the Chapter of
1850, made it possible for the Congregation of the Holy Family
Sisters to become affiliated with the Oblates, but this was not

accomplished for eight years. Father Noailles, the founder of
this congregation, had formed it progressively, and, like Bishop
de Mazenod, had gradually extended its activities. But the originality of Noailles' society consisted in the specializations of the different "branches," each of which was dedicated to a particular
activity and reached a specific community. The order had begun
in a small way and, as at Aix, with work among the poor in administering orphanages. However, it was equally important to
provide a Christian training for young girls of well-to-do families
who would one day become mothers of families in the so-called
leading class. Then too, the sick could not be left without physical and spiritual help, nor could one neglect young country
girls enticed to "abandon farm work in favor of the comforts
and corruption of the city"; nor could one ignore those girls who
work in shops where "very often they are given no examples or
lessons other than those which lead them from the path of
virtue." [96] And finally, there was a great need to provide domestic
help for communities of priests, colleges, and seminaries.

After establishing the Sisters of the Immaculate Conception
to administer orphanages and working-class schools, Father Noailles then created the Ladies of Loretto, the Sisters of Hope, the
agricultural nuns, the Daughters of Saint Joseph, and the Sisters
of Saint Martha, and to draw heavenly graces down upon these
different branches by their prayers and penances, he also established an order of contemplatives called the *Solitaires*. All these
groups comprised the Holy Family Society and followed a
common rule, but each group had its own habit, superior, and
constitution in accordance with its special type of work. Finally,
a group of religious, known as the Daughters of God, and
dedicated to complete self-denial, trained superiors for the different communities; as the need arose, these superiors could be
transferred from one branch to another. Noailles, who had conceived this structure, excelled in managing this whole intricate
machinery in a manner intended to assure variety in uniformity.
But, because he had failed to establish a similar congregation of
men which could take charge of the sisters' ecclesiastical and
spiritual direction, he could not but be worried about the fate
of his society after his death. In 1857, he decided, therefore, to
provide for a successor but was concerned about the one to whom

he should entrust the Holy Family Society. In view of its "great increase of numbers," confiding its care to the archbishop of Bordeaux would be placing "an immense burden upon a diocesan administration already taxing the strength and the time of the cardinal." Then, too, Cardinal Donnet, in whom Father Noailles had complete confidence, would not live forever. "Men pass on, and only rarely do those of outstanding merit have comparable successors. The thinking and acting of a leadership which passed from one archbishop to another and even to the different appointees each might choose to make would be affected by the diversity of those leaders; sooner or later, this constant changing would provoke crises as harmful to peace of soul as they would be to stability within the various groups. To be governed efficiently, the Holy Family Society needed the cohesion and unity that could be found only in a society living under a rule." Consequently, it was necessary to "seek help from a religious society," one which could offer some assurance that it would endure, one which would have "no other community of women" to hinder it "from giving undivided attention to the Society of the Holy Family," and one which would offer, in addition to this last advantage, a sort of kinship of purpose and mind. After praying and reflecting for a long time, Father Noailles decided on the Oblates and asked Bishop de Mazenod to affiliate the Holy Family Society with them.

Accompanied by two of his assistants general, the Bishop of Marseilles went to Bordeaux, fully disposed to accept a proposal which would bring honor to his Oblate Congregation, and just as surely bring advantages to both religious families, since their union would result in a veritable increase of strength and greater means of insuring the salvation of souls. Before they would conclude the agreement, however, it was important for them to determine precisely the conditions governing this spiritual partnership. A rough draft of the contract which Father Noailles had drawn up and submitted to Supreme Council of the Holy Family Sisters served as a basis for the negotiations:

Nothing would be decided without the agreement and collaboration of Cardinal Donnet. The Holy Family Society would not be entrusted to the bishop of Marseilles personally, but solely to the Society of the Oblates of Mary as represented by its present superior general or by his official delegate. Father Noailles would continue to direct the institute he had founded and until his death or retirement; only then would its direction pass to the superior general of the Oblates. To exercise this jurisdiction, the superior general could appoint a representative to govern in his name; to this end, Father Noailles should arrange to initiate an Oblate of the Talence community into the workings of the Holy Family Society, thus enabling him to assume whatever share of its government or work the founder of the Holy Family Society might assign him; in this way, he would be in a position to render a few services to the various groups and become better acquainted with the principal heads of the Association. The general and individual rules for the organization and the progress of the societies of the organization, as well as the prescriptions and usages which determined their spirit or their directional course, would remain the same, with the exception of those modifications deemed necessary by common agreement.[97]

Agreement about these modifications to harmonize the joint activities of the two societies, and about the other matters of the contract was reached without any difficulty, and the affiliation contract of 29 articles was signed on January 11–14, 1858.[98]

In conformity with the terms of this contract, Father Noailles continued to administer the Holy Family Society and remained in full control of it—assisted by Father Bellon, the delegate of Bishop de Mazenod—until his death on February 8, 1861. The Bishop of Marseilles then succeeded him, but by that time he himself was too ill to take personal charge of the Society. He accepted it, however, and on February 12, 1861, wrote to Cardinal Donnet:

Although the pledges I made were exclusively mine, perhaps I should wait until I am fully recovered before I accept the duties they impose on me. But, since it is the superior general who is obligated, I felt that I should send a reply today to the Council of the Holy Family Society and inform them that, as of this moment, I shall abide by my pledge. Therefore, according to the wishes which these women have formally made known to me, I have appointed Father Bellon, who is already known to Your Eminence, to reside at Bordeaux; and to be my representative with the Holy Family Society. I did not hesitate, Your Eminence, to grant this request which the Holy Family Council sent

me since I remembered that you had personally encouraged this affiliation and had caused me to hope that it would result in greater opportunities to promote the glory of God and the welfare of souls. . . . As
far as my health is concerned, I am in God's hands. The doctors and
those close to me give me hope that I shall recover my health. God's
will be done! [99]

Bishop de Mazenod did not long survive Father Noailles, and
at his death a few months later, left his cherished Oblate Society
permanently consolidated and strengthened by this additional
support. In France where the Holy Family, until then, was
principally established, and in distant mission fields to which
it would later extend its activities, the Society of Bordeaux would
provide the Oblate Congregation with the strong reinforcement
of its apostolic and sisterly devotion. [100]

Chapter Six

Natural and Supernatural Virtues of Bishop de Mazenod

DEATH OF THE FOUNDER

In spite of his advancing age, Bishop de Mazenod did not lessen any of his numerous activities nor discontinue any of the harsh austerities of his ascetical life. What was particularly amazing was his ability to remain so strong physically and so alert mentally. He delighted in boasting that his colleagues were unable to match his youthful vigor; he felt sorry for Jeancard, his auxiliary bishop, who was "threatened with loss of eyesight," and for Tempier who "had us worried for a few days." [1] This "minor idiosyncrasy," which Timon-David detected and of which he made use occasionally, was the only sign which betrayed his old age. Otherwise, everything indicated a healthy and productive longevity.

Toward the middle of December, 1860, however, a sudden illness whose cause and nature seem to have mystified the doctors alarmed his associates. Whether it was caused by two unfortunate falls which could have resulted in an accumulation of "body fluids," as the official diagnosis stated, or in a proliferation of small cells which had caused no suffering until then, is not certain; whatever the case, "the sharp stabs of pain" which he felt in his chest seemed serious enough to Father Fabre to warrant seeking a medical examination. This, the recalcitrant old bishop deemed unnecessary. Overly confident in his vigor and physical stamina, the bishop attributed his pains and aches to overwork and judged that the best way to treat them was to ignore them. Since he stubbornly refused to seek the services of the "men of art," as doctors were called in those days, subterfuge had to be employed. Under pretext of an urgent business matter, he was called to the major seminary where Doctor d'Astros awaited him. D'Astros diagnosed the trouble as a "tumor on the lower left side of the chest" and declared that an operation would be necessary: the large amount of pus released by the lancet revealed a more deep-rooted disease which had existed longer than the cursory examination had indicated. Nonetheless, it was hoped that by keeping the incision open all the pus could be drained, and that rest, good nourishment, and the approaching spring weather would help nature to assert itself. Unfortunately, these optimistic expectations were not realized. Although the incision was kept open and repeatedly dressed, the "poison steadily increased." A second operation was performed to enlarge the opening, but it resulted only in a high fever and some nervous spasms and did not halt the maturation.[2] Pleurisy developed, seriously complicating the condition and increasing the concern of the doctors. Bishop Jeancard sent an anxious letter to the pastors of Marseilles, prescribing public prayers; Tempier informed the Oblates and ordered that a novena and a Mass be offered in all houses of the congregation.[3] A third operation, more serious than the first two, brought no improvement. By the end of January, Doctor d'Astros considered the patient's condition so desperate that he felt the Last Rites should be administered and so notified Archbishop Guibert who had rushed to Marseilles from Tours. Until that time, Bishop de Mazenod, whose optimism had been nurtured by his staff, had had no suspicion that his life was in danger. Thus, when his beloved Guibert tried very tactfully to prepare him for this last service, the prelate's first reaction betrayed his great surprise. Quickly composing himself, however, he embraced the archbishop, manifested inspiring serenity and resignation, and simply asked whether the danger was imminent or whether he could wait three days in order to prepare himself for the reception of the Last Sacraments. Assured that there was no great urgency, he then allowed himself the delay but summoned Father Tempier to hear his general confession immediately.[4]

At that time, customs carried over from the *Ancien Régime* prescribed that the Last Rites for a bishop be administered with full pontifical solemnity. Thus, on January 28, a long procession proceeded from the temporary cathedral of Saint Martin to the episcopal palace; taking part in it were "the Confraternity of the Most Blessed Sacrament, the Christian Brothers, the Capuchin Fathers, the members of the major seminary, the Oblates of Mary Immaculate numbering more than seventy, and priests from all the city parishes. The cathedral chapter and Bishop Jeancard immediately preceded Archbishop Guibert, who was assisted by the vicars general of the diocese, Fathers Tempier and Fabre." [5] While the good people crowding the route stood in a silence that was all the more impressive since it was not the usual style of Marseillais demonstrations, the procession arrived at the episcopal palace where only the clergy was allowed to enter the patient's bedchamber. Tradition prescribed a sermon, but Archbishop Guibert, who was chosen to convey Bishop de Mazenod's feelings to the bystanders, was so overcome that his tears expressed his feelings more forcefully than words. After Extreme Unction and Viaticum had been administered, each one present received an individual blessing from the prelate along with a few words of affection. An eyewitness recalled: "We were all in tears and were sobbing, while he himself remained placid and smiling, happy in the love of his sons." [6]

Contrary to the fears of the doctors, the prelate recovered from the pleurisy. After remaining in critical condition for several days during which tremors, convulsions, and fainting spells seemed to presage the end, the patient showed a noticeable improvement, but it was only a respite. The prelate's "iron constitution" [7] prolonged his life for four months, but it was only at the cost of terrible suffering. In the Lenten pastoral letter addressed to the clergy and faithful of the diocese, Bishop Jeancard noted the great courage and spirit of faith with which the dying bishop accepted this prolonged suffering:

Although his body suffers, his spirit is undaunted and his patience remains strong, even in periods of great suffering and throughout painful operations. He bears everything as though he were insensible to the sharpest pain. Not a murmur, gesture, or sigh betrays the suffering he experiences in those agonizing periods. At such times, he raises his heart to God and thanks Him for these sufferings, looking upon them as graces sent to him for his sanctification. He pictures himself upon the Saviour's Cross and it is that thought which often prompts him to say: "When one is on the Cross, one must remain there. It means grace." [8]

While remaining upon his cross in a close union with Christ, the bishop-founder offered his sufferings for all the causes which were the sole objects of his solicitude: Holy Mother Church, which, wrote Jeancard "is dearer to him than life itself" and the Holy Father, whose spiritual independence he had fought so constantly to defend. As for the Roman question, he finally conceded that all his illusions about Napoleon III had vanished: "He is no emperor; he is a tyrant who persecutes the Church," the bishop declared to Father Mouchette. "You are still young, my child, and you will see him cause much evil and come to an evil end himself; but before that happens, he will cause many tears to flow." [9] On several occasions, Bishop Jeancard sent Cardinal Barnabo a request from the Bishop of Marseilles that His Eminence convey to Pius IX the expression of his filial devotion,[10] and one of the last joys the dying bishop experienced was the blessing the Holy Father sent him.[11] The prelate gave many touching expressions of affection to his Oblate sons who were standing watch at his bedside. To one of them, Father Fabre, he declared: "You know full well, my child, that I am attached to nothing in this world. And yet, leaving my children; Ah! that will indeed be a great sacrifice. There are still several things I should do for you." [12] One day, tears came to his eyes at the thought of this parting, and he explained: "It is not because I am going to die that I am weeping. Ah no! It is because I am leaving dear souls like yourself. . . . All of you must certainly know that the good God has given me a heart of immense capacity and with it an immense power to love my children. When I have gone, you will have another to take my place of authority, who will esteem you according to your merit; but will he love you as I have loved you? Never!" [13]

If we were to quote everything his sons have written about the marks of affection and the edifying examples he gave them to the very end, the account would be endless. The testimony of the diocesan clergy, however, is much sparser since, to the great regret of the bishop, visits to his bedside were restricted by order of the doctors. Nonetheless, the apostolic and spiritual renown of two priests to whom we are indebted for such testimony, their well-known objectivity of judgment, and their strong individuality, give an inestimable value to what they have to relate. The first account comes from Timon-David; he succeeded in forcing his way in, as it were, much to the joy of the bishop who "gladly welcomed anyone able to reach his bedside":

I had discovered a secret staircase . . . which led directly to his rooms, and by using it I eluded his guards. The first few times I visited him, he would be in his armchair, his beautiful white hair falling over his shoulders, and admirably cared for by the good Sisters of l'Espérance. The day finally came when he could no longer leave his bed and he was given the Last Rites. . . . A few days after that, I came to his bed and knelt beside it without saying a word. He opened his eyes and drew me to him, speaking to me very tenderly. Archbishop Guibert wanted me to leave since all this was tiring the bishop, but the bishop kept a firm hold on me as I remained kneeling beside him, with my head on his chest.

"Monseigneur," he said to the Bishop of Viviers [sic], "he has built a chapel which is actually a cathedral and which I myself consecrated. He has also founded an admirable society. You should go to see his church."

I was with him again on the evening of May 20, but he was motionless—perhaps unconscious. I left, brokenhearted and in tears. A business matter made it necessary for me to sleep that night at La Viste, and when I awoke the following morning, the south wind carried the sound of the doleful tolling of the great bell at Notre Dame de la Garde. It was a great misfortune for our society. We had lost our friend, our protector, our father; our only memory of him as a superior was of the kindness he had shown us.[14]

In the case of Father Jean, the heroic ascetic of the Victims of the Sacred Heart, whose love the bishop had won by settling him in his life's work, it was not in stealth nor by way of a secret staircase that he entered the bishop's room since he was not the assertive type. The "worthy Tempier," who constantly encouraged his efforts, had made an exception, wishing to give him the "consolation of seeing Bishop de Mazenod for one last time." Father Jean wrote:

It was three days before his death. The night before, he had been unable to speak for a long time, and it was felt that the end was near. But on that day, since he was in a clear, edifying, and amiable frame of mind, I knelt at his bedside. He gave me his hand to kiss and invited me to sit down.

"Here you are, back from your rounds," he said to me.

"Yes, Monseigneur."

"You still have much time left, but I—I have reached the top of the mountain."

"We are all praying for you, Monseigneur."

"Thank you. I need it. I am about to give an account of my stewardship. I am counting very much on God's mercy and very little on my own merits."

"Monseigneur, you will be judged by One you have always loved." At these words, the prelate's face brightened.

"Yes, I have loved Him," he replied, "and have labored to have Him loved. Whenever I presided at the Divine Office, it always delighted me to see the canons, pastors, and vicars passing back and forth in front of the Blessed Sacrament and bowing to it. Yes, that always gladdened me. But the Blessed Sacrament deserves more than that."

During those fervent words, two large tears rolled down his face.

"Jesus is even more beautiful in heaven," I said.

"Ah yes! but after such a long episcopate, the way to heaven will be long. I hope my children and my friends come to my assistance."

"Yes, Monseigneur. But it is precisely our deficiencies which bring God's mercy upon us."

The bishop gave a friendly word of reply. Then a convulsion terminated our conversation.[15]

On May 21, after giving his Oblate sons a last blessing and a final exhortation to be charitable to each other and zealous for souls in their work, the old bishop died at the very moment those at his bedside were reciting the last words of the *Salve Regina*: *O clemens! O pia! O dulcis Virgo Maria!*[16] Although, on the preceding days, he had been in a coma much of the time, the dying prelate regained consciousness when his last hour arrived as he had hoped and prayed. In his lucid moments he had frequently murmured: "How I would like to see myself die so that I might freely accept the will of God!" On several occasions, he had insisted with those keeping watch at his bedside: "If I drop off to sleep and become worse, awaken me, I beg you. I want to die knowing that I am dying."[17] The old warrior wanted to make the supreme sacrifice, conscious to the end. And God refused him neither the merit nor the happiness of doing so.

In his lengthy and glowing account of the funeral, Rambert, an eyewitness, describes in great detail the seemingly endless cortege which accompanied the body from the episcopal palace to Saint Martin's church, diocesan priests carrying the remains upon a silver stretcher, the face uncovered. Minute protocol dictated the sumptuous arrangements of the funeral procession which was to be preceded by the police and a line of infantry and followed by a large detachment of infantry-engineers and a detachment of cavalry. Directly behind the police and infantry were the pious sodalities and confraternities of Penitents in their penitential robes and carrying their banners, to be followed by the clergy separated from the venerable chapter by the 42nd Infantry band. Three palls were to be carried by eighteen pallbearers chosen from the administrators of La Providence and the oldest pastors, rectors, and canons. Directly preceding the bier were the prefect, the generals, the president of the Civil Court, and the mayor of Marseilles, and behind it the vicars general, the family, and civil and public authorities. More touching than these official honors, however, was the outpouring of the good people of Marseilles who had flocked to pay honor to the eighty-year-old prelate whom God had just called to Himself. Wrote Rambert:

More than an hour before the procession began, the population of this great city, eager to give a last public demonstration of gratitude, affection, and esteem to its saintly bishop, had assembled along the route of the funeral procession. In spite of the heat from the blazing sun, a dense crowd had jammed the entire stretch of the way from the episcopal palace to Saint Martin's Church; the windows and rooftops, even the yardarms and decks of the ships, were black with spectators, calmly and reverently waiting to view the funeral procession. It was a veritable triumph; a last homage paid by an entire population to one who had been its glory and the object of its love during the twenty-seven years of his episcopate.[18]

Thus, Rambert's account, which was meant to give evidence of a general grief, unwittingly brings out the difference between what, for some, was simply a propriety which had to be observed, and what, for the good people of Marseilles, was a spontaneous outpouring of affection. Certainly, the grief was not universal; but this is always the case, especially when a long episcopate comes to an end. While it is indeed true to say that people "like to see a change, like to discover the unknown and look forward to an entirely new regime," should it be concluded, therefore, as Timon-David did, in defending the memory of Bishop de Mazenod, that "the only fault of his regime was that it lasted too long"? [19] To do so would be to forget that opinion and feeling were divided regarding the prelate during his life, long before he would normally have suffered the fate common to time-worn leaders and institutes. The present biography has shown that he had been a controversial figure during his entire career; but this same biography, without concealing the darker side in favor of the brighter, has honestly attempted, in placing the story of the Bishop of Marseilles in its proper historical and social perspective, to emphasize the effect each side had upon the other. Such, after all, is the only way to understand how the prelate could have been so differently appreciated.

THE MAN AND HIS CONTRASTS

One is mystified by Bishop de Mazenod's contrasts. No sooner have a few harmonious traits been fixed than others suddenly appear, giving the physiognomy an entirely different expression; and, since all these traits are extremely clear-cut, rather than dissolving and blending into one another, they are emphasized. In Bishop de Mazenod's case, the counterpart which always accompanies human qualities actually suited the richness of the human qualities which he possessed and which Timon-David termed "exceptional." [20] In discovering them, one should not be deterred by what is strongly antithetical to them. Very often, the bitterest rind encloses the most savory of fruits.

To add to the complication, his personality which in itself is difficult enough to grasp, went through progressive changes in the day-to-day experience of living in a society in the full process of evolution. Nothing better illustrates this than the three portraits shown here, as different as the dates on which they were made. The first shows a young priest, characterized by provocative austerity; neglected hair-styling, drawn face, and piercing black eyes;

the composite revealing the resolute look of a Restoration missionary, ready to hurl himself into the struggle for souls in order to
reshape a society spiritually deformed by the Revolution. The
second portrait, made when he became Bishop of Icosia, accentu-
ates his self-assurance; he is every inch a bishop of the time of
Charles X; long sideburns, innate authority, firm determination;
less austerely dressed, he reflects his aristocracy, although he still
retains the same intensity and the same lack of gentleness found in
the first portrait. Completely different, however, is the photograph
of the old man, which shows him marked by his trials: it leaves an
impression of a man of fatigue and sad weariness; the forcefulness
is still there but one guesses that it lacks any illusions about human capabilities and that it is mingled with meekness and serenity; in the deep-set and half-closed eyes, what was once a flame has
now become a glow.[21]

However, in spite of the contrasts and variants, which are
more than mere shadings, it is possible to discover the essential
traits of that complex and mobile nature which seems to defy all
the classifications of scientific characterology. Nobility stands out
above all others. Even physically, the prelate made a striking appearance with his tall stature, his regal bearing, his dignity and
air of distinction, and, during liturgical functions, his pontifical
stateliness. Morally, he preserved the best of what was found in
the ancient nobility, elevating it through grace to what theolo-
gians term the virtue of magnanimity. Meanness and mediocrity of
mind and manner made him bristle. He could not tolerate doing
things or seeing them done half-way on the human level, but he
was particularly intolerant of this in the service of God and of the
Church; he set no restrictions on either his generosity or his views;
hence the exacting demands he made upon himself and upon
others whose potential he did not always gauge accurately. And
yet, in spite of appearances, there was nothing distant about him,
for, faithful to the noble traditions of his class, he proved accessible, simple, and, in fact, easygoing; genuine aristocracy was revealed even "in his dignified simplicity with his inferiors," which,
as Brassevin wrote, "was an exclusive prerogative of a bygone society." [22]

His nobility was enhanced by his straightforwardness. This
does not mean that he lacked the skill of diplomacy. At the time

of the Rossi mission, for example, he came to the rescue of the papal Secretary of State by composing a note which settled a very ticklish situation; and there were other undertakings just as skillfully directed and other negotiations just as successfully carried out. His type of diplomacy, however, countenanced no underhanded methods, no hedging and no evasive language, and never, during his entire administration, did he resort to the clever little ruses in which his uncle, good Fortuné, excelled. In his opinion, it was far preferable to go straight to the point, to express his mind frankly, and not to substitute the timid and shifty *perhaps* for the straight *yes* or *no*. Far from hiding behind formulas that were as vague as they were insincerely unctious and pious, he couched his arguments and categorical refusals in trenchant and blunt expressions. It was a costly error, therefore, for anyone to try to play mean tricks upon him while feigning an innocent look, or to try to hoax him or to alter the truth by picturing things to suit his purpose, or to break his word. At such times, his indignation exploded and his letters became veritable thunderbolts. Eventually he always forgave, but not without first making it unmistakably clear that he was perfectly right in feeling as he did, and that the individual was to guard against making the same mistake a second time.

This intransigent and even blunt frankness inevitably earned him opposition and criticism which, in turn, caused him great suffering. By nature, he was extremely sensitive; only those who did not know him well and who judged him by his outward severity, doubted his tender heart, little suspecting that this severity was merely a defense mechanism he employed in order to combat the deep-rooted inclinations of a nature all too fiery and prone to extreme enthusiasm. In his private notes and examinations of conscience, he readily admitted that he had to be on his guard to discipline himself in this matter. He likewise admitted that he needed to feel loved in order to open up, to give of himself, and to permit his inner richness to flow freely. The least coolness, even simple reserve, hurt him, and prevented his real qualities from manifesting themselves. Consequently, one had to ignore first impressions which were sometimes not encouraging, for, later, the individual concerned would be treated to a brusque but nonetheless touching demonstration of affection. Because they could not overlook a seemingly icy attitude, or wait for his second mood which more or less quickly followed the first, many people misjudged him, deceived by the outward appearances which corresponded so little to the hidden reality. Timon-David, who knew him better, gives the following picturesque account of how he found a way to unmask Bishop de Mazenod's affectionate kindness:

One day, my heart was very heavy, for in this work, troubles have always depressed me. I went to the bishop's palace. I was told that His Excellency was at Saint-Louis. I took a carriage; I arrived; no one at the door, the place wide-open. I went up to his room on the second floor; no sign of a servant; his bedroom door open. Hearing a sound, I drew back to the opposite end of the hallway, but he had heard me.
"Who's there?"
At that question, made snappishly, I started meekly towards his door.
"It's me, Monseigneur."
"Who told you I was here? Can't a bishop have a moment's peace?"
Etc. I didn't know which way to move and my knees were knocking. I then replied:
"I'm sorry, Monseigneur. I'll leave."
"No! As long as you're here, wait for me in the hallway."
A moment later, I heard a formidable *Entrez!* Stammering, I tried to explain what had brought me there, and as I went along, there were clear signs that his heart was softening. The storm was passing. He became kind again, then affectionate, and finally fatherly.
"But my child! When you have troubles like this, why don't you come and tell me about them? Am I not your father?"
And with these words, he embraced me, and my cheeks were moistened by his tears. No one I ever knew could mesmerize me as he could.[23]

On certain days—so Timon-David attests—it was more than mere brusqueness, but real "blasts of the mistral," for, like his compatriots, in fact, like the land of Provence itself, he had his stormy days. On such occasions, all that could be done was to wait out the storm patiently.
One day, writes Timon:

I touched a very sore spot. I had gone to Notre Dame de la Garde to say Mass. At that time, there were only three altars in the wretched shed that was being used as a temporary chapel. If you intended to say Mass there, you wrote your name on a slate in the sacristy. I was the

fourth one to sign and, therefore, should have been the first of the
second three. I had a strict right to that place. But when I came into
the vestry, three Oblates were there ahead of me. That was unfair.
Father Aubert, the chaplain, made a thousand apologies, explaining
that they were three missionaries about to set out on a journey. I
returned to the sanctuary. At the *Pater Noster,* I again went to the
sacristy to vest. Three other Oblates had already put on the vestments.
This was a plot. I could no longer bear it, and I complained bitterly
that we seculars no longer amounted to anything in our diocese and
that the Oblates were everything. I then ended with this peroration:
Indundatio camelorum operiet nos! This burst of ill temper need not
have had any sequel, had not the Oblates immediately reported the
incident to the bishop. Such anger! I had struck the apple of his eye.
A few days later, he officiated at a confirmation at the Brothers' school
on Villiers Boulevard. After the ceremony, we were all standing around
in a large parlor; His Excellency kept pacing back and forth, talking
to no one, his face dark with anger. Everyone was waiting for the storm
to break when, coming straight at me, he said in a low voice: "You
behaved disgracefully the other day at Notre Dame de la Garde. You
called the Oblates camels."

"Monseigneur," I answered, "this is not the time to discuss it. But
when you hear my side. . . ." But he had already turned his back on
me, and for the remainder of the time we were there he was in a
charming mood. There you have the blustery mistral of Marseilles.
Now for the warm sunshine. Some days later, I was sponsor at an investiture at the Refuge. With a friendly smile, His Excellency said to me:

"You will serve my Mass?"

"I can't Monseigneur. I have to sing the Chapter High Mass at
nine-thirty.

"No matter; you'll still have time."

At the *Sanctus,* I motioned to the chaplain to come to take the stole.
Noticing it and not hesitating to talk during his Mass, he said to me:

"You're leaving now? Come back for breakfast."

"I won't be able to, Monseigneur; it's too far away; I'll be too
late."

But he still insisted with that charming graciousness in which he
excelled during his good moments. He evidently wanted to make
amends for his fit of temper two days before.[24]

Since he knew Bishop de Mazenod well, loved him, and was
loved by him, Timon-David took little umbrage at these tantrums
ignoring them mostly on the grounds that the prelate was a "true

Provençal." [25] As far as Timon was concerned, the prelate's quickness of temper and petulance, both of a very local color, in no way detracted from the work accomplished by the episcopal administration; under the next four episcopates, it inflicted the third of the "Seven Sorrows" upon the director of the Working-Boys' Society.

As much a victim as anyone to these outbursts, good Father Tempier had his own method of calming the "mistral" immediately. Without saying a word, he allowed the prelate to blow off steam, and when everything became quiet simply asked: "What then? . . ." Nothing further was needed to restore calm immediately.[26] To those who overlooked these outbursts and accepted him as he was, Bishop de Mazenod was deeply grateful, for never would he have deliberately or needlessly hurt anyone. In fact, whenever the responsibility of his office obliged him to give a reprimand or a just punishment, it actually pained him to do so. But once his duty as superior was fulfilled, he made every effort to encourage and console.

Quick-tempered, he was also quick-witted. His intellectual formation, it is true, had its gaps; during his emigration—except for a short time at Turin—he had been unable to follow the usual courses in grammar and the humanities and as a result lacked an essentially classical culture; the lessons he received from the Zinellis in Venice gave him only the briefest introduction to the material the usual unbroken course of studies at a college would have provided. His ecclesiastical studies at Saint Sulpice were likewise incomplete since a shortage of priests at that time prompted a reduction in the number of years of seminary training so that the number of effectives in the various dioceses might be increased as quickly as possible. After his ordination, his consuming zeal and very active life hardly permitted him time to broaden and deepen his knowledge of the sacred sciences. So many deficiencies imputable to circumstances and common to the clergy of his time! His natural bent, however, more than compensated for the methodical training he had been unable to receive. Intuitive by nature, he went straight to the heart of problems, discerned their factors, gauged their importance and difficulties, their proximate and remote consequences, and then, without any delay, supplied "a clear and precise solution." [27] His rapidity in evaluating situations confounded experts accustomed to lengthy reflection, for speculation was entirely foreign to this man of action who wanted to bring things to actuality and much preferred realizing to theorizing. In his many and diversified undertakings, just as in his sermons, the prelate excelled in improvisations which a given situation suggested to him, and, without any minutely devised plan, made the fullest use of everything which could arouse or sustain a desired enthusiasm. In initiating or broadening his activities, he excelled in seizing opportunities as they occurred, including the most unforeseen.

Such spontaneity might prompt one to think that, with little concern for reflection or consideration, Bishop de Mazenod would act precipitately, like a fiery cavalry officer who recklessly urges his men forward. In reality, he had great difficulty in making decisions, particularly in matters of some importance, as was the case in choosing his priestly vocation, in founding his missionary society, and in seeking the approval of the Holy See for his Oblate Rules. As a young priest, he admitted his irresolution to Janson who deplored such "dilly-dallying." Was this the price he had to pay for a perspicacity which paralyzed his will in the face of reasons for and against, as sometimes happens with men of keen intelligence? The explanation is different: when Janson dubbed his friend a "lazy rump," he had, in crude terms, expressed the difficulty exactly. Bestirring himself was Bishop de Mazenod's biggest difficulty, and as proof of this it is necessary only to cite the letter which he, still the Bishop of Icosia, wrote to Father Tempier on August 25, 1835, when he was being considered for promotion to the coadjutorship of Marseilles:

Those people who are always making wrong judgments have concluded that, because I have accomplished many difficult things in my life where others perhaps would have failed, I am enterprising by nature and that I have a compulsive desire to be active and moving about. It is just the opposite. If I have been active, if I have exerted myself, and if I have undertaken difficult things with successful results, I did so only from a sense of duty—because it was impossible for me to reject a kind of evidence which proved to me that such and such an undertaking was a mission Divine Providence was entrusting to me. But, deep down, I have always had a great aversion for all kinds of undertakings. . . . Also, you may have noticed that in the stress of a very turbulent life, whenever I was able to conceal my whereabouts and to keep out of sight—in short, to retire into solitude—I felt that I was in my proper element, and I had to do violence to myself to tear myself away from it.[28]

Thus yet another interior tension appears and a new contrast between what the Bishop of Marseilles seemed to be and what he actually was.

But, if the prelate did not easily arrive at decisions, his decisions, once made, could not be checked. When he finally decided to found his Society of the Missionaries of Provence, he wrote to Janson: "I have committed myself to the utmost." [29] These were no empty words. The very laborious beginnings and the very slow progress of his Congregation bear this out. And what is true of his cherished Oblates is true of everything he did. Contradictions, disappointments, and frustrations, unable to dishearten him, seemed rather to stimulate him. His iron will enabled him to defy all obstacles, even to tackle them head-on instead of circumventing them. Time, which consumes as it passes, could not diminish his unflagging energy. Admittedly, with experience and age, and even more, with the efforts he expended to master his fiery temperament,[30] his manner of doing things became less aggressive. Nonetheless, although he measured his strokes more carefully where before he had inflicted them too vigorously, and although he adopted less extreme positions, his resoluteness never wavered, and, far from laying down his arms, the valiant old bishop stayed in the fight to the very end. He was criticized for various things, but no one could ever accuse him of failing to uphold his convictions, or, once stirred to action, of losing his enthusiasm and retreating because of discouragement or lassitude.

HIS SPIRITUAL LIFE

Such a rich and mercurial temperament demanded that he raise to the level of charity the best of his natural instinctive actions, and to discipline the fiery impulses which could be even more detrimental to his personal sanctification than to the fruitfulness of his ministry. Aware of the task he had to accomplish within himself if he were to attain to his priestly, spiritual, and apostolic ideal, Bishop de Mazenod never relaxed in his efforts.

That these efforts were an integral part of the general movement of the Church in France where the religious life was being reanimated, and that they conformed to the style of that period without adding anything very new, no one can deny. In no way did the Bishop of Marseilles consider himself a master of a school of spirituality. Nor is this particularly remarkable since, until the time of Bishop Gay in 1874, with the exception of Gerbet, there was no master of the spiritual life to be found in France. Nonetheless, there was great spirituality—and at times it was intense—as a few experimental soundings will indicate until such time as a deeper and broader investigation succeeds in discovering the full force of the current. But for what did exist, there was neither the necessary time nor method available for formulating it and for devoting works of value to it. For the scarcity of priests was growing and the many restorations that had to be accomplished absorbed all the activity of those who were available; and, too, the prevalent insufficiency of learning prevented the proper syntheses and the necessary art of presentation. Under these circumstances, the Bishop of Marseilles was no exception. Although he wrote much concerning the paths leading to communion with God, he did so in a completely haphazard fashion—that is, through his episcopal acts, through the Rule of his Congregation and through his correspondence—and never did it occur to him to organize what circumstances led him to counsel into a compact body of teachings.

Furthermore, his teachings are neither exclusive nor systematic. In fact, this improvisor was not concerned with theories; rather, being a man of action, he borrowed indiscriminately from the various schools, selecting whatever seemed to suit his purpose without any pretence at anything original. Of his first spiritual formation at Venice, the founder retained certain elements of the Ignatian method, which he had learned from the Zinellis as a young boy. Father Magy, who convinced him of his vocation, also exercised a similar influence on him, and the seminary at Paris failed to offset this original orientation. Father Tronson had imitated Father Olier, and Father Duclaux, Eugene's spiritual director, had devoted his efforts to formalizing a method of meditation to be used by priests. But Father Émery, who took the young cleric under his wing, gave him a deeper insight into the *Méta-*

physique des Saints. Steeped in the great masters of the French school of spirituality, "the little priest" left his personal mark upon Eugene de Mazenod, and it was a strong one. It is not surprising therefore to recognize Émery's spirit and his love of the interior life *(in Christo Jesu)* in the founder's daily schedule or to recognize much of Saint Sulpice in the Congregation of the Oblates. A final factor in his spiritual formation—since we are limiting ourselves to essentials—was the contribution of Saint Alphonsus Liguori. During his emigration to Naples and Sicily, the young de Mazenod had seen the Redemptorists at work and their zeal had left a lasting impression on him. The ministry to which the Missionaries of Provence at first devoted themselves exclusively was quite similar to that of the Redemptorists, for Bishop de Mazenod shared the great Italian Doctor's aversion for Gallicanism and Jansenism. "Oriented in thought and desire toward the conversion of sinners and their final perseverance," [31] the Liguorian spirituality was ideally suited to the members of the Aix community who specialized in preaching the Four Last Ends and who sought to open paths to perfect charity by instilling fear. In that spirituality, asceticism took precedence over mysticism; the saint's preference leaned toward active contemplation, and, in discussing passive contemplation and to explain its steps, he advised distrusting extraordinary states. This idea the Bishop of Marseilles found hard to accept since his experiences in the ministry eventually inclined him toward a certain "pessimism" [32] which may have contributed to making him less rigorous than the confessors of his day in discouraging the weaknesses of sinners.

Thus, the style which the spirituality of the nineteenth century was to assume, and even stress, was already emerging. Like the pastoral action of that time, particularly that found in the renowned missions of the Restoration, this spirituality was actually inspired by a defense reaction to a society born of the Revolution. The world of which Christ had spoken generically by alluding to all countries and ages without specifying any particular one now became clearly individualized in the mind of the clergy, who had survived the Revolution or were still suffering from it, because of its opposition to the beautiful periods of faith in the past. It was impossible to love that world and therefore there was no need to understand it. It had to be rejected and escaped until such time as it could be restored to its former state and be totally regenerated. Hence there was a stiffness and a severity which were intended only to be safeguards.

We can understand, therefore, why Bishop de Mazenod, like other religious founders and seminary directors of his day, multiplied the rules and regulations of his congregation; for in so doing, he felt he could more surely prevent any dangerous infiltration of the modern spirit by imposing tighter restrictions upon his subjects. On the other hand, since, in order to combat the satanic work of the Constitutionals and Jacobins, it was necessary not only to remedy dechristianization but also to replace the suppressed monasteries which had been devoted to penance and prayer, Father de Mazenod, in 1818, intended that his congregation undertake this two-fold aim. An harmonious combination of these two aims was not to be accomplished without the creation of onerous problems. But it was here that the man came into his own; not concerned with trying to solve problems theoretically by discussing the comparative excellence of contemplative orders, active orders and the combinations of the two, he used his talent for improvizing and his common sense, fully confident of succeeding. Besides this, his magnanimity induced him to reject any choice which would simplify his task and lessen his sacrifice. By committing himself "to the utmost," he had intended to give his all. But, though he had no doubts about himself, did he sufficiently gauge mankind at that time? Naturally, he expected that with experience and time, and without changing his mind, he would have to make adjustments. Moreover, several years passed before his constitutions, put to the test, were approved by the Holy See. No matter how unique his personality may have been, Bishop de Mazenod's case is quite similar to that of the other founders of the period. They all bore marks common to their time, although in style, the style of the nineteenth century, there should be some allowance made for the peculiarities of the style of Provence. For the Congregation of the Oblates, these peculiarities of Provence would grow proportionately fainter as it broadened its recruitment and extended its work, but it would still preserve intact the spirit which had originally inspired the Aix community.

In the beginning the founder had planned to adopt the title Oblates of Saint Charles for his congregation. It is important to emphasize this in order not to underestimate the prelate's debt to the model of pastors and reformers of the Tridentine era. Like all the de Mazenods, he was given Cardinal Borromeo as his patron saint; this was a family tradition, inspired more by social considerations than by spiritual preferences, since the originator of the noble line who was admitted at Marseilles to hereditary nobility, bore the Christian name of Charles, and giving each of his descendants this name seemed an additional guarantee of their authentic aristocracy. The other Christian names which distinguished one from the other always came second. The firstborn of the president of the Court of Accounts, baptized Charles Joseph Eugene, always honored this precedence of Charles in a more Christian spirit than did his ancestors. While there is nothing to prove that he showed any particular devotion to Saint Eugene, there is abundant evidence to prove his devotion to the Cardinal of Milan. Although his godparents obviously had no such thing in mind, the prelate esteemed as providential a patronage which proposed the attainment of such a high degree of perfection and which assured him such powerful protection. He favored seeking the intercession of Saint Charles. On his feast day, when best wishes were extended to him through speeches or letters, he replied by asking the well-wishers to pray to the saint for his intentions. The oratory in the episcopal palace and that of the major seminary were dedicated to the saint whose first name he bore. His *Journal* brings out what consolation he experienced when "celebrating the Sacred Mysteries in the crypt where the body of the sainted archbishop reposed."

I am going back there in a few minutes to make a careful examination of this chapel which is all lined with silver and to see the exposed body of the saint which is enclosed in a silver casket. If I can obtain a relic, I shall be very pleased, for all those which were given to me at Rome are only pieces of his purple robes and did not greatly enrich my devotion.[33]

The prelate frequently stated his determination to walk in his patron's footsteps. This was the case during the missions in Provence, when he used Borromeo as a model to carrying the cross personally in the penitential procession;[34] and especially so during his episcopate. In 1817, he wrote to his uncle Fortuné, when the latter was designated for the see of Marseilles: "We shall take Saint Charles and Saint Francis de Sales as our patrons and models." [35] While fully regretting that he was personally inferior to that ideal, he intended to equal his model by realizing in his own diocese what the cardinal had accomplished in his locality. "I remember," he wrote in his retreat notes prior to receiving his uncle's succession,

that there was a time when I felt such vigor of soul on reading the life of Saint Charles, that it did not seem beyond my power to do as much as he did in his position. I am less rash today, now that I have learned through experience how weak I am and how little help must be expected from others when work must be done.[36]

Again, on the authority of the archbishop of Milan he took a stand to justify certain of his attitudes and decisions as vicar general. When he was reproached for proving more rigorous than certain bishops regarding the fast, Father de Mazenod wrote:

Personally, I see in all these dispensations, which·are in no way demanded by necessity, an act of weakness, a veritable sacrificial offering made to this anti-Christian century in order to wheedle the tiger. Do you want my true opinion on the matter? They want to be considered softhearted and compassionate, and now that the trend has started, it has become a question of who will grant the most dispensations so as not to lag behind the others. Saint Charles would not have acted thus, nor will I, who am no Saint Charles, just plain Charles.[37]

Another time he was accused of being too lenient in the quarrels about freedom of education; after noting that the too-absolute ideas and the verbal excesses of unauthorized lay people were playing into the hands of the enemies of the faith, the prelate added:

So as not to give our enemies such an advantage, I very gladly consent to being accused of making a pact with my century and, in that, I am imitating my patron, Saint Charles, whose zeal for the Faith has never seemed to me to be suspected of weakness.[38]

Finally, in answer to the criticisms about the dominant role of the Oblates in his diocese and the preference he was showing them, he recalled that, to restore discipline and reinforce his clergy, Saint Charles Borromeo had founded a society of Oblates in his diocese and had favored them far more than the Bishop of Marseilles favored his.[39] Evidently, then, in spite of what the young missionary of Provence wrote to his uncle in 1817, his manner, during his episcopate, was influenced less by Saint Francis de Sales than by Saint Charles, whose character more closely mirrored his own than did that of de Sales, who was always gentle and cheerful even in his strictest demands. Like the cardinal of Milan after the Protestant Reformation, Eugene de Mazenod, especially at the beginning of his ministry following the revolutionary crisis, set himself as a counter-reformationist. In fact, he derived from his patron not so much a spirituality as an indomitable energy, a program of action, and a certain manner which suited his natural temperament. However, though strength dominated the exterior, as it did with Borromeo whose example he wanted to imitate, that strength swelled from an interior fullness which he derived from his intimate union with Christ Jesus.

The intensity and depth of Bishop de Mazenod's spiritual life could not go unnoticed by the people of his diocese. His austerity especially impressed them. His intransigence in the matter of abstinence was common knowledge, even at official receptions, including those of His Imperial Majesty. Whenever meat was served at these receptions on days of abstinence, the bishop refused every course, and even refused to unfold his napkin. It was commonly known that he increased his fasts and observed them so strictly that his evening collation on days of fast became restricted to a glass of water and a few mouthfuls of bread. Even in his old age, the prelate refused to reduce either the number or the rigor of his fasts and to those who cited his old age as a justification for lessening or mitigating them, he replied: "My eighty years might dispense me from fasting, but they do not dispense me from doing penance for my sins." [40] As for his corporal chastisements, he never ceased inflicting them on himself from the days of his seminary training.

The rich pomp which his episcopal functions obliged him to display during public ceremonies contrasted with the poverty of his private life. When he had to appear in public as bishop, he conformed to the requirements of the liturgy in religious ceremo-

nies, and, at civil receptions, he insisted on the rights which protocol demanded. On such occasions, it was not he, personally, but the
plenitude of the priesthood which had to be respected and honored. In his private life, however, there was nothing more simple
than his complete and quasi-monastic manner of living surrounded
by his Oblates. Naturally, in the episcopal palace of Marseilles,
certain rooms had to be properly outfitted for important occasions
and official receptions; the prelate's bedroom, however, had only
scant furnishings, including a bed which was as wretched as it
was uncomfortable. Well-groomed when making a public appearance, he was quite happy when, at his country retreat of Saint
Louis, he was able to wear an old patched cassock more or less
short of buttons and braiding. "I am a bishop, but I have also
taken the vow of poverty." [41] Father Avignon recalls, "One would
have mistaken him for a poor country pastor in purple." [42] The
prelate was amused by the remarks occasioned by his unceremonial
attire and sometimes joked about it; once in discussing it with
Father Jean, the ascetic, he compared his attire with the latter's
sorry frock-coat and made no secret of the fact that the rest of his
clothing was even less dazzling: "If they could only see what's un-
derneath!" he exclaimed with a hearty laugh.[43] All this was in
keeping with his style of asceticism which was by no means stiff
and gloomy; in the spirit of the Gospel, he preferred the unrestrained and joyful type.

The poverty which Bishop de Mazenod practiced in his personal life made him all the more compassionate and generous toward the poor, and thus he maintained the traditions of his own
family and of the *grand seigneur* bishops of the *Ancien Régime*,
who, though criticized for many things, are unanimously ap-
plauded by historians for their inexhaustible charity. The prelate,
who was often accused of being difficult to approach, actually threw
open his door, his heart and his purse to all who came seeking
help. "What a trying day!" he wrote in his *Journal*, September 3,
1838. "Such a stream of unfortunates whose miseries, much to my
regret and heartache, I was able to relieve only slightly even
though I gave out a large sum of money!" Two days later, when
there followed in succession a widow "without a penny," a young
Belgian who had "only ten francs" to get him back to his country,

an "old woman, the sister of a priest" who "doesn't have a farthing to her name," and many more equally to be pitied, the Bishop of Marseilles reached the point of avowing: "If mornings like this one and several others like it were to happen too often, I doubt if I could bear it." Giving money away "meant nothing" to him, but "not being able to provide for every need and trying to do the impossible" is what wore him down. "It is more than I can bear! . . . With all that staring you in the face, sit down and eat if you can." [44] The prelate's help was not limited to the many who came to his door seeking alms; he also cared for those destitute who said nothing of their misery and who, very often, were the most deserving of help and the most pitiful of cases. Father Mouchette related: "There was a kind lady, I think she was called *Grande-Marie*, whom he delegated to distribute his alms secretly to the poor who were too ashamed to ask for help. This woman sought them out diligently, then reported back to the bishop, informing him of her discoveries, and went off again, bringing them his help." [45]

Although he wrote that "giving money away meant nothing," there were times when Bishop de Mazenod found himself without any to give, for, after allocating his bishop's salary for diocesan projects, and donating his senator's salary to his congregation, he had to find at least 14,000 francs a year to take care of his almsgiving.[46] "I never have a cent," he wrote to Tempier, March 10, 1859.[47] Consequently he was all smiles when his purse was replenished for then he was able to empty it again. "One day," relates Father Mouchette, who witnessed the quaint scene, "two Little Sisters of the Poor visited his office."

"We were making our rounds in the neighborhood, Your Excellancy, and our Reverend Mother gave us strict orders not to miss seeing you today."   .

"She has a good guardian angel, this mother of yours," said the smiling bishop; but she must also have some problems"; then he opened the right-hand drawer of his desk and took out a hundred-franc note which he handed to the sister; then a second one, a third, and so on up to ten. Each time he gave her one, the sisters, bowing, thanked him and started to leave. This playful little game evidently tickled the prelate's fancy since he was all smiles. When the sisters had gone, the Bishop said to me:

"That's odd; you'd think that they knew that my desk drawer was well-stocked. They must have needed that money badly since I happened to have it so handy." [48]

Another incident, this one related by Father Brandouin, seems like something straight out of the Fiorettis.

I heard this from a priest who is thoroughly trustworthy; he related the incident at my table in the presence of several other priests when I was pastor of l'Éstaque; with his own eyes, he saw Bishop de Mazenod, dressed like a simple priest and divested of all the insignia of his dignity, remove his shoes in the very middle of the street—this in the dead of winter, mind you—and after making a pauper put them on, he went in his stocking feet to buy a new pair at a nearby shoemaker's.[49]

Although it was less spectacular than such acts of charity, the self-renunciation exacted by an overwhelming amount of work which he regularly performed day after day just as truly suggests rare virtue. But, then, the duties of one's state in life are always one of the essential touchstones used in judging the genuineness of a spirit of sacrifice. Bishop de Mazenod's time was never his own: in addition to the already burdensome and complex task of directing a diocese which included the second most important city in France, he assumed the responsibility for the direction of his congregation and of all the religious matters of France and Rome which he was called upon to handle. Upon his shoulders, too, rested the burden of protecting the interests of his diocese and of the Church in France and of Rome as well as those of the distant regions where his missionaries were laboring.[50] On his chancery desk, there was always a mound of letters, and at the episcopal palace a flood of visitors; constantly interrupted and forever exposed to the danger of the unforeseen, he had to deny himself sleep in order to settle the most urgent matters and to handle his correspondence. What the Oblates have preserved of that correspondence and what is contained in public and private archives constitute a veritable mountain of letters, all the more impressive in view of the fact that these letters were not mere notes, hastily composed. In that era, long letters were the custom, and the improvising bishop who allowed his pen to wander was not gifted with the skill of conciseness in expressing his thoughts or the outpourings of his heart. His sojourns at Saint Louis—supposedly vacations—were devoted to his mail which kept him at his desk for four or five hours at a time. But, the country retreat at least afforded him an enjoyable calm and tranquility. From the moment he returned to Marseilles, his routine was once again determined by the countless obligations which comprised his busy schedule; for, in addition to his many duties at the palace, there were visits to be made to parishes, organizations and sick people, matters to be discussed with local civil authorities, trips to be made outside his diocese when the interests of his congregation and those of the Church demanded them, and sojourns to Paris necessitated by his duties as senator. His tasks, rather than lessening with the passing of the years, grew heavier as his prestige and influence increased, for he was regarded as one of the most forceful personalities of the French episcopacy. His old age, in fact, was the most active period of his long career, and long before Father Chevrier formulated his celebrated definition of a priest as "a man devoured," the prelate had verified it.

Not that this "devoured" man excelled any less in maintaining and developing his spiritual activity without which even the most tireless apostolate is fatally drained of its substance; however active he may have been in public life, Bishop de Mazenod always gave first consideration to the interior life, for without it he would have remained, in the words of Saint Paul, "a sounding brass and tinkling cymbal." He spared no pains in safeguarding and nourishing it, adhering strictly to the schedule of spiritual exercises which he had originally devised for himself at Saint Sulpice and which his Oblate Rule imposed on him. If, in order to adhere to it, it was necessary for him to take from his sleeping hours, already greatly reduced by prolonged vigils, the prelate advanced the hour fixed for his rising. Efforts sometimes made upon him to consider his health and, toward the end of his life, to consider his age were to no avail. Besides becoming slightly peeved at this belittling of his physical vigor which the years had treated kindly, he turned a deaf ear to these counsels, claiming that they were inspired by misplaced prudence. Does not the grace of God permit a man to grow proportionately stronger as he realizes his own weakness? Man of action though he was, Bishop de Mazenod desired especially to be a man of prayer.

It is impossible to know if he always remained faithful to good Father Duclaux's simple method of meditation, or whether he escaped its restrictions and gained access to mystical paths. We do know, however, that the people of his diocese were deeply impressed by his devout reflection and by the intensity of his prayer life. Of course, they had no way of knowing what went on each morning when, in his palace, the prelate knelt at his prie-dieu or silently paced back and forth in his room. During ceremonies, especially during pontifical services at the cathedral, they were all so forcefully impressed watching him officiate that it took little searching on their part to discover the source of his great, simple, and deeply religious dignity. It is true that those who were near him at choir sometimes heard him intersperse the liturgical texts with a side remark in Provençal which hardly conformed to the traditional ejaculatory style of prayer since he could not tolerate any violation of rubrics; however, although these reproaches could be provoked by the least mistake in ceremony, they were unfailingly attributed to his praiseworthy concern to honor the Lord in a faultless fashion. Besides, on such occasions, he quickly gained control of himself and resumed a union with God which then became even more perceptible. As for the outward pomp so favored in church services at that time, it was not for itself that he loved it, and still less for the prestige he gained from it personally, but because it was intended to mirror as closely as possible the infinite perfection of the Most Holy Trinity.

During the forty hours' devotions which he established in his diocese toward the end of his life, both the clergy and the faithful had greater opportunity to watch him at prayer. Bishop de Mazenod greatly prized this popular form of devotion to the Eucharist because it was intended as a reparation for the errors and sins of a society perverted by the Revolution and because it fostered a close contact with the Eucharist; and consequently, in 1859, he ordered every parish to take its turn in maintaining an unbroken observance of the devotion throughout the entire diocese.[51] He was always delighted with the ceremony that accompanied it, and the more the exposed monstrance was surrounded by tapestries, flowers, and lights, and the higher it was raised to attract eyes and hearts to it, so much the more did he express his edification and delight. So greatly did the bishop esteem these devotions that he set the example by participating in them personally, and in spite of his multiple occupations, he made it a rule to attend them in each church in Marseilles when its turn came. He remained on his knees for an hour, so filled with the divine presence that he fell into ecstasies,[52] and sworn testimony given in this regard leaves no doubt that, at times, God had publicly favored him with genuine mystical states. If he experienced any privately in his morning meditations, humility and discretion would have prevented him from revealing them.

Once, during Holy Thursday night and Good Friday services, when a question arose about observing the traditional adoration before what was then improperly called "the tomb," Bishop de Mazenod pushed intransigence to the extent of imposing a mortifying lesson upon the clergy of the cathedral who were planning to cancel it. Since they were obliged to be present at the cathedral at 5.30 on Good Friday morning for a sermon on the Passion, the pastor and curates felt that such a long vigil on Holy Thursday night would be too exhausting. The bishop then sought to rekindle their zeal by informing them he would preside personally. Thus, they were forced to attend in a body, although they had already instructed the parishioners to the contrary. In fact, it was not until some time after 11 P.M. that the prelate sent them off to bed; he remained there himself until dawn, animating the prayers of the faithful by his exhortations and by readings from Louis de Grenade,[53] and this, in spite of the fact that he was scheduled to pontificate at the Good Friday services and in spite of the fatigue which his fearful fasting of Holy Week had accentuated.

HIS APOSTOLIC ACTIVITY

This intimate and profound union with God inspired, animated, and sustained Bishop de Mazenod's apostolic life. To that union he owed his devouring zeal in the service of the Church and of souls. During his entire life and under all political regimes, he never ceased the fight to defend the Church from the perils which threatened it from without since he allowed no temporal government, not even that of the legitimate king, to violate the rights of the spiritual; and this was never more the case than at the time of the 1828 Ordinances. After his reconciliation with Louis-Philippe, the prelate broke away from him over the issue of freedom of education. Though sympathetic with the aims of the Revolution of 1848, he no less vehemently protested its projected laws concerning religious worship. The Roman Question, which prevented him from voting for Prince Bonaparte at the time of the presidential election of 1848, once again put him into the opposition after 1859, in spite of the honors which the Empire had showered upon him. His last address to the Senate, an effort to save the Papal States, signalled the end of his public career. On the local scene as well, he always played a major part in repelling subversive attacks or violent uprisings against the clergy and the sodalities or of checking all administrative measures prejudicial to his diocese.

In his determination to make the Church stronger against the powers of evil, the Bishop of Marseilles attempted to concentrate all the forces of Catholicism under the direction of the hierarchy, convinced that such authority belonged to the hierarchy by divine right. Convinced, too, that all the political and religious authority which the Revolution had destroyed should be restored in its entirety, the prelate was militant in his ultramontanism and in his support of the cause of the Holy Father: more than ever before, Peter had to be Head. These convictions, too, prompted the vigor with which the Bishop of Marseilles dominated his priests and flock and his vigilance in checking all initiatives, especially those of the laity, which would presume to substitute their individual, zealous innovations for the directives of their chief shepherd.

There is no denying that, under the circumstances, his supernatural views were more or less influenced by the French Catholicism of his day and by his own natural tendencies. In fact, he had not escaped what one might call "the obsidional mentality" of his absolutist contemporaries. In his eyes, the Revolution was still effecting its antireligious work of disintegration; the Church, like a besieged fortress, had to defend her lost or regained positions against massive attacks or crafty infiltrations. But his temperament, his education and what remained of his extremist spirit inclined him toward absolutism. Though at one time he had resigned himself to living under a parliamentary regime, he could not allow democracy to be introduced into ecclesiastical institutions at the expense of indispensable discipline. But, rather than minimizing what the spirit of his times and his personal preferences injected into his theological principles and his ardent struggles, we ought, on the contrary, to stress their importance, in order to bring into bold relief the attitude he always adopted as priest and bishop toward the successive forms of governments he saw in France.

None of the testimony gathered after his death about this delicate and vital issue is of greater value than the statement made by M. de Foresta, grandson of the former sub-prefect of Aix:

In his spirit of faith, [Bishop de Mazenod] put religion in the first place and then extended the hand of loyalty to all governments, to the degree that they remained true to their obligations, deeming it unworthy of a bishop to play the role of either critic or flatterer. By holding to such conduct, he truly gained much merit, for I know . . . that his birth bound him to the nobility, his family traditions to the royalty, and his heart to the older branch of the Bourbons to the very end of his life. . . . Like his father, President de Mazenod, he retained a personal preference for the legitimate kings of France, but, as bishop, he had no wish to be systematically opposed to any government, if religion and the common good were safeguarded. For that reason, in supporting the Empire, at the time of my birth, just as formerly in other periods he had supported the Republic and the constitutional monarchy, he was never a courtesan or an obsequious lackey. He would never have allowed his gratitude to the emperor for the favors he had received . . . to detract from his rights as a priest and a bishop. . . . According to the traditions in my family, the Servant of God, therefore, was admirably skilled in reconciling his political preferences with his patriotic duties and with his duties as priest and bishop, without considering any personal interests and generously placing the interests of the Church and of souls above all others. Few people of his time appreciated this magnanimous attitude: certain of his legitimist friends, watching him rally to the good side of the Empire and of the Republic, accused him of ambition and ingratitude, and, at the same time, certain friends of the Empire and the Republic accused him of hypocrisy and calculation—all this because he knew how to maintain a happy medium and because he always refused to allow himself to be drawn into the maelstrom of party politics, believing that he had enough to do to defend the faith of his people.[54]

Thus, the Bishop of Marseilles proved completely true to the principles of Father Émery who, during the Revolution and later during the reign of Napoleon, was determined to remain on religious terrain exclusively, to be nothing but a priest, and, for the good of souls and the independence of the spiritual, to break the ties binding the Church to the *Ancien Régime*. To reach that same mental attitude, Émery's "Mazenod" of 1815 had to escape from a mentality restricting him too narrowly to concepts of a bygone era, and for him this was a truly painful sacrifice for this new attitude could only earn him (as it did his teacher Émery who described himself as the "the most decried man in France") the criticism and even the hostility of the many legitimists in Marseilles. Though it meant incurring unpopularity in a city of fiery political passions, the prelate, guided by his supernatural spirit, refused to swerve from the line of conduct he had permanently adopted in 1837. Although his heart remained deeply sympathetic to the old monarchy, he rose above all parties and willed to serve only the cause of the Church.

In effect, the triumph of this cause meant the salvation of souls to which, from his youth, Father de Mazenod had firmly devoted himself. A missionary by vocation, he remained one all his life, devoting himself by preference to the poorest and most abandoned souls. This aristocrat who shocked the Aix drawing-rooms by isolating himself in that very "uncouth" ministry and who was so little inclined toward democracy maintained a touching solicitude for the common people. He loved them and was loved by them, understood them and was understood by them. Certainly, he cannot be accused of having made Catholicism a religion for the wealthy classes; that would be failing to recognize that the prelate showed a deeper attachment to the common people in Marseilles than to the local bourgeoisie who had remained fiercely loyal to the Bourbons and found it difficult to accept his successive rallyings to usurping regimes. The beneficiaries of the Revolution, on the other hand, those who had been converted to liberal ideas and, as a whole, de-Christianized, felt no liking for him. As a consequence, the prelate was not comfortable with either group and somewhat formal and distant when he was among them. His manner, however, was entirely different when he visited the homes of the poor to confirm their sick children. Whenever he climbed their rickety stairways—sometimes to the sixth story— every landing was filled with people waiting to welcome him, and he made it a point to stop to chat at each door and to bless the *nistons,* the little ones; afterwards, when he went back down the stairs, he was beaming and brimming with joy. What was most typically Marseillais, however, was the manner in which the fish-wives of the Port district showed him marks of favor without any regard for protocol. Their queen, Babeau, who was not shy, some-times would force his carriage to come to a stop,[55] stand in front of his door, and begin a conversation in the Provençal dialect which is more than direct, although its lilting harmonies will soften what might otherwise be too blunt a remark. Her cronies would rush up to add their bit to the conversation, and, in his witty and hearty manner, Bishop de Mazenod would reply in rough and ready fashion, using expressions no less colorful, while at the same time slipping in a few spiritual ideas. He would then drive off again, after giving his blessing to the ladies of the fish-market as they knelt devoutly on the ground. The women es-teemed him so highly that they "had arranged to ask for him personally each time any of them became ill," and, in 1848, they appointed themselves his guardians and protectors and rushed to the episcopal palace when it was rumored that the Republicans, furious over the election results, planned to attack him. "Don't be afraid, Monseigneur," they told him; "we are here to guard you." [56] Actually, he had little need of such "protection" since there were only threats; but had there been more than just threats, the determination of these *femmes terribles* would have halted the assailants for they would not have confined themselves to heap-ing the spiciest and strongest morsels of their choice vocabulary upon their heads.

It should not be concluded from these unique demonstra-tions, however, that only the fishwives appreciated the prelate's innate goodness. Testimony proves that when he passed by on foot, "the common people and the poor surrounded him, greeted him, talked with him, and ran after him." [57] Generally less de-monstrative when in the presence of the clergy, the men were no exception. A single incident confirms this—and it is one to which we must limit ourselves to avoid an anthology of thoroughly Provençal anecdotes—and it deserves mention as a particularly typical example since it involves La Ciotat, a town that had been violently divided by anti-religious politics. On confirmation day, while walking through the streets of the town, Bishop de Mazenod came upon a group of men who were rather awed by his dignity and noble bearing. A conversation began, and each of the men was quickly attracted to the prelate's simplicity, kindness, and jovial manner. Surprised and delighted to discover his true character, these good men remarked: "Did you notice how gracious he was? And people say that he is haughty!" [58]

No less astonished was Father Aillaud one evening when he saw the prelate, who was known to be so particular in matters of liturgical solemnity and pomp, disregard all protocol and, without the least ostentation, take part in a rather jumbled swirl of a procession he had improvised in honor of the Immaculate Conception:

It was about ten o'clock in the evening. A large crowd had flocked to the Jesuit church on Tapis-Vert Street. The preacher began his text *Et nox sicut dies illuminabitur* but soon there was great confusion; His Excellency then rescued him from his predicament by announcing that a procession would start immediately from the Fountain of the *Fainéants,* and like any of the ordinary faithful, the old man joined the crowd. I happened to be with a dockworker, a member of our society, and His Excellency took hold of both of us, saying: "You at portside and you at starboard." And there we were, starting off at the side of the bishop, joyfully singing the hymn, *De Marie qu'on publie,* . . . and roaming through the city for two hours.[59]

In this spontaneous and disorganized procession, with his two chaplains at port and starboard, Bishop de Mazenod felt closer to his good people than when, with cope, crozier and mitre, he found himself surrounded by his canons.

The zeal of the prelate extended beyond his own diocese which he attempted to organize to meet the needs of a rapidly increasing population and to evangelize it through the combined efforts of the clergy, the religious congregations, and the schools and sodalities, utilizing to the fullest all the means at his disposal. From the time of his seminary days, however, he had yearned to go to pagan territory to bring the Gospel to souls even more abandoned than those in a civilized country threatened by de-Christianization. Consequently, although Pius VII's formal directives kept him among the *domestici fidei,* and although he had founded his Congregation of the Missionaries of Provence specifically for the apostolate of the poor in Provence, he included in the Rules of his religious family a loophole to provide for more distant destinations. Although he could not fulfill his dream as quickly as he should have liked, from the very moment his congregation took root in Marseilles, he watched for every opportunity since the very location of that city, a doorway to the Orient, in fact, to the world, seemed to indicate to him that Divine Providence was beckoning him, telling him, as it were, to "cast out into the deep." [60] Thus, it should be stressed that in robbing his meagre effectives to send the first Oblates to Bishop Bourget he was influenced far more by the prospect of converting the Indians than by the spiritual distress of Canadian Catholics in scattered townships and lumber camps. So true is this that he became rather impatient when he saw his Oblates too frequently engaged solely in ministering to Catholics; only when they finally began to contact the nomadic tribes were his evangelical yearnings satisfied, and, though indomitable daring worried him, it delighted him as well. The same was true in other foreign missions, as his reproaches to good Father Semeria—who allowed his time to be monopolized by sinful Christians instead of devoting his efforts to the Buddhists whom Bishop de Mazenod rather summarily classed as genuine pagans—bear witness. One would have to read all his correspondence with the missionaries in Canada, the United States, Ceylon, and Natal, to evaluate the outstanding role he personally played in this extraordinary expansion of his Congregation. Rather restricted in the diocese of Marseilles, which was hampered by the burden of a long history, his innate dynamism was given free play on new soil. His concepts broadened and he became more liberal in his outlook; now less attached to a past as burdensome as it was rich, he was able at times to look farther ahead into the future. The advice he gave his missionaries about the Indians proves very clearly that he favored the spread of the faith through a supplementary means of a purely human order.

Instead of considering the instruction of savages in their social responsibilities as foreign to their ministry, the members of the Society will, on the contrary, regard it as an essential complement to the beneficent work of their missions and one capable of producing excellent results. They will make use of every means, therefore, to prevail upon the nomadic tribes to abandon their wandering life and to choose some site where they will learn to build houses for themselves, cultivate the soil, and practice the basic skills of civilization. Furthermore, Superiors, in preparing workers for the foreign missions, will take great pains to recruit those who are particularly qualified in these areas and will assign as their companions coadjutor brothers who are also experienced in these skills and who can, in this respect, not only be of assistance to the missionaries, but substitute for them if necessary. Since, moreover, the progress of civil society depends especially on the early education of youth, it will be necessary, as often as possible, to establish a school in each mission where, under the direction of an experienced teacher, the children will learn secular subjects as well as the rudiments of Christian doctrine and will be given useful training in various skills. The concern of the missionaries must extend to everything which affects the progress—even the material progress—of the tribes initiated in the duties of Christian and social life. The missionary will make sure, therefore, that these tribes maintain peaceful relations with neighboring tribes and harmony among themselves, that they safeguard unity in their homes, and lastly, that they become accustomed, through work and skill, to preserving and even increasing their family possessions. The missionaries will make frequent visits to each of the neophytes, especially those who are sick, either to assure them of spiritual assistance or to provide for their return to health. They will never, however, seek to govern these domesticated tribes. Rather, each tribe will freely choose one or several of its members to manage its common interests; no pressure will be exerted upon them except to insure orderly elections and to guarantee that the one elected is qualified for the post and capable of governing in conformity with the laws of religion and justice and of promoting the welfare of the country and of its inhabitants.[61]

Undoubtedly, when he wrote these words, Bishop de Mazenod was influenced by information he had received from his Oblates and by the methods of the Jesuits in Oregon. The fact still remains, however, that he was keenly aware of the problems created in adapting natives to new living conditions and that he officially endorsed the solutions offered for these problems.

HIS APOSTOLIC SELF-DETACHMENT

The same spirit of faith to which Bishop de Mazenod owed his apostolic verve induced him to adopt an austere practice of self-renunciation which grew increasingly more profound as his long and difficult career, marked by so many struggles and setbacks, added to his disappointments and crosses. His *Journal* reveals at one and the same time how much he suffered when he was misunderstood and in what manner his magnanimous soul reacted to it in the peace and light that came from God. On March 31, 1839, just as he was about to go to the cathedral for the pontifical celebration of the Easter ceremonies, a young lawyer, M. Bourgarel, rushed into the palace to inform him that "the shameful woman, Arbieu," was having a suit drawn up against him "by some shyster lawyers, listing every calumny imaginable." What she actually wanted was revenge for having been reported to the procurator by the episcopal administration which had accused her of "conducting a house of prostitution, falsely using the holy name of Mary, and wearing a religious garb, the better to deceive the parents who thought that they were putting their young daughters in a boarding-school." Wrote the bishop:

I should have preferred it if this warning had come two days earlier; it would have been proper food for thought in Holy Week, a thorn from Golgotha, but certainly not a subject for meditation on the day's celebrations. But, then, every day is good for sharing the ignominy of the Cross we must carry daily in the Savior's footsteps. I thank our Good Master for the way He has providentially guided me. Although I feel that I am not prone to vanity, perhaps the devil would have eventually tempted with that detestable vice by exaggerating the little good I have been able to do, the credit for which, thank God, I have never thought of attributing to myself. Oh well! The Good God leads the way. He allows men to show no gratitude to me for anything, but rather to misrepresent my intentions and distort them when they cannot refute the evidence of actions that speak for themselves.

The prelate, who was then fifty-seven, profited from this providential trial on Easter Sunday to review his life and to mark out all the other trials which had more or less painfully struck his most sensitive and most vulnerable spot so that he might remedy a strong inclination toward personal gratification which could vitiate his apostolate.

But, though I have always felt invulnerable where my thinking is concerned, in the sense that I have always considered it folly to take credit for any good that might be done, I cannot say as much where my heart is concerned. On that score, I am not free of reproach. I once thought it was all right for me to enjoy a feeling which I was convinced was lawful and natural, and the example of which, I felt, was given by Our Lord Jesus Christ, the model of all perfection. I sometimes had the temerity to tell myself that I perfectly understood the love God has for man, that He loves each one according to his merit without detriment to anyone. Nourished by these thoughts, my soul, so to speak, gaped, opened, and expanded, in proportion as it continued to find food for this supposedly instinctive feeling. In my illusion, it seemed to me that by following God's example I could love every man in such a way that not a single one of them could complain of giving me more affection than I gave to him. I felt within me something resembling immensity, a well of justice and equity, which allowed me to divide my affection in proportion as each one deserved it and returned it.

For many years, Bishop de Mazenod had felt that this love which ardently yearned to give and devote itself to everyone (allowances being made for the claims each one had upon his beneficent generosity) would be matched by those upon whom he had lavished the treasures of his heart. While at Saint Sulpice and later when ministering to the prisoners, directing the youth sodality at Aix, and preaching missions in Provence, the young priest's illusions had been fostered by the trust and affection he felt all around him; his soul then opened up and expanded:

Everything, therefore, contributed to my conviction that it was impossible for me not to be loved, and, with the way my heart was always disposed, that is to say, wishing no harm to anyone, desiring to do good to everyone and always to be ready to show affection to everyone who could appreciate it, I would not have thought it possible to find a single person who, after making my acquaintance, would wish to hurt me or even sadden me. Sweet but deceitful illusion of a heart that loves too much! I did not realize the flaw in this all too natural feeling; so little did I realize it that I was willing to glory publicly in it just as I inwardly rejoiced in possessing it.

Undoubtedly the "petty jealousies" that occurred in his native city should have cooled his ardor and turned him in upon himself. But he was so "greatly compensated by the people's enthusiastic attachment to him," that these discords were drowned in flows of harmony.

Good city of Aix, would that I had never left your soil! I would have spent my life sanctifying your children and all your people, and I would have reaped nothing but consolation as a reward for my devotion. But what of that saying, "No man is a prophet in his own country"? It was verified, if indeed not in my native city, at least in the city I was forced to adopt. It was in Marseilles that I was to encounter the resentment which was the price I had to pay for the delights of my early years, spent so joyfully in the sweetness of mutual love and in the realization that my heart held sway over a large, grateful, and devoted population. And not just the people of Aix; I should also include all those places I had evangelized in the span of the nine years I devoted to the holy missions. Was there even one of them who did not show me proof of the most sincere gratitude for the blessings I obtained for them and for the devotion with which I sacrificed my way of life—one could say life itself—in order to bring them back to God? And yet, the time came when I was forced to recognize that all men are not like me. Merely consider Marseilles; it looked indifferently upon an outstanding service rendered to three of its poorest and most populous parishes by my Congregation during the city-wide mission we gave with other outside missionaries, who apparently produced more of a sensation than we—but not more fruit—in the more fashionable quarters of the city. Our labors among the people of Saint Laurence's parish, the Grands Carmes parish, and Saint Victor's parish went unnoticed. And yet, I did not spare myself. Undoubtedly, the good people in these three parishes were not insensible to our zealous efforts. No indeed!—and they proved it in the course of our ministry. But I must admit that the rest of the city failed to make that acknowledgment unanimous, since, less than three years later, all had been forgotten and I was welcomed like a foreign invader, although I came with my hands full of blessings and my mind full of plans inspired by divine grace, all of them most useful, most advantageous, and most necessary for the spiritual welfare of the city and of the whole diocese.

By dispelling Father de Mazenod's illusions, this painful lesson had put him on his guard against anything too natural which his inclinations had been injecting into his apostolic action. He then admitted his fault with as much honesty as humility:

I went to extremes in the love I showed my fellow man from my earliest youth. I went to extremes, especially, in supposing that I deserved a similar attitude from those for whom I wanted to do so much good and to whom my heart was ready to dispense still greater love in return for the love they were willing to give me. In spite of what my misguided reason might urge me to believe, this right to people's love belongs only to God. Whatever my reason may allege for expecting men's gratitude, it is wrong. Men may do wrong by not reciprocating the good which has been done for them or the good which a person might wish to do for them. But, for myself, I must not complain about this sort of thing, unjust though it might be. And the same rule which applies to external actions and services must also apply to the feelings and dispositions of the heart. Each man, according to the measure he has received, must, after he has exhausted his affections and his strength, say in all simplicity: *Servi inutiles sumus. Quod debuimus facere, fecimus.* I had always felt this way toward God and toward what one does in His service, but I needed further reflection to apply this feeling to men, or at least to include in it what one does for men over and above the strict duty of Christian charity. And so, I shall forego any reciprocation or gratitude from men. To count on that would simply be preparing sorrow for myself; I shall spare myself that sorrow by sacrificing it in advance.

I thank God for having enlightened me in this regard through many harsh experiences. In my vanity, had I not told myself many times that although so many people suddenly rose up against me because of a clearly unjust and blameworthy prejudice, it was due perhaps more to the fact that I was misunderstood than to the jealousy and hatred which useful ideas and salutary reforms, even necessary ones, provoke. *Et vidi quod hoc quoque esset vanitas.* Have I not been misunderstood, misjudged, mocked, calumniated, and despised by those who do not know me well, or at least who could have known me—living, as they were, near me and seeing me in action with their very eyes—and by those who had been not only witnesses of my excessive kindness but also the recipients of it, and by those upon whom I had lavished many favors? *Vanitas vanitatum, et omnia vanitas. Et vidi quod hoc quoque esset vanitas.* What possessed me to write all these things? *Eructavit cor meum.* Here I have opened up my heart to express very feebly what I thought I would never be able to say! [62]

We can only rejoice that the prelate allowed himself to write these things. These perfervid and doleful pages shed a strong light upon his psychology and plumb to the depths the agony that was involved in this self-evaluation, which served to direct his spiritual life and pastoral action along a path completely opposed to the one his inexperienced youth had long believed to be a good one. Far more than his extraordinary austerities, this interior and hidden struggle, intensified by his daily tasks and lack of human appreciation, is proof of his ascent to God. For progress in union with Christ, there must indeed be self-renunciation. With contemplatives, God provides this through the dark night of the senses and the mind, as he detaches them from sensible consolations and, in the words of Saint Catherine of Siena, forces them to seek the Giver instead of the gift. With apostles immersed in activity, He accomplishes this purification through that very same activity which reserves so many disappointments, heartaches, and sufferings for them. Thus, with those who, in spite of many personal sufferings, will to continue their efforts, unsustained by apparent, often illusory success, a self-renunciation is achieved, which gives free access to grace in foregoing those self-centered actions which are influenced too greatly by natural impulses.

Although Bishop de Mazenod was a man of prayer and reached mystical heights at times, and although he practiced penance to an uncommon degree, his spiritual ascent is best revealed, not by the extraordinary—clearly the more apt to impress—but by the ordinary. Considered from this viewpoint, he was far more indebted to Marseilles than to Aix. The crosses of his episcopate and the fulfillment of his pastoral duties, such as he conceived them, were a genuine school of sanctity for him.

A MEMORY WHICH CANNOT GROW

If they are considered from the level from which he himself judged situations and things, his all-too-human deficiencies and those of his diocese which, in both cases, were evident in the great work accomplished through the common although unequal effort of Bishop de Mazenod and his clergy, become faint indeed. Although Eugene de Mazenod seems to have been more successful as the founder of the Oblates when we judge him according to the astounding missionary expansion accomplished through the heroic zeal of his sons in Canada, the United States, Ceylon, and Natal, and although his Oblate sons seem to have been given a greater share of his confidence and affection than that given to his diocesan priests, it remains true that the grandeur and stability of the reconstruction effected in his diocese is no less remarkable. Local historians, who are well qualified to judge, pay a glowing tribute to that reconstruction by noting that "at the time of the breaking of the Concordat, a half century after his death, the whole diocese bore the stamp of his personality." [63]

The criticisms which were leveled unsparingly against Bishop de Mazenod during his lifetime, and especially those which appeared at the time of his death with a violence and indecency that were termed "scandalous," have now lost much of the virulence which the heated rancors gave them at the time. The "frightful" reaction marking the episcopate of his successor, Bishop Cruice, who was "unaware of the nature of his actions" because of a "horrible disease" [64] and who was spurred on by Father Guiol, soon resulted only in increasing the glory of the deceased prelate, from whom, at first, some felt they were fortunate in being delivered. Even the prefect stated in his official report that Bishop de Mazenod's method had been the right one and that nothing certainly had been gained from the change in administration: "Under Bishop de Mazenod, [the clergy] was dominated; under Bishop Cruice, it dominates." [65] Timon-David showed that he was more farsighted than were his fellow priests, all too visibly relieved, when he warned them: "You will mourn his loss," as was the vice-president of the civil court when, in his welcoming address at the Marseilles Academy, he left to time the task of giving that noble figure its true proportions. "His memory will but grow brighter." [66] As for the *vox populi*, it too bore witness, though in a more summary fashion: "Ah! what a bishop! Will we ever again see his like!" [67]

We judge a tree not by the thorns and buds on its branches but by its fruit. Now, no one can deny the prelate credit for accomplishments as magnificent as they are lasting, and only by utilizing with the greatest possible objectivity every document capable of shedding a different light on the subject, was it possible to determine under what conditions and in what manner he was able to bring these accomplishments to a happy conclusion. Bishop de Mazenod had nothing to lose from a presentation of the whole truth, as long as he was pictured within the proper framework; otherwise, his true image would have been completely distorted. In order to set him within his time and his country and to give this accurate picture of him, it was necessary to reconstruct the religious, psychological, political, social, and even the economic background. Such a reconstruction was also required by the recently revised idea of hagiography[68]—the purpose and the method to be followed in this genre which for too long a time has been stilted, and, many times, even falsified; and genuine edification cannot but be gained from it. In his allocution at the beatification of Saint Leonard Murialdo, Pope Paul VI, well-versed in this new orientation, posed the question:

What do we desire to know of a beatified or a saint? If we were only superficially curious or were influenced by a kind of medieval and naïve devotion, we might propose searching into the life of such an extraordinarily exalted man for the marvelous deeds and signal favors which certain privileged servants of God sometimes enjoy: the mystical phenomena, the miracles. But today, we are less avid for these exceptional manifestations of Christian life. . . . And as a consequence the question is answered more simply. We want to know the history of the glorified man, his biography, and, from the characteristic viewpoint with which modern hagiography is concerned, we prefer to know his human side rather than his mystical or ascetical traits. We want to discover in the saints whatever brings them close to us rather than whatever sets them apart; we want to put them on our level as human beings, plunged into the sometimes unedifying experiences of this world, and to find in them sharers of our labor and, perhaps also, of our misery so that we might have confidence in them and share with them the common and burdensome state of our earthly existence.[69]

The author of this long and laborious work could not wish for a more appropriate or more authoritative conclusion for the biography of Bishop Eugene de Mazenod.

Notes

Chapter One

1. On this subject, cf. the Administrative Compilations of the Bouches-du-Rhône Department, for the years 1837, 1843, 1847 & 1862; for the census of 1851 and 1856, cf. Municipal Archives of Marseilles, 2F 161 and 162A.
2. G. Rambert, *Marseille. La Formation d'une grande cité moderne.* Marseille, 1934, p. 446.
3. R. Blanchard, Trois grandes villes du Sud-Est in *Recueil des travaux d l'Institut de géographie alpine,* Vol. VI, pp. 181–182.
4. G. Rambert, *Marseille. La Formation d'une grande cité moderne,* p. 396.
5. Ch. Poutmas, *La Population française pendant la première moitié du XIX siècle.* Paris, 1956, p. 103.
6. M. Roncayolo, Intervention at the *Deuxième semaine sociologique organisée par le Comité d'Études sociologiques (C.N.R.S.),* a collection published in 1953, pp. 167–168.
7. G. Rambert, *Marseille. La Formation d'une grande cité moderne,* p. 465.
8. See the files of these new succursal parishes in the A.N.P., F[19] 2131, 2135, 2137, 2144.
9. Bishop de Mazenod, Ordinance of October 30, 1855. *Ibid.,* F[19] 2140.
10. Bishop de Mazenod to Berryer, December 25, 1846. A.A.M., Admin. Correspondence, Reg. V, p. 133.
    The concourse of new circumstances to which Bishop de Mazenod alluded had reference to the construction of the Saint Charles station in the vicinity of this neighborhood.
    The *Place du Chapitre,* the land of which formerly belonged to the Cathedral Chapter, is known today as Stalingrad Square, and is at the end of the Cannebière, at the left of the Reformés Church.
11. For the ordinations, see the diocesan Ordos of 1849 and 1861. For the deaths, cf. A. Ricard, *Souvenirs du Clergé marseillais.* Marseilles, 1881. Also the necrology composed by Father Long (Canon Espeut Library).
12. Nigon de Berty, *Résumé des documents statistiques de l'administration des cultes,* September 23, 1861, pp. 26–27. A.N.P., F[19] 7205, ms.
13. *Id.,* pp. 26, 19. *Ibid.*
14. "I am compelled," wrote Bishop de Mazenod in 1843, "to use nearly a hundred Spanish priests and about thirty Corsican priests, all equally incapable of being pastors, rectors or curates because of their ignorance of our language and their different customs." Bishop de Mazenod to

the Minister of Cults, February 27, 1843. A.A.M., Administrative Correspondence, Reg. IV, p. 214.

15. From 1850 on, the personnel of the diocese, appended to the *Ordo* for each year, makes it possible to follow the order of new appointments.

    In the city itself, while the cathedral, Saint Laurent's, Les Carmes, Saint Martin's and Saint Victor's continued to have four curates, and while Saint Lazare's, Saint Theodore's and Saint Charles' continued to have three and les Chartreux' one, les Réformes and la Trinité were given a fifth curate, beginning with 1852, and Notre Dame du Mont, as well as Saint Cannat a fifth beginning with 1853; Saint Ferreol's and Saint Joseph's gained a fourth curate beginning with 1852, Saint Michael's was given a second in 1851 and a third in 1857; the chapel-of-ease connected with Saint Jean Baptiste's received two curates in 1852, and the new parish of Saints Hermès and Adrian, furnished with one curacy in 1857, was given a second the following year. All together, 12 new curacies.

    In the suburbs, les Aygalades, Mazargues, Saint Henri's, Saint Loup's, Chateau-Gombert's, Saint Julien's and Saint Marcel's each remained with one curate. One apiece was given to Saint Jerome's in 1851, Saint Barnabas' and Saint Charles' *extra muros* in 1854. Les Crottes in 1855, Saint Margaret's in 1856, La Capelette's in 1859 and Saint Eugene's in 1860. Allauch always had three. The creation of these 7 new curacies tallied with the demographic thrust which took place on the outskirts of the city.

    Finally, in the other cantons, which were more stationary, Aubagne held on to its 4 curates, with one apiece added to Cuges and Gémenos; La Ciotat kept its three with one other at Cassis. Roquevaire, which had only one, received a second in 1860, while Auriol remained with only its two regular curates.

16. 139 of the priests who occupied these 173 parochial posts in 1861 were natives of the diocese; of these 139, 86 were natives of Marseilles, 12 were from Auriol, 11 from Allauch, 8 from Aubagne, 6 from La Ciotat, and 16 from the different other places in the arondissement; only 26 others came from outside the diocese; finally, the birthplace of 8 others could not be determined precisely.

17. J. Leflon, *Eugene de Mazenod* (Engl.-language edition), Vol. II, p. 219.

18. Cf. Administrative Reports of the Bouches-du-Rhône department for the years 1837 and 1862; also lists of the clergy for the diocese of Marseilles, A.N.P., F19 2401, 2424.

19. Cf. Lists of ecclesiastical students of the diocese of Marseilles, A.N.P., F19 2416–2424.

20. Bishop Fortuné de Mazenod to the Minister of Cults, September 1, 1836. A.A.M., Admin. Corresp., Reg. III, p. 121.

21. Bishop de Mazenod to the Minister of Cults, November 7, 1843. *Ibid.*, Reg. IV, p. 255.

22. Bishop de Mazenod to M. Giraud-Saint-Rome, August 3, 1853. *Ibid.*, Reg. VI, p. 98.

23. Father Rey to Father Fabre, August 21, 1859. A. G. R., Rey file.

24. Beginning with 1853, the lists of ecclesiastical students give the number of ecclesiastical students at the rectory schools but with no indication of

what parishes they were in; the number varied from 15 in 1854 to 40 in 1861. Cf. A.N.P., F¹⁹ 2418–2424.

25. Cf. lists of ecclesiastical students of the diocese, *ibid.*, F¹⁹ 2419–2424.

26. Fr. Rey to Fr. Fabre, August 21, 1859. A.G.R., Rey file.

27. Fr. Rey to Fr. Fabre, August 2, 8, 1859. *Ibid.*

28. Fr. Fabre to Fr. Rey, August 11, 1859. *Ibid.*, Fabre file.

29. Fr. Fabre to Fr. Rey, September 19, 1860. *Ibid.*

30. Cf. Ch. Marcilhacy, *Le Diocèse d'Orléans au milieu du XIXᵉ siècle. Les hommes et leurs mentalités.* Paris, 1964, pp. 236–237.

31. Y. Beaudoin, *Le grand séminaire de Marseille sous la direction des Oblats de Marie Immaculée (1827–1862).* Rome, 1964, doctoral thesis at the Gregorian University, pp. 79–80.

    The only certain data concern the number of ordinations to the priesthood: a total of 169 from 1837 to 1861, that is, an average of seven a year; based upon the number of those admitted to tonsure, the total of entrances to theology would amount to 229 during the same period, that is, an average of 9 a year; this would tally with an annual average of about forty seminarians for the three years of theology and one year of philosophy. Cf. registers of *Insinuations* which mention each ordination along with the names of those ordained. Marseilles, Archiepiscopal Archives.

32. Of the 244 known seminarians who entered from 1836 to 1861, 41 were incardinated into the diocese; the other 203 belonged to it. Of these 203, the city of Marseilles furnished 106, Allauch 12, and the rest of the diocese 44; for the other 41, their place of origin in the arondissement could not be determined precisely.

33. "The clergy," wrote Father Stanislas, "came neither from the poorest class nor from the wealthy bourgeoisie and it is easy to understand why. The children of the poorest class could not attend schools or institutions where they would have been able to learn Latin and as far as I know, there were no benefactors willing to help them. The children of the rich bourgeoisie, as has been seen, were not so inclined, although there were a few rare and happy exceptions. The clergy therefore were generally recruited from the class known as storekeepers . . . ; this class was able to send its children to institutions where they could take classes in Latin and it was rather flattered to see its sons enter Holy Orders." Fr. Stanislas, *Souvenirs et impressions,* note-book I, Chap. XLII, pp. 225–226. Paris, Capuchin Fathers archives, ms. nᵒ 1654.

    In regard to the children of the poorest class, especially for the suburbs of Marseilles and the other parishes of the diocese, Father Stanislas' appraisal must nonetheless be corrected since it concerns the city of Marseilles; there were recruits from the above mentioned class by way of the rectory schools about which, unfortunately, we have no precise data.

34. *Histoire de l'institut et de l'oeuvre de la jeunesse* de M. Allemand, Third period (1844–1857), Chaps. IV and VI. Marseilles, Arch. of the Allemand Society.

    Timon-David, *Annales de l'oeuvre de la jeunesse pour la classe ouvrière,* Vol. III. Marseilles, 1881, Chap. XIII, *Onzième année,* 1857–1858, p. 21.

35. Vital Grandin to his brother Jean, January 17, 1853. P.R. Grandin.
36. *Correspondance de Rome,* July 14, 1851.
37. *Notice historique et statistique sur la Congrégation des Oblats,* 1854–1855, p. 8. P.R., DM IX–8.
38. Rambert, Vol. I, p. 479.
39. From 1837 to 1860, there was a succession of 7 professors in moral theology, 9 in dogmatic theology, and as many in philosophy, and 15 in Sacred Scripture. It is true that Fathers Rey, Rambert, Fabre and Martinet taught several of these courses successively. Cf. list composed by Y. Beaudoin, *Le grand séminaire de Marseille sous la direction des Oblats de Marie Immaculée,* p. 44.
40. L. Foucher, *La philosophie catholique en France au XIXe siècle avant la renaissance thomiste.* Paris, 1955, p. 13.
41. Tempier to Father Ch. Baret, October 16, 1847. Quoted by Yenveux, *Saintes Règles,* Vol. VIII, p. 183.
42. Father Victor Baret to Father Fabre, August 25, 1855. A.G.R., Baret file.
43. This abridged summary was the *Summa theologica minuta,* in two volumes in 8° published in Paris by Louis Bordes in 1849.
44. The notes for a five-year course in Sacred Scripture (3 for the Old Testament and 2 for the New) which Father Rambert left after him, contain several quotations from Dom Calmet and some scriptural commentaries from Saint Thomas Aquinas. A.G.R., Rambert.
45. Bishop de Mazenod to Bishop Dupanloup, August 27, 1851. A.A.M., Administrative Correspondence, Reg. VI, p. 23.
46. *Id., ibid.*
47. U. Chevalier, *Notice sur la vie et les oeuvres du chanoine J.M.H. Albanès* (1822–1897). Paris, 1919.
48. Bishop de Mazenod to Bishop Dupanloup, August 27, 1851. A.A.M., Admin. Corresp., Reg. VI, pp. 23–24.
49. Vital Grandin to his brother Jean, June 16, 1853. P.R. LG Grandin.
50. F. Pozzolo, *Notice biographique sur le très regretté Messire P.H. Carbonel.* Marseilles, 1891, p. 21.
51. Chapitres gènèraux de 1843, 1850, and 1856. A.G.R., Reg. of the General Chapters, Reg. I (1818–1856) pp. 72, 85, 144.
52. Rey, Vol. I, p. 428.
53. Cf. A. Pascal, *Le Clergé du diocèse de Marseille pendant le XIXe siècle.* Aix, 1926, pp. 39–55.
54. Bishop de Mazenod to Bishop Parisis, September 23, 1846. Langres, Episcopal Arch., Bishops' Letters from 1836 to 1848.
55. Bishop de Mazenod to the Minister of Cults, March 17, 1852. A.A.M., Admin. Corresp., Reg. VI, p. 38.
56. Bishop de Mazenod to the mayor of Marseilles, November 5, 1852. A.A.M., Admin. Corresp., Reg. VI, p. 64.
57. Bishop de Mazenod to the Minister of Cults, March 17, 1852. *Ibid.,* pp. 38–39.
58. Reports of the Casuel Committee, 1841–1856. A.A.M., files 682, 684–685.
59. Bishop de Mazenod to Bishop Parisis, September 23, 1846. Langres, Episcopal arch., Bishops' Letters 1836–1848.
60. Bishop de Mazenod to Bishop Pavy, December 19, 1853. Quoted by Yenveux in *Les saintes règles de la congrégation des Oblats de Marie Immaculée.* Paris, 1903, Vol. I, pp. 74–75.

61. Bishop de Mazenod, *Journal,* December 6, 1838. P.R., JM.
62. Timon-David, *Les douleurs d'un fondateur d'oeuvres, 3e douleur: l'Évêché.* Marseilles. Arch. of the Fathers of Timon-David.

It was for the private use of his community that Timon-David undertook "the account of the great sorrows which the foundation of our works cost me." He wanted thereby to encourage his co-laborers and to teach them how to surmount every difficulty "by patience, moderation and above all by seeking the help of God." This, as well as his independent and unique character, explains the picturesque and unrestrained originality with which he portrayed prominent characters and brought out "sincerely, without emotion, without acrimony, without rancor" and yet with humor, the setbacks of an instructor of working boys.

63. What gave rise to such a criticism at first was the presence of the Oblate scholastics among the diocesan seminarians; the scholastics were presumed to be living there at the expense of the diocese, since each year, the pastors and rectors of the city took 2,500 to 3,500 francs out of their casuel fund for the seminary budget. The truth of the matter was that the Congregation regularly paid an annual sum of money for its students who were lodged with the seminarians of Marseilles; from 1852 to 1854 this sum amounted to 300 francs a year for each of them. *(Journal de la caisse générale, 1852–1854, A.G.R.).*

However, this rumor was accredited even more by the deceased prelate's last will; even the Aix procurator-general echoed the fantastic rumors that were circulating by writing to the Keeper of the Seals: "The faithful were amazed to learn that [the bishop] left an enormous fortune, valued at from 7 to 8 millions, the major part of which is to go to the Congregation of the Oblates of Provence." Rigaud to the Keeper of the Seals, July 8, 1861. A.N.P., BB[30] 370.

In effect, Bishop de Mazenod had made Fathers Tempier and Fabre his general legatees, "orally instructing" them to divide the property he left after him among the diocese, his religious congregation and his natural heirs since all this property had always been listed together under his own name, either because his Congregation possessed no legal status or because the episcopal revenues, whose juridical reality was poorly defined, were subject to the meddlesome formalities of Napoleonic legislation for their operations and transactions. This grouping of property gave rise to the belief that there was an exceptionally large estate, and the appointment of the two Oblates as legatees gave rise to the supposition that their Congregation would derive substantial profit from it.

The truth of the matter was that Bishop de Mazenod left 1,200,000 francs in money and real estate to his diocese; to this sum must be added the sum of 200,000 francs accruing from properties which the Oblates gave up, and about 100,000 francs represented by the bequests and donations which the prelate in his will left to various soceities, parishes or confraternities. (Report presented in 1862 by Canon Carbonnel and Fathers Rey, Tempier and Fabre regarding the administration of Bishop de Mazenod.) P.R. DM XVI.

In a memoire, the notary, Monsieur Gavot, rightfully concluded: "This is not the time to recall all the charitable works of Bishop de Mazenod's episcopate; history will do it far better than I could. It will suffice to recall what [the diocese] was spiritually and financially in 1822 and what it was in 1861 at the time of Bishop de Mazenod's death, in order to have some idea of all the difficulties . . . met by this illustrious prelate in building anew, or almost entirely rebuilding, more than fifty churches in the city and the suburbs, in sustaining, revivifying and creating that large number of religious houses, congregations, charitable institutions and establishments of every kind . . . The money bequeathed by Bishop de Mazenod for the special use of the diocese and put at the disposal of his successors, or the money he bequeathed to the seminary amounts to 2 or 3 million in value . . . In view of such results, could one seriously say that Bishop de Mazenod managed to enrich the Oblate Congregation which he founded, to the detriment of the diocese? . . . Not only did he never use any diocesan funds for the benefit of the Congregation, but one can say that he sometimes compromised the interests of the Oblates by mortgaging their property in order to borrow money for the diocese . . ." Memoire of Monsieur Gavot, notary-public at Marseilles, January, 1862.

64. Deposition of Canon Aillaud, June 3, 1926. P.R., DM XIX-1a.

Father Casimir Aubert, however, was never part of the secretarial staff of the cathedral; however, Bishop de Mazenod had appointed him in 1845 as his "private secretary for matters pertaining to the Congregation" of the Oblates. (Bishop de Mazenod to Father Courtès, January 4, 1845. P.R., LM Courtes). He entrusted Aubert with several canonical visitations to England and it was only beginning with 1856 that Father Aubert, elected assistant-general by the Chapter, resided permanently at Marseilles until his death on January 17, 1860.

65. Timon-David, *Les douleurs d'un fondateur d'oeuvres, 3e douleur*. Marseilles, Arch. of the Timon-David Fathers.

66. Brassevin, *La grande histoire des prêtres du Sacré-Coeur à Marseille*, Vol. II, IVe part, p. 124. Marseilles, Arch. of the Priests of the Good Shepherd. ms.

67. Timon-David, *Les douleurs d'un fondateur d'oeuvres, 3e douleur*. Marseilles, Arch. of the Timon-David Fathers.

68. Deposition of Canon Aillaud, April 3, 1913. P.R. DM XIX-1a.

69. Timon-David, *Les douleurs d'un fondateur d'oeuvres, 3e douleur*. Marseilles, Archives of the Timon-David Fathers.

70. Deposition of Canon Aillaud, June 3, 1926 and November 26, 1911. P.R., DM XIX-1a.

71. Timon-David, Report made on July 1, 1858 to the Statistical Society of Marseilles regarding Antoine Maurel's work, *Résumé des délibérations du grand conseil des sociétés de secours mutuels*. Marseilles, Chamber of Commerce Arch., copyright Société de Statistique.

72. Deposition of Canon Aillaud, June 3, 1926. P.R., DM XIX-1a.

73. Timon-David, *La vie du serviteur de Dieu Louis Maulbon d'Arbaumont, en religion le Révérend Père Jean du Sacré-Coeur*. Marseilles, 1887, pp. 137–138.

74. Deposition of Canon Aillaud, June 3, 1926. P.R., DM XIX-1a.

75. Brassevin, *La grande histoire des prêtres du Sacré-Coeur*, Vol. II, IVe part.; p. 122. Arch. of Priests of the Good Shepherd.

76. Deposition of Canon Aillaud, June 3, 1926. P.R., DM XIX-1a.

77. Brassevin, *La grande histoire des prêtres du Sacré-Coeur*, Vol. II, Part IV, p. 123. Marseilles, Arch. of Priests of the Good Shepherd.

78. Bishop de Mazenod to a priest of Marseilles, June 5, 1857. Quoted by Rambert, Vol. II, p. 609. This was probably Father Albanès, who left to study at Rome in 1857.
79. Bishop de Mazenod to a priest of Marseilles, May 6, 1854. A.A.M., Administr. Corresp., Reg. VI, p. 122 (loose leaf attached to this page.)
80. Cf. *Monita* from 1834 to 1835, Art. XIII.
81. Bishop de Mazenod to a pastor of the diocese, June 30, 1845. Quoted by Rambert, Vol. II, p. 658.
82. Bishop de Mazenod, *Journal,* November 4, 1848. Quoted by Yenveux, Saintes Règles, Vol. V, p. 81.
83. The 1854 cholera epidemic was the occasion for recalling this obligation already inscribed in article XIII of the *Monita* of 1834–1835. Cf. Carbonnel's letter to a pastor of Marseilles, July 17, 1854 and Bishop de Mazenod's letter to a pastor of that city, July 25, 1854. P.R., Collection of Mandates, pp. 519, 521.
84. Rey, Vol. II, p. 503, note 1.
85. Louis Guiol to Bishop de Mazenod, July 27, 1854. Quoted by Rey, Vol. II, p. 508, note 1.
86. Bishop de Mazenod, *Journal,* August 17, 1856. *Ibid.,* p. 614. Notebook of Episcopal Councils, July 26, 1856. *Ibid.*
87. Rey, Vol. II, p. 614.
88. Bishop de Mazenod, opening address of the Synod, September 28, 1856, in *Ordonnances synodales du diocèse de Marseille.* 1857, p. 341.
89. *Id., ibid.,* p. 338.
90. *Id., ibid.,* pp. 80–86.
91. Bishop de Mazenod, Journal, October, 1856. Quoted by Rey, Volume II, p. 615.
92. Bishop de Mazenod, closing address of the Synod, October 1, 1856, in *Ordonnances synodales du diocèse,* pp. 376–378.
93. *Ordonnances synodales du diocèse,* p. 378.
94. Rey, Vol. II, p. 616, note 1.
95. After the death of Bishop Cruice, Jonjon published a series of articles in the *Messager de Provence,* which he compiled in a booklet entitled, *Réponse aux frères quêteurs ou conférence entre le Messager de Provence et Monsieur Louis Guiol.* Marseilles, 1867.

   Guiol was violently taken to task for the double dealing he carried on at the time of the Synod and during the reaction which followed the death of Bishop de Mazenod.
96. Timon-David, *Les douleurs d'un fondateur d'oeuvres, 3ᵉ douleur.* Marseilles, Arch. of the Timon-David Fathers.

Chapter Two

1. Négrel-Féraud, Memorandum regarding the agricultural topography of the Bouches-du-Rhône department, in *Répertoire des travaux de la société de statistique de Marseille,* Vol. XVI (1853), p. 81.
2. 1851 census. A.D.M., M¹⁰ 17.
3. M. Chaudouin, Report to the Board of Health, 1850, in *Rapport général des travaux des conseils d'hygiène et de salubrité,* 1848–1851. Marseilles, 1851, p. 522.
4. Allibert, Report on the agricultural fair of Aubagne in 1851, in *Réper-*

toire des travaux de la société de statistique de Marseille, Vol. XVI, p. 96.

5. *Enquête sur le travail agricole et industriel de 1848,* report of the Justices of the Peace of Marseilles, October 29, 1849. A.N.P., C 947.

6. Ch. Pouthas, *La Population française pendant la première moitié du XIXe siècle,* p. 185.

For the value of the 1845 enquiry published by *La statisque de France, Industrie,* Vol. II, Paris, 1848, cf. J. A. Laurent, *L'Enquête pour la statisque industrielle à Marseille de 1839 à 1852,* in *Provence historique,* Vol. XIII, pp. 280–288.

7. Prefect Crèvecoeur to the Minister of the Interior, November 18, 1853. A.N.P., F^{ic} III Bouches-du-Rhône. 7.

8. The use of illuminating gas began in 1837 with the establishment of three companies; from 1841 to 1851, the Imperial and Continental Company alone enjoyed a definite monopoly, providing service to public establishments, shops and the principal streets of the city. Two others then competed with it, the Provençal Gas works of Felix Lopez and Co., and the Marseilles Gas works of Féraud & Co. In 1853, the Marseilles Gas works was bought over by the firm of Mires & Co. and the Imperial and Continental Company as well as Provençal Gas works went out of existence. The workers, most of whom were Piedmontese or Italians worked from 6 P.M. to 6 A.M. for an average wage of 3 francs 50 centimes. M. Toulouzan, Report of the Industrial Committee, March 3, 1853, in *Répertoire des travaux de la société de statistique de Marseille,* Vol. XVII (1854) pp. 74–79.

9. For all these figures concerning the above-mentioned people earning a living from the various trades, cf. Census of 1856, A.D.M., M¹⁰ 28, and census of 1861, A.N.P., F²⁰ 427³.

10. Cf. L. Campi, *Notice biographique sur Joseph Grandval . . .* Ajaccio, 1879. J. Billioud and G. Rambert, *Une industrie marseillaise, la raffinerie de sucre,* in *Marseille,* no. 9, January-April, no. 10, May-July, 1950.

11. Cf. files of Board of Health, A.D.M., M⁷ 253; files of Statistique de France, A.N.P., F²⁰ 501; P. Guiral, Le Cas d'un grand port de commerce, Marseille, in *Aspects de la crise . . . française au milieu du XIXe siecle,* p. 220.

12. P. Guiral, *Les Bouches-du-Rhône. Histoire et Géographie.* Grenoble, 1945, p. 121.

13. Imperial Procurator Mouriès to the Minister of Justice, July 12, 1861. A.N.P., BB¹⁸ 1633.

14. Prefect Crèvecoeur to the Minister of the Interior, November 18, 1853. *Ibid.,* F^{ic} III, Bouches-du-Rhone 7.

15. *Id., ibid.*

16. Cf. Census of 1851. A.D.M., M¹⁰ 17.

17. Prefect to the Minister of Interior, November 18, 1853. A.N.P. F^{ic} III, Bouches-du-Rhone 7.

18. Parochial enquiry, 1862–1863, Saint Jean Baptiste parish, September 9, 1862. A.A.M., 236.

19. F. Mazuy, *Essai historique sur les moeurs et coutumes de Marseille au XIXe siècle.* Marseilles, 1853, pp. 179–180.

20. Procurator-General Rigaud to the Minister of Justice, October 5, 1859. A.N.P., BB^{30} 370.

21. Ch. Marcilhacy, *Le diocèse d'Orléans sous l'épiscopat de Monseigneur Dupanloup 1849–1878.* Paris, 1962, p. 316.

22. Parochial enquiry 1862–1863, St. John Baptist Parish. A.A.M., 236.

23. Rey, Vol. II, pp. 306, 698, 723, 774.
    The records for the episcopal councils for 1856 mention one that was to be given at St. John Baptist's parish in Marseilles. *Ibid.*, p. 613.

24. *Ordonnances synodales du diocèse de Marseille,* p. 105.

25. *Examens à l'usage des membres de l'association pour la défense de la religion catholique établie à Marseille.* Marseilles, 1852, pp. 5–16.

26. Bishop de Mazenod to the mayor of Marseilles, November 2, 1853. A.A.M., Administr. Corresp., Register VI, pp. 103–105.

27. Minutes of the Episcopal Council, November, 1853. Quoted by Rey, Vol. II, p. 481.

28. Bishop de Mazenod, Circular letter to the rectors and pastors of Marseilles, November 8, 1853.

29. Prefect Crèvecoeur to the minister of cults, November 14, 1853. A.N.P., F^{19} 5822.

30. Ministry's note regarding Bishop de Mazenod's circular letter of November 8, 1853. *Ibid.*

31. L. Guiol to Bishop de Mazenod, March 21, 1855. Quoted by Rey, Vol. II, pp. 541–542.
    To give this religious defense society a durable impulsion, Guiol recommended forming a "Central Committee presided over" by the bishop or one of his vicars-general "and composed of a dozen somewhat influential laymen"; this committee "would carry on correspondence with the Paris Committee"; he also recommended creating a committee in each parish of the city; this committee "would obtain lists of members" and would transmit them each month to the central committee.

32. J. Timon-David. Report for his reception into the Statistiques Society, September 4, 1854. Marseilles, Chamber of Commerce arch., files *Société de statistique. Œuvres philanthropiques.*

33. J. B. Duroselle, *Les débuts du catholicisme social en France,* p. 493.

34. *Id.* pp. 503–504.

35. A. Maurel, *Grand conseil des sociétés de secours mutuels,* 2nd series Marseilles, 1865, p. 215.

36. J. B. Duroselle, *Les débuts du catholicisme social en France,* p. 534.
    In accepting the "title of honorary chairman of the Supreme Council," Bishop de Mazenod replied to Maurel on April 15, 1852, that he was delighted "with the religious spirit of the members of these societies. I dare to say," he added, "that you do justice to my own feelings which are inspired by the constant interest I take both in the good workers of our city and in all their associations formed under the auspices of religion." A.A.M., Administ. Corresp., Reg. VI, p. 40.

37. J. B. Duroselle, *Les débuts du catholicisme social en France,* pp. 534–535.

38. Lists of religious communities, Diocese of Marseilles, 1861. A.N.P., F^{20} 726.

39. L. Picard, *Émile de Valar, fondatrice des religieuses Saint Joseph de l'Apparition*. Paris, 1924, pp. 155, 162.

40. L. Giraud, *Monsieur Vitagliano . . . (1801–1871)*. Marseille, 1949, p. 146.

41. *Id.*, p. 147. Also cf. Pascalis, *La vie et l'oeuvre du chanoine Vitagliano*. Marseille, 1893, p. 159.

42. Bishop de Mazenod, Circular letter to the bishops of France, March 12, 1855. A.A.M., Administr. Corresp. Reg. VI, p. 150.

43. Bishop de Mazenod, *Journal*, December 16, 1856. Quoted by Rey, Vol. II, p. 624.

44. *Id., ibid.*

45. Rey, Vol. II, p. 700.

46. J. C. Cousson, *Paul de Magallon d'Argens*. Lyons, 1959, pp. 288, 261–264.

47. Bishop de Mazenod to Sister Geray, August 26, 1840. A.A.M., Administr. Corresp. Register IV, p. 99.

48. Bishop de Mazenod, *Journal*, June 29, 1845. Quoted by Rey, Vol. II, p. 209.

49. Bishop de Mazenod to Cardinal Della Genga, May 6, 1855. A.A.M., Administr. Corresp., Reg. VI, p. 160.

50. *Id., ibid.*

51. M. Deves, *Le Père Dassy, fondateur à Marseille de l'institut régional des jeunes aveugles et sourds-muets et de la congrégation des soeurs de Marie Immaculée*. Marseilles, 1938, pp. 185–274.

52. Lists of religious communities, diocese of Marseilles, 1861. A.N.P., F[20] 726.

    The most important communities resided at Marseilles. In the city were 150 Sisters of Saint Vincent de Paul, 127 Sisters of the Christian Retreat, 115 Sisters of the Holy Names of Jesus and Mary, 109 Hospital Sisters of Saint Augustine, 90 Visitandine Sisters occupying two monasteries, 75 Sisters of Saint Charles, and 60 Sisters of Good Hope (a branch of the Holy Family of Bordeaux.)

    Of the men religious, the Brothers of the Christian Schools were by far the most numerous, with 200 members; next to them were the Oblates with 94 (scholastics included), Capuchins 32, Religious of Saint Peter-in-Chains 30, Brothers of Saint John of God 27, Jesuits 17, Doctrinaire Fathers and Marist Brothers 10 for each community, Blessed Sacrament Fathers 5, and lastly, Religious Victims of the Sacred Heart and Brothers of Saint Gabriel with 4 in each community.

    The last to arrive in the diocese were the Blessed Sacrament Fathers, who were installed in 1859 in the old monastery of the Friars-minim. Their Founder, Father Eymard, began his religious life with the Oblates. Cf. *Le bienheureux Pierre Julien Eymard (1811–1868)*. Paris, 1928, Vol. II, pp. 153–192.

53. Rey, Vol. II, pp. 291–292. Cf. S. Vailhé, *Vie du Père Emmanuel d'Alzon (1810–1880)*. Paris, 1926, Vol. I, pp. 454–455.

54. Father Tissier to the Lyons provincial, September 19, 1852. Paray-le-Monial, Jesuit Arch. of the Lyons province, Collect. Prat, Nouvelle Compagnie, Vol. VIII, fol. 121–122.

55. Beneficent and Charitable Societies appearing in the budget of 1878. A.A.M., dossier 538.

56. P. de Thury, Report on the agricultural settlements, in *Annales de la charité,* Vol. VII (1851) p. 576.

57. J. Timon David to the Statistical Society, June 20, 1855. Marseilles, Chamber of Commerce arch., files *Société de statistique. Oeuvres philanthropiques.*

58. L. Bergasse, *Conférence de Saint Joseph. Histoire d'un siècle.* Marseilles, Arch. of the Saint Vincent de Paul Conferences, Saint Joseph's parish, ms.

59. *Id. ibid.*

60. *Tableau statistique de 1860.* Paris, Arch. of the Saint Vincent de Paul Society, *Conseil central de Marseille 1851–1894.*

62. Ch. Verger to M. Baudon, September 22, 1853. *Ibid.* Cf. J. M. Maurin, *Les derniers jours d'Ozanam à Marseilles,* in *Provence historique,* Vol. IV, July-September 1954, pp. 200–216.

63. *Tableau statistique de 1860. Ibid.*
    Three other conferences existed at Aubagne, Roquevaire and La Ciotat, numbering 56 active members, 14 honorary and 2 aspirants.

64. G. Jarlot, A Century of Social Apostolate, in *Lettres de Fourvière. Province de Lyon,* series 3, no. 9. Lyons, 1936, p. 450.

65. Father Tissier to the Lyons provincial, September 19, 1852, Paray-le-Monial, Jesuit arch. of Lyons, Collect. Prat, Nouvelle Compagnie, Vol. VIII, fol. 121–122.

66. Notice regarding the Marseilles residence in *Lettres de Fourvière,* Series 3, no. 9, p. 646.

67. Report of one of the Fathers of Marseilles, May 11, 1861. Paray-le-Monial, Jesuit Arch of Lyons, Collect. Prat, Nouvelle Compagnie, Vol. VIII, fol. 127–130.

68. *Courrier de Marseille,* September 21, 1858.
    Regarding the Saint Joseph Conference, see the list of its activities given by J. B. Duroselle in *Les débuts du catholicisme social en France,* p. 536.

69. G. Jarlot, *Un siècle d'apostolat social* in *Lettres de Fourvière,* Series 3, no. 9, pp. 452–453.

70. Father Tissier to the Lyons provincial, September 19, 1852. Paray-le-Monial, Jesuit arch. of Lyons, Collect. Prat, Nouvelle Compagnie, Vol. VIII, fol. 121–122.

71. *Id., ibid.*

72. *Id., ibid.*

73. *Id., ibid.*

74. *Id., ibid.*

75. Notice regarding the residence of Marseilles in *Lettres de Fourvière* series 3, no. 9, p. 646.

76. J. Timon-David, *Annales de l'oeuvre de la jeunesse pour la classe ouvrière de Marseille,* Vol. I, Marseilles, 1878, pp. 43–44.

77. *Id., ibid.,* pp. 72–74.

78. *Id.,* p. 72.

79. *Id.,* p. 74.

80. Relative to this matter, see J. B. Duroselle, *Les débuts du catholicisme social en France,* pp. 577–585.

81. J. Timon David, *Annales de l'oeuvre de la jeunesse,* Vol. III, Marseilles, 1881, p. 45.

82. J. Timon-David, *Méthode de direction les oeuvres de jeunesse,* Marseilles, 2nd edit., Vol. I, 1875, p. 25.

83. J. B. Duroselle, *Les débuts du catholicisme social en France,* p. 566, according to a register dating back to about 1870.

    Statistics drawn up by Timon-David himself for the first five years of the society (1847–1852) justifies reaching the same conclusions. Cf. *Statistique de la jeunesse pour la classe ouvrière pendant les cinq premières années, du 1er novembre 1847 au 31 octobre 1852.* Marseilles, 1854, Chamber of Commerce arch., files, *Société de statistique. Oeuvres philanthropiques.*

    Of the 1,387 enrollments, 251 give no information regarding their entrance into the society; 786 attended 68 schools in the city, 350 practiced various trades; chief among these were 56 clerks and store-workers, 27 manual or day laborers, 27 *porte Romaines,* 23 shoe-makers, 19 locksmiths, 15 masons, 15 rope-makers, 9 foundry workers. Of the 934 families of these children, more than a third (352) were employed in dock-work (70), masonry (69), shoe-making (67), manual and day-laborers (51), carpenters (44), carters (26) and tailors (25).

84. J. Timon-David, *Méthode de direction des oeuvres de jeunesse,* Vol. II, p. 171.

85. J. Timon-David, *Annales de l'oeuvre de la jeunesse,* Vol. I, p. 85.

86. *Id.,* Vol. II, pp. 119–120.

87. Admittance of the society to the Head Confraternity of the Sacred Heart of Rome, July 7, 1852, in *Annales de l'oeuvre de la jeunesse,* Vol. II, pp. 206–209.

88. Ordinance of Bishop de Mazenod canonically erecting the Youth Society and the Sacred Heart Society, November 20, 1852. *Ibid.* pp. 190–193.

89. J. Timon-David, *Annales de l'oeuvre de la jeunesse,* Vol. II, pp. 18–20.

90. *Id.,* p. 24.

91. *Id.,* p. 22.

92. J. Timon-David, *Annales de l'oeuvre de la jeunesse,* Vol. II, p. 23.

93. Brunello, Rector of Saint Henri-de-Séon parish, to Bishop de Mazenod, May 19, 1840. A.A.M., 293 (Saint Henri).

94. Grégoire, rector of Saint André-de-Séon parish, to Bishop de Mazenod, April 14, 1844, June 17, 1855. A.A.M., 245 (Saint André).

95. Taurel, rector of Les Caillols parish, to Bishop de Mazenod, January 11, 1840. *Ibid.,* 265 (Les Caillols).

96. Bishop de Mazenod, Pastoral visitation notes, Mazargues, May 24, 1856. *Ibid.,* 236.

97. *Id.,* Saint Marcel, May 27, 1856. *Ibid.*

98. *Id.,* Allauch, August 26, 1838, 1851, May, 1852, May 3, 1856. *Ibid.*

99. *Id.,* Plan de Cuques, June 27, 1854. *Ibid.*

100. *Id.,* Aubagne, June 1, 1854. *Ibid.*

101. *Id.,* Cuges, May 19, 1851. *Ibid.*

102. *Id.,* Roquevaire, 1851. *Ibid.*

103. *Id.,* Auriol, May 4, 1856. *Ibid.*

104. *Id.,* La Ciotat, 1851. *Ibid.*

105. *Id.,* Cassis, May 17, 1851. A.A.M., 236.

106. Rouden, rector of Ceyreste, to Bishop de Mazenod, May 20, 1856. *Ibid.,* 274 (Ceyreste).
107. Circular letter of Bishop Cruice to the pastors and rectors of the diocese, September 6, 1861.
108. Bishop Cruice, ordinance regarding visitation of parishes, March 1, 1862, in *Bref des oeuvres du diocèse de Marseille.* Marseilles, 1862, pp. 23–25.
109. Questionnaire for the visitation of parishes. *Ibid.* pp. 26–40.
    Compare this with the questionnaire Bishop Affre sent on February 1, 1846 to the pastors of the diocese of Paris for the purpose of re-organizing the archives of the archiepiscopal palace. Also cf. *Statistique religieuse du diocèse de Paris. Mémoire sur l'état présent du diocèse,* by G. Darboy, Paris, 1856.
110. H. Sarrazin, *Marseille, 1860. Structures religieuses,* in *Marseille sous le second empire. Centenaire du palais de la bourse. 1960* Paris, 1961, p. 171.
111. Percentages arrived at, based upon the number of those attending Mass, furnished by the notebooks of the enquiry from 1862 to 1863. A.A.M., 236.
112. Figures listed on a sheet attached to the enquiry dossier of 1861. *Ibid.*
113. Questionnaire of Saint Laurent, enquest of 1862–1863. *Ibid.*
114. F. Charpin, *Pratique religieuse et formation d'une grande ville. Le geste du baptême et sa signification en sociologie religieuse.* Paris, 1964, pp. 123–124.
115. Based on the Enquest of 1862–1863. A.A.M., 236.
116. F. Charpin, *Pratique religieuse et formation d'une grande ville,* Tables XIV, a and b, pp. 156–157, Map XIV, p. 159.
117. *Id.,* pp. 121–128.
118. *Id.,* pp. 51–55.
119. Cf. records of the enquiry of 1862–1863, answers regarding the religious life and the societies of the parishes. A.A.M., 236.
120. J. Timon-David, Development of religious societies in Marseilles since 1789, Marseilles, 1866, p. 10. Extract from *Répertoire des travaux de la société de statistique,* Vol. XXIX (1865).

Chapter Three

* A map of missions in Canada will be found in Vol. III, facing p. 123. For geographical orientation regarding missions in the United States, see the map in the present volume facing p. 113.
1. Bishop Taché, *Vingt années de missions dans le Nord-Ouest de l'Amérique,* Montreal, 1866, p. 44.
2. Bishop de Mazenod to Bishop Guigues, October 8, 1852. Quoted by Yenveux, *Saintes Règles,* Vol. I, supplement, p. 125.
3. D. Fremont, *Monseigneur Provencher et son temps.* Winnipeg, 1935, pp. 262–263.
4. *Id.,* p. 265.
5. *Id.,* p. 262.
6. *Id.,* p. 265.
7. *Id.,* p. 266.

8. *Id.*, p. 267.
9. *Id.*, *ibid.*
10. Bishop Provencher to Bishop Turgeon, July 21, 1851. Quoted by Dom Benoît, *Vie de Mgr. Taché, archevêque de Saint-Boniface.* Montreal, Vol. I, p. 206.
11. Bishop Provencher to Bishop de Mazenod, November 29, 1849. *Ibid.*, pp. 202–203.
12. Bishop de Mazenod to Bishop Taché, January 19, 1851. Quoted by Yenveux, *Saintes Règles,* Vol. IX, p. 205.
13. Bishop Taché, *Vingt années de missions* . . . , p. 38.
14. *Id.*, pp. 39–42.
15. Bishop de Mazenod to Father Faraud, November 24, 1851. P.R., LM Faraud.
16. Bishop de Mazenod to Bishop Provencher, January 24, 1852. Quoted by Yenveux, *Saintes Régles,* Vol. IX, p. 206.
17. Bishop de Mazenod to Canon Loewenbrück, October 26, 1848, Rome, Propagand. Arch., S.C., *America Centrale,* vol. 14, fol. 750.
18. Bishop Norbet Blanchet, *Mémoire sur l'établissement d'un siège métropolitain avec plusieurs suffragants dans la vaste étendue de l'Orégon,* February 23, 1846. *Ibid., Acta,* vol. 209, fol. 190.
19. *Id.*, *ibid.*, fol. 188.
20. Bishop Blanchet, *Mémoire sur l'établissement d'un siège métropolitain* . . . Rome, Propagand. Arch., *Acta,* vol. 209, fol. 188–189.
    On April 16, 1846, Bishop Blanchet renewed his attempt with the Propaganda "by asking that a nucleus of native secular clergy be formed before any religious novitiates would be allowed to be established," and "that there be a oneness of jurisdiction over all missionaries indiscriminately in what pertained to the exercise of the apostolic ministry." Bishop Blanchet to the cardinals of the Propaganda, April 16, 1846. *Ibid.*, fol. 160.
21. Bishop Blanchet to Cardinal Fransoni, February 18, 1852. *Ibid.*, S.C., *America Centrale,* vol. 16, fol. 57.
22. As early as 1846, Father Roothaan foresaw the difficulties which Bishop Norbert Blanchet would create for his religious. Cf. Roothaan to Joset, June 7, 1846, quoted by G. J. Garraghan, *The Jesuits of the Middle United States,* New York, 1938, Vol. II, p. 289.
    A year later, Father de Smet feared that "as a result of the archbishop's interference and harassment" he and his companions would have to abandon their missions much to the great misfortune of the poor Indians. "Several of the men fear that Bishop Blanchet is the victim and dupe of a few conniving Canadian, French and Belgian clergy who are seeking to create trouble for religious orders, particularly the Society of Jesus, and are trying to detach religious from the obedience they owe to their superiors." Extract from a letter of Father de Smet (1847). Rome, Propagand. Arch., S.C., *America Centrale* vol. 14, fol. 581.
23. Bishop Guigues to Bishop Bourget, August 2, 1848. Montreal, Archiepiscopal Arch, dossier Ottawa 1848–1865.
24. Bishop de Mazenod to Father Ricard, May 12, 1853, P.R. LM Ricard. Bishop de Mazenod to Father Ricard, November 15, 1856. *Ibid.*, Corresp. Regist. 1855–1861, pp. 80–81.

In the latter letter, Bishop de Mazenod recalled the superior of the Oregon missions to France.

25. Bishop Bourget to Bishop Norbert Blanchet, October 24, 1849. Montreal, Archiep. Arch., Reg. Letters, vol. V, pp. 377 et seq.
26. Bishop de Mazenod to Bishop Barnabo, December 29, 1849. Rome, Propag. Arch., *Acta*, vol. 212, fol. 283.
27. Cardinal Fransoni to Bishop de Mazenod, August 16, 1850. P.R., LM Fransoni.
28. Bishop de Mazenod to Cardinal Fransoni, July 25, 1850. Rome, Propag. Arch., S.C., *Anglia*, vol. 12, fol. 545.
29. Congregation of the cardinals, April 22, 1850. *Ibid., Acta*, vol. 212, fol. 259.
30. Bishop de Mazenod to Bishop Barnabo, July 8, 1851. *Ibid., S.C., America Centrale,* vol. 15, fol. 817–818.
31. Bishop Norbert Blanchet to Cardinal Fransoni, February 23, 1852. *Ibid.,* vol. 16, fol. 54.
32. Bishop de Mazenod to Cardinal Fransoni, December 8, 1851. *Ibid.,* vol. 15, fol. 929.
33. *Id., ibid., America Centrale,* vol. 15, fol. 930.
34. Father Roothaan to Cardinal Fransoni, September 14, 1850. *Ibid.,* fol. 584.
35. Father d'Herbomez to Bishop de Mazenod, October 19, 1854. A.G.R., d'Herbomez.
36. Council of April 14, 1858, *Ibid.,* Register of General Councils, vol. 2 (1857–1859).
37. Bishop de Mazenod to Bishop Bourget, June 7, 1844. Montreal, Archiepisc. Arch., dossier Oblates.
38. M. Quéré, *Bishop de Mazenod and the Foreign Missions,* Rome, 1960, p. 45.
39. Bishop de Mazenod to Cardinal Barnabo, March 27, 1861. P.R., Corresp. Regist. 1855–1861, p. 288.
    Bishop Bourget wrote to the same effect: "Your eminence knows that it is of an immense advantage to these new dioceses to have religious as bishops." Bishop Bourget to Cardinal Barnabo, August 24, 1860. Montreal, Archiep. Arch. Reg. Letters, vol. 11, p. 427.
40. M. Quéré, *Monseigneur de Mazenod et les missions étrangères.* Rome, 1960, p. 45.
41. *Id.,* p. 46.
42. Cf. Letters of Bishop de Mazenod to Cardinal Barnabo, April 28, 1858, July 12, 1859, March 16, October 6 and November 29, 1860. P.R., Corresp. Reg. 1855–1861, pp. 171, 233, 278, 280 and 283.
43. The Bishop of Philadelphia was John Nepomucene Neumann, beatified in 1963.
44. G. Carrière, *Histoire documentaire de la Congrégation des Missionaires Oblats de Marie Immaculée dans l'Est du Canada,* Part I.
45. Cf. *Id.,* p. 166.
46. Father Telmon to Mother Marie-Rose, October 29, November 15, 1848. *Ibid.,* p. 167.
47. Bishop de Mazenod to Bishop Guigues, September 15, 1848. Quoted by Yenveux, *Saintes Règles,* Vol. I, supplement, p. 71.

48. Bishop de Mazenod to Father Telmon, November 5, 1848. *Ibid.*, Vol. VII, p. 36.
49. Father Telmon to Mother Bruyère, January 3, 1849. Quoted by G. Carrière, *Histoire documentaire* . . . , part 1, Vol. IV, p. 168.
50. Father Telmon to Sister Charlebois, January 3, 1849. *Ibid.*, p. 169.
51. Bishop Bourget to Bishop de Mazenod, June 11, 1849. Montreal, Archiep. Arch, Reg. Letters, vol. 5, p. 235.
52. G. Carrière, *Histoire documentaire* . . . , part 1, Vol. IV, p. 171.
53. P. Cauvin to Bishop Guigues, March 23, 1849. *Ibid.*
54. Bishop de Mazenod to Father Telmon, June 1, 1849. Quoted by Yenveux, *Saintes Règles*, Vol. I, supplement, p. 111.
55. *Gazette de Québec*, October 15, 1842.
56. Father Honorat to Bishop de Mazenod, August 9, 1844. A.G.R., Honorat.
57. Bishop Bourget to Bishop de Mazenod, October 10, 1844. Montreal, Archiepisc. Arch. Reg. Letters, vol. 3, p. 433.
58. Bishop de Mazenod to Father Guigues, December 5, 1844. Quoted by Yenveux, *Saintes Règles*, Vol. VII, p. 37.
59. Bishop de Mazenod to Bishop Bourget, February 6, 1845. Montreal Archiep. Arch. dossier Oblates.
60. Council of November 6, 1845. A.G.R., Reg. General Councils, Vol. I, (1844–1857).
61. Bishop de Mazenod to Father Guigues, November 19, 1845. Quoted by Yenveux, *Saintes Règles*, Vol. VII, p. 40.
62. Father Gaudet to Bishop Guigues, November 16, 1854. Ottawa, Archiep. Arch., Reg. Letters, vol. VI, p. 49.
63. *Id. ibid.*
64. Father Honorat to Bishop de Mazenod, April 5, 1856. A.G.R. Honorat.
65. Bishop Guigues to Bishop de Goesbriand, October 20, 1856. Ottawa, Archiep. Arch., Reg. Letters, vol. VII, p. 366.
66. Bishop Bourget to Bishop de Goesbriand, November 13, 1856. Montreal, Archiep. Arch., Reg. Letters, vol. 9, p. 461.
67. Council of December 4, 1856. A.G.R., Reg. General Councils, Vol. I, (1844–1857).
68. Bishop de Goesbriand to Bishop Guigues, October 15, 1856. Montreal, Provincial Arch., dossier Burlington.
69. Bishop de Mazenod to Bishop Guigues, November 27, 1856. P.R. Reg. Correspondance, 1855–1861, pp. 84–85.
70. Father Bernard to Father Rey, November 19, 1862, in *Missions*, Vol. II (1863) p. 123.
71. Father Bernard to Father Rey, November 19, 1862. *Ibid.* p. 124.
72. G. Carrière, *Histoire documentaire* . . . , part 1, Vol. IV, p. 201.
73. Bishop de Mazenod to Bishop Guigues, November 24, 1857. P.R. Reg. Correspondance 1855–1861, p. 142.
74. Council of January 4, 1850. A.G.R., Reg. General Councils, Vol. I (1844–1857).
75. Council of September 2, 1850. A.G.R., Reg. General Councils, Vol. I.
76. Bishop de Mazenod to Bishop Guigues, January 10, 1851. P.R. LM Guigues.
77. Agreement between Bishop Timon and Father Tempier, July 31, 1851. A.G.R., dossier Buffalo.

78. Father Santoni to Father Aubert, August 14, 1851. *Ibid.,* Santoni.

79. G. Carrière, *Histoire documentaire* . . . , part 1, Vol. IV, p. 226.

80. Act of Visitation of April 28, 1852. Montreal, Provincial Arch. O.M.I., *Actes officiels concernant la province du Canada,* p. 40.

81. Father Casimir Aubert to Father Santoni, May 21, 1855. P.R. Reg. Correspondance 1855–1861, p. 15.

82. Bishop de Mazenod to Father Aubert, June 17, 1854. Quoted by Yenveux, *Saintes Régles,* Vol. V, p. 60.

83. Father Tempier to Father Chevalier, March 15, 1855. P.R., Reg. Correspondance 1855–1861, p. 7.

84. Bishop de Mazenod to Father Santoni, May 29, 1855. *Ibid,* p. 17.

85. Father Santoni to Bishop Timon, July 27, 1855. Montreal, O.M.I. Provincial Arch., Provincial's Letters 1849–1863.

86. Act of Visitation of June 6, 1857. *Ibid., Actes officiels concernant la province du Canada,* pp. 91–92.

87. Father Chevalier to Cardinal Barnabo, October 11, 1861. Rome, Arch. of Propaganda, S.C. *America Centrale,* vol. 19, fol. 421–422.

   Bishop Timon, after demanding the promissory note of $5,000 from Father Chevalier, a note the prelate had signed and which was "neither negotiable nor of any legal force," threw it into the fire and told Father Chevalier that he owed him nothing.

88. Bishop de Mazenod to Father Santoni, October 8, 1855. P.R., Reg. Correspondance 1855–1861, p. 30.

89. Father Tempier to Father Chevalier, March 24, 1856. *Ibid.,* p. 55.

90. Father Chevalier to Father Mauroit, November 16, 1860. Montreal, O.M.I. Provincial Arch., Buffalo 1858–1860.

91. Father Fabre, Report to the council of the Lyons Propagation of the Faith, March 27, 1860. P.R., Reg. Correspondance 1855–1861, p. 266.

92. Father Chevalier to Bishop de Mazenod, April 15, 1861, in *Missions,* Vol. II (1863) pp. 114–115.

93. Father Chevalier to Father Tempier, July 27, 1860. A.G.R., Chevalier.

   Father Chevalier wrote, however, that there were 1050 Communions at that mission and that he was "quite happy" about bringing back "some apostates."

94. Father Chevalier to Bishop de Mazenod, April 15, 1861, in *Missions,* Vol. II, p. 116. Hammondsport is at the southern end of Crooked Lake.

95. Bishop Odin to the Council of the Lyons Propagation of the Faith, July 8, 1846. Fribourg, Arch. of the Prop. of Faith Council.

96. Bishop de Mazenod, *Journal,* November 10, 1849, quoted by Yenveux, *Saintes Règles,* Vol. III, p. 124.

97. Father Soulerin to Father Rey, 1862, in *Missions,* Vol. I, (1862), p. 459.

98. *Id. ibid.,* p. 461.

99. *Id., ibid.,* p. 460.

100. Letter from Father Soulerin in the obituary of Father Telmon. *Notices nécrologiques,* Vol. III, Paris, 1879, pp. 504–507.

101. Bishop Odin to Bishop de Mazenod, March 18, 1850. A.G.R., Odin.

102. Council of September 2, 1850. *Ibid.,* Reg. General Councils, Vol. I, (1844–1857).

103. Bishop de Mazenod, *Journal,* May 1, 1837, P.R., JM.

   Telmon was mentioned several times during this month.

358 EUGENE DE MAZENOD

104. Bishop Odin to Father Tempier, s.d. (1852). A.G.R. Odin.
105. Minutes Book of the Propagation of the Faith Council (1851), p. 137, Fribourg. Arch. of the Propagation of the Faith Council.
106. Agreement between Bishop Odin and Bishop de Mazenod, November 14, 1851. A.G.R., dossier *Fondation du Texas*.
107. B. Doyon, *The Cavalry of Christ on the Rio Grande 1849–1883*. Milwaukee, 1956, pp. 36–37.
108. Bishop Odin to the Council of the Lyons Propagation of the Faith, July 1, 1853. Fribourg, Arch. of the Council of the Propagation of the Faith.
109. M. Chambodut, vicar-general of Galveston, to the Propagation of the Faith Council, August 10, 1853. *Ibid.*
110. Bishop de Mazenod to Father Verdet, September 2, 1852. Quoted by Yenveux, *Saintes Règles*, Vol. II, p. 27.
111. Bishop Odin to Bishop de Mazenod, May 15, 1857. A.G.R., Odin.
112. B. Doyon, *op. cit.*, p. 52.
113. Father Gaudet to Bishop de Mazenod, received on January 22, 1857. A.G.R., *Journal de la correspondance générale* (1857–1859), p. 6.
114. Council of January 22, 1857. *Ibid.*, Reg. General Councils, Vol. II (1857–1859).
115. Bishop Odin to Bishop de Mazenod, May 15, 1857. *Ibid.*, Odin.
116. Bishop de Mazenod to Bishop Odin, June 20, 1857. P. R. Reg. Correspondance 1855–1861, pp. 110–111.
117. Father Verdet to Father Viala, August 31, 1853. A.G.R., Verdet.
118. E. Domenech, *Journal d'un missionnaire au Téxas et au Méxique 1846–1852*. Paris, 1857.
119. Quoted by B. Doyon, *op. cit.*, p. 63, note 13.
120. Father Gaudet, Historical Report, 1863, in *Missions*, Vol III (1864) p. 69.
121. W. Passmore, quoted by B. Doyon, *op. cit.*, p. 63, note 13.
122. Father Gaudet to Bishop de Mazenod, April 25, 1859, in *Missions*, Vol. I (1862), p. 491.
123. *Id., ibid.*, p. 490.
124. Father Gaudet to Bishop de Mazenod, June 13, 1859. *Ibid.*, pp. 495–496.
125. Father Gaudet to Bishop de Mazenod, April 25, 1859. *Ibid.*, p. 492.
126. Bishop de Mazenod to the Oblates in Texas, November 26, 1858. P.R. Reg. Correspondance 1855–1861, p. 206.
127. Father Gaudet to Bishop de Mazenod, October 3, 1859, in *Missions* Vol. I, pp. 500–501.
128. Father Gaudet to Bishop de Mazenod, March 12, 1861. *Ibid.*, p. 525.
129. Father Parisot to Bishop de Mazenod, September 3, 1858, in *Missions*, Vol. I, p. 470.
130. Father Gaudet to Bishop de Mazenod, December 24, 1858. *Ibid.*, pp. 482–483.
131. Father Casimir Aubert to Father Gaudet, April 20, 1858. P.R., Reg. Correspondance 1855–1861, p. 165.
132. Father Gaudet to Bishop de Mazenod, December 24, 1858, in *Missions*, Vol. I, pp. 483–484.
133. Father Parisot to Bishop de Mazenod, September 3, 1858. *Ibid.*, p. 470.
134. Bishop de Mazenod to Father Gaudet, August 28–September 3, 1858. P.R., Reg. Correspondance 1855–1861, p. 199.

135. Don Musquiz, Pastor of Matamoros, to Bishop de Mazenod, March 14, 1859. San Antonio (Texas) O.M.I. Provincial Arch.
136. Father Gaudet to Bishop de Mazenod, December 24, 1858, in *Missions,* Vol. I, p. 482.
137. Bishop de Mazenod to Don Musquiz, October 10, 1859. P.R. Reg. Correspondance 1855–1861, pp. 249–250.
138. Father Gaudet to Bishop de Mazenod, November 13, 1859, in *Missions,* Vol. I, p. 503.
139. Father Sivi to Brother Bournigalle, 1860. Ibid, pp. 517–518.
140. *Id., ibid.* p. 519.
141. Father Sivi to Father Mouchette, April 20, 1861. *Ibid.,* pp. 530–531.
142. Father Gaudet to Father Fabre, March 12, 1861. *Ibid.,* p. 524.
143. Don Musquiz to Bishop de Mazenod, March 14, 1859. San Antonio, O.M.I. Provincial Arch.
144. Father Parisot to Bishop de Mazenod, March 19, 1860, in *Missions,* Vol. I, p. 510.
145. Father Parisot to Father Gaudet, March 16, 1859. *Ibid.,* p. 487.
146. Father Parisot to Bishop de Mazenod, March 19, 1860. *Ibid.,* p. 510.
147. Father Parisot to Father Gaudet, March 16, 1859. *Ibid.,* p. 487.
148. Father Parisot to the Junior Seminarians of Notre Dame de Sion, February 10, 1880. A.G.R., Parisot.
149. Father Parisot to Father Gaudet, March 16, 1859, in *Missions,* Vol. I, p. 488.
150. Father Parisot to Bishop de Mazenod, March 19, 1860. *Ibid.,* p. 510.
151. Father Parisot to Father Gaudet, March 16, 1859. *Ibid.,* p. 489.
152. Father Parisot to Bishop de Mazenod, March 19, 1860. *Ibid.,* p. 510.
153. Account of the Texas and Mexican missions, May 31, 1867. A.G.R., *Rapport 1867, Texas.*
154. Father Gaudet to Father Fabre, March 12, 1861 in *Missions,* Vol. I, p. 528.
155. Father Gaudet to Father Fabre, December 10, 1861. *Ibid.,* p. 537.
156. Father Gaudet to Father Fabre, February 12, 1861. *Ibid.,* p. 522.
157. Father Gaudet to Father Fabre, March 12, 1861. *Ibid.,* p. 525.

Chapter Four

1. Bishop de Mazenod to Father Vincens, August 12, 1847. P.R., LM Vincens. Regarding Bishop de Mazenod and the Oblates at Ceylon, cf. "Bishop de Mazenod and Ceylon" in *Études Oblates,* Vol. XI, (1952), pp. 168–178, 312–322.
2. Cf. A. Lourenço, *Utrum fuerit schisma Goanum post breve multa praeclare usque ad annum 1849?* Goa, 1947, Part 3, Chapter II, *Utrum oppositio fuerit schisma?* pp. 111 & seq. Doctorate thesis at the Gregorian University.
3. The first vicar-apostolic appointed in 1835, Bishop François-Xavier, died before his consecration. Succeeding him were Bishop Vincent de Rosario who died in 1842, and Bishop Gaetano Antonio Musulce, appointed in 1843; all three were from the Saint Philip Neri Oratory of Goa.
4. Bishop Bettachini, bishop *in partibus* of Toron, arrived at Ceylon in 1842; he, too, was an Oratorian, but belonged to the Rome Oratory.

5. Bishop Bettachini to Bishop Barnabo, March 9, 1850. Rome, Propag. Arch., S.C., *Indie Orientali*, vol. 12, fol. 756.

   "*Ora le faccio sapere che chi m'istigava sempre contro i Goani era appunto lui [Bravi], e nelle sue lettere a me scritte chiamava i Goani demoni, diavoli neri, negromanti, ecc., ecc . . .*"

6. M. Quéré, *Monseigneur de Mazenod et les missions étrangères*. Rome, 1958, p. 109. Typewritten thesis.

7. The division of Ceylon into two vicariates, decided upon in 1847 with the boundary lines defined, became effective only in 1849. At that date, Bishop Bettachini, the vicar-apostolic of Jaffna, ceased to be coadjutor to Bishop Gaetano, and the Sylvestrine, Bravi, was appointed in his place as coadjutor of Colombo, much to the indignation of Bettachini, who accused him of reaching the episcopate *sulla mia rovina*. Bishop Bettachini to Cardinal Fransoni, December, 1849. Rome, Propaganda Arch., S.C., *Indie Orientali*, vol. 12, fol. 707.

8. Bishop de Mazenod to Cardinal Fransoni, August 11, 1847. Rome, Propagand. Arch., S.C., *Indie Orientali*, vol. 11, fol. 402.

9. Bishop de Mazenod to Cardinal Fransoni, September 25, 1847. *Ibid.*, fol. 478.

10. *Id., ibid.*, fol. 479.

    In his letter of August 11, the Bishop of Marseilles pointed out to the Cardinal the rather strange situation of a Greek priest, Macario Spira, who was under the jurisdiction of the Propaganda, and who, not finding enough work in the Greek parish of Saint Nicolas de Myre at Marseilles, had just left that city for an unknown destination.

11. Bishop Semeria, *Journal*, December 3, 1847, p. 13. A.G.R.

    The original, preserved in the episcopal Arch. of Jaffna, is divided into three parts: 1) *Histoire de notre établissement à Ceylan 1847–1852.* 2) *Annales du Vicariat depuis 1852 jusqu'en 1855.* 3) *Annales historiques du Vicariat de Jaffna de juin 1855 à août 1861.*

    A copy was made from the register in 1907 by Father Batayron, and is preserved in the archives of the Oblate General House in Rome. The references are made from that copy.

12. Bishop Semeria, *Journal*, November 28, 1847, p. 12, A.G.R.

13. *Id.*, pp. 12–13. *Ibid.*

14. *Id., ibid.*

15. Bishop de Mazenod to Father Semeria, January 25, 1848. P.R., LM Semeria.

16. *Id., ibid.*

17. Bishop Semeria, *Journal*, May 18, 1848, pp. 20–22. A.G.R.

18. Bishop de Mazenod to Father Semeria, July 10, 1855. P.R., Reg. Correspondance 1855–1861, p. 25.

19. Bishop Semeria, *Journal*, November 28, 1847, p. 12, A.G.R.

20. J.A. Otto, *Gründung der neuen Jesuitenmissionen durch General P. Johann Roothaan*. Freiburg-im-Breisgau, 1949, pp. 343–345.

21. Bishop Semeria, *Journal*, September, 1848, p. 26. A.G.R.

22. *Id.*, May 22, 1848, p. 22. Ibid.

23. *Id.*, September 23, 1848, p. 23. A.G.R.

24. *Id.*, September, 1848, pp. 26, 23. *Ibid.*

25. *Id.*, p. 26. *Ibid.*

26. Bishop de Mazenod to Father Semeria, November 3, 1848. P.R., LM Semeria.
27. Bishop de Mazenod to Father Roothaan, October 28, 1848. Rome, Arch. S.J., Madure I-XIII, 14.
28. Father Roothaan to Bishop de Mazenod, November 7, 1848, recopied in Bishop de Mazenod's letter to Semeria, November 22, 1848. P.R., LM Semeria.
29. Bishop de Mazenod to Father Semeria, November 3 & 8, 1848. *Ibid.*
30. Bishop Semeria, *Journal,* January, 1848, p. 16. A.G.R.
31. Bishop de Mazenod to Father Semeria, May 9, 1848. P.R., LM Semeria.
32. Bishop Semeria, Journal, December, 1850, p. 81. A.G.R.
33. Bishop de Mazenod to Cardinal Fransoni, August 11, 1847. Rome, Propagand. Arch. S.C., *Indie Orientali,* vol. 11, fol. 401.
34. Bishop Semeria, *Journal,* January, 1853, p. 158. A.G.R.
35. *Id.,* December, 1849, pp. 58–59. *Ibid.*
36. Bishop de Mazenod to Father Semeria, February 21, 1849. P.R., LM Semeria. The figure of "more than 30,000 idolaters" is given by Bishop Bettachini in a letter of June 5, 1846, published in the *Annales de la Propagation de la Foi,* Vol. XIX (1847) p. 91.
37. Bishop de Mazenod to Father Semeria, March 12, 1851. P.R. LM, Semeria.
38. Cf. Letters of Bishop de Mazenod to Semeria, *passim. Ibid.*
39. Bishop de Mazenod to Father Semeria, January 21, 1852. *Ibid.*
40. *Id.,* November 8, 1848. *Ibid.*
41. *Id.,* March 12, 1851. *Ibid.*
42. Bishop de Mazenod to Father Semeria, October, 1855. *Ibid.,* Reg. Correspondance 1855–1861, p. 29.
Bishop Bettachini to Semeria, October 30, 1854 in Semeria *Journal,* p. 265. A.G.R.
43. Bishop de Mazenod to Father Semeria, May 9, 1848. P.R., LM Semeria.
44. Bishop de Mazenod to Bishop Barnabo, February 27, 1850. Rome, Propagand. Arch, S.C., *Indie Orientali,* vol. 12, fol. 741.
45. Bishop Bettachini to Cardinal Fransoni, May 5, 1851. *Ibid.,* vol. 13, fol. 434.
46. Bishop de Mazenod to Father Semeria, March 25, 1851. P.R., LM Semeria.
47. Bishop de Mazenod to Father Semeria, June 3, 1851, *Ibid.*
48. Bishop de Mazenod to Father Semeria, July 27–August 5, 1851. *Ibid.*
49. *Id., ibid.*
50. Bishop de Mazenod to Father Semeria, April 16, 1852. *Ibid.*
51. Bishop Bettachini to Cardinal Fransoni, January 7, 1852. Rome, Propagand. Arch., S.C., *Indie Orientali,* vol. 13, fol. 785.
52. Bishop Bettachini to Cardinal Fransoni, January 25, 1856, (confidential letter). *Ibid.,* vol. 15, fol. 896.
53. Bishop Semeria, *Journal,* August, 1850, p. 61. A.G.R.
54. *Id.,* Reflections at the beginning of 1854 and report to Bishop de Mazenod regarding the year 1853, April 1, 1854, pp. 187, 210. *Ibid.*
55. Father Semeria to Bishop de Mazenod, quoted by Father Duchaussois, *Sous les feux de Ceylan.* Paris, 1929, p. 92.
56. Bishop de Mazenod to Father Semeria, July 2, 1852. P.R., LM Semeria.

57. Bishop Semeria, *Journal*, July, 1857, p. 334. A.G.R.

58. Id., September, 1857, p. 341. A.G.R.

59. Father Duchaussois, *Sous les feux de Ceylan*, p. 101.

60. Bishop Semeria, *Journal*, January, 1859, p. 356. A.G.R.

61. Bishop de Mazenod to Bishop Semeria, February 18, 1860. P.R. LM Semeria.

62. Bishop Semeria, *Journal*, January, 1860, pp. 367–368. A.G.R.
    Regarding the native clergy and Bishop Semeria, cf. N. Kowalsky, Mgr. Semeria, O.M.I., "Apostolischer Vikar von Jaffna (1857–1868) zur Frage des einheimischen Klerus," in *Neue Zeitschrift für Missionswissenschaft*, 1951, pp. 273–281.

63. Bishop de Mazenod to Bishop Semeria, February, 1860. P.R., LM. Semeria.

64. Bishop de Mazenod to Bishop Semeria, July 8, 1860. *Ibid*.

65. Bishop Semeria, *Journal*, January, 1861, p. 391. A.G.R.

66. *Id., ibid.*

67. *Id.,* October, 1854, p. 266. A.G.R.

68. Bishop de Mazenod to Cardinal Barnabo, December 15, 1860. Rome, Propagand. Arch., S.C. *Indie Orientali*, vol. 17, fol. 1547.

69. Bishop Bravi to Cardinal Fransoni, August 14, 1851. Rome, Propagand. Arch, S.C. *Indie Orientali*, vol. 13, fol. 568.

70. In effect, Bishop Bravi was convinced that his conciliatory policy was the only good one in the South of Ceylon, and he boasted of having established real peace there. He feared that the arrival of the Oblates, employing the methods of the North, would rekindle the quarrels and would throw the Goanese priests back into schism. He constantly repeated that neither the Propaganda nor Bishop de Mazenod knew the real situation and that their appraisal of it was based upon the false reports sent by the Oblates.
    Don Beda Barcatta, a Sylvestrine O.S.B. made himself the fervent apologist of Bishop Bravi in his doctorate thesis, *L'Apostolato dei Missionari Silvestrini O.S.B. nel Ceylon (1845–1883)*. Rome, 1948, Typewritten thesis.

71. Bishop de Mazenod to Father Semeria, June 3, 1851. P.R., LM Semeria.

72. Bishop de Mazenod to Father Semeria, March 25, 1851. *Ibid*.

73. Bishop de Mazenod to Father Semeria, March 12, 1851. *Ibid*. Bishop de Mazenod to Bishop Barnabo, December 18, 1850. Rome, Propagand. Arch., S.C., *Indie Orientali*, vol. 12, fol. 1141.

74. Bishop de Mazenod to Father Semeria, March 12, 1851. P.R. LM Semeria.

75. Bishop de Mazenod to Bishop Barnabo, June 15, 1851. Rome, Propagand. Arch. S.C., *Indie Orientali*, vol. 13, fol. 515.

76. Bishop de Mazenod to Father Semeria, July 27–August 5, 1851. P.R., LM, Semeria.

77. Bishop Bravi to Father Semeria, July 26, 1851, recopied in Semeria's *Journal*, p. 108. A.G.R.

78. Bishop Bravi to Father Semeria, August 4, 1851. Ibid., pp. 108–109.

79. Bishop Semeria to Bishop de Mazenod, August 7, 1851, in *Journal*, p. 112. *Ibid*.

80. Father Mouchel to Father Semeria, August, 1851. *Ibid.*, p. 114.

81. Bishop de Mazenod to Father Semeria, September 19, 1851. P.R., LM Semeria.

82. Bishop Semeria, *Journal,* August, 1851, p. 114. A.G.R.
83. Bishop de Mazenod to Father Semeria, October, 1855. P.R., Reg. Correspondance 1855–1861, p. 28.
84. Bishop Semeria, *Journal,* pp. 130 & 136. A.G.R.
    In this passage, Bishop Semeria speaks of the river Kaimel, a name designating the mouth of the Maha Oya.
85. Bishop Semeria, *Journal,* pp. 136–137. A.G.R.
86. *Id.,* May, 1852, pp. 139–140. *Ibid.*
87. Quoted by Semeria, *Id.,* August, 1854, p. 262. *Ibid.*
88. *Id., ibid.*
89. Father Semeria to Cardinal Fransoni, September 30, 1854, Rome, Propagand. Arch., S.C., *Indie Orientali,* vol. 14, fol. 1332–1333. Cf. Semeria, Journal, pp. 263–264. A.G.R.
90. Bishop de Mazenod to Father Semeria, November 28–December 8, 1854, in *Journal,* p. 264. *Ibid.*
91. J. Rommerskirchen, *Die Oblatenmissionen auf der Insel Ceylon 1847–1893.* Hünfeld, 1931, p. 41.
92. Bishop Semeria, *Journal,* May 1853, p. 163. A.G.R.
93. Missionaries of Jaffna to Cardinal Fransoni, August 28, 1853, Rome. Propagand. Arch, S.C, *Indie Orientali,* vol. 14, fol. 583.
94. Bishop Semeria, *Journal,* June, 1853, p. 163, A.G.R.
95. Father Semeria to Cardinal Fransoni, June 6, 1853, in *Journal,* pp. 163–166, *Ibid.*
96. Bishop Bravi to Cardinal Fransoni, August 11, 1853. Rome, Propagand. Arch., S.C., *Indie Orientali,* vol. 14, fol. 524.
97. Bishop de Mazenod to Cardinal Fransoni, September 20, 1853. Rome, Propagand. Arch., S.C., *Indie Orientali,* vol. 14, fol. 636–637.
98. Bishop Bravi to Father Semeria, March 7, 1854, in *Journal,* p. 194. A.G.R.
99. Regarding this Negombo conference, see Father Semeria to Bishop de Mazenod, June 4, 1854, in *Journal,* pp. 198–205. *Ibid.*
100. Congregation-General of April 2, 1855. Rome, Propagand. Arch., *Acta,* vol. 209, fol. 276–281.
    Regarding the decree of the Propaganda, cf. Semeria's *Journal,* pp. 296–297.
101. Bishop de Mazenod to Bishop Barnabo, July 12, 1855. Rome, Propagand. Arch. S.C., *Indie Orientali,* vol. 15, fol. 543.
102. Bishop de Mazenod to Bishop Semeria, September 17, 1860. P.R., LM Semeria.
103. Bishop de Mazenod to Cardinal Barnabo, April 15, 1860. Rome, Propagand. Arch., S.C., *Francia,* vol. 4, fol. 479.
104. Bishop de Mazenod to Cardinal Barnabo, July 12, 1859. *Ibid., Indie Orientali,* vol. 17, fol. 601.
105. Bishop Bonand's report, May 16, 1860. *Ibid.,* fol. 1240–1243.
106. Bishop Bravi to Cardinal Fransoni, March 3, 1855, Rome. Propagand. Arch., S.C., *Indie Orientali,* vol. 15, fol. 352.
107. Bishop de Mazenod to Bishop Barnabo, August 2, 1855. *Ibid.,* fol. 599.
108. Bishop de Mazenod to Cardinal Barnabo, August 30, 1856. *Ibid.* fol. 1209.
109. Bishop de Mazenod to Cardinal Barnabo, July 20, 1860. *Ibid.,* vol. 17, fol. 1268–1269.

Same to the same, October 21, 1857. P.R., Reg. Correspondance 1855–1861, p. 133.

110. Bishop de Mazenod to Bishop Barnabo, November 15, 1855. *Ibid.*, p. 37.

111. Bishop de Mazenod to Cardinal Barnabo, July 4, 1860. Rome, Propagand. Arch., S.C., *Indie Orientali*, Vol. 17, fol. 1292–1293.

112. Bishop de Mazenod to Bishop Semeria, September 17, 1860. P.R., LM Semeria.

113. Bishop Jeancard to Cardinal Barnabo, March 2, 1861. Rome. Propagand. Arch., S.C., *Indie Orientali*, vol. 17, fol. 1606.

114. Bishop de Mazenod to Cardinal Barnabo, April 6, 1861. *Ibid.*, fol. 1676.

115. J. Rommerskirchen, *Die Oblatenmissionen auf der Insel Ceylon*, p. 166, note 13.

116. Bishop de Mazenod to Cardinal Pedicini, April 10, 1832, in *Missions*, Vol. LXXII (1938), p. 391.

117. Bishop de Mazenod to Father Dassy, July 18, 1848. Quoted by Yenveux, *Saintes Règles*, Vol. I, supplement, p. 86.

118. Bishop de Mazenod, retreat for the episcopate, October 7–14, 1832. P.R., DM IV-3.

119. Bishop de Mazenod, *Journal*, October 29, 1842, in *Missions*, Vol. XII (1874), p. 431.

Undoubtedly, Bishop de Mazenod was relying on the assertions of Prince de Mir, made in 1838, which gave first impressions regarding the religious attitude of the Arabs: "The prince averred that there was nothing so easy as winning over through virtue all these infidels who are separated from us only because of the impiousness of our colonies." Bishop de Mazenod, *Journal*, February 15, 1858. P.R. JM.

This Polish prince, returning from Algiers where he had formed an establishment 7½ miles from the city, conceived the idea, along with Father Landmann, of founding a Christian Association for the colonization of Algeria. In fact, two meetings were held at the bishop's palace in Marseilles, on November 29 and December 3, for the purpose of composing the statutes and placing the association under the patronage of Bishop Dupuch and Bishop de Mazenod. After several other meetings, the plan was abandoned, particularly since the Bishop of Algiers put his Marseilles colleague on guard against the prince, who, he said, "cannot be our man." Bishop Dupuch to Bishop de Mazenod, in *Journal*, February 19, 1839. *Ibid.*

Regarding this affair, cf. Bishop de Mazenod's *Journal*, December 4, 5, & 8, 1838, January 22 & 24, and February 28, 1839. (A.A.M., Administrat. Corresp., Reg. IV, pp. 26–27.) Father Landmann later on resumed this project. Cf. Duroselle, *Les débuts du catholicisme social en France*, pp. 441, 603.

120. Bishop de Mazenod to Father Dassy, July 18, 1848. Quoted by Yenveux, *Saintes Règles*, Vol. I, supplement, p. 86.

121. Bishop de Mazenod to Bishop Pavy, December 4, 1848. *Ibid.*, Vol. III, p. 143. Cf. E. Lamirande, *Les Oblats en Algérie (1849–1850)* in *Études Oblates*, Vol. XIV (1955), pp. 154–183.

122. Bishop de Mazenod to Bishop Pavy, January 5, 1849. Quoted by Yenveux, *Saintes Règles*, Vol. I, supplement, p. 107.

123. Bishop de Mazenod to Father Viala, April 5, 1849. *Ibid.*, Vol. V, p. 232.

124. Bishop de Mazenod, *Journal*, November 30, 1849. *Ibid.*, Vol. I, supplement, p. 86.

125. General Council, February 22, 1848. A.G.R., General Councils, Vol. I, 1844–1857.

126. Bishop de Mazenod to Bishop Pavy, February 4, 1850, Algiers, Archiep. Arch.

127. Bruneau, vicar-general of Mans, to Father Tempier, January 26, 1850, transcript to the council of February 4, 1850. A.G.R., General Councils, Vol. I, 1844–1857.

128. Bishop de Mazenod, *Journal*, February 22, 1850. Quoted by Yenveux, *Saintes Règles*, Vol. IX, p. 86.

129. *Id.*, March 27–April 1, 1850. *Ibid.*, Vol. VII, pp. 62–63.

130. Bishop de Mazenod to Bishop Barnabo, May 24, 1850. Rome, Propagand. Arch., *Acta*, vol. 212, fol. 513.

131. Bishop de Mazenod to Father Allard, December 4, 1850. P.R., LM Allard.

132. Bishop de Mazenod to Bishop Guigues, April 18, 1851. Quoted by Yenveux, *Saintes Règles*, Vol. III, p. 49.

133. Bishop de Mazenod to Father Baudrand, March 25, 1851. P.R., LM Baudrand.

134. Bishop de Mazenod to Bishop Guigues, January 10, 1851. *Ibid.*, Guigues.

135. Th. Ortolan, *Les Oblats de Marie Immaculée durant le premier siècle de leur existence*, Vol. II, Paris, 1915, p. 541.

136. Bishop de Mazenod to Father Allard, April 18, 1851. P.R., LM Allard.

137. Bishop de Mazenod to Bishop Guigues, August 7, 1851. Quoted by Yenveux, *Saintes Règles*, Vol. IX, p. 18.

138. Bishop Allard to Bishop Devereux, January 21, 1852. A.G.R., Register of Natal correspondence, no. 10. Bishop Devereux resided at Port Elizabeth, Bishop Griffith at Capetown.

139. Bishop Allard to Blancheton, the consul, April 25, 1852. *Ibid.*, no. 18.

140. Bishop Allard to Bishop de Mazenod, November 10, 1853. Ibid., no. 176.

141. Bishop Allard to the Lyons Propagation of the Faith, October 10, 1852. *Ibid.*, no. 54.
     Father Sabon's death notice, in Notices nécrologiques, Vol. VI, Bar-le-Duc, 1895, pp. 89–90.

142. Bishop Allard to the Lyons Propagation of the Faith, October 10, 1852. A.G.R., Reg. Correspondance Natal, no. 54.

143. Bishop Allard to Bishop de Mazenod, July 14, 1852. *Ibid.*, no. 34.

144. Father Barret to Father Martinet, May 24, 1873. A.G.R. Justin Barret.

145. Bishop Allard to Bishop de Mazenod, June 10, 1854. *Ibid.*, Reg. Natal correspondence, no. 204.

146. Bishop Allard to the Lyons Propagation of the Faith, February 28, 1857, in *Annales de la propagation de la foi*, XXX (1858), p. 33.

147. Father Gerard to his parents, May, 1856. *Ibid.*, XXIX (1857), pp. 99–100.

148. Bishop Allard to the Lyons Propagation of the Faith, February 28, 1857. *Ibid.*, Vol. XXX, pp. 34–35.

149. Bishop Allard to M. Kepstone, June, 1856. A.G.R., Register of Natal correspondence, no. 307.

150. Bishop Allard to Father Gerard, July 23, 1856. Ibid., no. 320.

151. Bishop de Mazenod to Bishop Allard, May 30, 1857. P.R., Reg. Correspondance 1855–1861, pp. 108–109.
152. Bishop Allard to Bishop Griffith, January, 1857. A.G.R., register of Natal correspondence, no. 338.
153. Bishop de Mazenod to Bishop Allard, June 11, 1855. P.R. Reg. Correspondance 1855–1861, p. 23.
154. Bishop de Mazenod to Bishop Allard, May 30, 1857. *Ibid.*, p. 109.
155. Bishop de Mazenod to Bishop Allard, November 10, 1857. *Ibid.*, pp. 139–140.
156. Father Gerard to Bishop de Mazenod, April 5, 1858, in *Missions*, Vol. I (1862) p. 352.
157. Bishop Allard to Bishop de Mazenod, August 21, 1859. *Ibid.*, pp. 319–322.
158. Father Gerard to Bishop de Mazenod, June 10, 1860. *Ibid.*, p. 357.
159. (Translator's note). Since the publication of Monsignor Leflon's work, new data were supplied to the translator by Father Howard St. George, O.M.I., of Natal, South Africa, regarding the exact location of this third mission. These data were found in Bishop Allard's *Journal*. An entry, dated August 23, 1861, recording the abandonment of that mission, states: "After preaching nine months to the Zulus living in the *Evete* River valley, where there are about eight kraals, we accomplished nothing, nor did we see any hope of Christianizing the people."
160. Father Gerard to Bishop de Mazenod, April 12, 1861, in *Missions*, Vol. I, pp. 364–365.
161. Bishop Allard to Father Fabre, October 26, 1861. *Ibid.*, p. 340.
162. Bishop de Mazenod to Father Gerard, September 4, 1860. P.R., LM Gerard.

Chapter Five

1. List composed by J. Perlioz, O.M.I., in *Chapitres Généraux (1818–1861)*. Rome, 1962, Vol. II, pp. 732–739. Typed work.
    91 of these Oblates "worked in the missions of Red River, Oregon, British Colombia, Texas, Natal and Ceylon; 47 belonged to the Canadian province, and 60 worked zealously in Ireland and England." *Id.*, p. 740.
2. Death notice of Father Leonard Baveux, in *Notices nécrologiques,* Vol. I, p. 224.
3. Bishop de Mazenod to Bishop Bourget, November 7, 1846. Montreal, Archiep. Arch., dossier Oblates.
4. Bishop de Mazenod to Father Leonard, April 2, 1847. P.R., LM Leonard.
5. Bishop de Mazenod to Father Leonard, June 10, 1847. *Ibid.*
6. Bishop de Mazenod to Father Leonard, August 15, 1847. *Ibid.*
7. Bishop de Mazenod to Father Leonard, October 27, 1847. *Ibid.*
8. Bishop de Mazenod to Father Leonard, November 8, 1847. *Ibid.*
9. Bishop de Mazenod to Bishop Sergent, July 22, 1856. P.R., Reg. Correspondance 1855–1861, p. 70.
10. Bishop de Mazenod to Bishop Sergent, October 28, 1856. Quimper, Grand Seminary Arch.
11. Bishop de Mazenod to Father Soullier, December 9, 1856. P.R., LM Soullier.

12. Bishop de Mazenod to Bishop Sergent, January 8, 1857. *Ibid*. Reg. Correspondance 1855–1861, p. 86.

13. Father Lagier to Bishop de Mazenod, January 15, 1857. A.G.R., *Journal de la correspondance* 1857–1859.

14. Council of May 26, 1857. *Ibid*., Reg. Councils General, Vol. II, 1857–1859.

15. Bishop Guibert to Bishop de Mazenod, August, 1857. Quoted by Rey, Vol. II, p. 649.

16. Bishop Sergent to Bishop de Mazenod, August 1, 1857. Quimper, Grand Seminary Arch.

17. Bishop de Mazenod to Bishop Sergent, August 6, 1857. P.R., Reg. Correspondance 1855–1861, pp. 120–121.

18. Bishop de Mazenod to Bishop Sergent, August 25, 1857. Quimper, Major Seminary Arch.

19. Bishop de Mazenod to Father Lagier, August 17, 1857. P.R., Reg. Correspondance 1855–1861, p. 124.

20. Bishop Sergent to Bishop de Mazenod, August 14, 1857. Quimper, Major Seminary Arch.

21. Bishop Sergent to Bishop Jaquemet, October 30, 1857. Nantes, Episcop. Arch., dossier Quimper.

22. Bishop Dufêtre, Bishop of Nevers, to Bishop Sergent, August 6, 1857. Quimper, Major Seminary Arch.

23. Bishop Casanelli d'Istria, Bishop of Ajaccio, to Bishop Sergent, August 26, 1856. *Ibid*.

24. Bishop de Mazenod to Father Lagier, October 17, 1857. P.R., Reg. Correspondance 1855–1861, p. 124.

25. Father Berthuel to Father (Tempier), June, 1856. A.G.R., Berthuel.

26. Father Lancenay to Bishop de Mazenod, April 21, 1857. *Ibid*., Lancenay.

27. Father Lancenay to Father Vincens, September 12, 1857. *Ibid*., Lancenay. Father Lancenay to Bishop de Mazenod, September 24–October 1, 1857. *Ibid*.

28. Father Lancenay to Father Vincens, October 4, 1857. *Ibid*.

29. Bishop Lyonnet to Bishop de Mazenod, October, 1857. Quoted by Burnichon, *La compagnie de Jésus en France. Histoire d'un siècle*, Vol. III, p. 514.

30. Father Lancenay to Bishop de Mazenod, September 24–October 1, 1857. A.G.R. Lancenay. Bishop de Mazenod wrote the following notation on this letter: "Extremely odd letter, written on the eve of our expulsion which they had already planned."

31. Account of this conversation given by Bishop de Mazenod to Father Beckx, General of the Jesuits, October 12, 1857. P.R., Reg. Correspond. 1855–1861, p. 128. The Jesuit General, informed of these underhanded dealings, had recommended prudence without making a decision on the plan. Later, on October 21, he informed Bishop de Mazenod of the answer he had given to the Lyons provincial: the matter is "a very delicate one, for how would Bishop de Mazenod look upon our being substituted for his Congregation? Before all else, we must avoid offending a prelate who, in most critical times, proved to be the protector of our house at Marseilles and of our Society." Report regarding the Congregation in 1857–1858, p. 28, note 1.

32. Bishop de Mazenod to Bishop Lyonnet, October 10, 1857. P.R., Reg. Corresp. 1855–1861, p. 127.
33. Bishop de Mazenod to Father Beckx, October 12, 1857. P.R., Reg. Corresp. 1855–1861, pp. 127–129.
34. Father Gautrelet to Bishop de Mazenod, October 18, 1857. Quoted by Burnichon, *La compagnie de Jésus en France*, Vol. III, p. 513.

On October 18, Father Gautrelet wrote to the General of the Jesuits that, during his visit to the prelate, he had "made it clear: first, that we had not taken the initiative; second, that we had not entered into any contract, and third, that although we had given hopes for the future, it was only after expressing our fears and reluctance and on the basis of what Bishop Lyonnet, who realized our difficulty, had promised us, namely, that he would settle everything with the Bishop of Marseilles when circumstances were favorable." *Ibid.*

35. J. Burnichon, *La compagnie de Jésus en France*, Vol. III, p. 513.
36. Bishop Lyonnet to Bishop de Mazenod, October, 1857. *Ibid.*, p. 514.
37. J. Burnichon, *La compagnie de Jésus en France*, Vol. III, p. 514.
38. Bishop de Mazenod to Father Gautrelet, October 20, 1857. P.R., Reg. Corresp. 1855–1861, pp. 132–133.
39. Bishop de Mazenod to Father Beckx, October 21, 1857. *Ibid.*, p. 134.
40. *Historia domus Massiliensis ab anno 1856 ad annum 1862.* Paray-le-Monial, Arch. S.J. of the Lyons province, Col Prat Nouvelle Compagnie Vol. VIII, p. 142.
41. Father Vincens to Bishop Lyonnet, October 26, 1857. P.R., Reg. Corresp. 1855–1861, p. 134.
42. J. Burnichon, *La compagnie de Jésus en France*, Vol. III, p. 515.
43. Father Beckx to Father Gautrelet, October 26, 1857. *Ibid.*
44. Father Tortel to Father Fabre, October 24, 1857. A.G.R., Tortel.
45. Bishop de Mazenod, allocution to the members of the chapter, August 26, 1850. *Ibid.* Reg. General Chapters, Vol. I, p. 83.
46. *Constitutiones et Regulae Congregationis Missionariorum Oblatorum* . . . Marseilles, 1853, pp. 25–34.
47. Although the lease signed in 1818 granted Laus to the Oblates for 29 years' duration and although the contracting parties had orally agreed to an indefinite renewal of the lease, the Oblates had to give up this shrine as early as 1841; next to Aix, it was the oldest establishment of their Institute. Actually, Bishop de la Croix d'Azolette, former superior of the Chartreux (diocesan missionaries) of Lyons, as soon as he took possession of the See of Gap in 1837, resolved to form a society of missionary priests in the Hautes-Alpes, and, in consequence, requested the Bishop of Marseilles to withdraw his Oblates from the post they had been occupying at Laus. (Bishop de la Croix to Bishop de Mazenod, October 24, 1839. Notre Dame du Laus Arch.) Furthermore, a petition was circulated among the clergy at the time of the pastoral retreats of 1839, requesting that a retreat house for aged or infirm priests be opened "in that pious solitude." (*Annales de Notre Dame du Laus*, Gap, 1876, Vol. II, p. 315–316.)

Thus, the friendly relations established between the Oblates and the episcopal administration under Bishops Miollis and Arbaud, deteriorated completely. However, when the Founder remonstrated, the

Bishop of Gap, who anticipated his transfer to the archiepiscopal see of Auch, promised to make no changes in the *status quo* and to leave the solution up to his successor. (Father Depery to Father Martel, January 6, 1840. Notre Dame du Laus Arch.)

Meanwhile, a memorandum from Parisian jurists, who had been consulted in this matter, furnished the diocese with the expedient whereby the 1818 lease could be broken; the memorandum stated that on the day the bishop himself would appoint a pastor and curate, chosen from outside the Oblates, Bishop de Mazenod would be in the impossible position of "fulfilling the principal condition of the contract," which obliged him "to maintain two priests for the service of the shrine," and the lease would thus become voidable. (*Annales de Notre Dame du Laus,* Vol. II, pp. 320–321.) Shortly after his arrival, Bishop Rossat used this subterfuge, appointed two new titulars for the parish and notified Father Mille, superior of the house at Laus, to leave the property. While communicating this decision to the Superior-General, he also took all faculties away from the missionaries, through an ordinance of September 30, 1841, placed them under a personal interdict which he extended to any member of the Congregation who might go to Laus. Warned of these measures, the Bishop of Digne hastened to advise the Oblate Fathers that they could cross the Durance River without any fear and celebrate Mass in his diocese.

Owing to such procedures, Bishop de Mazenod counselled Father Mille to be calm and moderate, instructed him to leave all discussion of the matter to the general administration of the Oblates, while he proposed to Bishop Rossat that the latter send two representatives to Marseilles who would open discussions with his own representatives. (Jeancard to Father Rua, November 5, 1841. Notre Dame du Laus Arch.) These drawn-out conferences, which were held in November of that same year, resulted in an agreement granting the missionaries lodging in a cottage near the shrine. The Bishop of Gap did not feel that he could agree to this clause and the Superior-General finally had to resign himself to recalling his religious, leaving it up to Father Mille to safeguard the material interests of the Congregation. (M. James to Jeancard, December 5, 1841; Bishop de Mazenod to Bishop Rossat, March 15, 1842. *Ibid.*)

48. Bishop de Mazenod, Act of Visitation for Notre Dame du Laus, October 18, 1835, in *Circulaires administratives,* Vol. I, Paris, 1887, pp. 319–321.
49. Father Martin to Father Fabre, June 12, 1862, in *Missions,* Vol. I, pp. 428–429. For the history of Notre Dame de Bon Secours, cf. V. Gaben, Chronique de Notre Dame de Bon Secours, Vol. I, 1846–1898. Manuscript, 1961. A.G.R.
50. Notes on the shrine of Notre Dame de la Garde, July, 1864, in *Missions,* Vol. III, pp. 436–437.
51. *Id., ibid.,* pp. 439–443. Cf. G. Arnaud d'Agnel, *Marseille, Notre Dame de le Garde,* Marseilles 1923.
52. Bishop de Mazenod to Father Dassy, October 29, 1850. Quoted by Yenveux, *Saintes Règles,* Vol. VII, p. 151.
53. For all these facts, cf. E. Mangenot, *Sion, son pélérinage, son sanctuaire.* Nancy, 1919, pp. 379–514.

Regarding the novel by Barrès, see J. Barbier's thesis, *Les sources de la Colline inspirée de Maurice Barrès.* Nancy, 1957.

54. Father Martin to Father Fabre, June 12, 1862, in *Missions,* Vol. I, pp. 430–433.

55. Father Roux to Father Fabre, August 17, 1862. *Ibid.,* pp. 575–576.

56. Report on the house at Autun. *Ibid.,* pp. 566–567.

57. Report on the house at Talence. *Ibid.,* pp. 558–563.

58. Father de l'Hermite to Father Fabre, May 21, 1863, in *Missions,* Vol. II, pp. 468–469.

59. Father de l'Hermite to Father Fabre, May, 1862. *Ibid.,* Vol. I, pp. 439–443.

60. Ch. Marcilhacy, *Le diocèse d'Orléans sous l'épiscopat de Monseigneur Dupanloup.* Paris, 1962, pp. 293–297.

61. For these missions of la Haute Vienne and la Creuse, cf. reports in Reg. *Maison de Limoges, Missions, jubilés, retraits.* Paris, Arch. Oblate Provoncial House.

62. Father Coste to Father Fabre, June, 1862, in *Missions,* Vol. I, p. 436.

63. Father Bise, Account of the mission at Mezières. Paris, Arch. Oblate Provincial House, Reg. *Maison de Limoges.*

64. Father Magnan to Father Fabre, June 21, 1863, in *Missions,* Vol. II, pp. 243–244.

65. Bishop de Mazenod, *Journal,* July 16, 1841. Quoted by Rambert, Vol. II, p. 97.

66. Father Richard, foundation of the missions in England. A.G.R., Reg. *Chroniques de la Province d'Angleterre,* p. 13.

67. Bishop de Mazenod, *Journal,* July 16, 1841. Quoted by Rambert, Vol. II, p. 97.

68. *Id., ibid.*

69. *Id.,* quoted by Rey, Vol. II, p. 106.

70. Bishop de Mazenod to Father Aubert, June 11, 1844. P.R., LM Aubert. At this period, Father Casimir Aubert had gone back to France with a few Irish novices.

71. Seven of these establishments were only temporary. Penzance had to be abandoned in 1846. Grace-Dieu was closed in 1848, Everingham and Manchester in 1851, Aldenham and Maryvale in 1852, and Galashiels in 1860. Liverpool, Leeds and Sicklinghall in England, Leith in Scotland, Inchicore, Glencree and Glen-Mary in Ireland, all lasted.

72. Bishop de Mazenod, Pastoral Letter prescribing public prayers for the return of England to Catholic unity, December 21, 1845.

73. This suit stirred up public opinion in England and caused Newman enormous expenses by reason of the witnesses he had to bring to England from Italy in order to refute Achilli and expose, not his errors in doctrine, but his moral lapses; regarding this suit, cf. Wilfred Ward, *Life of Cardinal Newman,* Vol. I, pp. 273 ff. also see L. Bouyer, *Newman, sa vie, sa spiritualité.* Paris, 1952, pp. 399–401. It was not the Holy Office, as Achilli claimed, but the Roman Civil Court which had prosecuted him.

In behalf of Father Newman and the "English Congregation of Saint Philip Neri," Fathers Dalgairns and St. John thanked the Bishop of Marseilles for saving their founder "from an imprisonment which, although it would have done honor to him, would have deprived us for a time of his presence and counsel." Dalgairns and St. John to Bishop de Mazenod, April 27, 1853. Quoted by Rey, Vol. II, p. 469.

74. Bishop de Mazenod to Father Arnoux, July 20, 1849. Quoted by Rey, Vol. II, p. 312.

75. Bishop de Mazenod to Father Boisrame, July 7, 1860. P.R., LM Boisrame.

76. Bishop de Mazenod to Father Aubert, August 28, 1851. *Ibid.*, Aubert.

77. Bishop de Mazenod to Father Richard, May 1, 1853. *Ibid.*, Richard.

78. Bishop de Mazenod to Father Courtès, June 30, 1852. *Ibid.*, Courtès.
    He was readmitted to the novitiate in 1892 and died in the Institute in 1894. Cf. *Missions*, Vol. LXVI, pp. 587–589.

79. Bishop de Mazenod to Father Noble, July 21, 1858. *Ibid.*, Noble.

80. Bishop de Mazenod to Father Tempier, August 1 & 5, 1857. P.R., LM Tempier.

81. Bishop de Mazenod to Father Tempier, July 1, 1850. *Ibid.*

82. Bishop de Mazenod to Father Tempier, June 23, 1850. *Ibid.*

83. Bishop de Mazenod to Father Tempier, August 1, 1857. *Ibid.*

84. Bishop de Mazenod to Father Tempier, July 1, 1850. *Ibid.*

85. Bishop de Mazenod to Father Tempier, July 15, 1857. *Ibid.*

86. Bishop de Mazenod to Cardinal Barnabo, October 1, 1857. *Ibid.*, Reg. Correspond. 1855–1861, pp. 126–127.

87. Bishop de Mazenod wrote to Father Fabre: "Curiosity, more than anything else, brought me to enter [the church] of a sect, whose name I didn't even know. They call themselves Apostolic Catholics, claiming that we have lost apostolicity which was revealed by divine revelation and that we have also lost the communication of the Holy Spirit which has been renewed in their chief; they call him Saint Ange. They also claim they have received the power to perform miracles. Nothing resembles one of our churches as much as their place of worship: baptismal font, confessional, altar surmounted by a crucifix, sanctuary lamp, exactly like ours, hanging in front of the altar in the middle of the sanctuary."
    Regarding this Protestant community, founded at the start of the nineteenth century by the London banker, Henry Drummond, and continued by Edward Irving, cf., A. Humbert, article "Irvingiens," in *Dictionnaire de Théologie catholique,* Vol. VII, col. 2566–2570.

88. Bishop de Mazenod to Cardinal Barnabo, October 1, 1857. P.R., Reg. Correspond. 1855–1861, pp. 125–126.

89. Bishop de Mazenod to Father Noble, July 21, 1858. P.R., LM Noble.

90. Cf. R. Cooke, *Sketches of the Life of Bishop de Mazenod.* London, 1882, Vol. II, pp. 271–306.

91. Bishop de Mazenod, allocution to members of the chapter, August 26, 1850. A.G.R., Reg. General Chapters, Vol. I, p. 83.

92. Regarding these points, cf. *Constitutiones et Regulae.* Marseilles, 1853, part 3, Chapter I, paragraphs 7 & 8.

93. *Id., ibid.* paragraph 9.

94. Death notice of Bishop Guigues, in *Notices nécrologiques,* Vol. III, p. 95.

95. Chapter of 1850, session on August 30. A.G.R., Reg. General Chapters, Vol. I, pp. 101–102.

96. Notice regarding the Holy Family Association, in *Annales de l'association de la Sainte Famille,* Vol. I, August 1860, pp. 376, 385.

97. Father Noailles, Notes for an agreement to affiliate, in *Traité d'affiliation* between the Oblates and the Holy Family of Bordeaux. A.G.R., Dossier Holy Family of Bordeaux.

98. *Traité d'affiliation entre la congregation des Missionnaires Oblats de Marie Immaculée et l'Association de la Sainte Famille,* January 11–14, 1858. *Ibid.*

99. Bishop de Mazenod to Cardinal Donnet, February 12, 1861. Bordeaux, Archiep. Arch, dossier Oblates.

100. On the death of Father Noailles, the Holy Family, in addition to its General House at Bordeaux, numbered 223 establishments in France, 7 in Spain, 2 in Belgium and 1 in Algeria. Six of these houses belonged to the Sisters of Saint Joseph, 9 to the Ladies of Loretto, 128 to the Sisters of the Immaculate Conception, 36 to the Sisters of Hope, 38 to the Sisters of Saint Martha, 4 to the Agricol Sisters and 2 reserved to the Solitaires. The Association numbered about 2,000 religious altogether. Cf. List in *Vie du bon Père Noailles.* Bordeaux, 1889, Vol. II, pp. 561–569.

Chapter Six

1. Bishop de Mazenod to Archbishop Guibert, August 6, 1860. Quoted by Rey, Vol. II, p. 822.

2. For all these details, cf. Rey, Vol. II, pp. 831–834.

3. Bishop Jeancard to the clergy of the diocese, January 11, 1861. Father Tempier to the Oblates, January 17, 1861. *Ibid.,* pp. 834–835.

4. Rambert, Vol. II, pp. 692–693.

5. Rey, Vol. II, p. 837.

6. Bishop A. Ricard, *Monseigneur de Mazenod.* . . . , Paris, 1892, p. 452.

7. Doctor d'Astros' report, quoted by Rey, Vol. II, p. 851.

8. Bishop Jeancard, Letter for the opening of Lent, February 4, 1861, p. 6.

9. A. Mouchette, *Souvenirs,* Quoted by Rey, Vol. II, p. 847.

10. Bishop Jeancard to Cardinal Barnabo, February 2, 1861. Rome, Propag. Arch., S.C., *Francia,* vol. 4, fol. 641–642; the same to the same, March 2, 1861. *Ibid., Indie Orientali,* vol. 17, fol. 1606.

11. J. Fabre, circular letter to the Oblates, May 26, 1861, in *Notices nécrologiques,* Vol. I, p. 19.

12. Letter of Father Fabre, January 31–February 3, 1861. Quoted by Rambert, Vol. II, p. 695.

13. Quoted by Rambert, Vol. II, pp. 695–696.

14. J. Timon-David, *Annales de l'Oeuvre de la Jeunesse,* Vol. III, Marseilles, 1881, pp. 82–83.

15. Father Jean, *Souvenirs.* Quoted by N. de Chauffailles, *Vie du serviteur de Dieu Louis Marie Maulbon d'Arbaumont, en religion le R. P. Jean du Sacré Coeur.* Lyons, 1911, pp. 381–382.

16. On the first page of his will, Bishop de Mazenod had written on August 1, 1854: "I invoke . . . the intercession of the Most Holy and Immaculate Virgin Mary, Mother of God, making bold to remind her, in all humility but with consolation, of my lifelong filial devotion to her and the desire I have always had to make her known and loved and to spread

her devotion everywhere through the ministry of those whom the Church has given me as my sons and who have shared my wishes." P.R., DM XVI–1. This *Salve Regina* at the close of the Founder's life was the final salutation of this great servant of the sinless Virgin.

17. J. Fabre, circular letter to the Oblates, May 26, 1861, in *Notices nécrologiques,* Vol. I, pp. 19–20.

18. Rambert, Vol. II, pp. 712–714.

19. J. Timon-David, *La vie du serviteur de Dieu Louis Maulbon d'Arbaumont . . .* Marseilles, 1887, p. 355.

20. *Id., ibid.*

21. (translator's note). The three portraits mentioned appear in Volumes II & III of Monsignor Leflon's French edition. They are reproduced on the dust jackets; see also the frontispiece of this volume.

22. Brassevin, *La grande histoire des Prêtres du Sacré Coeur à Marseille,* Vol. II, part 4, p. 122. Marseilles, Arch. Priests of the Good Shepherd, ms.

23. Rambert, Vol. II, pp. 603–604. Rambert received this souvenir from Timon-David, himself.

24. *Les douleurs d'un Fondateur d'oeuvres,* by Timon-David. (3rd sorrow.) Marseilles, Arch. Timon-David Fathers.

25. J. Timon-David, *La vie du serviteur de Dieu Louis Maulbon d'arbaumont,* p. 173.

26. Canon Gabriel, deposition of June 4, 1927. P.R., Informative Process at Marseilles, vol. I, fol. 154.

27. Brassevin, *La grande histoire des Prêtres du Sacré Coeur,* Vol. II, part 4, p. 122. Marseilles, Arch. Priests of the Good Shepherd. ms.

28. Bishop de Mazenod to Father Tempier, August 25, 1835. Quoted by Rambert, Vol. I, pp. 706–707.

29. Cf. J. Leflon, *Eugène de Mazenod,* Vol. II, p. 38, (Plon edit.)

30. Father Mouchette records the following anecdote regarding the Bishop of Marseilles' constancy in keeping his resolutions: "One day in the country—that is, at the Saint Louis retreat—I was helping him go through some old papers. We came across the resolutions he had made during his retreat in preparation for his episcopal consecration; he bade me read them to him. With admirable frankness, he interrupted me after each resolution and said: 'That one I kept; this one took me twenty-five years before I was able to master it, but I finally made it! You see,' he added, 'in retreats, it is the Holy Spirit which inspires resolutions and it is also He Who ultimately enables a man to succeed in the designs He has inspired. Who would have told me then that it would take twenty-five years of struggle to fulfill that resolution? And yet, it was not too much.' " Quoted by Rambert, Vol. II, pp. 598–599.

31. Father Pourrat, *La spiritualité chrétienne,* Vol. IV, Paris, 1947, p. 461.

32. *Id.,* p. 479.

33. Father de Mazenod to Father Tempier, May 14, 1826, in *Missions,* Vol. X, (1872), p. 316. The body of Saint Charles reposes in the crypt of the Milan cathedral.

34. Father de Mazenod, *Journal de la mission de Marignane,* November 24, 1816. *Ibid.,* Vol. IV (1865), p. 283.

35. Father de Mazenod to Canon Fortuné de Mazenod, November 17, 1817. Quoted by Rambert, Vol. I, p. 241.

36. Bishop de Mazenod, Retreat Notes, May, 1837. P.R., DM IV–3.

37. Father de Mazenod to Father Tempier, July 9, 1832. Quoted by Yenveux, *Saintes Règles,* Vol. IV, p. 203.
38. Bishop de Mazenod to Bishop Dupanloup, June 15, 1852. A.A.M. Administr. Corresp., Reg. VI, p. 44.
39. E. Blanc, Deposition of October 3, 1936. P.R., Apostolic Process, p. 261.
40. E. Gandar, *Souvenirs de Montolivet,* September 8, 1926. *Ibid.,* DM XIX–1a.
41. F. X. Bonnefoi, Declaration of March 31, 1913. P.R., DM XIX–1a.
42. Father Avignon, March 30, 1913. *Ibid.*
43. J. Timon-David, *La vie du serviteur de Dieu Louis Maulbon d'Arbaumont,* p. 211.
44. Bishop de Mazenod, *Journal,* September 3 & 5, 1838. P.R. JM.
45. A. Mouchette, *Souvenirs,* Quoted by Rambert, Vol. II, p. 681.
46. Rambert, Vol. II, p. 680.
47. Bishop de Mazenod to Father Tempier, March 10, 1859. P.R., LM Tempier.
48. A. Mouchette, *Souvenirs,* Quoted by Rambert, Vol. II, pp. 680–681.
49. Ch. Brandouin, Declaration of November 27, 1911. P.R., DM XIX–1a.
50. He had written to Bishop Bourget, as has been seen, on February 15, 1844: "You are a Pontiff in the Church of Jesus Christ and consequently you have a share in caring for not only your own flock but that of the whole Church." Montreal, Archiep. Arch., file Oblates.
51. Bishop de Mazenod, Pastoral letter on the occasion of the establishment of the Forty-Hours Devotion in his diocese. December 21, 1859.
52. J. B. Bartet, Declaration of March 30, 1913. P.R., DM XIX–1a.
53. Bishop de Mazenod, *Journal,* March 21, 1856. Quoted by Rey, Vol. II, pp. 584–585. Father M. B. Couissinier, a professor at the minor seminary, had published, in 1855, a translation of Louis de Grenade's *Méditations sur la passion et sur les grandes verités de la foi,* and it was approved by Bishop de Mazenod.
54. Marquis Henri de Foresta, Declaration of 1928. P.R., DM XIX–1a.
55. L. de Chazournes, *Vie du R. P. Joseph Barrelle,* Vol. I, p. 432.
56. F. X. Bonnefoi, Declaration of March 31, 1913. P.R., DM XIX–1a.
57. *Id., ibid.*
58. Bishop de Mazenod, *Journal,* October 8, 1837. Ibid., J.M.
59. Canon Aillaud, Declaration of June 3, 1926. *Ibid.,* DM XIX–1a.
60. The financial contribution made by the diocese to the Society for the Propagation of the Faith merits being singled out. From 1841 to 1861, Marseilles donated 990,106 francs for the missions, that is, an average of 49,505 a year. In 1861, with the sum of 79,021, it ranked sixth among the dioceses of France, coming after Lyons, Paris, Cambrai, Nantes and Bordeaux. Cf. reports published in *Annales de la propagation de la foi, 1842–1862.*
61. Bishop de Mazenod, Directory for Foreign Missions, in *Constitutiones et Regulae Missionariorum Oblatorum . . .* Marseilles, 1853, pp. 179–180.
62. Bishop de Mazenod, *Journal,* March 31, 1839. P.R., JM.
63. A. Rampal, The Bishop's Palace of Marseilles, in *Le mouvement social,* Vol. X of the *Bouches-du-Rhône. Encyclopédie departementale.* Marseilles, 1923, p. 651.
64. J. Timon-David, *Les douleurs d'un fondateur d'oeuvres* (third sorrow).

Marseilles, Arch. Timon-David Fathers. As has been said previously, the majority of the curates of Marseilles, immediately after the death of Bishop de Mazenod, disregarded the synodal prescriptions regarding common life, rejoined their families or took apartments outside the rectories. The diocesan administration was changed from top to bottom. "Never," wrote Jeancard to Archbishop Guibert on October 3, 1861, "in any diocese at the change of a bishop, was there a more complete raid upon everything that had been. Not a single person was left in office, except the acting secretary of the Palace, Father Blanc." (Quoted by Rey, Vol. II, p. 871.) Furthermore, Bishop Cruice demanded that the former vicars-general give a minute accounting of the diocesan funds during the episcopate of his predecessor, suspecting that the Oblates had diverted them to their own profit. The Oblates had to transfer their general house to Paris and, shortly after, gave up the direction of the major seminary. "But," notes Timon-David, "when this reaction was seen going beyond all bounds, the Oblates shamefully expelled from the major seminary which they had been directing so ably and in which they had trained all the diocesan priests for such a long time, and expelled also from so many different chaplaincies, right-thinking priests were deeply grieved at seeing the vicars-general carry out Bishop Cruice's edicts with such harshness against the sons of him to whom they owed so much." According to the director of the Working Boys' Society, "Father Guiol especially" displayed unusual "harshness and ruthlessness."

65. M. de Maupas, prefect of the Bouches-du-Rhône, to the minister of cults, January 7, 1864. A.D.M., 6 V 1. Through a rather human recurrence, a reaction opposite that of 1861 was produced when Bishop Cruice, stricken mentally, had to be deprived of his office. "A minor revolution, or rather a minor *coup d'état*," wrote Eugene Audouard in the *Phare de la Loire* on January 16, 1866, "has just occurred at Marseilles, to the great joy, it seems, of the clergy of our city." The "omnipotence" of the vicars-general who have been governing the diocese in the name of Bishop Cruice, little by little engendered "rancors, and the opposition was soon more clearly marked" against their administration than against that of the preceding bishop. "As a result, the clergy looked back fondly on the days of Bishop de Mazenod and praise for his entourage, against which criticism had been hurled in days gone by, was expressed by all the members of the Chapter." In fact, on January 10, 1866, the Chapter, "exercising its prerogative," restored "the men of the former regime to diocesan positions" and named as "capitular vicars, three priests who had been part of Bishop de Mazenod's administration." "The clergy," concluded the reporter, "has generally approved the step." *Phare de la Loire,* January 16, 1866. (published at Nantes.)

66. A. Autran, Welcome Address to the Academy of Marseilles, June 2, 1867, in *Mémoires de l'Académie des Sciences, Belles-Lettres et Arts.* Marseilles, 1867, p. 271.

67. Canon Aillaud, Declaration of June 3, 1926. P.R., DM XIX–1a.

68. Pope Paul VI, Allocution for the beatification of Leonard Murialdo, November 3, 1963, in *Osservatore Romano* (French edition), November 15, 1963, p. 4.

69. *Id., ibid.*

Index